EDITED BY *John L. Fell*

Film Before Griffith

University of California Press

Berkeley Los Angeles London

University of California Press
Berkeley and Los Angeles, California

University of California Press, Ltd.
London, England

© 1983 by
The Regents of the University of California

Library of Congress Cataloging in Publication Data
Main entry under title:

Film before Griffith.

    Bibliography: p.
    Includes index.
    1. Moving-pictures—History—Addresses, essays,
lectures. 2. Moving-picture industry—History—Addresses,
essays, lectures. 3. Moving-picture plays—History and
criticism—Addresses, essays, lectures. I. Fell, John L., 1927–
DN1993.5.A1F48 1983   384′.8′09   82–8540
ISBN 0–520–04738–9   AACR2
ISBN 0–520–04758–3 (pbk.)

Printed in the United States of America

1 2 3 4 5 6 7 8 9

Today a fresh generation of film historians
is systematically reconsidering the claims,
appraisals, decisions, and conceits of past
books, many now fifty or more years old.
With respect and appreciation, this anthology
is dedicated to all the early authors,
however their views may be taken now. They
made new understandings possible.

Contents

PART III   *The Films*

Credits

Special thanks to the following sources for permission to print or to reprint articles:

"Fall Motion Picture Production," excerpted from *The Kinetoscope* (New York: The Beginnings of the American Film, 1966) by permission of Gordon Hendricks. "The American Vitagraph, 1897–1901," copyright © Charles Musser 1980. "Images of Canada," from *Embattled Shadows: A History of the Canadian Cinema, 1895–1939* (Montreal: McGill-Queens University Press, 1979). "In the Beginning, 1896–1911," from *Word and Image: History of the Hungarian Cinema* (Budapest: Corvina Press, 1968). "The Features Begin," from *Australian Silent Films* (Melbourne: Lansdowne Press, 1970), copyright © C. M. Reade 1970. "The Yorkshire Pioneers," *Sight and Sound* 46, no. 1 (Winter 1976–77).

"Contra the Chaser Theory," *Wide Angle* 3, no. 1 (1979). "Hale's Tours: Ultrarealism in the Pre–1910 Motion Picture," *Journal of History* 3 (1957), copyright © Smithsonian Institution; reprinted with permission of the author and the Smithsonian Institution. "Edwin J. Hadley: Traveling Film Exhibitor," *Cinema Journal* 28, no. 3 (Summer 1976). "Vitascope/Cinématographe; Initial Patterns of American Film Industrial Practice," *Journal of the University Film Association* 31, no. 2 (Spring 1979). "The Lumière Organization and 'Documentary Realism,' " copyright © Alan Williams 1980. "Motion Picture Exhibition in Manhattan, 1906–1912: Beyond the Nickelodeon," *Cinema Journal* 17, no. 2 (Spring 1979). "Copyright and Early Theater, Vaudeville, and Film Competition," *Journal of the University Film Association* 29, no. 3 (Summer 1977). "The First Motion Picture Audiences," *Journal of Popular Film* 3, no. 1 (Winter 1974).

"Cinema and the Romantic Tradition," *Millenium Film Journal* 1, no. 1 (1978). "Alexander Black's Picture Plays, 1893–1894," *Cinema Journal* 16, no. 2 (Spring 1977). "Georges Méliès and the *Féerie*," *Cinema Journal* 16, no. 1 (Fall 1976). "Paper Prints of Early Motion Pictures," *Journal of the University Film Association* 17, no. 4

Introduction

Every history claims to search for meaning to support its fragments. Such meaning is narrative. It proposes one among many possible stories linking "facts" together. Some histories simulate mysteries, promising last-minute rewards or solutions for the reader's diligent search, but much film history reads more like the impatient, encapsulated synopsis of an interminable serial. As if embarrassed by Greek and Latin polysyllables and nineteenth-century engravings, English-language film study streaks past the "primitive" period with token nods toward Leonardo da Vinci and Eadweard Muybridge, requisite homage to the Wizard of Menlo Park (Thomas Edison) and the Lumières, and reluctant descriptions of *The Life of an American Fireman, The Great Train Robbery,* and *Rescued by Rover.* Méliès is quickly acknowledged; then, with a kind of relieved sigh, the authors get on to real stuff, which is D. W. Griffith and Hollywood business. The Promethean Griffith rises like a slumbering giant, striding the American continent and dispensing gifts like the functional closeup, the flashback, and offscreen space. Hollywood businessmen are viewed as the first entrepreneurial wizards.

Several forces now join determinedly to challenge this combination of romance and avoidance behavior. One, of course, has been the academicization of film study itself. For the first time, people now writing "film history" have undergone basic training in techniques of historical research in centers such as New York University and the University of Iowa. In the process, they have encountered broad issues of historiography. Among the articles included in this anthology, a number were written by recent or soon-to-be Ph.D.'s (Tom Gunning and Charles Musser, for instance). Significantly, some of the articles in this volume originate on the East Coast, where many early film records reside, not only in archives (the Library of Congress, the Museum of Modern Art, George

Eastman House) but also in court records and business directories. Articles considering distribution and exhibition are scattered more widely across the country.

If, as the historian Douglas Gomery has proposed, film history must be rewritten monograph by monograph,[1] this volume modestly undertakes an early stage of the project. Knowledge about the pre-Griffith film world may be likened to an old, scattered jigsaw puzzle with many pieces missing. Enough has been organized so that we begin to sense the picture, foreground and background both, but whole areas are blank, their shapes implied at best by adjacent, recognizable images. Of course the jigsaw simile is itself misleading, for history is only partly archaeological. Much simply depends on conceiving thoughtful questions to ask about the past. The best questions are the simple ones: Who made films? Where and under what conditions? How were the films conceived as "entertainment"? How were they promoted, exhibited, and circulated? Who saw the films? How were the shows regarded? As time passes, can the narrative character of the movies, be quantified so as to evidence formal change? Can changes be explained?

In this respect, *Film Before Griffith* itself comprises a small compendium of methodologies for future work. Some articles in this volume use documents (correspondence, business records, legal briefs and findings) unattended for years. Others look to parts of the globe (Canada, Yorkshire, Hungary) little recognized as of interest with respect to the movies' past. Some pieces confront old shibboleths (the Chaser Theory, the exclusively immigrant audience). Some look to antecedent traditions, such as the *féerie* and the Picture Play, for unacknowledged shaping forces. Significant to almost all the work represented in this anthology is an impulse to contextualize findings within some broadly supporting and self-conscious research design. In such fashion we glean new understandings from the past through new sources, less exclusively dependent than earlier histories on aging memories and crumbling movie reviews.

Contemporary film work in many quarters has expanded its operative base, incorporating methodologies from other disciplines. As film history, like film theory, applies the tools of economics, linguistics, and psychology, perhaps too as younger scholars face the overwhelming number of film titles that now make up the accessible past, greater attention centers on the social, political, industrial, and cultural dimensions of film. The pre-Griffith period particularly lends itself to these approaches. When we learn to ask the right questions, we may view these formative years in such a way as to excavate the foundations of today's popular film culture.

Techniques of reputable historical research are not bound to designated periods. Useful ways to think about the turn of the century may eventually prove

---

[1]Douglas Gomery, "Books: *The Dream That Kicks* (Chanan) and *History Must Answer to Man* (Petrie),"*Wide Angle* 4 (1981): 78–81.

helpful to other decades. Yet of all periods, the late Victorian-Edwardian world seems especially fruitful for study because beginnings somehow always implicate endings. Urban demographics, patterns of distribution, and strategies of exploitation in early film history supply a context in which early film may be considered as something happening for the first time (a media phenomenon) yet as rooted in its society as lantern slides, camera batteries, and Wild West shows. Without daring to place ourselves in the minds of early filmmakers such as Wallace McCutcheon and James Williamson, we are able to examine the sorts of options available to them, the alternatives they had to choose from, the contradictions they had to reconcile.

Past film histories that make non-questions out of such items as the phenakistoscope and the Thanhouser Company customarily develop their narratives along a string of movie pearls, masterpieces authenticated by commendations from yet earlier studies. In a real sense, this approach is an application of the Great Man theory of history, in which a nation's fate may hinge on Napoleon's lust or Hitler's sanity. In such an approach the issue is the "significance" of *The Great Train Robbery* or *Fire*, because these "landmark" films "influenced" what followed through "innovations."

The film historian's curse is that the more movies he sees the more difficult it becomes to draw easy connections, lines as it were on which to string his newly discovered pearls. Whatever commendations it warrants, *The Life of an American Fireman* is shedding its uniqueness. As more early films surface, the committed scholar begins to understand how (and less often, why) the story forms emerged that are today simplistically described as the dominant narrative codes. Major factors in this strategy of reconsideration have been the riches of the Library of Congress Paper Print Collection (see Kemp R. Niver's "Paper Prints of Early Motion Pictures" in part 3) and increasing cooperation among international film archives in the sharing of holdings for the sake of film scholarship.

The result has been an embarrassment of riches in which particular benchmark films submerge now in a sea of titles. Traditional formal notations of narrative complication—measures such as scene breakdowns into component, sequential parts or camera angle shifts—are therefore being reevaluated. In consequence, a filmmaker such as Edwin S. Porter is not so much diminished as reassigned a different role on history's stage. See, for example, André Gaudreault's essay "Temporality and Narrativity in Early Cinema."

Impelled then by a new wealth of resources, by the rigors of more careful research, and by encompassing interests which include, but do not subordinate themselves to, esthetic considerations, sufficient work of estimable worth has appeared, meriting a compilation such as the present one.

To avoid misunderstanding, however, we must align the intentions of our project within wider fields of need and ambition. As quoted earlier, Douglas Gomery is right. Film history has yet to be written, and the current anthology betrays gaps and deficiencies of knowledge even as it shows new energy and self-confidence. *Film Before Griffith* does not presume to survey relevant subjects or chronological landmarks comprehensively. We urgently need wider coverage, but this waits on long-term, cooperative endeavors among the new scholarly band, supported not only by film archives and period records but by money. At best, this anthology helps point the way.

The book's primary intention is to introduce material more or less inaccessible to the younger student. *Film Before Griffith* does not judiciously balance its essays against an outline of relative significances. The attention, for example, devoted to circumstances of film's early production and exhibition in Canada, Australia, and Texas hardly suggests that these spots merit chapters in some future study. Rather, their inclusion emphasizes thoughtful, recent research; it encourages broader reconsideration of the ways in which isolated communities responded to common problems. Serious readers are urged to further investigate most subjects introduced here by means of the additional resources cited in the bibliography.

The book falls into three sections. Part 1, "Places and Productions," emphasizes a few early companies, filmmakers, and screenings. This field carries special present interest both because of the emergence of new data and because of the controversy attending ideas about the relation between early filmmaking and matters of ideology. Elsewhere, and each in his own way, Michael Chanan and Lary May have argued that the movies' first character was shaped by a conjunction of proletarian and bourgeois idioms of popular culture, themselves reflective of class relationships embedded in nineteenth-century society.[2]

Part 2, "Exhibition and Distribution," describes how and where the early movies were systematically viewed, and, too, how such situations were inflected by matters such as copyright law and distribution practices. Here the dateline moves more exclusively into the twentieth century as film consumption, like filmmaking, becomes regularized. In various ways, these essays ask the questions: Who saw the films? Where were these films shown? How was the entertainment arranged? What relationship existed between the choice of genre of entertainment and its exploitation?

Part 3, "The Films," concentrates on the product itself, early movies viewed now seventy or eighty years after their initial, often very transient, appearance, many not publicly screened since. Attention centers here on issues of both form and content; that is, the authors face problems of classifying their burgeoning subjects, of generalizing about the subspecies, of reading out social meanings of the period implicit in the imagery, and of conjoining these seemingly innocent little entertainments with such current concerns as feminism and the avant-garde.

---

[2]Michael Chanan, *The Dream That Kicks: The Prehistory and Early Years of Cinema in Great Britain* (London: Routledge and Kegan Paul, 1980); Lary May, *Screening Out the Past: The Birth of Mass Culture and the Motion Picture Industry* (New York: Oxford University Press, 1980).

Short introductions precede each major division. Several essays are usefully amended with citations contributed by George C. Pratt, Associate Curator of Motion Pictures at George Eastman House in Rochester. The editor is especially grateful to Mr. Pratt for his counsel and his accuracies, with the usual admonition that other, uncaught errors are the editor's own.

PART I

Place and Production

Introduction

After developing a photographic process that produced its image on silver-coated copper plates treated with iodine vapor, Louis Daguerre ceded rights for his invention to the French Academy of Science, thus rendering it public (except for in England) in 1839. By way of contrast, the cinema's first years, the early 1900s, were centrally affected by patent disputes.

The movies' appearance generated hastily competitive cries of "first," immediate forays into commerce, and not-so-gradual consolidations by business interests. Claims to inventive precedence were made variously in Germany (the Skladanowsky brothers), England (Le Prince, Paul, Acres, and Friese-Greene), France (Marey, Reynaud, the Lumières), and the United States (Muybridge, Dickson, Edison, the Lathams). Production companies sprang up almost immediately after the first publicly projected film events of 1895 and 1896.

Such units needed filmmaking equipment, whether leased, purchased, or pirated from some parent source. Initially, too, a filmmaker would serve equally as a film exhibitor (Vitagraph and the Lumières offer contrasting approaches), although size, complexity, and investment strategies soon encouraged specialization. However entrepreneurial, such combinations of production and distribution nevertheless had their precedents. We may turn to contemporary industrial models in search of illumination of such patterns.

It may be helpful to note, without diminishing the generosity of Daguerre's grand gesture, that industrial, social, and merchandising circumstances differed markedly after the sixty-year interim between the introduction of photography and the beginning of cinema. By the 1890s patents supplied vital ammunition to corporate warfare. With Edison attempting an economic stranglehold on competitive filmmaking in the U.S. by means of patents, other companies alternately resorted to bootleg operations[1] or unwieldy "original" equipment to avoid using the Edison designs.[2]

By the time of McKinley and Teddy Roosevelt American invention had assumed organized, strategic relations with the society it served. Indeed, invention had become part of the country's ideology. The Wizard of Menlo Park discovered what he understood the public wanted. Part of the country's merchandising plan was to incorporate, as far as possible, vertical industrial organization, the better to incorporate a full sequence of separate processes. Thus, with respect to film, Edison sequentially attempted to control (1) technology; (2) the production of the movie product (its "software"); and (3) distribution activities. Yet he remained dependent on John Corbutt of Philadelphia, then Blair Camera of Boston, and finally Eastman Company in Rochester for his celluloid-based strip film. In contrast, the Lumières in France both developed their own photographic raw materials and organized production and distribution. Both quickly undertook worldwide penetration of their markets.

Although film studios have traditionally tried to control exhibition of their product, neither Edison's nor the Lumières' patterns of control prevailed more generally. Elsewhere, what started as small-unit operations with employees doing multiple duty soon split into separate trades or businesses, like the Miles brothers' early distribution network in San Francisco or the similar network provided by Walker and Turner in Britain. The movie business redefined itself in terms of increasingly sophisticated marketing decisions as its volume increased. For example, by means of careful organization of its industrial base in relation to raw materials, quality-controlled mass production, and inventive relations with the consumer market, Eastman has maintained almost a century's domination of the film and processing business. Early in its history, the company made a considered decision to avoid film production so as not to antagonize its raw stock clients.

Technology's role in the American still photography industry is thoughtfully recounted in Reese V. Jenkins's *Images and Enterprise,*[3] which itemizes a repeated succession of historical trends: (1) the movement from decentralized to centralized factory production; (2) the separation and specialization of functions in producing photographs; (3) the emergence of a mass market for apparatus and materials; (4) an increase in scale and integration of enterprise;

---

[1]See, for example, Fred G. Balshofer, "Early Career with Shields, Lubin and Others," in Balshofer and Arthur Miller, eds., *One Reel a Week* (Berkeley: University of California Press, 1967).

[2]American Mutoscope and Biograph first built its picture-postcard Mutoscope to outmaneuver Edison, then constructed a huge camera and projector. See G. W. Bitzer, *Billy Bitzer: His Story* (New York: Farrar, Straus, and Giroux, 1973), pp. 8–9.

[3]Reese V. Jenkins, *Images and Enterprise* (Baltimore: Johns Hopkins Press, 1975).

and (5) a growing awareness of technology and a sophistication of its use in business competition.[4]

Such patterns apply equally to motion picture history. The period covered by this anthology, ending around 1908, largely accounts for items (1), (2), and (3). The increase in scale (longer films, studio systems, movie palaces) and developing technology (cameras, lenses, superior color, sound) of cinema fall more comfortably into subsequent phases.

In part 1, subjects for the Kinetoscope, which almost exclusively dominated popular film entertainment in New York at the time, are described by Gordon Hendricks in "Fall Motion Picture Production" within a context of technical refinement and the deteriorating personal relationship between W. K. L. Dickson and William H. Gilmore, Edison's business-minded assistant.[5] (Soon to expire, the Kinetoscope was clearly a money-maker at this stage.) Long a respected figure in film research, Hendricks is noted for the scrupulous precision and thoroughness of his work.

Some American companies, William Selig for example, turned to the Lumières Cinématographe design to escape Edison patent attorneys, while American Mutoscope and Biograph built its own machines. American Vitagraph's example poses other questions. If J. Stuart Blackton's account is to be believed, Vitagraph bought its equipment directly from Edison.[6] Albert Smith's version differs altogether.[7] Charles Musser's article, "The American Vitagraph, 1897–1901," questions the accuracy of both that company's founders. By such a discussion Musser reminds us how contemporary film historians must reexamine earlier "facts," recountings, and even metaphors that structure first-generation movie history. Smith's and Blackton's autobiographies retain meaning, but their significance changes when other motives surface. In conclusion, Musser challenges the accuracy of the technological model for film history when such a design pays insufficient attention to the product of such technology: the films.

Comparing the circumstances of film's first appearance in separate parts of the world—in Canada (Peter Morris, "Images of Canada"), Hungary (István Nemeskürty, "In the Beginning, 1896–1911"), and Australia (Eric Reade, "Australian Silent Films, 1904–1907")—we find striking similarities. Motion pictures were introduced in these areas by way of Lumière or Edison enterprises.

[4]Jenkins, *Images and Enterprise*, p. 6.

[5]Elsewhere, Hendricks describes various Kinetoscope films in greater detail, sometimes calling attention to Edward F. Madden, Buffalo Bill's press agent, who figured in the making of several. See Marshall A. Deutelbaum, ed., *"Image": On the Art and Evolution of the Film* (New York: Dover, 1979), pp. 9–19.

[6]Blackton's memories are quoted in Anthony Slide, *The Big V: The Beginnings* (Metuchen, N. J.: Scarecrow, 1976).

[7]Albert E. Smith, in collaboration with Phil H. Koury, *Two Reels and a Crank* (New York: Doubleday, 1952), p. 12.

Shows were often undertaken by traveling magicians, as in Canada and Australia. Indeed, the alliance between movie and stage magic is documented in a monograph by Erik Barnouw,[8] as well as in Lucy Fischer's study in part 3, "The Lady Vanishes: Women, Magic, and the Movies."

Occasional productions documenting local subject matter appeared before audiences eager to recognize local images: an arrival in Budapest, a yacht race on Albert Park Lake. Such short actualities were sometimes intermixed with fraudulent, staged news events. This kind of material intermixed with imported French, British, and American products. By 1910, film exhibition had established itself through regular scheduling in permanent locations among the world's major cities.

In Britain, as described in Allan T. Sutherland's study of the Yorkshire industry, "The Yorkshire Pioneers," film assumed an early pattern of regional production, although it was sometimes distributed to wider audiences through Cecil Hepworth, who came to film by way of magic lanterns and whose production and distribution system somewhat paralleled Edison's. Staged performances, comedies in particular, came to assume greater prominence, along with the usual actualities, faked actualities, and trick films.

Sutherland's research on Le Prince underscores the many optical and mechanical processes under development worldwide from the 1880s onward, independent of both Lumière and Edison. As we investigate such questions of place and production, simple lines of priority and chronology merge into webs of growing complexity.

---

[8]Eric Barnouw, *The Magician and the Cinema* (New York: Oxford University Press, 1981).

GORDON HENDRICKS

The Kinetoscope:

Fall Motion Picture Production

The Lathams had tried to match "Gentleman Jim" Corbett with Jim Fitzsimmons but had been unsuccessful. So on September 8, the anniversary of Corbett's fight with Sullivan (as a result of which he had become heavyweight champion of the world), Corbett met Pete Courtney, a Trenton heavyweight who was said to have "stood up against" Fitzsimmons for some rounds. They met in the Black Maria for six rounds of 1.16, 1.24, 1.12, 1.29, 1.23, and 50 seconds,[1] appropriate lengths for the Latham enlarged Kinetoscope. This fight served to focus, as no other event had yet done, national attention on the Kinetoscope and the motion picture.

Although Raff and Gammon's production schedule was nowhere nearly so spectacular as the Corbett-Courtney fight, it was nevertheless consistent and sometimes conspicuous. On September 13, the Glenroy Brothers, a comic vaudeville boxing team, met in the Maria for their boxing bout.[2] On September 20 a rats-and-terriers subject was shot.[3] On September 21, Layman, the "facialist," and another rats-and-terriers subject were shot.[4] On September 22 the Glenroy Brothers apparently returned, and still another rats-and-terriers subject was made.[5] On September 24 the Maria's stage was host to Buffalo Bill and an aggregation from his Wild West Show, which had just closed a long run at

---

[1]According to *The New York Herald*, September 8, 1894.

[2]Business correspondence of Norman C. Raff and Frank R. Gammon, Baker Library Collection, Harvard University, Cambridge, Mass.

[3]*Orange Journal*, September 27, 1894

[4]Ibid.

[5]Ibid. Also *Newark Evening News*, September 24, 1894.

Ambrose Park in Brooklyn.[6] Buffalo Bill was shot in a rapid-firing demonstration, and the Indians from his company were shot in subjects later called *Sioux Indian Ghost Dance, Indian War Council,* and *Buffalo Dance.*[7] On September 26 the Englehardt Sisters, lady fencers, were shot in two subjects.[8] On September 29 the Kinetoscope Company, deciding that the boxing business was the one that would bring rich commercial returns, arranged for Hornbacker and Murphy to meet for five rounds before the camera.[9] On October 1 a "Madam Rita" danced in the Maria.[10] October 6 was a big day: Walton and Slavin, comic boxers from *1492,* a popular Broadway musical; a "pickaninnies" dance from *The Passing Show,* another musical; four "Arab" numbers—*The Mexican Knife Duel, Lasso Thrower, Sheik Hadj Tahar,* and *Hadji Cheriff* from the Wild West Show and Cleveland's minstrel show; and another Glenroy Brothers subject.[11]

The E. E. Cowherd letter, of possibly the week beginning October 7, is very interesting in describing this atmosphere:[12]

> as pretty as can be.[13] I do not see why, but Mr and Mrs Dickson seem to take great interest in me, I suppose on account of Mr. Shepherd.[14] In the afternoon they asked me to go to New York with them, as they were going to the Theatre there, but I declined, as I was not dressed well enough to go in a box with a man, as prominent to the world as Mr D. He promises to take me to Niagara Falls soon, when he is going to photograph the falls for the Kinetoscope. I shall go if he foots the bill.[15]

---

[6]Ibid. Also *East Orange Gazette,* September 27, and *Orange Chronicle,* September 27.
[7]Ibid.

[8]Baker Library Collection. These ladies were called the Englehardt sisters, although there was only one Englehardt, the other being named Blanchard. This is according to a receipt signed on September 26, in the Baker Library Collection.

[9]Ibid. The Hornbacker and Murphy fight is also listed in an undated catalogue as a "Five Round Glove contest to a finish. Price per set . . . $100.00. Or single rounds, each $20.00."

[10]Baker Library Collection.

[11]Ibid. The October 16 balance sheet (see below) lists a number of these subjects and dates various reimbursements therefor. Newspapers of Orange, East Orange, and Newark also refer to the taking of these subjects.

[12]I have referred to this letter in "A Collection of Edison Films," *Image* (September 1959), pp. 158–63. Cowherd appears to have been a student at a New York electrical school who was also possibly known to Dickson through Virginia friends, since Cowherd wrote that he had seen a Virginia local newspaper at "Mr. D's."

[13]An intriguing fragment: the preceding sentences are missing.

[14]I have not found who "Mr. Shepherd" was; local directory listings are inconclusive.

[15]So far as I have determined, the first Edison-sponsored Niagara Falls excursion was in the fall of 1896—excepting a trip by Heise for Raff and Gammon in April of 1896. And the first such subject taken by Dickson was taken at the same time for the American Mutoscope

My life is very pleasant as every fair day we have some theatre troupe out to act for the photo [sic]; Mr D always sends for me in time to see the performance. Last week we had 4 negro's from Vᵃ. who danced the old Vᵃ. break down for the photographing machine [possibly the "picka-ninnies."—G. H.].

Cowherd wrote his father again on December 8:[16]

I think you do me an injustice by misconstruing my meaning as to my expenses. My board is $5.^{00} per week since winter, and only was 4. per week for the first few weeks through Mr D's request of Mr Petit.[17] Now I have to pay full price, which is the cheapest can be had in the Oranges, that is fit for a *gentleman* to have. West Orange is only a new town built by the employees of Edison . . . the people charge what they like for board. I now get it one dollar cheaper than any one in the house, owing to Mr D's influence. I only get $8^{00} per week now, as I do not work at night but very little. Our dep't has been shut down for the past week and I am the only one who has worked. . . . Mr. D. allowed me to put in my time. . . . Where my money goes to, is in necessary wearing apparel, of which I was very scarce. I can now save about $2^{00} per week. . . . If I keep my health, I will help you if you wish, or pay all my loans. . . . I bought a very nice warm overcoat for 9.00 and a suit for $10.00. Mr D. cashed the check. . . . I have been to N.Y. to the Theatre with ["one or two of Dickson's friends"] as a crowd, tickets & expenses by Mr D. He can get as many tickets as wants free, as theatre troupes are out here every day to be photographed for the kinetoscope.

I receive all the visitors for such purpose and see that they are attended to, look after the ladies with whom I have lots of fun, but for the time being of course, Theatre girls are a jolly set.

Company (see Gordon Hendricks, *Beginnings of the Biograph*. [New York: The Beginnings of the American Film, 1964]). This is probably a trip which was never seriously planned, considering the fact that such a trip would have involved the transportation of the ponderous Black Maria camera to the falls. It is also possible that Dickson, who had obviously impressed Cowherd with his importance, was doing more of the same. The phrase, "I shall go if he foots the bill" is poignant, in the light of the December 8 letter (see below).

[16]"Motion Pictures, 1894." E. E. Coward to his father, December 8, 1894, Document File, Edison National Historical Site.

[17]This could be the Petit of U. S. Phonograph Company fame, who was later to be granted a significant patent. This reference substantiates what that patent suggests: that Dickson and Petit were on friendly terms.

On October 11 Luis Martinelli, a contortionist, was "taken" in the Maria. And on October 16 four subjects of the bronco-busting contingent of Buffalo Bill's Wild West Show were shot. They had received expense money on October 12 and were to receive a total of $85, which included transportation on the Delaware and Lackawanna Railroad for two horses.[18] On October 17 Professor Tschernoff's performing dogs were taken in two subjects—*Skirt Dance Dog* and *Somersault Dog.*[19] On October 18 the Japanese tumbler Toyou Kichi was shot.[20] And on November 1 three subjects from the Broadway musical *The Gaiety Girls,* a trapeze artist named Alcide Capitaine, and Annie Oakley were taken—the last in apparently three subjects, only one of which must have been successful.[21] On November 26 two subjects of the Rixfords, an acrobatic team, were taken.[22]

Although the foregoing are the subjects I have specifically dated in the 1894 Black Maria season, the following were also shot before the end of the year: several dance subjects by Annabelle; apparently four subjects of athletes in calisthenics; Armand 'Ary; another (than Madame Rita) oriental dancer, possibly "Miss Rosa"; Topack and Steele; two barroom scenes (one in existence by June 1894 and a new one made in December); a Chinese laundry scene; a Chinese opium den scene; a "Cupid Dance"; a fan dance; two Elsie Jones dance subjects; a fire rescue scene; a Japanese dance; an Indian club swinger; a gun spinner; five subjects from the Broadway musical *A Milk White Flag;* a Ruth Dennis (i.e., Ruth St. Denis) subject; an Arab "human pyramid"; an Arab "sword combat"; a trained bear subject; Waring and Wilson, from *Little Christopher Columbus;* a wrestling dog; a wrestling and a boxing match; and, possibly before January 1, 1895, a dentist scene in which Dr. Colton, credited with being the first to administer gas, was starred.

In addition to the manufacture of Kinetoscopes and the production of motion picture subjects, experimental work was being done. For example, there was work on a "New Model Kinetoscope Motor" and a "Model Armature" for

---

[18]This information is from a receipt signed by Madden, their manager, in the Baker Library Collection. I referred to this matter in "A Collection of Edison Films," but I may have erred in my apportionment of this fee.

[19]*Orange Chronicle,* October 20, 1894.

[20]Ibid. Kichi is illustrated on pages 33 and 44 of the Dicksons' booklet (Laurie and William Kennedy Dickson, *History of the Kinetograph, Kinetoscope, and Kineto-Phonograph* (1895; New York: Arno, 1970), but is there misnamed "Shiekh Hadji Tahar."

[21]This information is from *The Orange Chronicle,* November 3, 1894. I have refuted Ramsaye's dating of the "Gaity Girl's" shooting on page 195 of *The Edison Motion Picture Myth* (Terry Ramsaye, *A Million and One Nights* [New York: Simon and Schuster, 1926]). *The Orange Journal* of October 18 announced an Annie Oakley visit for October 19, but this was apparently canceled.

[22]*The New York Clipper,* December 8.

such a motor.[23] In October, November, and December there was also work on a film puncher, a cutter, and a printer. In November and December an additional cutter and puncher were under way.[24]

On October 30 Gilmore wrote to Raff in Chicago, who had complained on October 23 that things were a bit slow:[25]

> I have your letter of the 23rd. Arrangements have been made to enlarge the film department, and new apparatus is now being made for same. The apparatus necessary to do the work, has, of necessity, to be very accurate, and some time will be consumed in getting same out. Within the next month, however, I see no reason why we should not be in a position to turn out all the film that may be required.

Raff and Gammon, not satisfied, urged further diligence on Gilmore, who tried to pacify them further on November 7:[26]

> I have your letter of October 31st and in reply would say that we continue to steadily increase the output of our film department. Last week we turned out a total of 120 films, and we hope to continue to increase this output steadily right along. Another set of printing apparatus was only put into practical use during last week, and when this machine gets running as it should, I see no reason why we should not be in a position to increase our output materially. In addition to this, I have other apparatus being made, which will more than double the present output, but as I wrote you several days ago this apparatus necessarily has to be made very accurately. . . . We are pushing ahead the work on this apparatus all that we can. You must also remember that this is an entirely new line of work, and necessarily it takes time to break in new help to do it in a systematic and thoroughly satisfactory manner. . . .
>
> I trust that our people here will soon be in a position to give you everything you want, not only in the way of films, but of machines, etc.

That Gilmore was "doing everything possible" is unlikely. The ore-milling business was still uppermost in Edison's mind, and it was to remain so until late

---

[23]John Randolph (accountant), letter book E1717, July 31, 1894–July 1, 1897, pp. 39, 54. [Presumably in the Edison Archives, West Orange, N. J.—ed.]

[24]Ibid.

[25]Letter book E1717, March 8, 1894–April 7, 1894.

[26]Ibid.

the next year when he said,[27] "I am getting close to the end of my mill biz & and will soon be able to come back to work."[28]

That Gilmore's relation with Dickson was going from bad to worse is also certain. A particular deterioration seems to have occurred not later than about November 10 and possibly not sooner than the deadline for the *Cassier's Magazine* article of December. Dickson did not claim projection in this article, whereas he did claim it in the late-1894 booklet. I have described elsewhere[29] the arrangement between Dickson, Raff and Gammon, and Albert Bunn, the printer of the Dicksons' *History of the Kinetograph Kinetoscope and Kineto-Phonograph.* I have said that Dickson's first claim for projection was made in this book, which appeared to have been "closed" about December 17. Although it is true that the book must have been closed on about that date, Bunn's note of November 10 to Raff and Gammon suggests that as of that date the text, and therefore the projection claims, had been completed:[30] "The Book is in hands & I am rushing it along—It is going to be a handsome & credible [*sic*] publication."

The phrase "The Book is in hands" suggests a completed text. Therefore Dickson, moving along with the Lathams in their projection efforts—at least a part of which predated October 30—felt he should take a stand concerning projection. That he made this claim now adds to the impression that he began to see the end of his association with Edison. We can be sure that he was being constantly nettled by Gilmore, a man who was being given free rein at the laboratory, often to the frustration of other long-time employees.

Meanwhile Tate was having *his* troubles with Edison. He had left Edison because of the phonograph concessions matter, but was still, in spite of the World's Fair debacle, hankering after Kinetoscope profits. A letter he wrote to Edison on October 22, offering to settle the affairs of the Chicago Central Phonograph Company, appears to be antecedent to clearing the record for a *rapprochement* with Edison concerning the Kinetoscope.[31] It is interesting to note that Tate used the letterhead of the Kinetoscope Company in inquiring about the matter.

---

[27] "Elec. St. G. E. Co. 1895."

[28] It is such remarks as these that have helped sustain the Edison legend of superhuman industry. There can be no doubt that Edison worked unusually hard, long hours for many years, but there also can be no doubt that he was constantly aware of the hard-work legend that he was living.

[29] In Hendricks, "A Collection of Edison Films." A microfilm of my more than forty-page research paper, published by the George Eastman House (Rochester, N. Y.) in connection with this study, contains my analysis of the Dickson-Bunn-Raff and Gammon matter.

[30] Baker Library Collection.

[31] Ibid. It will be remembered that the Chicago Central Phonograph Company was set up to handle World's Fair business and had been advanced $10,000 by Edison. It had repaid $8,207.

The North American Phonograph Company, of which Tate had been vice president, had failed in August, and Edison had forced it into bankruptcy. Tate was now assessing his prospects in the Kinetoscope business. A contract, found among Raff and Gammon's effects, appears never to have been implemented:[32]

THIS AGREEMENT, made in duplicate this twentieth day of November, 1894, by and between THE KINETOSCOPE COMPANY . . . hereinafter called the "Company", and Alfred O. Tate, of the City of New York, State of New York, hereinafter called "Tate".

WITNESSETH:—

Whereas, the said Tate is desirous of purchasing from said Company certain Kinetoscopes and supplies therefor, and

Whereas, the said Company desires to sell said Kinetoscopes and supplies therefor to the said Tate, upon the terms and conditions hereinafter stated, and

Whereas, it is agreed that said Tate, may assign this agreement to a corporation to be formed within thirty (30) days from the date hereof, and that this agreement shall be as binding between said Company and said corporation as if originally made between them;

NOW THEREFORE, in consideration of the premises and the covenants and agreements herein contained the parties hereto have agreed and do hereby agree as follows:

FIRST   The said Company agrees to sell and deliver at the factory of The Edison Phonograph Works, West Orange, New Jersey, to the said Tate, or his assigns, at the prices and under the terms and conditions hereinafter specified, such Kinetoscopes and Kinetoscopic supplies as may be required by the said Tate, or his assigns, during the life of this agreement. . . .

FIFTH   The said Company agrees to deliver to the said Tate or his assigns, all films for which orders are given by the said Tate or his assigns (except such films as are reserved by said Company for its exclusive use), as soon as the same are received by the said Company from the manufacturer. . . .

SIXTH   The said Company, to the full extent of such control as they now or may hereafter acquire, over Kinetographs of Thomas A. Edison, agrees to make, or cause to be made for the said Tate or his assigns, films from subjects furnished by said Tate or his assigns, to such extent as such Company may be able to control or dictate the taking of subjects by the Kinetograph, and barring breakage or other accidents, and further agrees that such films shall not be used by it, or sold, or otherwise

---

[32]Baker Library Collection.

disposed of to others, but shall be held for the exclusive use and benefit of the said Tate or his assigns; provided, however, that said Tate or his assigns shall pay all expense of whatever nature attached to the production and taking of such subjects. . . .

NINTH   The said Company agrees that if it shall obtain for use, one or more portable Kinetographs or Cameras for photographing exterior views or scenes, it will place one of the said instruments under the direction and control of the said Tate or his assigns, it being, however, expressly understood and agreed that such direction and control shall relate solely to the selection of views or scenes to be photographed, at the expense of the said Tate or his assigns, and shall not by inference or otherwise indicate any right of ownership in said instrument on the part of the said Tate or his assigns and said Company is bound only to such extent as it may be able to control or dictate the taking of such subjects by the Kinetograph.

There is little evidence that Tate ever managed much in the Kinetoscope business, although he tried more than once to get into it.

Meanwhile the profits of the Kinetoscope Company appear to have been solid. Their net profit, for example, from September 1 to October 1 was $8377.13.[33] On October 12, in a burst of confidence, the majority stockholders assigned half their prospective dividends to Raff and Gammon until the $10,000 paid at the time of the August 1894 contract had been repaid.[34]

An interesting abstract of the company's September 1 to October 16, 1894, finances is in the Baker Library collection. It lists office expenses, cash transactions, purchases from Edison, all film expenses in which the Hollands were involved, etc., and contained the following essential facts:

1. As of October 16, 1894, the Kinetoscope Company had paid Edison $7940 for Kinetoscopes and $369.35 for film subjects;[35]

2. As of October 16, 1894, the Kinetoscope Company had received $15,878.56 from customers;[36]

3. Such a subject as the "oriental dance" of October 1, costing $25, was

---

[33]Baker Library Collection. This is from a balance sheet of April 22, 1895.

[34]Ibid.

[35]It is easy to contrast this with modern motion picture production costs. Modern production may cost a million times as much, but in terms of viewer excitement, it is often difficult to credit an advance.

[36]It is difficult, without an analysis of facts somewhat beyond the reach of the researcher, to decide what part of this is from the sale of machines and what part is from films.

relatively expensive. It was two and a half times the amount paid the lady fencers and equal to the amount paid a prominent vaudeville act like Walton and Slavin;

4. B. M. Tate, A. O. Tate's brother, was a talent scout for film subjects, whereas Fred Harvey was an agent for many of these artists.

With the close of 1894 the Kinetoscope business was not working out in the way Raff and Gammon had expected. Business was good for the first six months after public exhibition began, but they did not enter the field until September, and although the fall sustained itself, the end of the year brought difficulties.

CHARLES MUSSER

The American Vitagraph, 1897–1901:

Survival and Success in a Competitive Industry

J. Stuart Blackton and Albert E. Smith, the original partners in the American Vitagraph Company, remembered the first years of their successful venture into moving pictures with nostalgic affection. As they grew older, the pair left behind an array of reminiscences about their youth, of which Albert Smith's *Two Reels and a Crank* is the best known and perhaps least reliable. These recollections have found their way into numerous film histories, from Raymond Fielding's *The American Newsreel,* Kenneth Macgowan's *Behind the Screen,* and Tino Balio's *The American Film Industry,* to Erik Barnouw's recent *The Magician and the Cinema.* Anthony Slide, in his history of Vitagraph, *The Big V,* relied on their recollections, and, in trying to reconcile contradictions in them, frequently offered two or more accounts of what was supposed to have happened.[1] Presumably he was aware that none of these different versions is necessarily accurate. This article, in contrast, relies on primary source materials, most previously overlooked or

---

[1]Albert E. Smith, in conjunction with Phil A. Koury, *Two Reels and a Crank* (Garden City, N. J.: Doubleday, 1952); Raymond Fielding, *The American Newsreel* (Norman: University of Oklahoma Press, 1972); Kenneth Macgowan, *Behind the Screen* (New York: Delacorte, 1965); Tino Balio, ed., *The American Film Industry* (Madison: University of Wisconsin Press, 1976); Anthony Slide, *The Big V: A History of the Vitagraph Company* (Metuchen, N.J.: Scarecrow, 1976); Eric Barnouw, *The Magician and the Cinema* (New York: Oxford University Press, 1981). Other histories which make use of this or other unreliable reminiscences by Blackton and Smith include Eric Barnouw, *Documentary* (New York: Oxford, 1974); Terry Ramsaye, *A Million and One Nights* (New York: Simon and Schuster, 1926); and Gerald Mast, *A History of the Movies,* 2nd ed. (Indianapolis: Bobbs-Merrill, 1976).

.ineffectually used, in order to test later statements against a framework of known facts. The purpose is not merely to produce a more accurate and detailed account of those early years, but to bring to the surface the problems and realities of the film world that have been concealed. Reminiscences are not necessarily inaccurate because of faulty memories; rather, they often have a legitimizing function and are created specifically to obscure the aspects of the film industry most revealing and characteristic of the period.

Within the overall context of an historical narrative, this study looks at key aspects of the moving picture world in the late 1890s. Then as now, cinema's mode of production involved three essential processes: film production, exhibition, and viewing; however, these processes and the relationships between the production companies, the showmen, and their audiences were very different in the 1897–1901 period than they would be even a few years later. The editorial function, for instance, was the responsibility of the showmen who selected short films, determined their order, and often tied them together with a narration. In many instances, spectators were supposed to bring a level of familiarity to their appreciation of screen narrative that later would be provided by intertitles. The tendency among film historians has been to treat film exhibition and the process of spectator appreciation as constants. They have read history backward in these two areas, using a framework of contemporary procedures. This equation of film production with the production of cinema assumes that change has taken place only in a limited area and has restricted our understanding of pre-Griffith cinema in general and the period of the 1890s most of all.

In tracing the rapid growth of American Vitagraph, which became the foremost exhibitor of 35 mm. films in New York City and one of the country's most important film producers by 1898–99, this article will pay particular concern to the relationship between exhibition and film production. These relations provide a valuable basis for analyzing not only the mode of production and representation during the 1890s, but Vitagraph's business strategies. Vitagraph began as an exhibition company but moved increasingly into production. The Edison Manufacturing Company was a producer that eventually, if indirectly, moved into exhibition. At first complementary, the two companies became increasingly competitive. Vitagraph's survival and growth in a highly competitive, rapidly changing industry was based on its ability to make "creative" use of business strategies which were representative of business standards employed by American capitalism at the turn of the century.

Before their involvement in cinema, Blackton and Smith worked in the same vein of entertainment as their contemporary, the Parisian prestidigitator Georges Méliès.[2] Blackton, like Méliès, was a cartoonist, an artist with a satirical pen. Smith

---

[2]See Maurice Bessy and Giuseppe Lo Duca, *Georges Méliès, Mage* (Paris: Jean-Jacques Pauvert, 1961); Paul Hammond, *Marvelous Méliès* (New York: St. Martin's, 1975), p. 27. The relationship between magicians and the cinema is explored at some length in Barnouw, *The Magician and the Cinema*.

had a career as a magician which eventually reached its highpoint in 1899, when his portrait appeared on the cover of *Mahatma*, a popular magazine for American magicians. The duo, often assisted by their friend and fellow Englishman, Ronald Reader, traveled the Lyceum circuit of churches and YMCA's, putting on an evening's entertainment made up of a variety of acts: sleight of hand, chapeaugraphy, ventriloquism, Blackton's lightning sketches and a magic lantern show which customarily closed the evening.[3] Blackton apparently painted many of the slides, which were projected onto a screen accompanied by his monologue. Others were probably stereopticon slides (i.e., photographs on a glass base suitable for projection) that were taken and developed by the two partners.[4] Lantern shows were a standard turn, not only in their Lyceum entertainments, but at Méliès's Théâtre Robert-Houdin and among prestidigitators in general.

The two young men, according to Smith's later reminiscences, became interested in expanding the lantern portion of their program by emulating Alexander Black's success with his "picture plays." These plays were presented by a series of stereopticon slides shown in rapid succession while the showman mimicked the lines of various characters in the play:

> Blackton and I had been considering something along this line to fit into our program. We even had reached the point where we had decided that "Rip Van Winkle" would be a good story to illustrate and present with magic lantern slides, but when we found this early kinetoscope exhibition we knew we had found what we had been looking for.[5]

Like many entertainers who began to work with film in the United States and Europe, Blackton and Smith saw moving pictures as an extension of the magic lantern with which they were already working.

Blackton and Smith's Initial Involvement With Cinema

Blackton and Smith had left us with conflicting versions of how they got started in the movies. In speeches and testimony, Blackton suggested that the wizard Edison was directly responsible for launching their careers. Blackton's

---

[3]See Slide, *The Big V*, pp. 3–5, for a reproduction of a Blackton/Smith/Reader program dated December 7, 1894.

[4]Account books for the Commercial Advertising Bureau indicate that they shot and developed their own slides. This expertise undoubtedly facilitated the move into film production. Account books of Commerical Advertising Bureau, January 5, 8, 1898, Albert Smith Collection, University of California, Los Angeles, courtesy Mrs. Albert Smith (henceforth abbreviated ASC).

[5]Albert E. Smith, unpublished manuscript for *Two Reels and a Crank*, courtesy Mrs. Albert Smith. Alexander Black was on the Lyceum circuit as well, making this statement credible.

engaging story has him visiting Thomas Edison as a nineteen-year-old cub reporter for the *New York World*. After interviewing Edison and drawing his picture, Blackton was taken around back to the Black Maria where Edison had him perform for the camera. The afternoon ended with the inventor taking an order for a projector from young Blackton.[6] There is an aura of being at the source, in the right place and at the right time. It is the stuff with which great legends are made: the recruitment of the "film pioneers." Blackton's story, as reported and legitimized in *A Million and One Nights* is one of those that "should have been true" and so one that Edison did not dispute.[7] Furthermore, there are important elements of truth in Blackton's account.

The three films made at the Edison Manufacturing Company which featured Blackton resulted from his work with the *New York Evening World*, where his sketches appeared between June 4th and October 26th, 1896.[8] Most were humorous "comics," although at least two were political cartoons. Although Blackton's newspaper sketches demonstrate a flair for comedy that can be found in later Vitagraph films, none of these newspaper sketches were of Thomas Edison. In fact, it seems exceedingly unlikely that the *World* would send a fledgling caricaturist to draw the "wizard" at the height of his popularity and even more unlikely that Edison would consent to see him. The only drawing of Edison in the *World* from this period that I have located appeared on the 12th of April and was "taken from a photograph."[9] Blackton was not the artist. Furthermore, this famous meeting was mentioned by neither Edison nor Blackton when they were fighting each other in the courts. Only when Edison and Vitagraph were sued by the United States for violation of the Sherman antitrust laws, did Blackton tell the story in court—almost twenty years after it supposedly occurred.

Other documentation suggests a different.explanation for Blackton's visit to the Black Maria. His work for Pulitzer's newspaper led to a benefit performance for the *Evening World*'s Sick Baby Fund, which helped the infants of poor New Yorkers survive the summer heat. The entertainment at the Brunswick Hotel Casino in Asbury Park, New Jersey, was given by the "Royal Entertainment Company of New York" on June 26th, raised $16.85, and was favorably reviewed by the *Evening World:* ·

---

[6]Slide, *The Big V*, pp. 5–7. Blackton's story was delivered at University of Southern California on February 20, 1929.

[7]Edison read the Ramsaye manuscript before its publication. Gordon Hendricks, *The Edison Motion Picture Myth* (Berkeley: University of California Press, 1961), p. 12.

[8]I went through issues of the *New York Evening World* from April 1896 to February 1897. Between June and October 1896, I found eighteen cartoons, on June 4, 6, 10, 12, 16, and 24; July 4, 8, 11, and 17; August 31; September 9, 12, 14, and 19 (two cartoons); and October 21 and 26. I went through the *New York World* from April to October 1896 and found a single cartoon of Blackton's on April 9, 1896 (colored supplement, p. 5).

[9]*World*, p. 6.

Albert E. Smith opened the programme with a series of skillful experiments in prestidigitation. Using no mechanical appliances and only such articles as he could borrow from the audience, the most wonderful results were produced. He terminated the first number with his humorous shadow-graphs—the swan dressing its plumage, the wolf swallowing a bone and a pigeon in flight were very natural in their motions, while the comical antics of six different characters in grotesque pantomime caused the audience to howl with delight.

J. Stuart Blackton, the well-known cartoonist and humorist, certainly has no rival in rapid cartoon and caricature work. He won his audience at the start by a series of humorous sketches of people in the audience, accompanying each drawing with a running fire of good-natured talk that kept everyone in a roar. His wonderful pencil fairly flew over the large sheets of paper, and the drawings were as finely finished in appearance as the illustrations in a comic paper.

The political cartoons were a series of striking likenesses, especially Senator Hill's sad expression and McKinley's smile, and his remarks apropos the political situation tickled the audience immensely. There was a rush for Mr. Blackton's signed sketches after the entertainment which netted a good round sum for the poor suffering little tots.[10]

This performance not only gave the duo an excellent press review but led to Blackton's appearance before the camera. The *World* had taken an active interest in moving pictures from the outset; at its request, May Irwin and John C. Rice had visited the Black Maria and were photographed executing their famous kiss from *The Widow Jones,* a musical then being staged at the Bijou Theater in New York City.[11] *The Kiss* turned out to be the most popular film on Vitascope programs. In July or early August Edison's cameramen took a film of the *New York "World" Sick Baby Fund* showing the children of poor people enjoying themselves in swings or on hobby-horses.[12] They also took three films of Blackton sketching portraits of Edison, McKinley, and a female figure. The films, numbers 93, 95, and 97 in Maguire and Baucus catalogues, were each 150 feet long, at a time when most films were only 50 feet in length.[13] On August 5th, the *Evening World* reported a

[10]*Evening World,* June 27, 1896.

[11]*World,* April 26, 1896, p. 21.

[12]*The Phonoscope* 1 (November 1896): 16. This film, which was listed by the International Film Company, was almost certainly a dupe (like many others on the list) made from an Edison print.

[13]Maguire and Baucus, *Lumière Films, Edison Films, International Films* (New York, Fall 1897), p. 14. The catalogue, however, lists him as Blackman.

donation to the Sick Baby Fund of $25.00 by the Vitascope Company. It was almost certainly connected with the production of these films.[14]

Titles given the film of Blackton drawing Edison suggested that the famous inventor was sketched "from life." It proved to be perfect for "The Wizard Edison's Marvelous Vitascope," which was presented as the headline attraction at Proctor's Pleasure Palace and Proctor's 23rd Street Theatre, two of the leading New York vaudeville houses. Proctor advertisements announced that seven films were to be shown at both theaters: *The Arrival of Li Huang Chang, Inventor Edison Sketched by* World *Artist, New Bathing Scene at Rockway, The Haymakers at Work, The New Skirt Dancer, Newsboys Scrambling for Pennies,* and *Shooting the Coney Island Chutes.*[15] The exhibition was favorably reviewed by the *Mail and Express,* with particular attention given to Blackton's sketch of Edison:

> The animation and realism of the moving scenes from local life pictures by Edison's Vitascope excited much enthusiasm at Proctor's houses.... The most curious and interesting of the new views was that showing the rapid sketching of Wizard Edison's portrait by a well-known cartoonist. Every stroke of the crayon was reproduced until the excellent likeness was perfected. The Vitascope will enjoy great and long continued popularity at the Palace.

When the program changed at the end of the week, Blackton's sketch of Edison was the only holdover. Again the *Mail and Express* singled out Blackton's film:

> No subject is allowed to grow stale and every view is new for the coming week except that which shows Edison's portrait developing beneath the rapid crayon strokes of a cartoonist, who turns and bows to the audience at the finish.[16]

What distinguished this film from the many other recordings of vaudeville acts, indeed from Blackton's sketch of McKinley, was the suggestion, further developed in Blackton's story, that Edison sat for his portrait just outside camera range. The film's effective use of offscreen space was valorized as an Edison production and by its projection on the Edison Vitascope.

---

[14]*Evening World,* August 5, 1896, p. 6.

[15]*World,* September 13, 1896, p. 14. Program of Proctor's Pleasure Palace, September 21, 1896, Harvard Theater Collection (HTC).

[16]*Mail and Express* (New York), September 15, 19, 1896. A version of the last quote also appeared in *The Phonoscope* 1 (November 1896): 13, but mentioned Blackton by name.

The new International Film Company paid Blackton the compliment of duping all three films and offering them for sale in the first issue of *The Phonoscope,* a new trade journal that began publication in September 1896:

> BLACKTON'S SKETCHES. The New York "World's" caricature artist, drawing sketches on a screen.
>
> No. 1 represents him as drawing a large picture of Mr. Thomas A. Edison.
>
> No. 2 showing the artist drawing pictures of McKinley and President Cleveland.
>
> No. 3 is a humorous selection, showing the artist drawing a life-size picture of a female figure, in which the expressions of the countenance are rapidly changing.[17]

As a result of such duping practices, Thomas Edison was soon copyrighting the films produced by his company.

The films of Blackton drawing Edison and other figures helped the artist move from the Lyceum circuit to vaudeville as a drawer of "Clever Crayon Caricatures." He appeared at Keith's Union Square Theatre for the week of February 22, 1897, and over a year later at Proctor's 23rd Street Theatre and Proctor's Pleasure Palace.[18] The success of this film and its effect on Blackton's career emphasized the potential of moving pictures to the young partners. The money gained from Blackton's appearance at Keith's may have even financed the acquisition of a machine for projecting films.

In *Two Reels and a Crank,* Albert Smith claimed to have projected motion pictures at Pastor's Theatre on 14th Street in March 1896, a month before the introduction of the Vitascope at Koster and Bial's. This latter-day claim to priority is contradicted by Smith's earlier and far more believable account of their entry into moving picture exhibition, offered as testimony in a court case initiated by Thomas Edison in 1898:

> J. Stuart Blackton, the other defendant, and myself were in business as entertainers prior to July 1898. He was a cartoonist and I was an impersonator and ventriloquist. We were partners. We were each much interested in the subject of motion picture photography, and in the early part of 1897, we bought an apparatus for taking and exhibiting moving

---

[17]*The Phonoscope* 1 (November 1896); 16.

[18]Program of Keith's Union Square Theatre, February 22, 1897. Courtesy Richard Koszarski. "Next Issue," program of Proctor's 23rd Street Theatre, May 30, 1898 (HTC); program of Proctor's Pleasure Palace, June 20, 1898 (HTC). (J. Austin Fynes had moved from Keith's as general manager to the Proctor houses in the intervening year.)

pictures from McAllister on Nassau Street, New York City. This apparatus was of the manufacture of the complainant, Thomas A. Edison, who I am informed does business under the name of the Edison Manufacturing Company.[19]

This apparatus was the Edison Projecting Kinetoscope ('97 model) which became available in late February 1897 at a cost of $100.[20] Its price was a substantial reduction in cost from earlier projectors on the market; the Projectograph, for instance, which was manufactured by the International Film Company, was advertised at a cost of $200 in January 1897.[21] The substantial reduction in cost allowed the young pair to become moving picture exhibitors.

Smith and Blackton formed a copartnership in March 1897 and called it the Edison Vitagraph Company.[22] In the minds of the public, the name associated (or confused) their concern with Edison and the Vitascope. Moving pictures became a new feature in their repertoire of Lyceum entertainments. Little documentation survives to indicate either the films they projected on the screen or the way they were shown. In his memoirs, Smith recalled projecting the *Black Diamond Express;* Blackton provided the introductory remarks and accompanied the film with sound effects from behind the screen.[23] Undoubtedly one of the films was Blackton drawing Edison, and it would not be too much to suppose that Blackton's story of interviewing Edison introduced the film. Such remarks allowed them to get maximum value from their small supply of films.

THE COMMERCIAL ADVERTISING BUREAU

Blackton and Smith decided to enter the field of motion picture advertising at the end of 1897, calling this new enterprise the Commercial Advertising Bureau. The use of projected images for advertising purposes predated cinema, although moving pictures were easily incorporated into its mode of exhibition. As C. Francis Jenkins observed,

---

[19]Deposition of Albert E. Smith, April 9, 1900, equity no. 6990, 6991, U. S. Circuit Court, Southern District of New York, Federal Archive and Record Center, Bayonne, N. J. (FARC-B); p. 1. The thrust of this deposition was that a projector could also be used to take moving pictures, and it must be interpreted from this perspective.

[20]Maguire and Baucus, "Preliminary Circular," February 16, 1897. It announces that the Projecting Kinetoscope will be available in ten days for $100.

[21]*The Phonoscope*, January–February 1897, p. 3.

[22]Dunn and Bradstreet, reports on American Vitagraph, Edison National Historic Site (ENHS).

[23]See Smith, *Two Reels and a Crank*, pp. 39–40.

The catchy character of "life motion pictures" was soon recognized by advertisers and they were not long in availing themselves of the opportunity offered, and now one can scarcely visit a large city anywhere in America without finding an advertising stand employing moving pictures wholly or in part as their attraction. The methods in vogue are but simple modifications of ordinary lantern advertising practice. Usually there are two lanterns, one to project moving picture advertising films, while the other lantern is employed to fill in the gap with single slide advertising pictures or pictures of purely entertaining character. Quite frequently a slide is used in the secondary lantern which projects above and below the moving picture on the screen the name of the article together with the address, etc., of the manufacturers. The moving picture is thrown upon the pre-arranged black blank on the screen.[24]

Others had demonstrated that this form of exhibition was popular and commercially lucrative the previous spring and summer.[25] It flourished during the warm months when people passing by on the streets were ready to stop and watch films and slides projected onto a well-placed canvas. The images customarily advertised local stores, services, and products. The partners found this kind of exhibition particularly attractive because its busy period coincided with the dull season for theatrical and Lyceum entertainments. To better service their customers, the two young men acquired an office on the ninth floor of the Morse Building at 140 Nassau Street in New York City, room 90, with a skylight. Signed on December 22, 1897, the lease ran for a year and four months, from January 1, 1898 to April 1899.[26]

The Commercial Advertising Bureau intensified Blackton and Smith's involvement in cinema as significant changes were taking place inside the institution of the screen. Cinema's era as a screen novelty, with its projection of discrete images, its emphasis on life-like movement, and its lack of interest in narrative had ended. By the 1897–98 season, it had become "last year's novelty." At the same time, a new form of projection technology was commercialized which indicates a shift in role of the motion picture exhibitor. This was "a combination moving picture machine and stereopticon."[27] Slides and films could easily be integrated into a continuous program using one lantern. The mechanics varied, but many machines had a swivel attachment mounted in front of the lantern

---

[24]C. Francis Jenkins, *Animated Pictures* (Washington, D.C., 1898), p. 90.

[25]*The Phonoscope*, July 1897, p. 9.

[26]Lease signed by Blackton and Smith, December 22, 1897 (ASC).

[27]W. B. Moore first offered this for sale in November 1897, advertising it as "something radically new." *New York Clipper*, November 1897, p. 617.

box/light source which could be swung back and forth by the operator, making a cut that was manifested on the screen. While some exhibitors had juxtaposed images before the development of the combination moving picture machine and stereopticon (either showing several films spliced end-to-end or projecting slides and films from separate lanterns), the machine indicates a heightened concern for the succession of images and with narrative in general. A whole range of editorial possibilities was now in the hands of the moving picture operator, although this "new" mode of exhibition was not so novel when placed within the larger context of screen history. Effectively, it involved the incorporation of cinema, until then a screen novelty, into the mainstream of screen entertainment.

Accounts for the Commercial Advertising Bureau document all income and expenditures during the first four-and-a-half months of the company's existence. After paying their January rent ($10), the partners began to furnish their modest office with a desk ($9.75), an arm chair ($1.49), two cane chairs ($1.26), a table ($.76), a hat rack and mirror ($1.50), and partition ($4). After purchasing stationary supplies ($8.25), they bought lantern plates, developer, two boxes of amaline colors ($3.25) for tinting slides and printed up a thousand circulars ($5.50). Expenses mounted in February as they paid rent on a roof uptown ($12), made a deposit with the Electric Company ($18), and bought a calcium lamp from the International Film Company ($30), which was on its way out of business due to a suit brought by Thomas Edison. A cinematographe or electric lantern was bought from Raff and Gammon ($20), and a mechanism for a picture machine (also $20).[28] Having spent $247.08 between January 1 and March 1, 1898, they were ready to start showing films with the first hint of warm weather.

In mid-March, the Commercial Advertising Bureau began to generate income, receiving payment from Munk's Shoe Store ($8), North Side Dental Rooms ($3), Lickmann's Cigar and Photo ($4), Mayer's Clothiers ($2), Wiener's Jewelers ($2), and Blackman's Bicycles ($2). In April 1898 they made slides for their customers but had to hire an outside film company to make two advertising films for Lickmann's and North Side Dental Rooms. Weekly income gradually moved up to more than $40 a week as the Commercial Advertising Bureau picked up a few additional customers.

Blackton and Smith's advertising enterprise was of short duration as other opportunities arose, created by the Spanish-American War. On April 12, 1898, Blackton and Smith sold "Branch No. 23" for $250. The sale of Branch No. 18 at 125th Street on May 16 for $125 closed the account. The books for the company suggest the enterprise required considerable work and yielded relatively modest

---

[28]These and other figures for 1898 and 1899 come from accounts of receipts and expenses for the period between January 1 through May 19, 1898 and checkbook stubs for the period between January 1, 1898 through August 5, 1899 (ASC).

profits. With the sale of their branches, the Bureau was able to break even with modest gains in film, equipment, and furniture.[29]

SHOWING WAR FILMS FOR VAUDEVILLE

Vaudeville theaters did not acquire or show their own films but hired an independent company to provide them with a complete service: projector, operator, weekly film program, and occasionally a lecturer. Such companies not only acted as exhibitors but effectively distributed the films they purchased from producers or their agents. Prior to the sinking of the *Maine* in February 1898, moving pictures were shown only at a limited number of vaudeville houses and then for a few weeks in between long hiatuses. With the Cuban crisis, most theaters showed pertinent "war films" for weeks and then months without interruption: in many cases moving pictures became a standard feature. This sudden increase in demand gave exhibitors like American Vitagraph new opportunities to move up to big-time showmanship. As tensions rose between Spain and the United States over Cuba, the Edison Manufacturing Company arranged for William Paley to go to Florida and Cuba to photograph the approaching war. On April 21 and 22, Edison copyrighted twenty of these films and put them on the market. On April 25, the day the United States declared war on Spain, Vitagraph purchased six to ten Edison war films for $87. On May 2, 1898, the Central Opera House opened at 67th Street and Third Avenue in Manhattan with a vaudeville program and played to a small house; American Vitagraph was on its bill.[30] Two of the last entries for the Commercial Advertising Bureau indicate the partners were paid $47.50 on May 7 and again on the 14th for these exhibitions, their first on the vaudeville circuit.

The rapid expansion of Edison (American) Vitagraph in the spring and summer of 1898 can be attributed to two additional developments taking place within the partnership. Smith converted a projector into a camera which allowed them to make their own films, and he made substantial improvements on the Projecting Kinetoscope. Together these factors enabled them to become an important force in the exhibition of motion pictures.

Smith's modification of the Projecting Kinetoscope, a reframing device, gave Vitagraph an important advantage over its competitors. The problem it solved was a persistent one in early exhibition:

> It not infrequently happens in use . . . that the rapid motion of the film as it is propelled past the aperture causes the holes of its edges to spring out of engagement with the sprocket on the propelling drum. This

---

[29]See n. 28.

[30]*New York Clipper*, May 7, 1898, pp. 160, 168.

immediately causes the picture projected on the screen to be out of register with the field of light... and produces the effect... where parts of two sections of the film are thrown upon the screen instead of the whole of one section.[31]

Smith solved this problem by mounting the actuating mechanism of the film on a moveable frame so that "no cessation of the forward motion of the film need to take place while the adjustment referred to is being made, a result which prior to my invention had not been accomplished."[32] This improvement can be accounted for, in part, by two ledger entries in mid-May, noted as "brass work for Vitagraph" amounting to $1.43 and "mechanical work for Vitagraph" coming to $8.69 and done by Herman Muller.[33]

Blackton and Smith's motivation for going into production was not to make money by selling prints to competing exhibitors but to make films for their own exclusive use. They were able to offer vaudeville managers a film program which included motion picture subjects no one else could provide. Their film service became more attractive as a result. In the spring of 1898, Vitagraph purchased another Edison Projecting Kinetoscope and adapted it "either to take, print or exhibit motion pictures."[34] Entries on May 19 in the Commercial Advertising Bureau account book total $2.13 for two naval books, a photo, fireworks, gunpowder and gypsum, and cards. Photographic chemicals came to $.90 and sensitized film was $31.75. These were undoubtedly the props, film, and developer for their *Battle of Manila Bay*, a miniaturized reenactment of Dewey's famous naval victory which had occurred two weeks earlier. Albert Smith later recalled that

At this time street vendors in New York were selling sturdy photographs of ships of the American and Spanish fleets. We bought a set of each and we cut out the battleships. On a table, topside down, we placed one of artist Blackton's large canvas-covered frames and filled it with water an inch deep. In order to stand the cutouts in the water, we nailed them to lengths of wood about an inch square. In this way a little "shelf" was provided behind each ship, and on this shelf we placed pinches of

[31]Patent specification by Albert E. Smith, application filed March 15, 1900, and granted April 30, 1901, as no. 673,329, p. 1. The delayed filing coincided with a break in the relationship with the Edison Company (see below).

[32]Ibid., p. 3.

[33]Accounts of Commercial Advertising Bureau, May 12, 17, 1898. Checkbook stub #138 of the Vitagraph Company, May 7, 1898. This work could also have been for the conversion of the projector.

[34]Deposition of Albert E. Smith, April 9, 1900.

gunpowder—three pinches for each ship—not too many, we felt, for a major sea engagement of this sort.[35]

Blackton is purported to have blown cigar smoke in front of the lens to conceal the tacky quality of the production.[36] Other purchases of sensitized film followed.

A small ad for "The American Vitagraph" in the June 4 issue of the *New York Clipper* emphasized the company's new assets by asserting that they had "a perfect picture machine" and were "exhibiting original and exclusive war films."[37] Blackton and Smith's successful move into vaudeville exhibition was integrally related to these two features. A major impediment to their entry, however, was financial. For the week of May 16, for instance, twenty-nine films were being shown at Proctor's 23rd Street Theatre, almost all of them having to do with the war. Twenty-five 50-foot films selling between $.20 and $.24 a foot could cost over $250.[38] J. Austin Fynes, who managed Proctor's vaudeville theaters, where Blackton and Smith were given their big break, helped them to acquire the working capital by first hiring Blackton as a caricaturist for two weeks in June. Blackton performed at Proctor's 23rd Street Theatre during the week commencing June 6 as a "cartoonist and monologist," mounting a show the *Clipper* found "entertaining." Two weeks later he was at Proctor's Pleasure Palace and deemed "decidedly clever in his crayon work."[39] A complete change in program at Proctor's 23rd Street Theatre for the week of June 27 suggests they commenced exhibiting films at that theater after Blackton's brief tour on the Proctor circuit came to an end.[40] It was not until Monday September 4, 1898 that the pair showed films at Proctor's Pleasure Palace.

AMERICAN VITAGRAPH BECOMES AN EDISON LICENSEE

Vitagraph's shortage of capital encouraged the young pair to engage in a questionable money-making scheme. The Vitagraph ad of June 4 also offered to sell "two sets of Edison War films. Brand new. At $7.00 while they last." Blackton and Smith were making dupes and selling prints at $5 under the Edison rate. Not

[35]Smith, *Two Reels and a Crank*, pp. 66–67.

[36]Ramsaye, *Million and One Nights*, pp. 390–91. As Eric Barnouw reminds us, another version (perhaps somewhat apocryphal) has Mrs. Blackton smoking a cigarette for the scene; *The Magician and the Cinema*, p. 77.

[37]*New York Clipper*, June 4, 1898, p. 233.

[38]Advertisement for Lubin, *New York Clipper*, June 25, 1898, p. 286; Edison Manufacturing Company, *Edison Films* (Orange, N.J., May 1898).

[39]*New York Clipper*, June 11, 25, 1898, pp. 244, 276.

[40]Program of Proctor's 23rd Street Theater, June 27, 1898 (HTC).

surprisingly, a number of people associated with Edison investigated, among them George Dutel, a salesman for the P. Z. Maguire Company which sold Edison "War Films." Eugene Elmore and Edwin S. Porter, his associate at the Edison licensed Eden Musee, also dropped by. Elmore describes his visit in a deposition.

> On June 2nd, 1898, and during the forenoon of that day, I called at the office of said American Vitagraph Company and found that it was in fact the office of J. Stuart Blackton and Albert E Smith. I was accompanied by Mr. Edwin S. Porter, who is associated with me in business. Our object was to inquire as to the matter advertised and to ascertain what photographs were being sold at said office, and possibly to purchase some if photographs and terms were satisfactory. On reaching said office, we found J. Stuart Blackton in conversation with Mr. George F. Dutel. Mr. Porter and I stated our errand, and during a conversation which ensued and which was had in the presence and within the hearing of Mr. Porter, Mr. Dutel and myself, Mr. Blackton said he had been selling a number of photographs known as "Edison War Films" and which had been printed from negatives made from a commercial Edison photograph forming one of this series of pictures. Mr. Blackton then procured and exhibited to us a negative illustrative of the Edison photograph entitled "Transport Whitney Leaving Dock. . ." Blackton also said that he had other negatives made in the same manner and illustrating other subjects in the series of war films, copies of which had been marketed for some time past by Mr. Edison. Blackton said that he did not at that time have on hand any copies made from the negative "Transport Whitney Leaving Dock," having sold the day before all such copies which had been made from that copied negative. He said, however, that if we were able to wait for a few days, he would be able to supply us with such copies.[41]

George Dutel did return a few days later and purchased two dupe films, *Transport Leaving Dock (Transport "Whitney" Leaving Dock)* and *Soldiers Leaving Train (10th U.S. Infantry Disembarking);* these would serve as evidence in the suit brought by Thomas A. Edison against Blackton and Smith a month later.

On July 12, subpoenas were served on "J. Stuart Blackton and Albert E. Smith, individually and as co-partners trading under the name and style of Commercial Advertising Bureau and American Vitagraph Company." There were three suits: one for copying copyrighted material and two for infringing on

---

[41]Deposition of Eugene Elmore, July 15, 1898, equity no. 6989, U. S. Circuit Court, Southern District of New York (FARC-B).

Edison's motion picture patents.[42] As soon as he received his subpoena, Blackton went to the office of Dyer, Edmonds, and Dyer, Edison's lawyers, and talked to S. O. Edmonds, who later testified that

> The defendant, Blackton, called upon me and asked why the suits had been brought. I explained the reason in very plain terms to the effect that he had violated Mr. Edison's copyright on the picture entitled TRANS-PORT WHITNEY LEAVING DOCK, and that, in addition to this, he and his partner had been using projecting machines and films infringing upon the Edison patents, Nos. 493,426 and 539,168, and that the object of the suits was to secure injunctions against them both on the grounds of pirating the copyright and on the ground of infringing said patents. During the conversation which ensued he explained the business which he and his partner were carrying on, and the character of the projecting machine which they were using and asked me what he should do. I told him that I could not advise him further than that he should put his affairs in the hands of counsel. He replied that he did not wish to go to that expense and that henceforth he would use nothing but apparatus and films purchased from the Edison Manufacturing Company. He then asked me what would be the effect if no attention were paid to the subpoenas and I replied that we would enter decrees *pro confesso* and issue injunctions in all three suits under those decrees. He asked if this would interfere with his using non-infringing Edison apparatus, and I told him that it would not. This seemed to satisfy him, and he went away after stating that he would probably go to Orange and see Mr. Gilmore, about the purchase of Edison apparatus. After he left the office, I wrote Mr. Gilmore as follows:

> W. E. Gilmore, Esq.
> Orange, N. J.
>
> Dear Sir:
>
> The subpoenas in the suits for infringement of the Edison patents and those in the suits for infringement of Mr. Edison's copyright were served on Messrs. Blackton and Smith this forenoon. This afternoon Mr. Blackton called and informed us that the Colt projecting machine which had heretofore been in operation in Proctor's 23rd St. Theatre had been replaced by an Edison projectoscope, and that all of the films in use both at that theatre and at the Pleasure Palace are genuine Edison films. . . . He seemed somewhat frightened at the three suits brought against him and promised that hereafter he would not infringe either by the use of

---

[42]Equity case nos. 6989, 6990, 6991 (FARC-B).

machines or films infringing Mr. Edison's patents or copyrights. Nevertheless, since the affidavits and exhibits on the proposed motion for preliminary injunction against Blackton and Smith have been prepared, we deem it wise to proceed with the motion even at the risk of defeat.[43]

The next day, Blackton went out to West Orange and talked with William Gilmore, vice-president and general manager of the Edison Manufacturing Company. After discussing the injunction, they came to an agreement, whereby Blackton and Smith would work as Edison licensees. Blackton later described the verbal agreement.

Towards the close of the conversation, after I had informed Mr. Gilmore that my previous experience as an actor was useful to me in devising new subjects for these moving pictures, he said that they would be glad to make a contract with us to make pictures for them on royalty; that if we would make negatives and they accept them, they would give us the right to use them for our own exhibition purposes and would pay us 30 cts. a piece for each 50 foot film they used or sold. He said that they had made a similar agreement with a person named Paley, and that I had better see him and see how generous Edison had been in making such an arrangement.[44]

On August 2, on their way to Martha's Vineyard, Blackton and Smith signed an agreement which allowed the decrees resulting from the suits to be entered against them. The decrees were filed on August 10, although the final injunctions were not actually served on the partners until October 28, 1898.[45] To the trade, however, the two young men appeared to contest the Edison suit:

The defendants enter a general denial, and as far as the transport is concerned, aver that they had their apparatuses on the dock while the ship was leaving, and that Mr. Edison cannot prevent them from taking photographs.[46]

The assertion that Smith and Blackton went to Cuba to film the Spanish-American War, an assertion that can be found in their reminiscences and many

---

[43]Deposition of S. O. Edmonds, April 9, 1900, equity nos. 6990, 6991.

[44]Deposition of J. Stuart Blackton, April 9, 1900, equity nos. 6990, 6991.

[45]S. O. Edmonds, April 9, 1900.

[46]*The Phonoscope*, August 1898, p. 13.

film histories, probably began as a face-saving gesture designed to conceal their duping activities.

Blackton and Smith's acceptance of the decree and their subsequent agreement with the Edison Manufacturing Company momentarily strengthened their position in the New York moving picture world—as it had for William Paley—by giving them a distribution outlet for their films and a quasi-legal status as Edison licensees. At the same time, Edison needed commercial allies. Sigmund Lubin, the Philadelphia producer of 35 mm. films, and the American Mutoscope and Biograph Company, a New York-based rival which produced and exhibited their own large-format films, continued to offer severe competition. William Paley's films from Cuba and Florida were a success, but the war was winding down, and films of a different sort would have to follow if the Edison Manufacturing Company was to take full advantage of their commercial position. As bright, attractive young men of tremendous energy and British birth, the pair had an advantage over other immigrants who were moving into the film world as producers and exhibitors. Edison personnel found men like Sigmund Lubin or Eberhard Schneider, a New York exhibitor, uncouth, and preferred not to do business with them. Perhaps more to the point, the Edison Company could afford to embrace Vitagraph since their failure to contest Edison's suit left the production company firmly in control of Vitagraph's fortunes. If Vitagraph's activities threatened the well-being and profitability of Edison's Kinetograph Department, their license could simply be withdrawn.

An assessment of Blackton and Smith's situation in August 1898 would suggest the following strengths and weaknesses. The Vitagraph partners had established themselves in vaudeville exhibition; they had real though still limited experience in film production and exhibition augmented by their background as entertainers; they had a secret reframing device and a modest though growing investment in machines and films including their own productions. On the other hand, their youth, which translated into business inexperience, was demonstrated not so much by their decision to sell dupes as by their handling of the lawsuit.[47] Men like Lubin contested Edison lawsuits and stayed in business unencumbered. The injunction against the pair potentially weakened their ability to act freely in the film world, although its ramifications were not fully apparent at the time. Perhaps most important, rapid growth on limited resources left Vitagraph strapped for funds. A lack of money prevented them from fully capitalizing on their strengths, forced them to take short cuts and to make mistakes. Their

---

[47]The legality of Edison's method of copyrighting film had not been established by the courts. This would happen in 1903 and only then on appeal to a higher court; Thomas A. Edison v. Sigmund Lubin, equity no. 36, April Sessions 1902, Circuit Court for the Eastern District of Pennsylvania, Federal Archive and Record Center, Philadelphia.

reluctance to hire a lawyer when they were sued was motivated in large part by a desire to avoid spending money they did not have. This weakness left them vulnerable to the machinations of their future partner, William T. Rock.

A THIRD PARTNER: WILLIAM T. ROCK

William T. Rock at forty-seven was substantially older than his partners-to-be and more experienced in the ups and downs of the moving picture world and the world of entertainment. With Walter Wainwright he had bought the rights to exhibit moving pictures in the state of Louisiana under the Armat Patents in 1896, and showed films at West End Park and Vitascope Hall in New Orleans on their Edison Vitascope. By 1898, he had moved to New York and continued to exhibit moving pictures, using his office as an exchange for second-hand films. He also owned some slot machines and called himself "a manufacturer of billiard tables and supplies."[48] (As with Blackton and Smith, Rock had not yet made moving pictures a full-time occupation.) As his ownership of a small exchange might suggest, Rock had films available for exhibition and some financial reserves, both of which the other two desperately needed. He was to lend the partnership at least $300.[49] Although Blackton and Smith had encountered Rock in early June, when they bought a few films from him,[50] this contact was more casual than those that took place later that summer. As Rock recalled,

> I became acquainted with Albert E. Smith and J. Stuart Blackton late in August or early in September of 1898. They were doing a small business in exhibiting films and they applied to me and asked me to lend them some of mine or to exchange some of my films for theirs. The acquaintance then ripened quickly into an intimacy, as a result of which, I was offered a partnership in their business.[51]

This quick ripening of friendship was not based on goodwill alone. In the summer of 1898, Rock remained on good terms with Thomas Armat, who was initiating suits to uphold his patents for projecting motion pictures. Rock, undoubtedly aware of Vitagraph's response to Edison's bill of complaint, decided they were an easy target and wrote Armat suggesting he take action. Armat responded in a letter dated August 18, 1898.

---

[48]Deposition of William T. Rock, April 9, 1900, equity nos. 6990, 6991.
[49]Checkbook stub #324 of American Vitagraph, April 17, 1899.
[50]Checkbook stub #150 of American Vitagraph, June 8, 1898.
[51]Rock, April 9, 1900.

Mr. Wm T. Rock
112 East 125th Street

Dear Sir:

You are hereby authorized and directed to initiate suit for ten thousand dollars damages against Proctor, of Proctor's Theatre and the party or parties who have the animated picture apparatus at said theatre, which said apparatus is an infringement upon my U. S. Patent No. 578,185 if they refuse to pay royalty.

Yours, (signed)

Thomas Armat[52]

Rock went to Proctor's Theatre, apparently threatening a court case if they did not give him Vitagraph's exhibition contract. Instead, Manager J. Austin Fynes urged a merger. Rock might have an untested patent behind him, but Blackton and Smith had other assets that Proctor's wanted to retain. Turning the Pleasure Palace over to an expanded Vitagraph copartnership which included Rock may have been part of the compromise.

Before coming to an agreement, Rock and his future partners went to West Orange to talk with Gilmore and James White, in charge of much of the film business, about Vitagraph's business dealing and legal status, vis-à-vis Edison According to Smith,

In September 1898, we admitted to our partnership Mr. William T. Rock, who had been engaged in similar lines of business. Prior to our making a contract with him, Mr. Blackton and he and I accordingly went out to the Edison factory to have Edison or his superintendent confirm the agreement with us. We met there Mr. J. H. White and Mr. Gilmore and had a general conversation with them. The agreement was then confirmed and amplified and was to the following effect:

We were to devise subjects for pictures and make the negatives and submit them for approval. If Edison accepted them, we were to receive $15.00 for each fifty (50) foot negative and were to receive from him one positive printed therefrom free and a length of blank stock equal to that used in the negative. Also we were to receive a royalty of thirty (30) cents for every positive made by him and sold from the negative.

We were to copy films for him or on his order, we were to pay for the originals and then for each negative furnished, we were to receive from Edison twice the length of blank film stock, and our original in blank.

---

[52]Thomas Armat to William T. Rock, August 18, 1898, Armat Letter Book, 1898, Thomas A. Armat/Glenn E. Matthews Collection, George Eastman House, p. 23.

We were to loan him our apparatus, which was an Edison apparatus, the mechanical details of which had been improved by me, and were to receive in return five (5) complete machines from him.

If in securing subjects we were put to unusual expense, he agreed to pay half the expense.[53]

The terms of this agreement were never formalized. Gilmore took the terms down in shorthand and dismissed Blackton's earlier request for a more official agreement, insisting that "we [Vitagraph] could trust him and that he could produce his notes at any time and that as we were going to be friends, there was no use of being so formal."[54] With this understanding, Rock decided to join the partnership. As Rock later testified,

After some little deliberation, I concluded to accept [their offer], provided I was not obliged to discontinue my own business and an agreement was made between us that I might continue to exhibit moving pictures and buy and sell films independent of the business conducted by us as co-partners.[55]

The new co-partnership was conducted under the name of the American Vitagraph Company with Blackton preparing the programs and making many of the films, Smith acting as cashier and bookkeeper, and Rock booking exhibitions in the theatres.[56]

THE MODE OF PRODUCTION

War films were popular throughout the summer and into the fall of 1898 as Paley continued to send films back from the war zone and others were sent from San Francisco. They were the most important part of Vitagraph's programs, not only in the large theaters but in the occasional Lyceum-type entertainments they continued to give. An Edison Vitagraph Circular for two evenings of entertainment on Martha's Vineyard for August 3 and 4 suggests the different ways Blackton and Smith exhibited their films.[57] The first evening was a lyceum entertainment featuring Blackton (distinguished cartoonist, artist, humorist, and monologist), Albert Smith (popular entertainer, shadowgraphist, and mimic), and Great Cuban War Pictures. A list of ten war films, all taken by William Paley,

---

[53]Smith, April 9, 1900.

[54]Blackton, April 9, 1900.

[55]Rock, April 9, 1900.

[56]Deposition of James White, April 30, 1900, equity nos. 6990, 6991.

[57]Broadside of Edison Vitagraph, August 3, 4, 1898, exhibit, equity nos. 6990, 6991.

are given with brief descriptions, followed by the suggestion that these war films would be supplemented by comic and startling subjects and by foreign war views. Within the film program itself, there was a structural tension between a variety approach that offered an eclectic gathering of diverse films and a unified program built around a single event or theme. In vaudeville theaters, Vitagraph showed similar programs of twelve to thirty films. Surviving playbills indicate comic and non-war scenes were often interspersed between films related to the Cuban war, while important events like the New York Naval Parade of August 20, 1898, were treated as a unified portion of a program. Such films were shown in the following order at Proctor's 23rd Street Theatre:

THE WAR-GRAPH
WITH NEW WAR VIEWS.
Including Pictures of the Great Naval Parade in the North River, Aug. 20.

After the Fire.	U.S.S. "Iowa."
Sixth U.S. Cavalry Horses.	U.S.S. "Indiana."
Negro Kiss.	U.S.S. "Brooklyn."
Thirteenth U.S. Infantry.	U.S.S. "Massachusetts."
Cavalry Charge.	U.S.S. "Oregon."
Seventy-first Embarking for Santiago.	U.S.S. "Texas."
President McKinley at Camp Alger.	Old Glory.[58]
Flagship "New York."	

Blackton and Smith's second program in Martha's Vineyard, an illustrated lecture, "With Dewey at Manila," was a unified account built around a single subject. It interwove films and lantern slides to form a narrative. Some of Vitagraph's vaudeville programs also used slides and films. Proctor's ads for this period indicate that their theaters were showing the "War-graph and New York Herald's Sensational Views of the late struggle."[59] Such programs were not unique to Vitagraph but were often advertised as stock shows in the *New York Clipper*.[60]

Blackton's "With Dewey in Manila," like most unified programs, had a narration, in this case Blackton posing as an eyewitness. Many of the vaudeville programs with their variety format probably did not. In April 1898, the *New York*

---

[58]Program of Proctor's 23rd Street Theatre, August 29, 1898 (HTC).

[59]*New York Herald,* August 21, 1898, section 2, p. 8.

[60]For instance, advertisement placed by W. B. Moore, *New York Clipper*, April 30, 1898, p. 168.

Clipper noted that "The Edison Wargraph still retains its hold on the public, the pictures it throws upon the screen eliciting signs of hearty approval or disapproval as they depict American or Spanish subjects."[61] Such reactions were common although noted less frequently by the time Vitagraph moved into Proctor's theaters. Under such circumstances, the lecturer's spiel was unnecessary and would have been lost in the roar of the crowd. Instead, there was developing a relationship between the viewer and the screen that would characterize much of early cinema. Audiences generally acquired prior knowledge of events shown on the screen through a variety of cultural forms, providing an explicit framework for appreciation. At the time of the Great Naval Parade in the North River, newspapers were filled with drawings of the participating ships. Detailed descriptions were given of their firepower, their commanding officers, and accomplishments during the war.[62] Unlike today's audience for television news, vaudeville spectators generally read the papers and could appreciate the films within this context. The cinema itself was increasingly looked upon as a visual newspaper.

Vitagraph's production of short films, several of which were hits, was important to its success as an exhibition company. Many of the films taken at the New York Naval Parade on August 20, 1898, and shown in the 23rd Street Theatre the following week were probably taken by Blackton and Smith. Beginning September 12, they were showing *The Vanishing Lady*, starring Albert Smith as the magician, at both Proctor theaters;[63] at the Pleasure Palace, it was one of four films held over for the following week.[64] Smith's *The Vanishing Lady* used stop action photography to perform a standard magic trick previously executed on stage by means of a trap door: a filmic device replaced a theatrical/profilmic procedure. Méliès's first trick film was also called *The Vanishing Lady* but he pushed the same trick to a new extreme by making the woman disappear and then replacing her with a skeleton: a trick that could only be executed filmicly. The manipulation of projected images using the principle of stop action substitutions had been popular in precinema magic lantern shows with hand-painted slip slides. Objects could mysteriously appear or disappear. In a flash, a man's head could be replaced by that of a horse. Viewed within the tradition of screen entertainment, it is evident that moving pictures led to several important "advances." The substitution was no longer performed by the exhibitor but executed by the cameraman, allowing for standardization and increased

---

[61]*Clipper*, April 30, 1898, p. 144.

[62]*Clipper*, July 30, 1898, p. 356.

[63]Program of Proctor's Pleasure Palace, September 19, 1898; Program of Proctor's 23rd Street Theatre, September 19, 1898 (HTC). This film was *not* shown at Proctor's 23rd Street Theatre the week of September 5.

[64]Program of Proctor's Pleasure Palace, October 3, 1898 (HTC).

complexity. Finally, in utilizing traditional stage tricks as subject matter and quickly elaborating on them, magicians like Smith expanded the screen part of their entertainment at the expense of stage sleight-of-hand.

By October 3, *A Burglar on the Roof*, with J. Stuart Blackton as the burglar, was being shown at Proctor's Pleasure Palace. Unlike most previous acted films which had excerpted play or vaudeville performances, *Burglar on the Roof* was indebted to the simple newspaper comic, evoking the format of mass media with its much larger audience. It remained on the Proctor program for at least three weeks and was featured in trade catalogues for many years.[65]

Both *Burglar on the Roof* and *The Vanishing Lady*, which survive in the paper print collection at the Library of Congress, were crudely made. Smith's magic film has several jumps from poor sprocket registration and was staged on the ground against a simple white sheet. *Burglar on the Roof* was staged informally as well, with several Vitagraph employees suddenly running out in front of the camera to beat their boss at the end of the film. While its photographic quality was substantially improved, it still was lacking in sharpness. Such "imperfections" were then acceptable, and the films were valuable assets. With Proctor's theaters as showcases, the trio could branch out and contract with outlying theaters in Brooklyn or neighboring cities.

THE EDISON/VITAGRAPH ALLIANCE IN PRACTICE

The American Vitagraph Company and the Edison Manufacturing Company were embarked on an uneasy but mutually beneficial relationship which lasted through January 1900. Thomas Edison copyrighted *Burglar on the Roof* on December 12, 1898, and *The Vanishing Lady* four days later. Once copyrighted the films were offered for sale. During the previous three months, they had been the exclusive property of American Vitagraph. After three months the exclusive value of these films was diminished, and Vitagraph benefited from sales to independent exhibitors through Edison's Kinetograph Department. Correspondingly, this arrangement gave the Edison Company a wider selection of films to market, and Vitagraph films, particularly their comedies, proved to be popular. Finding Vitagraph's printing and developing to be of a comparatively high quality, the Edison Company let the partners do a significant amount of their laboratory work.

Vitagraph thrived on this symbiotic relationship. By May 1899, Rock could say with a degree of self-assurance that "the American Vitagraph Company is probably one of the largest moving picture concerns in the United States."[66]

---

[65]Kleine Optical Company, *Catalogue* (Chicago, 1903).

[66]Deposition of William T. Rock, May 25, 1899, equity nos. 7124, 7125, Thomas Edison v. Eberhard Schneider, U. S. Circuit Court, Southern District of New York (FARC-B).

Frank B. Cannock, a machinist, projectionist, and cameraman for Vitagraph between March 1899 and May 1900, indicated that the major part of Vitagraph's business during this period was with Edison.[67] Later, Blackton described their dealings with Edison film people in terms designed to embarrass them:

> Thereafter [after the agreement] we did considerable business with the Edison Company. We bought of them dozens of films and made very many for them. He also asked us frequently to copy films for him, and by other people. I remember that we copied one made by Lubin of Philadelphia of which the subject was "A Cakewalk" and another made by Amet, of Waukegan, Ills., the subject of which was "Teaching Baby to Walk."[68]

The triumvirate gradually forgot that they were licensees dependent upon the good will of Edison and his associates.

The interaction between the Vitagraph and Edison companies on one hand and their competitors like Lubin and Eberhard Schneider was multifaceted. Vitagraph began purchasing substantial amounts of Lubin's films in January 1899, but also bought a "Demeny" camera for $100 from Walter Isaacs late in February 1899 which was used primarily for duping and printing.[69] Under the arrangement made with Gilmore and White, they were able to reduce the cost of their non-Edison film purchases by duping these subjects. Afterward Vitagraph was free to show the originals in their theaters. Unaware that Vitagraph was doing the actual duping, Lubin occasionally referred to their patronage in the trades, noting, for instance, that "the American Vitagraph Company of New York City are showing our fight films in the New York and Brooklyn Theatres with remarkable success."[70] Gilmore and White were attempting to eliminate Lubin's company in several different ways. While Edison lawyers were trying to enjoin him from interfering with Edison's patents and so put him out of business, they were also enjoining or threatening to enjoin exhibitors for showing Lubin's films. Yet these same exhibitors could often buy dupe copies of the Lubin films from the Edison company, courtesy of Vitagraph. That Sigmund Lubin could survive this commercial squeeze testifies to his business abilities and to the films he produced.

---

[67]Deposition of Frank B. Cannock, August 14, 1900, equity no. 6991. Cannock had been responsible for constructing the Eden Musee's highly regarded Cinematograph during the summer of 1897 and adding improvements during the succeeding year. Cannock was able to use this expertise to improve the quality of Vitagraph's projectors. *Moving Picture World*, February 22, 1908, p. 131).

[68]Blackton, April 9, 1900.

[69]Checkbook stub #286 of American Vitagraph, February 28, 1899.

[70]*New York Clipper*, July 8, 1899, p. 380.

Vitagraph, applying the strategy Rock used against Blackton and Smith with the Armat patents, encouraged Edison lawyers to bring suit against competing exhibitors and took an active part in many of these legal battles. S. O. Edmonds would testify that

> [they] seemed to have regarded themselves as identified with Mr. Edison's interests, and frequently called upon me or wrote me with respect to infringing exhibitions given by their competitors. Recognizing the fact that they had been enjoined under the Edison patents, they repeatedly urged that these other infringers be treated in the same manner and injunctions secured against them. Upon the information which they furnished, a number of infringers were warned and legal proceedings taken—in many cases, Blackton and Smith or Rock furnished the necessary proofs.[71]

Perhaps the most extensive example of Vitagraph's participation in these suits was the case of the exhibitor Eberhard Schneider.[72] Schneider showed films with his American Cinematograph at New York's Eden Musee from mid-April 1897 until June 14, 1897, when a fire started by his projecting machine led to his dismissal.[73] He exhibited films at Proctor's Pleasure Palace between June 20 and September 3, 1898, when his place was taken by American Vitagraph.[74] He had three or four projectors which were frequently hired by New York vaudeville theaters during 1898 and 1899. After being threatened by Edison lawyers in mid-July 1898, he tried to reach some kind of accommodation with them but failed. Subpoenas were served against him on December 21, 1898, and he responded by trying to obtain a license from Edison, again without success. After Schneider failed to appear in court (Schneider insisted that he had been tricked into going to West Orange to arrange for a license on his court date), a decree was entered against him on April 9, 1899. He subsequently tried to pay Edison royalties on a number of Lumière films he wished to show but was refused.

Vitagraph appears to have been the major impetus in the Schneider suit. While he was using the same mix of Edison/Lubin/Amet/Lumière/Houdin films[75] as everyone else, Schneider's position in the vaudeville circuit made him a desirable target for Rock, who was trying to expand their business. Edmonds observed that "[Schneider] has been put out of a number of theatres in New York

---

[71]S. O. Edmonds, April 9, 1900.

[72]Thomas A. Edison v. Eberhard Schneider, equity nos. 7124, 7125.

[73]*New York Daily Tribune*, June 15, 1897, p. 1.

[74]Program of Proctor's Pleasure Palace, July 11, 1898.

[75]Méliès's productions were known as Houdin films after the Théâtre Robert-Houdin, which he owned and operated.

because of the infringing character of his machines and films, and so far as I know, these theatres have since severing relations with Schneider respected the Edison patents, and when desiring to reproduce animated pictures have employed operators using Edison apparatus."[76] Vitagraph was the safe choice for any vaudeville manager just caught with an infringing exhibitor, and Rock was in a position to make timely appearances at the manager's office when the theater was looking for a replacement. The triumvirate was not only able to take over Schneider's engagements from the Dewey and other theaters, but picked up an occasional, well-trained projectionist like James O'Rourke, who started out with Schneider in July 1898 but moved to Vitagraph eight months later.[77] After Schneider had been enjoined, competitive pressures forced him to show infringing films. Finally Rock and Schneider's former employee O'Rourke went out to a festival of the German Soldier League in Sulzer's Harlem River Park and watched his exhibition, noting the infringing films. Afterward they tore down a poster from an outhouse for Edmonds to submit as evidence. Schneider was threatened with contempt, but continued to use infringing films (he obviously had no choice). He was hauled into court again in January 1900 and fined; his films were impounded and destroyed.

Vitagraph and Edison, while partners in these campaigns, were pursuing the same ends for different purposes. The Edison Company used such victories to threaten exhibitors who were inclined to buy films and projectors from Lubin, Amet, and its other competitors. For Edison it was an attempt to increase its market share indirectly by intimidating potential buyers into purchasing their products, rather than directly by successfully closing down their rivals' businesses, a process which was proving more difficult. Vitagraph's interest was more direct; it simply wanted to disrupt the business of its competitors, have crippling limitations imposed on them, and then take advantage of their misfortunes.

PRODUCTION AT VITAGRAPH, 1898–JANUARY 1900

In their reminiscences and in William Basil Courtney's "History of the Vitagraph,"[78] Blackton and Smith often cited a number of their earlier films, films which are presumed to have suffered the fate brought on by deteriorating nitrate. In his deposition of 1900, however, Blackton indignantly indicated that many of their films had been copyrighted by the Edison Company. This raises an important point ignored by previous historians: a substantial number of films made by Blackton and Smith survive in the paper print collection at the Library of

---

[76]Deposition of S. O. Edmonds, May 26, 1899, equity no. 7124.

[77]Deposition of James O'Rourke, May 25, 1899, equity no. 7124.

[78]William Basil Courtney, "History of Vitagraph," *Motion Picture News*, February 7, 1925, pp. 542e ff. Subsequent installments in succeeding issues.

Congress. Still other Vitagraph films can be traced to catalogue descriptions even when they were not actually copyrighted.

The Edison Manufacturing Company seems to have pursued an inconsistent policy in copyrighting Vitagraph films between December 1898 and January 1900 while the company was an Edison licensee. What follows here is a tentative attribution of Edison films (mostly copyrighted) to Blackton and Smith. Each film is assigned an attribution number from 1 to 4:

1 indicates a positive identification based on newspaper reports, contemporary references or through visual identification as to performer or location.

2 indicates that a film has been referred to as a Vitagraph film in such sources as Courtney's history. I have used these sources cautiously.

3 indicates there are reasons to believe a film is likely to be a Vitagraph film either because it was apparently referred to in Vitagraph material before it was copyrighted or because at the time it was copyrighted, its subject matter and its style suggest that this is a likely possibility.

4 indicates that a film could be a Vitagraph film because of the time it was copyrighted (Vitagraph films were often copyrighted in groups) or because of subject matter.

The following is a tentative filmography by copyright date except where indicated.

December 12, 1898	**Burglar on the Roof** (1), 50 ft. The roof is the roof of the Morse building, and Blackton is breaking into the Vitagraph office. Mrs. Olsen, the building superintendent's wife, is one of the women who catches the burglar. They are quickly helped by a number of Vitagraph employees and friends, one of whom may be Charles Urban.
	The Cop and the Nurse Girl (3), 50 ft.
December 16, 1898	**The Vanishing Lady** (1). Smith is the magician.
	Sleighing Scene (1).
	The Burglar in the Bed Chamber (3), 50 ft. (Is this the same burglar as *Burglar on the Roof*?)
	Cavalier's Dream (3). Trick film like *The Vanishing Lady*.
January 27, 1899	**Astor Battery on Parade** (1). An article on Smith in *Mahatma* indicates that "at the review of the Astor Battery on January 23rd, 1899, Mr. Smith broke all records in photography and caused considerable newspaper talk by taking an animated picture of the

parade on Union Square at 4:00 PM and developing, printing, and exhibiting it by 9 PM the same evening at several New York theatres."[79]

February 4 **Panoramic View of Brooklyn Bridge** (3).
Raising Old Glory over Morro Castle (2). This could be the often-referred-to Vitagraph film *Tearing Down the Spanish Flag*. The painted backdrop looks as if it were drawn by Blackton.
Willie's First Smoke (1), filmed on the rooftop of the Morse building. Blackton dashes into the frame at the end of the film.

ca. late March **Reproduction of Windsor Hotel Fire** (2). Shot in miniature. Referred to by William Courtney in his history of the Vitagraph Company. The fire took place on March 17. Edison first offered the film for sale on April 29.[80]

ca. July **A Quiet Smoke** (2), 50 ft. "Baby sits in his high chair and papa is playing with him. Papa is smoking his evening pipe. Baby claps his hands, points to pipe and wants it. So papa puts on baby's hood, and baby smokes papa's pipe. The child's face is full of expression, and is as pretty a picture of baby life as was ever made for a moving picture machine. Sure to delight the children."[81]

September 22 **New Brooklyn to New York via Brooklyn Bridge** (2). This is apparently described in a Vitagraph ad of May 13, 1899: "FROM BROOKLYN TO NEW YORK OVER THE BRIDGE, taken from a moving cable car leaving Brooklyn train yard, crossing entire span and arriving at New York Terminus in City Hall."[82]

(shot) September 29 **Presentation of Loving Cup at City Hall** (1). This is one of the films of Dewey's triumphal arrival in New York. It was not copyrighted, although it does appear

---

[79]*Mahatma*, February 1899, p. 81.

[80]Courtney, "History of the Vitagraph,"*Motion Picture News*, March 14, 1925, p. 1090; *Clipper*, April 29, 1899, p. 178.

[81]Warwick Trading Company, *Warwick Films* (London, 1901), p. 219. Listed under "American Films." The copy of this catalogue in the Albert Smith Collection has pencil marks referring to this film.

[82]*Clipper*, May 13, 1899, p. 217.

in the Edison catalogue for 1900. A letter on Vitagraph stationary submitted as legal evidence by James White proves they shot the film.
Other Films of Dewey's Arrival in New York.[83]

October 20   **America's Cup #1 and #2** (3). In a Vitagraph catalogue from 1900, a few America's Cup films were offered for sale, films the Edison Company apparently didn't choose to put in its catalogue or which Vitagraph kept for its own use.

October 24   **America's Cup #1 and #2** (3), same.

October 25   **America's Cup #1 and #2** (3), same.[84]

(shot) November 3   **Jeffries-Sharky Fight** (1). Blackton and Smith, accompanied by James White, head of the Edison Kinetograph Department, surreptitiously filmed the fight. Not copyrighted, a print of this film managed to survive.[85]

November 7   **America's Cup Race #1 and #2** (3).

(shot) ca. December   **A Visit To The Spiritualist** (1), 100 ft., was not copyrighted, but appears in both the Vitagraph and Edison catalogues for 1900. Although Edison claims to have copyrighted it, no records of this appear at the Library of Congress. It is described in the Edison catalogue as follows: "This is acknowledged by exhibitors to be the funniest of all moving magical films. A countryman is seen entering the office of the spiritualist and paying his fee. He is then mesmerized and sees funny things. He drops his handkerchief on the floor and as he races for it, it gradually grows larger and larger, dancing up and down, and going through funny antics until before the eyes of the spectator it turns into a ghost of enormous proportions. It then vanishes and as the countryman is in the act of sitting in the chair, the ghost suddenly

---

[83]Deposition of James H. White, April 30, 1900, equity no. 6991.

[84]American Vitagraph Company, *List of New Films* (New York, n.d.).

[85]The story of this film has been told many times in various film histories, notably Smith, *Two Reels and a Crank,* and Ramsaye, *Million and One Nights.* Most histories suggest that White stole the negatives. Under Blackton and Smith's agreement with Edison, they were Edison's property. The print that was given to Vitagraph was likewise part of this agreement. Vitagraph, however, apparently did not get the customary period of exclusivity.

appears and the countryman receives a great fright. He then jumps up and throws off his hat and coat, and they immediately fly back on his body. He repeatedly throws them off and they as often return. This scene finally closes by numerous ghosts and hobgoblins appearing and disappearing before the eyes of the frightened countryman, who finally leaves the room in great haste."[86]

Such films gave Blackton, Smith, and Rock a position as exhibitors that few companies could match. In early 1899, William Paley had yet to establish his own exhibition company, and his films were sold directly to exhibitors through the Edison Company. This was also true of the Edison films made by James White. Lubin was content to concentrate on manufacturing. Vitagraph was quite possibly the only East Coast exhibitor of 35 mm. films with a supply of exclusive subjects. Their only rival in this respect was the American Mutoscope and Biograph Company with its large format film. A Vitagraph ad in the *New York Clipper* of May 13, 1899, could proudly announce that

the American Vitagraph Co. has exhibited in almost every leading place of amusement in the United States and Canada, having given over seven thousand successful performances during the past year. We refer to the following: Proctor's Pleasure Palace, Proctor's 23rd St. Theatre, 42 weeks under the title of "Wargraph"; Bijou Theatre, Washington, John Grieves; Bijou Theatre, Richmond, Va., Jake Welles; Dewey Theatre, New York City, George Kraus; Brooklyn Music Hall, Novelty Theater, Brooklyn, Percy Williams; Bon Ton Theatre, Jersey City, T. W. Dinkins; Wonderland Theatre, New Haven Conn., S. Z. Poli; Harlem Music Hall, Hurtzig and Seamon; Theatre Royal, Montreal Canada; Harry Williams' Academy, Pittsburg, Pa.; and hundreds of other well-known houses. Also this season with Reilly and Woods' Show, Ed. F. Rush's enterprises, Joe Oppenheimer's Zero and Miss NY, Jr., Fred Riders' New Night Owls and White Elephant. Now in Fourth Season at West End Park, New Orleans, La. (refer to C. D. Wyman, General Manager, New Orleans Tracton Co.) where we have exhibited 20 consecutive weeks each year. Also booked for entire season of 1899 at Glen Echo Park, Washington, D.C. Commencing June 5th.[87]

On June 19, 1899, Blackton and Smith also moved into Tony theater on 14th Street, New York City, where they would continue to s

[86]Edison Manufacturing Company, *Catalogue No. 94, Edison Films* (Oran 1900), pp. 40–41.

[87]*Clipper*, May 13, 1899, p. 217.

until Pastor's closed nine years later.[88] Vitagraph had an exhibition network that covered much of North America. As the company grew, tension developed between it and the Edison Company.

The tensions between Edison and Vitagraph typified the conflict between producers and exhibitors; both were trying to expand their positions in the industry during the 1890s. From late 1896, the Edison Company had sold films to exhibitors on a first come, first served basis. Edison business strategy envisioned maximizing the number of exhibitors while centralizing production either in the company or under Edison's control through licensing agreements. A large number of comparatively small exhibitors dependent on the Edison Company for its product could have maximized potential outlets while leaving the film producer in a dominant position. Such goals were frustrated by independent producers like Sigmund Lubin and large exhibitors like Biograph, which produced its own films, and increasingly Vitagraph, which had several sources for films: foreign imports, domestic products, and its own productions. As its own productions increased in quantity and quality, the Vitagraph dependence on outside producers decreased. Under such circumstances, a production company like Edison was potentially vulnerable, and its legal advantage became central to the retention of commercial power in the industry. From this perspective, conflict between Edison and Vitagraph was almost inevitable.

Smith later insisted that relations between the two companies were strained from the beginning:

> From the beginning, our relations with the complainant [Edison] have not been satisfactory. He has constantly failed to credit us with goods delivered to him, has not paid us the royalties agreed and has never paid us any money, forcing us to purchase goods from him in order to secure remuneration.[89]

Rock echoed the complaint:

> The complainant has not kept his agreement. We have not been paid our several royalties and the accounts rendered to us have been ridiculously inadequate. Instead of furnishing us with five fully equipped machines as he agreed, he furnished only the drum gearings and connections, omitting the lenses, lamps, rheostats, boxes and other expensive parts, and early in this year, as our relations were so unsatisfactory, we demanded an accounting from him of the payment which was due us.[90]

Variety, June 13, 1908, p. 7; July 18, 1908, p. 1; August 29, 1908, p. 4.

lbert Smith, April 9, 1900.

:k, April 9, 1900.

When Vitagraph threatened to sue Edison for an accounting in January 1900, Edison canceled the agreement on the 29th of that month.[91] Without a license, Blackton, Smith and, Rock were suddenly in the position they had placed Schneider a few months before, and the Edison Company was just as persistent in court.

By January 1900, Vitagraph was no longer as essential to the Edison Company as it had been a year earlier. Paley had returned to New York and set up his Kalatechnoscope Company to exhibit films. He replaced Vitagraph at Proctor's 23 Street Theatre on October 8, 1899, and at the Pleasure Palace one week later. From Proctor's point of view, Vitagraph may have been overbooked on the New York vaudeville circuit, and Paley offered his own films plus a reputation established by his work as a cameraman during the Spanish-American War. He was also an Edison licensee. Perhaps more importantly, James White, manager of the Edison Kinetograph Department, and John Schermerhorn, assistant general manager of the Edison Manufacturing Company and Gilmore's brother-in-law, entered into an informal partnership with Percival Waters, a New York jobber of Edison films who had a modest position as an exhibitor. In a secret agreement reached in November 1899, they promised to favor him whenever possible in business dealings.[92] With the credit they extended Waters's newly formed Kinetograph Company, he was able to enter the exhibition field on a more competitive basis. This included making films available to the Kinetograph Company before selling prints to other exhibitors. Since Vitagraph was Waters's major adversary, it was also the adversary of White and Schermerhorn. Whatever the personal intrigues, the Kinetograph Company, which did not make its own films, was dependent on the good will of Edison's Kinetograph Department. It effectively represented an extension of the Edison Company into the field of exhibition.

After the rupture between the two companies and perhaps as part of Edison's tactics to harass Vitagraph and prevent it from putting films on the market, the Edison Company may have copyrighted a number of additional Vitagraph films at the end of February and early March:

February 28 **Faust and Marguerite**
       An Animated Luncheon
       A Dull Razor
       Ching Ling Foo Outdone
       The Magician

[91]Deposition of James White, April 30, 1900, equity no. 6990.

[92]James H. White and John R. Schermerhorn v. Percival L. Waters, Supreme Court, County of New York. This case considers the relationship between White and Waters at some length. Records for this can be found at the Archive for the City of New York as well as at the Edison National Historic Site.

March 21   **An Artist's Dream**
            Uncle Josh in a Spooky Hotel
            Uncle Josh's Nightmare
            The Mystic Swing[93]

Although the producer of these films remains open to conjecture, they could well have been part of Vitagraph's "Special line of Magical subjects." The above filmography does not include all the films made by Vitagraph during this period; other films copyrighted by Edison between September 1898 and March 1900 could also be Vitagraph films. Blackton and Smith also made films that did not get into the Edison catalogue but were shown in their theaters. From this group, however, a few conclusions can be drawn. Vitagraph generally specialized in topical films of news interest, mysterious films, and comedies. The partners would take films of newsworthy events and then rush them into their theaters ahead of the competition. By the time Edison could offer copies of these films for sale, the value for Vitagraph had been realized. Many of the trick films were imitations of Méliès's efforts. Their "best" work in this genre, films like *A Visit to the Spiritualist*, unfortunately do not seem to have survived. Comedies were their most distinctive contribution to the American screen, and a film like *A Quiet Smoke* was one of the few American films to be offered for sale in England. Although many of Vitagraphs featured "headliners" like *The Passion Play*, boxing matches, or bullfights were made elsewhere, original productions gave the company a mix of films which, as an asset for acquiring exhibition contracts, cannot be underestimated.

VITAGRAPH STRUGGLES TO SURVIVE

While film production and exhibition must have taken most of the trio's time and energy between 1898 and 1900, Blackton, Smith, and Rock continued to be involved in other parts of the entertainment industry. Smith pursued his career as a prestidigitator, meeting with a large degree of success on the Lyceum circuit. A circular printed in 1898 claimed that Mr. Smith filled over 180 church and YMCA engagements during the 1897–98 season.[94] A brief article in *Mahatma* (February 1899), a magazine for American magicians, claimed that "as a lyceum entertainer he has few if any equals, having appeared on every entertainment course of prominence in this country. Mr. Smith's repertoire is distinctly unique and original, being a clever combination of sleight of hand and invisible mechanical

---

[93]I have not been able to positively identify these films as Vitagraph films, but they were all made by the same company, using many of the same actors and sets.

[94]Reproduced in Courtney, "History of the Vitagraph,"*Motion Picture News*, February 7, 1925, p. 542d.

appliances of his own invention."[95] Blackton continued his chalk acts. Rock, as his arrangement with his partners clearly indicated, pursued other business interests. It was not until 1906 that he finally put his two hundred slot machines up for sale.[96] It is remarkable, at least in retrospect, that all three members of the copartnership that constituted one of the largest exhibition companies in the country would direct their energy into other areas. Yet the Edison Company's attempt to put Vitagraph out of business by withdrawing its license fully justified their caution.

Blackton, Smith, and Rock had created a highly successful and increasingly profitable business in a field that seemed certain to grow. They were not prepared to look elsewhere for a livelihood. After the termination of their agreement with Edison on January 29, 1900, Blackton and Smith placed the business in Rock's hands, who then sold it to a newly-formed corporation, the American Vitagraph Company, which was incorporated in the state of New Jersey on February 15, 1900, by Herman Meyer, Stephen Cox, and Howard Cox of Cranford, N.J.[97] Meyer and Cox transferred their stock and rights to George S. W. Arthur, Smith's father-in-law, who became the dominant stockholder and president of the company, and Ronald Reader, their partner in earlier Lyceum ventures.[98] An announcement was sent to the Vitagraph's customers:

> The co-partnership heretofore existing between the undersigned under the name and style of The American Vitagraph Company has been this day dissolved by mutual consent. All accounts due to us have been assigned and transferred by us to the American Vitagraph Company, a corporation organized under the law of the State of New Jersey, and our debtors will please make payments to the said corporation and its receipt with be therefore [sic].
>
> Dated February 15th, 1900
>
> > (signed) William T. Rock
> > J. Stuart Blackton
> > Albert E. Smith
>
> The American Vitagraph Company announces that it has purchased the business heretofore conducted by the above mentioned copartnership and respectfully requests the continued patronage of the customers and dealers with the firm, promising the best of service that skill and

---

[95]*Mahatma*, February 1899, p. 81.

[96]*Views and Film Index*, June 9, 1906, p. 8.

[97]Papers of incorporation of the American Vitagraph Company, February 15, 1900, exhibit C, deposition of James White, April 30, 1900.

[98]Deposition of Walter B. Arthur, May 7, 1900, equity nos. 6990, 6991; deposition of Ronald A. Reader, May 5, 1900, equity nos. 6990, 6991.

money can secure. Business will be conducted from the above address
(116 Nassau Street).

The American Vitagraph Company
by G. S. W. Arthur, President[99]

Walter Arthur, Smith's brother-in-law, became general manager. Rock
continued to book engagements for exhibition of motion pictures until the
beginning of March when he, too, was enjoined. Blackton and Smith were soon
back at work. According to Blackton,

> About the first of March 1900, having nothing to do, I tendered my
> services to the corporation in the capacity of a sort of artist. I felt that my
> previous experience as an artist would enable me to be of service to the
> company, entirely outside of the manufacture, use or sale of moving
> picture apparatus.
>   While I was employed by the corporation, I painted scenery, designed
> cuts and wrote advertisements.
>   Under the terms of my employment with the incorporated Company,
> I was permitted to use a considerable portion of my time upon private
> affairs of my own, including the business of lecturing, in which I have
> been engaged during the past six years. . . .[100]

Smith likewise secured the position of cashier and bookkeeper. Both were
officially paid a salary of $15 a week. For the moment, American Vitagraph was
able to continue much as before; it had successfully evaded Edison's attempt to
shut it down. Vitagraph continued to make pictures, although Blackton and Smith
did not actually operate the camera. Frank Cannock, a former employee, later
testified that

> I myself used a [Colt consecutive views] camera for the purpose of
> making a moving picture film on the occasion of the ceremonies
> attending the opening of the Rapid Transit tunnel in Manhattan. This
> was on March 24th, 1900. In the morning of this day, Messers. Blackton
> and Smith told me that they wished these ceremonies photographed,
> and instructed me to take the Colt camera and come with them.
> Thereupon Blackton, Smith and myself, taking the camera, went to City
> Hall Park and made the photograph, both Blackton and Smith being
> present during the operation and assisting me. The actual operation of
> turning the crank was performed by myself under their instructions, as I

[99]William T. Rock, et al., to exhibitors, February 15, 1900, exhibit G, deposition of James
White, April 30, 1900.
[100]Deposition of J. Stuart Blackton, May 5, 1900, equity no. 6991.

have said. The picture having been taken, the negative was taken back to the American Vitagraph Company's shop, and developed, and positives printed therefrom. That night I was engaged, as usual, in giving the picture exhibition at Tony Pastor's Theatre and a positive made from the negative taken as above described, was sent to me and projected upon a screen during the course of the exhibition that night. . . .[101]

Vitagraph not only continued to make films, but sold them directly to the trade, coming out with its first catalogue in April 1900.[102] Meanwhile, Edison had Blackton and Smith served with subpoenas to appear before John A. Shields as Master in Chancery to account for the profits and damages accruing to Edison for their acknowledged (August 10, 1898) infringement of his patents. The lack of company records (!) and Blackton and Smith's claims of poverty hampered Edison's efforts to receive compensation.

On April 9, 1900, Blackton and Smith submitted detailed depositions arguing that they had not been aware that they were being prosecuted for anything more than copyright infringement. With the American Mutoscope and Biograph Company and Lubin contesting Edison's patents in the courts, all three asked that "the decree herein be set aside and that Messers Smith and Blackton be permitted to come in and defend the same upon their merits."[103] Meanwhile, Edison lawyers tried to demonstrate that the incorporation of American Vitagraph and the apparent change in ownership was nothing more than a ruse to avoid the earlier rulings of the court. Frank Cannock testified that the only practical effect of the incorporation was to add Walter Arthur to the partnership. Circuit Court Judge LaCombe was sympathetic to Edison's point of view but not quite ready to hold Blackton and Smith in contempt of court. In his opinion, filed on August 3, 1900, LaCombe wrote that

The Court has very little doubt that all three of the defendants have deliberately conspired together to disobey the injunction by means of a colorable evasion of its terms, and that the alleged corporation was a mere sham or device to conceal their individual disobedience. . . . If the complainant chooses to go to additional expense, he may take an order of reference to a master, where a thorough overhauling of the books and papers of the defendants' alleged corporation, and a drastic examination of their so-called fellow-stockholders may develop enough to warrant a finding in contempt. The expense of this reference will have to be born by the complainant, because it seems quite apparent that the defendants

---

[101]Cannock, August 14, 1900.

[102]American Vitagraph Company, *List of New Films.*

[103]Rock, April 9, 1900.

are without funds which the marshal could reach, and in the event of a finding adverse to them the court *would punish not by fine but by imprisonment.*[104]

While Edison was pressing Blackton and Smith in court, a reconciliation was being worked out. Blackton and Smith were still able to take their customary August vacation in Martha's Vineyard and confidently wrote S. O. Edmonds:

> Cottage City, Mass.
> on Martha's Vineyard
> August 11th, 1900

Smith and myself will return from our vacation in a few days. Before leaving New York we attempted to reach you by phone many times but were never successful. We conversed with White the day before his departure and he stated that you would close the contract at any time. As we are now ready to get down to business and have on hand a large number of negatives of comedy subjects, etc., taken during the summer, we would like you to make an appointment as soon as possible in order that, after arrangements are satisfactorily concluded we may ship the said subjects to Orange, as we understood from White that comic pictures were greatly needed in that quarter. Please address all communications to my residence 966 E. 166th Street, NYC.

> yours truly,
> J. Stuart Blackton[105]

An accord did not come as quickly as Blackton had hoped. On September 10, Smith and Blackton submitted a proposition to Edison that was approved by West Orange a few days later, although not formally put into effect until October 10. This agreement basically reiterated the financial arrangement made in September 1898 but committed it to writing and also elaborated on the licensing arrangements.[106]

---

[104]Opinion of Judge C. J. Lacombe, August 3, 1900, equity nos. 6990, 6991.

[105]J. Stuart Blackton to S. O. Edmonds, August 11, 1900, legal box 100 (ENHS).

[106]J. Stuart Blackton and Alfred E. Smith to Edison Manufacturing Company, proposed contract, September 10, 1900.

1. We (Blackton and Smith) will secure and hold, during the continuance of any arrangement which you (the Edison Mfg. Co.) may make with us, all of the capital stock of the American Vitagraph Company of New Jersey. We will operate said Company as a moving picture exhibiting concern in the City of New York, will grant to you such right of direction, supervision or inspection of our plants, books, methods of doing business, etc. as you may desire, and will, to such an extent as you see fit, advertise the business so carried on by us in connection with the name *Edison* or *Edison Manufacturing Company.* The business of said Company shall consist solely of the giving of exhibitions of moving

Faced with the alternative of prison, Blackton and Smith once again had to surrender a large degree of independence to work as Edison licensees. It is doubtful, however, that Edison executives ever saw this arrangement as anything more than a short-term convenience in which they gave little and gained much. Vitagraph provided the Edison Company with films while Edison's rooftop

---

pictures, and shall not extend to the taking of photographic negatives, or the development thereof, or the printing of positives therefrom, or to the duplicating or sale of either positives or negatives. The apparatus and films used shall be exclusively Edison projectoscopes and Edison films, save as stated in the next succeeding paragraph hereof.

2. It being desired to make use for a limited time of 246 positive picture films now in the possession of said Vitagraph Company and a schedule of which marked "Schedule A" is hereto annexed, which films are of other than Edison productions, we will make use of such of these films as may be desired in the giving of moving picture exhibitions during the period of 90 days next ensuing your acceptance of this proposition. During that period we will not sell, loan, or in any wise encumber or part with the possession of these films, and at the expiration of the said period will turn them over to you at a price to be agreed upon between you and ourselves, which price is to be given us as a credit upon your books against such supplies or other material as we may, order of you at current rates. Said films, when so turned over shall be your property to do with as you see fit.

3. Mr. Edison or the Edison Manufacturing Company to bring suits (such as were brought in the summer of 1898 against ourselves) against the American Vitagraph Company (corporation) and against Walter Arthur individually and as general manager of said Company, under the Edison patents Nos. 493,426 and 589,168. As soon after the service of subpoenas in said suits as you may see fit, we will procure the Consent of Counsel for said Company and of said Arthur himself, to the entry and filing of decrees in such suits in substantially the same form as the decrees entered in the suits against us hereinabove referred to.

5. We personally, and not as the American Vitagraph Company, will make photographic moving pictures, negatives and turn the same over to you, or to such person or concern as you may elect, undeveloped, or will, should you so require it, ourselves develop the same at such place or places as you may designate. . . .

8. Should you accept this proposition, we agree that the arrangement evidenced hereby may be terminated by you at any time upon ten hours notice in writing served upon us or either of us, or at your election printed in any newspaper published in the County of New York. We further consent that the proceedings now pending in the suits brought against us in the summer of 1898 as herein before referred to, shall not be dismissed, but shall be stricken from the calendar under a stipulation to be entered into by the attorneys' for the respective parties thereto, that the same may be restored to the calendar and heard, either upon the showing now made by both parties or upon additional showing as they may see fit, on ten days formal notice of the calling up of such proceedings for argument. We further agree that nothing herein contained shall disturb, prejudice, or otherwise influence the present standing of such proceedings.

studio at 41 East 21st Street was being built and production commenced now, under Edwin Porter. It was also a way to enjoin Walter Arthur and the new Vitagraph Company under the decrees agreed to by Blackton and Smith on August 10, 1898.

The agreement is a fascinating document not only because it details the relationship between the two companies but because it lists 246 non-Edison films by production company. Vitagraph made selections from these for its exhibitions.

56 films distributed by Warwick, an English company run by an American, Charles Urban. The films are primarily news and actuality footage plus a few comedies.

45 films by Georges Méliès made between 1897 and early 1900. All but two were trick films like *Dining Under Difficulties* or fairy tales like *Cinderella*.

42 films by Sigmund Lubin. They varied from news/actuality footage to trick films, vaudeville acts, and dramatic recreations.

31 films by Robert Paul, the English filmmaker, including trick films, documentaries, comedies, and dramas.

29 films by G. A. Smith of Brighton, England.

16 "Elge" films from Gaumont in Paris.

5 Lumière films.

1 film by Birt Acres, England.

1 film by William Selig.

20 films produced by Vitagraph, made and exhibited between June 1899 and September 1900.

Edison Films were not listed because they were covered by Edison patents and considered "non-infringing." If one were to speculate that Vitagraph exhibited a selection of thirty to fifty non-Vitagraph Edison films as well as a significant number, perhaps fifteen to twenty-five, of Vitagraph subjects made under the old arrangement, their reliance on foreign productions still remains striking. While all films shown by Vitagraph in 1900 were made in the three major producing countries, 117 of the 246 films listed were English and 66 were French. The largest number of films were from England, perhaps because of the company's ties to that country; all three copartners had been born there, and Walter Wainwright, Rock's first partner in his Louisiana Vitascope venture, was acting as a special London agent. Méliès was the most popular French producer, although interest focused on his mysterious and fantasy subjects rather than the actualities and reenactments he was also producing.

Significantly, the only major producer of infringing 35 mm. films in the United States other than Vitagraph was Sigmund Lubin. Using the legal weapon of his patents, Edison was close to curtailing all American production not supervised by West Orange. Nevertheless, it remained relatively easy for major exhibitors like Lyman Howe, Burton Holmes, George Spoor with his Kinodrome, and Vitagraph to buy films from abroad or to purchase foreign films duped in the United States. Edison's legal battles resulted in the domination of the American screen by European productions.

The twenty Vitagraph films in the agreement were listed as follows: (Alternate titles appearing in Edison catalogues are given in parentheses.)

> *Mysterious Cafe* † *
> *Jeffries Skipping Rope**
> *Dewey Arch** (*Panoramic View of Dewey Arch, New York City*)
> *Harry Thomson's Imitations*
> *Inquisitive Clerks*
> *Such a Headache**
> *Artillery Firing*
> *Smallest Train** (*Miniature Railway*)
> *Speedway*
> *Boat Race on the Harlem River*
> *Polo Game*
> *Panorama of Broad Street, Richmond*
> *Broadway Panorama*
> *Jeffries Throwing Medicine Ball**
> *Fun in Training Quarters*
> *Oceanic*
> *Sousa Leading the Band, Thomson* † (*Harry Thomson's Imitation of Sousa*)
> *Leaping Dogs* † (*Leaping Dogs at Gentry's Circus*)
> *Washing the Dogs*
> *Roeber Wrestling Match* † (*The Great Wrestling Match Between Ernest Roeber and August Faust*)

*Indicates film is listed in later catalogues of Edison Films.

† Indicates film was later copyrighted by Edison and is in the paper print collection at the Library of Congress.[107]

Smith and Blackton also made a series of comedies during the summer of 1900 which starred J. Stuart Blackton as Happy Hooligan. These were among the comedy subjects Smith was anxious to place with Edison. An ad in the October 13 issue of *The New York Clipper* lists seven Happy Hooligan films for sale.

The Adventures of Happy Hooligan

> *Hooligan and the Summer Boarders* (1)   75 ft.
> *Hooligan in Central Park* (1)   75 ft.

---

[107]These films were copyrighted in mid-December 1901 by Thomas A. Edison. Blackton can be seen at the conclusion of *Roeber Wrestling Match*, copyrighted December 16, 1901.

Hooligan at the Seashore (1)   100 ft.
Hooligan has Troubles with the Cook (1)   60 ft.
Hooligan Takes His Annual Bath (1)   75 ft.
Hooligan Causes a Sensation (1)   100 ft.
Hooligan's Narrow Escape (1)   75 ft.[108]

None of these films were copyrighted.

The Happy Hooligan series continued the tramp character first portrayed by Blackton in *Burglar on the Roof*. The series loosely referred to the well-known cartoon character (their appearances were different) which also inspired toys, waxworks at the Eden Musee, and a play. As with the earlier *Burglar on the Roof*, each film's simple gag was commensurate in structure and complexity to the strips of cartoon panels then appearing in the Sunday Supplements of New York's leading newspapers. Audience appreciation of these gags was facilitated by the viewer's ability to place the experience within the context of strips like "Happy Hooligan" or "Burglar Bill."

The Happy Hooligan series could be shown either singly or as a group. Shown over a period of several weeks on a vaudeville program, it acted like an ongoing cartoon strip at a time when the cinema was increasingly seen as a "visual newspaper" with news features as well as cartoons. Grouped together as *The Adventures of Happy Hooligan*, the series resembled later "feature" films like Porter's *The Buster Brown Series* (1904), which was made up of a series of discrete scenes and based on a cartoon strip character.

Under the new contract, Blackton and Smith resumed their production of films for Edison. In September 1900, they photographed a series of eight films in Galveston, Texas, of the devastated city which had been destroyed by a hurricane and floods. Eight of the films were subsequently copyrighted by Edison on September 24, 1900. A credit memorandum dated October 31 was sent to the pair; it totaled $71.40, based on a 30¢ per 50 ft. royalty on films sold. They were

Panorama of East Galveston   50 ft.   35 copies sold
Searching Ruins on Broadway, Galveston, for Dead Bodies   50 ft.   35   "
Panorama of Wreckage on Waterfront, Galveston   50 ft.   26   "
Panorama of Orphans' Home, Galveston   50 ft.   22   "
Panorama of Galveston Powerhouse   50 ft.   23   "
Panorama of Tremont Hotel, Galveston   50 ft.   17   "
Launching of a Stranded Schooner   75 ft.   20   "
Birds-Eye View of Dock Front, Galveston   75 ft.   18   " [109]

---

[108]*Clipper*, October 13, 1900, p. 740.

[109]"Credit memorandum" of Edison Manufacturing Company to Blackton and Smith, October 31, 1900, defendants' exhibit no. 115, testimony of J. Stuart Blackton, United States v. Motion Picture Patents Company, U. S. District Court, Eastern Pennsylvania, printed record, p. 1988.

On November 16, 1900, Thomas Edison copyrighted the following films by Blackton and Smith. They, too, survive in the paper print collection (Vitagraph attributions as previously coded).

> *The Enchanted Drawing* (1), starring Blackton.
> *Congress of Nations* (1), starring Smith.
> *Maude's Naughty Little Brother* (1), starring Blackton's son Buster.
> *Hooligan Assists the Magician* (3).
> *The Clown and the Alchemist* (3).

Three months after the new agreement between the Edison and Vitagraph companies, White asked Dyer, Edmonds, and Dyer to cancel the licensing arrangement because the licensee had failed to pay a 10 percent royalty on exhibition fees. Blackton wrote a final plea to William Gilmore:

> We went over this matter [of the royalty] with Mr. White and, after submitting a statement of our business for two months showing amount taken in and amount of running expenses we demonstrated that we could not possibly pay ten per cent. of our gross receipts and still remain in business, as we are under extremely heavy expense in maintaining our present premises until the expiration of our lease on June 1st, 1901. At the time of our conversation with Mr. White we understood that he was to confer with the Edison Co. and in submitting our case for their consideration, was instructed to state that we were willing to pay a reasonable royalty on our business, and we have been daily expecting an answer.[110]

Blackton's last ditch attempt at a compromise was rebuffed, and American Vitagraph lost its license.

Vitagraph was subsequently forced to confine itself to exhibitions. Even here there were problems. Because Blackton and Smith could only stay in business by showing non-Edison films, they were constantly risking a legal move on the part of Edison lawyers that would place them in contempt of court. At one point they tried to sell out to Lyman Howe.[111] Fortunately for them, he declined. In the meanwhile, Edison lawyers were preoccupied with their patents case against American Mutoscope and Biograph Company, which resulted in an Edison victory on July 15, 1901. While Biograph operated under court supervision as the case was appealed, Lubin closed his American office and moved to Germany.

---

[110]J. Stuart Blackton to William Gilmore, January 12, 1901, defendants' exhibit no. 116, testimony of J. Stuart Blackton, pp. 1989–90.

[111]Testimony of Blackton, p. 1879.

Edison had a virtual monopoly in moving picture production within the United States.[112]

Film production for Vitagraph was impossible between late January 1901 and March 2, 1902, when the Biograph suit was reversed on appeal, throwing out the ruling that had previously been entered against Blackton and Smith. Thereafter, Vitagraph produced subjects for its own use, particularly newsworthy topicals. It was not until September 1905 that Vitagraph sold original productions to the trade, a timely move taken at the beginning of the nickelodeon era.[113] Within a year of this move, Vitagraph was the most important production company in the United States.

CONCLUSIONS

The history of the Vitagraph Company offers a case study which allows us to grasp many of the essential characteristics of the film industry in the late 1890s. At first glance the company's expansion appears to conform to the historical model utilized by Douglas Gomery and other film historians primarily interested in the institution of cinema as a business. This approach is based on industrial organization economics, "an economic theory of technological innovation, which posits that a product or process is introduced to increase profits in three systematic phases: invention, innovation and diffusion."[114] Such a perspective sees Smith's development of the reframing device as a key innovation which enabled Vitagraph to enter the world of vaudeville exhibition. It does not constitute, however, a sufficient basis for constructing the history of American Vitagraph, nor does it adequately account for the company's success.

Vitagraph's survival and continued growth in the world of vaudeville exhibitions was sustained by Blackton and Smith's output of films, which enabled them to offer attractive programs to theater managers and to please the public. Although Smith's technical improvements were available to anyone willing to buy the '99 Projecting Kinetoscope, its diffusion does not seem significantly to have affected Vitagraph's business position. Vitagraph's constant production of exclusive quality subjects was enough to assure continued ascendency. When this supply of films disappeared early in 1901, however, the company was plunged into a crisis so severe that the trio tried to sell the business. More than most of their competitors, the Vitagraph partners understood the possibilities inherent in the interaction and interdependence between film production and exhibition during the late 1890s.

---

[112]See Charles Musser, "The Early Cinema of Edwin Porter," *Cinema Journal* 19 (Fall 1979); 12–13.

[113]*Clipper*, September 23, 1905, p. 795.

[114]J. Douglas Gomery, "The Coming of the Talkies: Invention, Innovation, and Diffusion," in *The American Film Industry*, Balio, ed., pp. 193–94.

Vitagraph's success in the late 1890s, its problems in the early 1900s, and rapid expansion in the post-1905 period suggest a more useful framework for analysis: the examination of business activities in relation to a mode of production rather than simply in terms of technology. This approach is dialectical rather than cyclical, and it rejects the notion of technological determinism which is implicit in the model offered by industrial organization economics. While the technological basis for a process like cinema remains an essential aspect of the mode of production, it is often not the crucial one in accounting for change and new economic opportunities. It would be a mistake simply to see the nickelodeon form of exhibition as a result of improved technology—the reduction of flicker. Rather, it was made possible by the production of an increasing number of longer films which could be used interchangeably by theaters. Vitagraph's rapid expansion into film production after 1905 was based on its astute assessment of this new development. A methodology such as Gomery's, which translates technological innovation directly into business strategies, patterns information in certain ways that are not always useful or accurate. This model, in fact, shares many characteristics with the biological model of older film historians and its notion of birth, growth, and development.

A second, related weakness in Gomery's model is that it ignores the films as cultural products. Unless historians understand how individual films are produced, exhibited, and appreciated, we cannot fully account for the economic history. Films are not like steel. With steel, the mode of production can change, but the product remains constant. In cinema, when the mode of production changes, the product (as evidenced in its mode of appreciation) changes, and *vice versa*. One cannot help but be impressed by Gomery's ability to write insightful historical narrative, but until he treats the films as a source of documentation commensurate with the written material he has located, his historical insights will be unnecessarily limited.

Finally, the history of cinema as an industry must be framed in terms of the specific economic system in which it operates, in terms of the mode of production in the largest sense. Vitagraph's success was not simply based on Smith's technical wizardry or Blackton's short film comedies, but on their ability to operate within the business standards of American capitalism at the turn of the century. With William Rock as their mentor, they used legal coercion to gain theatrical outlets and to weaken their competitors. They were also victims of similar machinations. Albert Smith later suggested that the constant anxiety of their predicament, their fear of going to jail, contributed to the death of his child.[115] Cooperation often turned to competition and subterfuge. Frank Cannock brought his technical expertise to Vitagraph, then left and testified against his former employers. Blackton and Smith bought films from Lubin even as they

---

[115]Ramsaye, *Million and One Nights*, p. 384.

were trying to put him out of business. Rapacious economic competition in the film industry during the 1890s affected not only the pattern of invention, innovation, and diffusion, nor only the modes of production and representation, but finally social relations.

PETER MORRIS

Images of Canada

The first films made in Canada, as elsewhere, were "interest" films, brief scenes of Canadian points of interest. Niagara Falls, "the mecca of all early motion picture cameramen,"[1] was the first featured attraction—filmed, separately, by three cameramen in September and October 1896: Felix Mesguich for Lumière, W. K. L. Dickson for the American Mutoscope and Biograph Company, and an unknown cameraman for Edison.[2] Another popular subject was the Rockies. Scenes were most often photographed from a moving railway train, with the friendly cooperation of the Canadian Pacific Railway. G. W. ("Billy") Bitzer— later famous as D. W. Griffith's cameraman—photographed a series of five films for American Mutoscope and Biograph in October 1899.[3] Edison's cameraman

---

[1]Gordon Hendricks, *Beginnings of the Biograph* (New York: Arno, 1964), p. 38.

[2]The titles for the American films were *American Falls from Above, American Side; American Falls from Bottom, Canadian Side; American Falls from Incline R.R.; Horseshoe Falls—from Luna Isle; Horseshoe Falls—from Table Rock; Whirlpool Rapids—from Canadian Side; Rapids Above American Falls.* Those for the American Mutoscope and Biograph were *Canadian Falls Table Rock; Canadian Falls Table Rock No. 22; Falls from Michigan Central Railway No. 23; American Falls from Luna Island; American Falls from Goat Island No. 25; American Falls from American Side No. 26; Niagara Gorge from Erie Railroad; Lower Rapids Niagara Falls; Pointing Down Gorge, Niagara Falls; Taken from Trolley in Gorge Niagara Falls; Upper Rapids from Bridge; Panorama of American and Canadian Falls Taken Opposite American Falls.* See Hendricks, *Beginnings of the Biograph,* pp. 38–39, 48–51.

[3]Titles were *The Gap (CPRR); Fraser Canyon; Fraser Canyon, East of Yale; Down Kicking Horse Slide; Under Shadow of Mount Stephen.* Another series of railway films were photographed by F. S. Armitage in May–June 1900: *Gilead (Grand Trunk Railroad); Victoria Bridge Montreal (Grand Trunk); Approach to Lake Christopher (Grand Trunk).*

shot another series of six films on the Rockies in 1901.[4] Not surprisingly, films of Canadian winter scenes were also a popular attraction, as were "newsreels" of visits by royalty together with other Canadian activities that might interest American audiences.[5] Among these were films of Canadian troops leaving for the Boer War in 1899 and films of the visit of the Duke of York to Canada in 1902, all released by Edison.

The names of many of the early cameramen who filmed Canadian subjects have not survived. Certainly some, such as Billy Bitzer, were sent into Canada by the parent company; others may have been Canadians who photographed scenes on a freelance basis and sold their films to Edison, Biograph, or another company. One such may have been Robert Bonine. In October 1897, the Edison Company began releasing a series of films on the Klondike Gold Rush, scenes first of the loading of baggage and horses and later scenes in the Klondike itself.[6] Eight films in all, priceless records of one of the most extraordinary events of modern times. The photographer was Robert Bonine, a cameraman who supplied film to both Edison and Biograph. Nothing is known of his origin, but his name and the fact that most of the material he obtained for these companies was of Canadian origin suggest that he was himself Canadian. The films of life in the Klondike were not released by Edison until May 1901, presumably after Bonine's return from the gold fields. In early 1902, both Edison and Biograph released an unusually large number of films set in Montreal and Quebec. The records of Biograph show that Bonine photographed three films for the company in February 1902: *Run of a Snowshoe Club, Quebec Fire Department on Sleds,* and *What Ho, She Bumps!* [7] At the same time, the Edison Company released several very similar films: *Skiing in Quebec, Skiing in Montreal, Tobogganing in Canada,* and *Coasting at Montmorency Falls.* It seems likely that Bonine also photographed these, as it does that he was the cameraman for *Arrival of the Governor General, Lord Minto, at Quebec* (February 1902).[8] Bonine's work immediately after this was entirely outside Canada; in August 1902 he photographed the coronation of King Edward VII, and in 1906 he filmed the San Francisco earthquake, but his later career is unknown.

---

[4]The films are all various views of Kicking Horse Canyon.

[5]The earliest of these "winter scenes" were *Sleighing—Ottawa* (1898), *Snowstorm, Quebec* (1898), and *Skating, Montreal* (1898). The cameramen are unknown.

[6]Titles were *Horses Loading for Klondike, No. 9; Loading Baggage for Klondike, No. 6; S.S. "Williamette" Leaving for Klondike; Rocking Gold in the Klondike; Packers on the Trail; Pack Train on the Chilcoot Pass.*

[7]Kemp R. Niver, ed., *Biograph Bulletins, 1896–1908* (Los Angeles: Locare Research Group, 1971).

[8]Bonine may also have photographed the Kicking Horse Canyon films for Edison in December 1901, since from July to September 1901 he was filming in Asia and could have shot the railroad films on his return to eastern Canada.

Almost certainly the first Canadian to produce his own films was James S. Freer, a farmer from Brandon, Manitoba, who had purchased an Edison camera and projector. Freer, a former printer and newspaper publisher in Bristol, England, had settled in Manitoba in 1888.[9] By the fall of 1897 he was filming scenes of life in Manitoba, including harvesting and the arrival of the CPR trains, and by April 1898 was on tour with his films in Britain.[10] Freer's tour was sponsored by the Canadian Pacific Railway Company, and his show, "Ten Years in Manitoba," included not only movies but lectures on "the value of agricultural pursuits in Canada . . . the richness of the Canadian soil and the large free grants of land which are given to emigrants by the Canadian government."[11] How the CPR became involved with this venture is not known.[12] However, William Van Horne, builder and then head of the CPR, was a great believer in modern promotional methods; it appears not unlikely to have been his personal decision to back Freer's tour. Certainly, this was only the first involvement by the CPR in using film as a tool in its land settlement policies. Over the next two decades the company was to be increasingly involved in motion pictures, eventually establishing its own production company in Montreal.

Freer's films included *Arrival of CPR Express at Winnipeg; Pacific and Atlantic Mail Trains; Harnessing the Virgin Prairie; Canadian Continental Jubilee; Premier Greenway Stooking Grain; Six Binders at Work in Hundred Acre Wheatfield; Typical Stooking Scene; Harvesting Scene, with Trains Passing By; Cyclone Thresher at Work; Coming thru' the Rye* [children playing in the hay]; *Winnipeg Fire Boys on the Warpath;* and *Canadian Militia Charging Fortified Wall.* While in Britain, Freer photographed *Canadian Contingent at the Jubilee* and *Changing Guards at St. James Palace,* which he added to his program. His tour was a great success, drawing praise from newspapers for the novel use of the motion picture as an "emigration agent." The London *Daily Mail* admired Freer's "capital series of cinematograph pictures," while the Norwich *Eastern Daily Press* described his films as "reproducing in realistic manner the conditions of life in the Far West from the interior of a

---

[9]*The Dominion Illustrated* 24 (December 15, 1888): 372, 374.

[10]This dating is taken from the fact that his public tours began in the spring of 1898; his films included harvesting scenes which must have been photographed in the fall of 1897 at the latest.

[11]*Optical Magic Lantern Journal and Photographic Enlarger* 9 (April 1898): 54. Henry Hopwood, *Living Pictures* (London: Opticians and Photographic Trades Review, 1899), p. 232.

[12]The Canadian government and the CPR had for some time been using lantern-slide lectures to promote emigration from Britain to Canada. Agent for these was Alfred Jury, who later bccame British distributor for the films of the Canadian Government Motion Picture Bureau. Following the CPR's lead, the Northwest Transportation Company in the United States used films in 1899 to encourage potential immigrants to settle in Alaska.

bachelor's shanty to Mr. Freer's pretty and attractive family residence with the family assembled outside."[13]

How many Britons were convinced to emigrate to Canada as a result of Freer's films and lectures is unknown. They must have had some effect because, in December 1901, the federal minister of the interior, Clifford Sifton, agreed to sponsor a second tour, "under the auspices of the Canadian Government."

James Freer had returned to Manitoba in the spring of 1899. He attempted to make additional films but without much apparent success, and increasingly he turned his activities toward exhibitions, showing films of the "Old Country" in Manitoba. He attempted to obtain the federal government's cooperation in his planned filming of the Duke of York's visit to Ottawa.[14] He received no reply to his letter, and the visit was filmed instead by a cameraman for Edison, films which Freer then had to purchase for his collection. He may have attempted other film projects but, if so, they failed. For his 1902 tour, Freer used again the films he had used in 1898–99 with the addition of new films purchased from other producers: *Canadian Mounted Rifles Cutting Off a Boer Commando; Arrival of the Duke of York in Canada; Shooting the Chutes.* The only new Freer film was of a trip across the Atlantic from Liverpool to Quebec City, probably photographed on his return from the 1898–99 tour. This second tour was less successful than the first, possibly because Freer visited many of the same towns, and audiences must have been disappointed to discover they were watching the same scenes they had seen three years earlier. In any case, neither the Canadian government nor the CPR repeated the experience with Freer. When the CPR, liking the idea but wanting new films, decided to sponsor their own, they went not to James Freer but to a British producer, Charles Urban. Freer himself returned to Manitoba and apparently abandoned film production, though he continued running film shows.

The CPR was not alone in discovering the potential of motion pictures for promotion and advertising. By 1898, several commercial companies (notably the soap companies) were taking advantage of films to promote their products.[15] Among the first was the Massey-Harris Company of Toronto, which, in 1898, commissioned the Edison Company to produce films of its agricultural machinery at work on Ontario farms.[16] A by-product of Walter Massey's interest in photography, the films were shown at the Toronto, Ottawa, and Montreal exhibitions of 1898 and later exported to Britain, from where it was "anticipated that large orders for goods will follow." This early involvement by both

---

[13]Quoted in Freer's promotional leaflets, copies of which are in the National Archives, Ottawa.

[14]Files on Clifford Sifton, Public Archives, Canada.

[15]*Optical Magic Lantern Journal and Photographic Enlarger* 9 (March 1898): 37–38.

[16]*Optical Magic Lantern Journal and Photographic Enlarger* 9 (February 1899): 18; Merrill Denison, *Harvest Triumphant: The Story of Massey-Harris* (Toronto: Collins 1949), p. 157.

commercial companies and government is of interest because it, too, set a pattern that continued to mark Canadian production over many decades. Indeed, it seems to have been realized almost from the beginning in Canada that film could be used for more than just entertainment. The Massey-Harris films are an example of this, as are the two tours by James Freer to promote immigration. In fact, the CPR's inevitable need to promote settlement of "The Last Best West" was to be a key element in Canadian film production until 1910.

"BUT NO SNOW OR ICE SCENES"

At the turn of the century, Canada had a population of just over five million. Between then and 1914 the combined efforts of the CPR, other railways, and the federal government lured more than three million immigrants to Canada. "Nothing to compare with the great mass migration into Western Canada during the first decades of the twentieth century ever happened before. . . . Nowhere were more people enticed, cajoled, persuaded, induced, gulled, or just plain bamboozled into tearing themselves up by their roots to journey . . . to a land where not a single constructive step had been taken by anybody to prepare for their arrival."[17]

In this process of persuasion, the motion picture was to play a key role, being used first by the CPR and later by governments themselves and other railways. The effectiveness of these films was to be remembered later by officials of the federal government when they were considering the establishment of a permanent government film bureau in 1917.

Most of the films were directed principally at British audiences. This was a deliberate policy decision. In the first five years of the century immigrants from the United States outnumbered those from Britain. There was concern in Ottawa that the "British" character of the Canadian west might be lost, indeed that the west itself might be lost to the United States, if British immigration were not stepped up.[18]

First in the motion picture field was the CPR, whose commercial viability depended on the rapid settlement of the Canadian west. In 1902, soon after Freer's second tour, the CPR hired a British group to travel across Canada filming scenes of Canadian life. The films were guaranteed release in Britain through the Charles Urban Trading Company and were designed to stimulate emigration from Britain.[19] Charles Urban also supplied the personnel of the

[17]James H. Gray, *Red Lights on the Prairies* (Toronto: Signet Books, 1973), p. 15.

[18]J. W. Dafoe, *Clifford Sifton in Relation to His Times*, quoted in Gray, *Red Lights on the Prairies*, p. 16.

[19]In 1902, Charles Urban was heading the Warwick Trading Company. He left there early in 1903 and established his own company, the Charles Urban Trading Company. Urban was an American who originally went to Britain in 1894 to manage the London office of

group: F. Guy Bradford, a cameraman, technician, and later an executive with
Urban's company; Clifford Denham, Bradford's brother-in-law; and Joe Rosenthal, the most famous cameraman of his day, whose reputation had been
established by his coverage of the Boer War in South Africa. The group called
themselves the Bioscope Company of Canada, following Urban's general practice.[20] They had strict instructions from the CPR, according to Cliff Denham, "not
to take any winter scenes under any conditions." Canada was—already—
thought of too much as a land of ice and snow. CPR liaison for the filming was
handled by Mr. Kerr, general passenger agent, and Mr. Armstrong, colonization
agent.[21]

Filming began in the early fall of 1902, continued through the summer of
1903, and covered the country from Quebec to Victoria—following, of course,
the CPR railroad. "The railroad scenes were taken from a flat car pushed by
an engine and the others were usually picked out by Tourist Bureaus, etc., as we
visited different cities in turn."[22] Guy Bradford set up processing facilities in
downtown Montreal to print the film as it was shot. His assistant was Maurice
Metzger, who later became superintendent of Associated Screen News' film
laboratory.

The first films to arrive in Britain in January 1903 were given a major
première at the Palace Theatre, London, in the presence of the Canadian high
commissioner, Lord Strathcona (formerly Donald Alexander Smith of the CPR),
who "has so materially assisted in developing the resources of Canada."[23] The
series, eventually to be called *Living Canada*, pictured Canada from coast to coast,

---

Edison's Kinetoscope. When he reorganized the company in 1898 as the Warwick Trading
Company he also began producing films. Warwick had a staff of itinerant cameramen who
traveled around the world and were the first war cinematographers. The most famous of
these was Joe Rosenthal. Urban was a businessman and entrepreneur rather than a
producer. It was to his initiative that the early British film industry owes such achievements
as Kinemacolor, the scientific film, and travel and war films. He was also expert at securing
financial backing for his itinerant cameramen, from both commercial companies and
governments. For example, the North Borneo Company financed "the Urban Bioscope
Expedition through Borneo" in 1903 and through Malay in 1904. The CPR, of course, did
the same thing in Canada. Urban also had cameramen on both sides of the Russo-Japanese
War in 1904–5.

[20]The name came from their use of the "Bioscope" camera manufactured by Urban.

[21]Material derived from H. H. McArthur to Hye Bossin, March 31, 1951, Bossin
Collection, National Film Board of Canada; and from Cliff Denham to Hye Bossin, quoted in
Canadian Film Weekly, July 11, 1951.

[22]Cliff Denham, quoted in *Canadian Film Weekly*, July 11, 1951.

[23]*The British Journal of Photography*, January 23, 1903, p. 70. Lord Strathcona was high
commissioner for Canada to Britain from 1896 to his death in 1914. He was most certainly a
supporter of Freer's tours and his CPR films.

from the arrival of immigrants at Quebec City, through the Canadian Shield, across the prairies, and down the Fraser River Canyon to Vancouver. The first night audience gave the films a "hearty reception"; London's critics were also kind. The films "included some of the finest we have seen; the Fraser River 'run' took twelve minutes to pass through, and, photographically was remarkably good. The harvesting, ranching, and lumbering views are, besides, full of instruction in characteristic phases of Canadian life, and altogether we congratulate those concerned on a display of animated photographs which, for technical excellence and deep interest, we have not seen excelled."[24]

True to his convenant with the CPR, Charles Urban diligently avoided displaying any winter scenes at that première performance. The CPR itself and Canadian immigration agents used that series in special presentations throughout Britain, often accompanied by a lecturer, in the manner of James Freer. But when Urban came to release the films of his own account for general theatrical release in June 1903, it was apparent that the trio at work in Canada had not taken the CPR's instructions too seriously. Such films as *Montreal on Skates, Ice Yachting on the St. Lawrence,* and *The Outing of the "Old Tuque Blue" Snow-Shoeing Club of Montreal* were listed in Urban's catalogue under the heading *"Living Canada* by Joseph Rosenthal."[25] Other films were more what had been expected, including items on the lumber industry, threshing wheat, Indian canoe races, the Labour Day Parade in Vancouver, CPR trains in the Rockies, and, inevitably, *Niagara, the World's Wonder.* The trio also took advantage of additional financing from the Anglo-British Columbia Packing Company to produce *Catching Fifty Thousand Salmon in Two Hours.* In all, Charles Urban released thirty-five *Living Canada* films in 1903–4. In 1906, several of the films were reedited, condensed, and rereleased under the title *Wonders of Canada.*[26]

Living Canada was also exhibited in Canada in programs organized by Denham and Bradford.[27] Their two and a half hour show opened at the Windsor Hall in Montreal in 1903, ran for six weeks, moved to Massey Hall in Toronto for two weeks, and then toured the country. Joe Rosenthal left Canada at the end of his assignment in order to film the Russo-Japanese War. Both Bradford and Denham remained in Canada, and both developed careers in exhibition. Denham settled in Victoria, B.C., and eventually managed several theatres for Famous Players Canadian Corporation. Bradford, "a very fine type of cultured English gentleman with a real genius for creating enthusiasm," moved to the Maritimes

[24]Ibid.

[25]*Charles Urban Trading Company Catalogue,* November 1903, pp. 16–17, and January 1904 *Supplement,* pp. 5–8 (British Film Institute copies).

[26]*Charles Urban Trading Company Catalogue,* 1909, pp. 287–89 (British Film Institute copies). *The Optical Lantern and Kinematograph Journal* 2 (1906): 227; *Moving Picture World* 1 (April 27, 1907). *Wonders of Canada* was 725 feet.

[27]Cliff Denham, quoted in *Canadian Film Weekly,* July 11, 1951.

and was instrumental in starting St. John's first deluxe movie theatre, the Nickel.[28] Later he opened other theatres in the Maritimes and became a distributor himself.

While in Canada, Rosenthal produced what is certainly the first film drama in Canada: "Hiawatha," The Messiah of the Ojibway. Released by Urban in the fall of 1903, it was described as a dramatized presentation of Longfellow's poem The Song of Hiawatha "enacted by North American Indians of the Ojibway Tribe at Desbarats, Ontario." The makers are unknown, but Urban's catalogue acknowledges the conception as the work of Mr. E. A. Armstrong of Montreal—who may well have been the same Armstrong who was the CPR's colonization agent. At 800 feet (fifteen minutes) Hiawatha was considerably longer than the usual production of 1903, which rarely exceeded 200 feet. Urban subtitled the film The Passion Play of America ("There is but one Oberammergau. There is but one Desbarats."), and it is evident that the film was largely a photographed stage play, though set in natural surroundings. The nine-page description which Urban included in his catalogue is in fact a rapturous description of the original stage play since it includes references to the play's music (by Frederick R. Burton) and the spoken words of Longfellow's poem. The anonymous author concluded: "Never had play such a setting. Never had actors such splendid distances, such a glorious background. The picture stamps itself indelibly upon the mind of every beholder, a perpetual memory, odorous with the unameable [sic] fragrance of pine and cedar and balsam, and shelving rock and shimmering water."[29] While on the West Coast Rosenthal also made a short one-minute drama, Indians Gambling for Furs—Is It Peace or War?, released also in September 1903.

---

[28]McArthur to Bossin, March 31, 1951.

[29]Charles Urban Trading Company Catalogue, November 1903, pp. 31–39 (British Film Institute copy). The catalogue number 1091 would date the release in September 1903. Rosenthal is credited as director in the British Films Catalogue. (London: British Film Institute, 1948).

ISTVÁN NEMESKÜRTY

In the Beginning, 1896–1911

Of Budapest's many cafés the Velence was not the most splendid, but it was one of the most enterprising—and it had a good site. It was on busy Rákóczi Street, where the present Tisza Cinema stands. In this café the Hungarian cinema began its history.

The café is a remarkable institution developed by bourgeois society in the last century. It used to be—and sometimes still is—a place where merchants, businessmen, artists, clerks, and even radical intellectuals could mingle. At a Budapest café you were served more than coffee; food and other drinks were available, but that was not its chief attraction. One came here for companionship, business appointments, political discussion, and the exchange of ideas. To attract more patrons to come more regularly the owner was obliged to stimulate conversation and keep alive the various interests of his customers. For one thing there was always plenty of newspapers; every Budapest café subscribed to as many important European newspapers as the owner could afford—this was as vital as the quality of the coffee beans he bought. Habitués of each café knew that their favourite paper always awaited them.

There were cafés with literary programmes, musical recitals, and solo comedians; there were cafés with floor shows and full variety programmes, music halls reduced in scale. No extra fee was charged, either for this entertainment or for the always available newspapers. If the café owner wanted regular patrons, he had to keep them well entertained.

No wonder that films also found their way into the café. It was the Grand Café on the Boulevard des Capucines that gave the first commercial performance of the Lumières' films. Immediately cafés in Berlin and Rome threw their doors open to the filmmakers, and patrons poured through the same open doors. Now the café owner could say: Come to us for tea, to talk business, to chat with your friends, to read the papers, and every day from five to six we also show moving pictures. At first this novelty was included for the patrons without charge; only later was a special room prepared to admit visitors for a very modest entrance fee. Here people could come who were more interested in films than in coffee—and these patrons, shopkeepers, salesmen, clerks, poets, prosperous stallkeepers, people who were killing time before their suburban trains left Budapest, these were the nucleus of the film audience that was soon to swell to astonishing numbers.

That was what induced Mr Ungerleider, the owner of the Velence Café, to go in for films. Mr Bécsi, the head waiter, let down a clean sheet in the middle of the café—the guests could enjoy the film from both sides, so nobody need change his table—and brought out the projection machine, which he had learned to operate; under the table he placed a wastepaper basket where the shown reel could be caught as it came through the machine, and the performance began.

Later, when this projector was converted into a film camera, József Bécsi handled it with equal zeal; he was the first Hungarian cameraman.

In 1898 Mór Ungerleider, the café owner, founded a firm together with his business partner József Neumann, a former stage performer. This firm, operating under the name of Projectograph, provided films for its own cinema, sold and rented projectors and cameras, and even rented the films of major foreign companies to provincial cinemas. Projectograph was the first Hungarian firm which traded in films and ran a cinema.

In the first decade of the present century Projectograph also made newsreels and educational films. These films were offered in a catalogue which may be of interest to quote:

The Races at Alag, 88 metres;
Hare Hunting in the Plain, 150 metres;
Parade in Vienna in Homage to the Emperor's Jubilee, 200 metres;
View of Budapest, 190 metres;
Arrival of the Bulgarian Ruler at Budapest, 65 metres;
Pigeon-shooting Tournament on Margaret Island, 85 metres;
Demonstrations in Budapest During the Ides of March, 100 metres;
Vine-growing at Szekszárd, 115 metres;
The Spanish King Hunting at Féltorony, 140 metres;
Fire at the Kovald Factory, 77 meters;
The Funeral of Ferenc II Rákóczi at Budapest and at Kassa, 265 metres;
Lake Balaton, the Lower Danube, and the Tátra, 135 metres.

And there were also a few funny pictures among them:

Károly Baumann, 65 metres;
The Inebriated Cyclist, 120 metres;
Max and Maurice on the Turf, 120 metres.[1]

The text of a contemporary handbill gives a good idea of the dramatic composition of reconstructed (or staged) newsreels:

The Life of Vagrant Gipsies. The Robbers of Dános, a film of 136 metres, was described by the firm in the following terms: "Arrival of Strolling Gipsies in the Village. Life in the Tents. Stealing Hens and Horses. Gipsy Women Excel in Snatching Chickens, the Men in Stealing Horses. It is shown how deftly a gipsy woman can snatch a chicken from a coop and hurry with her prey to the tent where she throws it into a steaming cauldron prepared in advance by the other gipsies."[2] The farmer snores while the thieves ride off with his horse; then, complaint at the police station; "Pursuit over Hill and Dale and Water"—then the picture of the Dános murderer, Tuta Kolompár Balog, is shown at his trial.

The process of "creative work" can be now clearly seen: at that time it was easier to fool filmgoers, and such reconstructions were being made everywhere. Obviously, the only *real* part of this "newsreel" was what was taken at the trial of Tuta Kolompár Balog; the rest was played by actors, exactly as if a fictional film were being made.

The "exceedingly humorous, irresistibly funny film" entitled *Chess Maniac* (A sakkjáték őrültje), played by the members of the Modern Stage and directed by Endre Nagy, is also worthy of notice. The film is about a passionate chess player so absorbed in the game at a café that when he leaves he judges everything in the town by the moves permitted on the chess board. That is how he walks along the street, how he contemplates the wares displayed in the market, where goods and market-women suddenly change into chessmen and pawns. He boards the omnibus with a knight's move; he gets home; "when he is about to plunge his fork into the roast it vanishes and in its place he finds a knight"—and so on. We know the contents of approximately a dozen similar Projectograph films made between 1905 and 1910. Quite likely more were made, but only some of these films received any public notice. Beside the firm Projectograph, there were one or two other enterprising persons who made a few films at this time. A good many cafés were converted into cinemas, but the new cinema proprietors showed no inclination to make films themselves. They had neither capital nor experience to encourage them. For the time being Projectograph could meet the demand of the Hungarian public to complete satisfaction.

At the time a scientific educational society was active in Hungary under the name of Urania. Founded in Germany, it maintained theatres where lantern-slide

---

[1]This price-list advertisement of Projectograph was published in the review *Mozgófénykép Hiradó* and its photograph reprinted in my monograph, where all details of this chapter and of the Hungarian silent film are elaborated in greater detail. István Nemeskürty, *A Mozgóképtől a filmmüvészetig* (Budapest, 1961).

[2]*Mozgófénykép Hiradó* no. 7, 1908.

lectures were presented about scientific expeditions, about remote countries and continents, about literature, music, and acting. Urania also had its own theatre.

On one occasion Gyula Pekár, a writer and politician, was to give a lecture on dancing. He asked the chief projectionist of the institute, Béla Zsitkovszky, to make a motion picture which might be projected to illustrate his lecture. In answer to this request was made *Dancing* (A tánc) in 1901. This film was followed by a dozen or so similar "lecture-films," about which we know only from vague reports. These films served to illustrate the lectures of a well-organized educational society. As such, they did not belong to the category of film merchandise, produced in all parts of the world—in Hungary by the Budapest firm Projectograph—but represented a new initiative; on the other hand, this fortunate start—including *Dancing*—remained an isolated phenomenon.

There is not much to be said about the other experiments. Hungary has her own date of 1896: at the Millennial Exhibition a clever businessman, Arnold Sziklay, took pictures of Franz Joseph opening the exhibition, inspecting Mihály Munkácsy's painting *Ecce Homo* and congratulating the artist. The film has been lost; it is said to have been a failure, a failure perhaps due to the fact that the scene was taken with a camera put together largely by the cameraman himself and on an American strip of film perforated also by himself. The theatre where it was shown soon went bankrupt as did the other theatres, opened at Budapest in the nineties, including the cinema of the Lumières in the Hotel "Royal."

At the Millennium Exhibition in 1896 there was also a cinema building, opened for Edison's kinetoscope: "The kinetoscope pavilion has the character of an opera hall which has been designed in a fine style by the architect Ignác Alpár. The hall of 50 square metres has been built at a cost of nearly 6,000 forints by Ödön and Marcell Neuschlosz."[3]

However, various kinds of cinemas in tents, showbooths of itinerant cinematographers, ever increased in number. In Budapest the Apollo Cinema of Ungerleider and his partners stood on the site of the present Corvin Department Store; for a long time it was the largest and the grandest of our cinemas. The tent cinema opposite the Film Museum of our days was also famous. The excited audience thronged inside a big circus tent after listening to the enticements of a barker. Poets and authors fond of night life in the capital visited quieter small cinemas which had been converted from cafés. The well-known reporter-writer of that time, Árpád Pásztor says: "I also joined the circle of authors, painters, and musicians who frequented the New York café, went to films at a time when there were only two cinemas on the boulevard and it was 'the thing' to see both programmes on the same evening."[4]

---

[3]In the book *Az ezredéves kiállitás erdémenye* [Results of the Millennial Exhibition of 1896] (Budapest, 1897), p.108. Ignac Alpar was the best Hungarian architect of the time.

[4]Viktor Lanyi-István Rado-Albert Held, *A 25 éves mozi* [The 25-year-old cinema] (Budapest, 1920), p. 37.

A few years later the first film critics came from among the members of this circle: Zoltán Somlyó, Frigyes Karinthy.

According to contemporary statistics, there were 270 permanent cinemas in Hungary around 1912. In relation to the size and population of Hungary at the time, this figure may be regarded as normal by contemporary European standards. In Budapest there were 92 cinemas seating 26,332 spectators altogether. (Újpest, Kispest, Pesterzsébet, Csepel, etc., are not included. These suburbs now are parts of the capital.) Thus a cinema had approximately 300 seats. The population of the capital having been 970,000—about half of the present—there was a cinema for every 10,500 inhabitants.[5] Berlin, with three million inhabitants at the same time, had 300 cinemas. Hence the ratio was similar to that of Budapest.

As a rule provincial towns had one, sometimes two cinemas, but some had none. In the larger towns there were four or five cinemas. Kaposvár was a remarkable exception: this small town of 26,000 inhabitants had three cinemas seating 1,600 people. It was at Kaposvár that the first book on films in Hungarian appeared (a translation of the German cinematographer Paul Liesegang's book, translated by Sándor Kozma, cinematographer of Kaposvár, in the year 1911). Let us compare another big provincial town of Hungary with a German town of similar size. At Szeged there were four cinemas seating 1,250 people. The town had 125,000 inhabitants, i.e., a cinema for every 31,000 inhabitants. Mainz, having a population of 110,000, had also four cinemas.[6] If a cinema is assumed to have held 300 people on the average, daily attendance may have amounted to 243,000 people in the case of three performances a day at the 270 cinemas of Hungary.

On the evidence of contemporary observers the number of cinemas tended to increase, so that a regular Hungarian motion picture industry must have seemed to have a promising and lucrative future. Lucrative even if the National Association of Hungarian Cinematographers founded at the time counted altogether sixty-seven members in 1909;[7] and lucrative even if the products of the Hungarian film industry had to share the market with those of foreign competitors. Obviously, cinemas flourished and their owners were getting rich. Still no regular Hungarian motion picture production industry developed in those initial years, though a weekly attendance of a million and a half could be counted on.

In fact, the early stages of development, when a film industry is taken in hand by cinema owners themselves to produce their own products, failed to set in in Hungary. This may be ascribed to the absence of major capital concentration. Every cinema owner thought in terms of one, namely his own, cinema, and it is extremely risky to make films for one cinema. The purchase of a

[5]Lajos Körmendy-Ékes, A mozi [The cinema] (Budapest, 1915), pp. 102–4.

[6]Körmendy-Ékes, A mozi, pp. 74 and 102.

[7]Mózgófénykép Hiradó no. 11, 1909.

ready film, on the other hand, involved only the payment of the price for one copy. Moreover, the cinematographer could afford to pick and choose, and buy attractive films of a high standard. That is why no major production enterprise was launched in Hungary at this early date; a new industry of wholesale "dealing" in films began to thrive instead. Projectograph and other firms went in chiefly for distributing films. On their yearly two or three trips abroad the distributors bought what they liked best from French, Italian, American, Danish, occasionally German and Austrian motion picture studios. Even a Film Exchange was founded where deals were made and prices were quoted. In the spring of 1911, when Mór Ungerleider saw the first Asta Nielsen film of Nordisk, *Avgrunden,* he quickly published a scathing review, lest somebody else should conceive the idea of purchasing this treasure, but he quickly bought his railway ticket to Copenhagen, where in a few days he secured an option on all Nordisk films for years to come.[8]

---

[8]*Mózgófénykép Hiradó* nos. 4, 13, 1911.

ERIC READE

Australian Silent Film, 1904–1907:

The Features Begin

In Sydney in 1904 the only activity of any consequence, apart from the Cyclorama, was at the Queen's Hall, Pitt Street, where the screening of the 1904 Melbourne Cup was referred to by one critic as one of the finest on the programme. But in Melbourne during the same year there was a definite feeling in the air that big things were about to happen. January began sedately enough with the Grand Biograph at the Athenaeum, under the banner of John H. Tait. (Looking back, one soon realised that this hall was being groomed for stardom.) Included in the lineup of films were pictures of the wrecked steamer *Coogee*. The Opera House continued to feature moving films throughout January, and at the end of the month introduced "coloured" bio-pictures.

Although the motion picture industry in Australia had developed a lethargic attitude, the Salvation Army's cinematographic division had blossomed into a thriving unit that both covered Army work (for which purpose it had been originally set up) and featured the subject commercially as well. In fact it appears that the Salvation Army kept the moving picture camera turning during those formulative years.

A glass-roofed studio had been erected at the rear of the Army Headquarters at 69 Bourke Street, Melbourne, to produce films that were developed on the premises by Perry himself. A series of Victorian beauty spots, such as the Gembrook District, were taken for the Railways Department and were screened nightly above Princes Bridge Railway Station. Industrial documentaries included Chaffey's Irrigation Scheme at Mildura and a visit to MacRobertson's confectionary factory. Other Perry films covered the fishing fleet at Port Fairy and coaching in New Zealand.

Meanwhile, Orrie Perry, the "front legs of the lion" in *Soldiers of the Cross*, had followed in his father's footsteps. Accompanying a scientific expedition to

King Island, he photographed the bird life in the area. This was ultimately screened in the Church Hall, Collins Street, Melbourne, and throughout the world.

Grand Open Air Concerts were held at the Melbourne Cricket Ground every Monday, from 15 February to 25 April, and it was here that Alex Gunn's Royal Bioscope was featured. Gunn is a name that has been perpetuated in the picture business right to the present day, under "Gunn Slides."

The Opera House continued to feature the Bio-Graph on its bill fairly regularly throughout the year. On 4 June it was advertised

For the First Time—a local biographic picture, depicting with marvellous realism—a Yacht Race on the Albert Park Lake.

The Town Hall on 17 September provided a bill that was startlingly different—a combination of records of Madame Melba and Enrico Caruso and the New Biograph. Admission prices were 2/- and 1/-. It was stated that every record could be heard distinctly. The show was transferred to the Athenaeum for one week, and had a one night stand at the Masonic Hall in October. During this period Edison's Moving Pictures were being screened in the most unusual of venues—the Aquarium.

Meanwhile, Joseph Perry returned from Europe, where he had used his moving camera industriously. At the Melbourne Town Hall he screened films taken by him on the trip. Projected on to a sheet 20 feet square, his bill of fare included *In Sunny France, Amsterdam—Land of Windmills,* and scenes of Sweden and Germany. English subjects covered views of Crystal Palace and slum work in London.

J. C. Williamson and his Bio-Tableau returned to the Athenaeum on 22 October and a week later revived the 1904 Melbourne Cup film, claimed to be an "absolute triumph" and "the very finest film of the Melbourne Cup and Flemington Racecourse ever yet displayed in Australia." After the final screening on 22 November, Mr Williamson then took his Melbourne Cup film to Sydney.

On Boxing Day the Athenaeum was occupied once again when John H. Tait came back with his American Biograph and remained until 14 January 1905. This year new forces were coming into focus, giving a new significance and impetus to the flickering screen in both Sydney and Melbourne.

In April the Sydney Cyclórama stated with pride that it had just imported a "professional Chrono Cinematograph." Meanwhile, James McMahon at the Lyceum seemed to sense a revival of interest in the movies and paved the way with Grand Concerts and the Bioscope. Then came the all-important announcement—"For a short season only, C. Spencer will present his Great American Theatrescope at the Lyceum, on Saturday July 1st."

This advertisement was no different than many that had appeared in the past, but Spencer was to become the first of a new breed of showmen who would greatly influence the future of the film industry in Australia. Spencer didn't take long to demonstrate that he was there to do something about local production too—and more to the point, to make it a profitable occupation. In the early 1900s it was possible to combine production and exhibition.

On 22 July Spencer announced that he would film the sculling championship race on the Parramatta River, between ex-champion George Towns and James Stanbury. "At great expense and difficulty, it has been arranged to reproduce this Herculean struggle, within 5 hours of this historic event. The effort is unparalleled in the annals of animated art—a triumph of scientific and human ingenuity." This gives some indication of what to expect from Cousens Spencer. Later, Spencer toured the other states and returned to the Lyceum "after a triumphal tour of Western Australia."

But there were other forms of activity as it became apparent that the moving picture industry was showing more signs of life. On 24 June J. Baker at the Criterion Theatre, Park Street, advertised that he had "cinematograph films for sale, hire, or exchange."

A fortnight later, the Cyclorama proudly announced that its cinematograph machine was the only one that didn't flicker. In fact, events were so vividly and distinctly portrayed that the hundreds who saw it nightly left thinking that they were really there on the eventful occasion.

By 16 September another great showman, T. J. West, was knocking on Sydney's door, and took the trouble to pay for newspaper space proclaiming that "West's Pictures aren't in Sydney—they're still in New Zealand. West's—pre-eminent in the animated picture world."

During the following month there was a great deal of activity on the Sydney screens. J. S. Phelan and his Big Biograph were at the Centenary Hall, Pitt Street. It was the only biograph operated in Australia by electricity, although not the first. On 7 October, J. C. Williamson, an American who had been in Australia for a number of years, transferred his Bio Tableau activities to the Palace Theatre, and not to be outdone showed that he too could provide film highlights of everyday activities in this country. He screened a *Busy Day at the Homebush Cattle Market; A Trip from Post Office Place to Redfern* (taken from the top of a George Street tram); *Panoramic Views of Circular Quay as Viewed from a Ferry Boat; The Championship Wood Chopping Contest at Devonport, Tasmania; Shearing Sheep on a N.S.W. Station.*

Melbourne, for its part, was making startling advances in motion picture activity—and was adding a purely Australian touch into the bargain. At the Open Air Concerts in the Melbourne Cricket Ground, the bioscope again figured prominently. This time it was under the direction of Millard Johnson and W. A. Gibson—names that would soon become well known in the production of Australian full-length pictures. Meanwhile, Johnson & Gibson were taking giant strides in the distributing and exhibiting fields.

Millard Johnson was originally a chemist on the corner of Nelson Street and Punt Road, St. Kilda. His main claim to fame had been "Old Shoe Corn Cure." He was joined by his brother-in-law, William Alfred Gibson, an astute businessman. Strangely enough, the Australian film industry owes a great deal to one of the queer quirks of fate that put Johnson & Gibson into the business in the first place.

An Englishman who was appearing in a vaudeville show approached Johnson & Gibson for materials required to operate a magic lantern that projected moving figures on to a screen. Then in true show-business style, his manager, and the takings, disappeared. The Englishman, being loath to join the unemployed show people on Melbourne's "poverty row," sold his lantern to Gibson for £40.

At first, Gibson merely used it to entertain his friends on the roof of the shop. He showed his short lengths of film on a makeshift screen erected under the stars. What he didn't realise was that his picture show could be seen from the street. However, an irate policeman soon made him aware of the fact, demanding that the performance be terminated as a congestion in the street below was being caused.

Gibson was an astute businessman, and, sensing public interest, he took his projector and films to St. Kilda Beach. Success was immediate and Johnson and Gibson set up a film exchange in the Temperance Hall, Russell Street, where they hired out projectors and films. They soon began repairing the machines and gathered a staff of trained projectionists to show the pictures. These operators were men who worked throughout the day in other jobs but were anxious to earn a few extra shillings at night. But in those early days Gibson was kept so busy himself that he often projected at two different places in one evening, covering three separate shows—an early and a late one at the first location, and an intermediate show at a second ground or hall.

Johnson & Gibson's name appeared on programmes for the People's Concerts at the Temperance Hall; Sacred Concerts at Fitzgerald's Circus Building on a Sunday; Sunday Concerts at the Collins Street Masonic Hall; Sunday Evenings for the People at Fitzgerald's (where late in the year the new electric bioscope was used); and at Sunday Services of Song at the Masonic Hall. They also screened the *Port Fairy Fishing Fleet* (Perry's film) on 27 March at the Open Air Concert in the Melbourne Cricket Ground. Another J. &. G. accomplishment was in operating the Great American Bioscope at the Athenaeum Hall. They were billed as the "best bioscopic operators in Australia."

1905 was the year that Joseph Perry and his Biorama Company paid yet another visit to New Zealand. It was also the year that posed a problem. A four-minute meldodrama made by Edwin J. Cole, *A Maiden's Distress* or *Saved in the Nick of Time,* has been referred to as being produced in 1902 in one record, and 1904 in another. But a reliable source states that the baby in the film, Mr Ossie Wilson, wasn't born until 1905. He has since died, and his widow, who resided in North Sydney, moved in April 1969, leaving the mystery unanswered. However, the National Film Library in Canberra received a copy of this film from Mr Ossie Wilson in 1962.

A Maiden's Distress was an Australian western with all the players dressed as Red Indians. A knife thrower had a squaw tied to a tree and was trying to force some deep secret from her when the hero arrived and she was "saved in the nick of time."

In early October 1905 at the Palace Theatre Sydney J. C. Williamson's Bio Tableau and All Star Picture Show featured the Australian Cricketers in England.

Williamson arrived back in Melbourne on 14 October, where he offered the "magnificent series of eye motion-picture studies of the Australian cricketers, with his newly constructed Bio Tableau." *The Argus,* commenting on these living pictures, noted that the Australian cricketers were watched with deep interest. The recognition of the different players was the signal for hearty applause. Included were such memorable players as Darling, Gregory, Trumper, Armstrong, and Noble.

On Saturday 21 October *Australia by Biograph* was taken by Williamson's bioscopists for special presentation in England and America. Scenes and incidents of Australian life covered George Street, Sydney; Collins Street, Melbourne; shearing sheep in New South Wales; buckjumping; views of the Hawkesbury River; woodchopping in Devonport.

By October 1905, Johnson and Gibson had extended to the suburbs, showing in the Malvern Town Hall and in Fitzroy. In November and December the circuit was enlarged to cover Williamstown and Footscray.

J. C. Williamson provided a coverage of the 1905 Melbourne Cup on 7 November, when Blue Spec won from Scot Free and Tartan. A very brief season of the Animatograph opened at the Athenaeum in December, followed by Best and Baker's Moving Pictures. "Direct from England, the no-flicker, new life-o-graph machine" was the main feature.

1906 was a busy year for Joseph Perry and the Biorama Company in New Zealand. There, Perry exhibited the first "talking" pictures with the Cinephone. This was a combination of gramophone and film, the identical procedure used in the late 1920s with the "sound on disc" talkies. He took films of the Christchurch Exhibition and some of its special attractions, including Fijians doing a war dance and the Maoris with their hakas and poi games.

Perry met T. J. West, founder of West's Pictures, in Christchurch. A bond of mutual admiration developed between the two showmen, and when West finally began exhibiting in Australia many of his films (usually scenic views of various Australian cities) were developed in the darkroom of the Salvation Army.

Another interesting Perry picture was of Pelorus Jack, the famous pilot fish. This was the first time "Jack" had been photographed. By courtesy of the captain of the *Arahura,* a special platform was fitted over the bow of the ship near the water line to take the moving pictures of Pelorus Jack as they sailed through French Pass. Excellent photographs of Milford Sound were other highlights of the New Zealand trip.

Orrie Perry showed some of his father's skill with the moving camera when the *Maheno* ran into a fierce storm and huge waves threatened to engulf the ship. Orrie captured the drama of the scene on film.

The film game was now on for every cinematograph operator. Sydney offered shows at the Lyceum, Queens Hall, Centenary Hall in York Street, and the Palace Theatre. Melbourne's picture attractions were screened at the Athenaeum, the Town Hall, and Wirth's Olympia.

Names that appeared were varied and colourful. Cook's Living Pictures; Morton's Living Pictures; West's Pictures—the missionaries of healthy amusement; Spencer's American Theatrescope; J. C. Williamson's Bio Tableau; Best and Baker's Life-o-Graph; Macdermott's New Zealand Biograph Company, with John H. Tait, Cowards, and Sudholz added for good measure.

Spencer remained at the Lyceum, Sydney, until 10 February. Then on 29 March J. & N. Tait took over this theatre to screen *Living London.* However, films with the same title were shown at various theatres in Sydney—each version being billed as "the original."

On 21 April T. J. West followed his screening of *Living London* at the Palace with his own version of *Living Sydney.* This covered the turn out of the fire brigade; scenes in George and Pitt Streets; and views of Manly, Mosman, and North Shore ferries. Contained in the advertisement was the following memo to the employees of Anthony Hordern: "You left business at 1 p.m. today. Come and see yourself doing it again tonight."

Also in April, Bland Holt staged the play *Besieged at Port Arthur,* written by Arthur Shirley and Sutton Vane, at the Theatre Royal. This play has been recorded as a 1906 film, but a check through newspaper files has shown only the play. If such a film had been made in this year it would have automatically deserved the distinction of being the first feature film in the world.

Meanwhile, Cousens Spencer had yet to establish regular residence at the Lyceum. When he took over the Palace Theatre from West's in June, MacDermott's were at the former theatre, but as the newcomers gained strength, Sydney noted the passing of an old friend when the Cyclorama closed on 18 August.

Now the strength was coming into the industry and new names were appearing that would mean a great deal to Australian film production in later years. At the Criterion Theatre on 19 September, "A Feast of Pictures" was advertised by the Unique Pantoscope Company. This entry is important only for the name of the representative, W. Franklyn Barrett, a man who would make his mark as a cameraman and director.

The following Saturday, Edison's Popular Pictures were locum tenens at the Lyceum. Their importance to the record of Australian films—and then only as an interesting sidelight—lies in this advertisement dated 8 November: "Edison's have secured excellent pictures of the Melbourne Cup, but cannot present them at the Lyceum. The Management and Board of Directors of this theatre have refused permission to screen them." (The Management and Board of Directors were members of the Methodist and Presbyterian churches.)

Cousens Spencer arrived back from Queensland on 18 December and took up his "pictorial residence" at the Lyceum. Senora Spencer, "the only lady projectionist in the world," was one of the special attractions.

In 1906 most of the action was in Melbourne, yet strangely enough, four months had elapsed before this city recorded its first important entry.

In early May J. & N. Tait at the Melbourne Town Hall were exhibiting *Living London*. Then on 11 May a change of programme included *Moving Melbourne* (taken the previous Wednesday). This was the first of a series taken for exhibition in London—one of the highlights being the reception given by His Excellency the Governor to the officers of the Japanese Navy.

In the afternoon of Saturday 12 May, Tait's operators took crowds in the block from Swanston to Elizabeth Streets. Two hours later, they set up their cameras in Smith Street, Collingwood, then journeyed to Chapel Street, covering the strip between Commercial Road and High Street.

Moving Melbourne created such a favourable impression that it was screened at Parliament House on 15 May. At the end of its run at the Town Hall on 26 May all those in the audience were presented with a portion of this biograph film.

Meanwhile, West's Pictures made their Melbourne debut on 12 May at the Athenaeum Hall. T. J. West and Henry Hayward were listed as managers, and Edwin Geach as director. They opened with a pictorial record of the *Welcome to Our Gallant Allies—the Japanese*, which showed the arrival of the Japanese warships in Hobson's Bay, under the command of Rear Admiral Shimamura. These were specially photographed by T. J. West. The subsequent programme featured *Marvellous Maoriland* (again photographed by West—this time by special arrangement with the New Zealand Government). A short on the same bill showed Australian swimmer, Annette Kellerman, performing in London.

In June, Melbourne football fans visiting West's Pictures eagerly viewed scenes of a match between Carlton and Fitzroy. "See these champion teams fighting their battle over again," urged the advertisement. "The play, the players, and the roaring crowd come to life, every time the film is projected."

Early the next month West's screened scenes of the San Francisco earthquake taken by their own operator Edward Hardy, who was in the city at the time. The season closed on 7 July and the Athenaeum was reoccupied by Best and Baker's Moving Pictures at the beginning of September. Five days later their screen captured all the excitement and spectacle attached to Melbourne's Agricultural Show. This 2,000 feet of film was claimed as a film footage record for Australia and showed many of the 50,000 jostling people entering the grounds. Special attention was paid to the Trotting and the Grand Parade. The advertisement for the feature naively proclaimed that "a few amusing incidents were included." It had a successful run of one month.

Johnson and Gibson had built up a handsome business distributing overseas films in Australia—and probably would never have entered the production field but for the fact that the earnings of one of their releases suddenly went into a decline when pitted against a stage production. As already stated, Gibson was a businessman, and when his bank balance was affected he did something about it.

Living London (the version no doubt screened by J. & N. Tait in Melbourne and Sydney), a Johnson and Gibson release, was a box office success until it was booked into towns simultaneously with the Australian "flesh and blood" show—*The Kelly Gang*. As J. & N. Tait held the rights to the play, the rest became a happy and very profitable business arrangement, and Johnson and Gibson became pioneers in Australian film production.

The Story of the Kelly Gang—a triumph for Australian film production—was photographed for J. & N. Tait by Johnson and Gibson. Billed as "The Sensation of the Year—the greatest, most thrilling, and sensational moving picture ever taken," it was to justify its claim at the box office and in motion picture history. It took six months to make—and was "upwards of three quarters of a mile long."

Now comes the comparison. The American film *The Great American Train Robbery*, made in 1903, is usually quoted as the world's first feature film—but this was only 800 feet long and ran for 20 minutes. Comparing the Kelly film on these grounds it is easy to justify the claim that the Australian film was the world's first full-length feature. The film was screened at the Athenaeum Hall, Melbourne, in the afternoon, and the Melbourne Town Hall at night. The demand for admittance was so great that hundreds had to be turned away.

The *Argus* critic wrote:

Necessarily the events have had to be created and for dramatic reasons many liberties were rightly taken which the public will pardon, as they serve to make the exploits all the more convincing.

The police are always seen in uniform, which they never were, being in fact dressed to resemble ordinary bushmen as much as possible.

Ned Kelly when taken was got up in dandy bushman style—yellow cord pants with slate cross barred pattern cloth coat, very thin soled and high heeled kangaroo skin riding boots with spurs; white Crimean shirt with large black spots; vest of the same material as the pants; and a long white mackintosh closely buttoned.

The best scene in the film is the attempt to wreck the special train beyond Glenrowan, by tearing up the metals and sleepers.

Authentic details of *The Story of the Kelly Gang*, like those of *Soldiers of the Cross*, are extremely hard to obtain. But the legends that have arisen grow taller with every telling. Orrie Perry has been given full credit for shooting the film in Studley Park,

Melbourne, but this is an impossible feat as Orrie was with the Salvation Army Biorama Company in New Zealand at the time. However he did film additional scenes in 1910 for a reissue of *The Story of the Kelly Gang*.

As late as March 1967, a Melbourne suburban paper under the heading of "Pioneers" mentioned the fact that *Soldiers of the Cross* was in dispute as the world's first full-length silent film, even though it was made in Melbourne in 1904. (Actually it was screened, as already stated, in 1900.) The article goes on to state that Mitcham was closely associated with another very early film, *Ned Kelly*, which was produced in 1907. (The writer was improving. He was only a year out in his facts this time.) The closing portion of the entry states, "An old cottage in Whitehorse Road, in the vicinity of the present police station, was set up as the 'Glenrowan Pub,' scene of the famous last stand." At that time Mitcham was a struggling community of holdings along the road to the Dandenongs.

It would be colourful and charitable to hope that the legend concerning the Mitcham cottage at least was correct—even though numerous inquiries have failed to substantiate the claim. The paper in question no doubt published the article in good faith, but fact and fiction associated with Australian films are extremely hard to separate.

Another example is the tearing up of the railway lines in the Kelly film, which according to many sources took place at Eltham. Lady Tait, however, while doing research for her own book on the theatrical achievements of J. & N. Tait, established that the incident was filmed at Rosanna.

Now to the Studley Park myth. Most of the shooting was done on Charles Tait's property Chartersville, Heidelberg. Various outdoor location shots set around the stables have been attributed in turn to the area behind the present Y.M.C.A. Building in South Melbourne and to the building used for the darkroom by Johnson and Gibson. Legends certainly can be colourful.

A Canadian in the Bland Holt company, whose name has not been recorded, appeared as Ned Kelly for a considerable portion of the film, and then disappeared, leaving an extra to complete the picture. Consequently, the concluding action had to be taken in long shots, as closer views would have revealed the imposter. Apparently Ned often put his beard aside to swell the ranks in many of the crowd scenes.

Charles, John, Frank, and Ivan Tait all played extras in the production, and Elizabeth Veitch, wife of Charles Tait, portrayed Kate Kelly. Another notable member of the cast was Mrs Gibson, an excellent horsewoman who added realism to many of the sequences in the film.

The Story of the Kelly Gang was made for £400. Full production costs were recovered from the first week's screening, with the final gross takings being estimated at £25,000. The Victorian Railways cooperated to the fullest extent and actually placed a train and workmen at the film company's disposal to reenact the pulling up of the line near Glenrowan and the arrival of the troops.

One of the big scenes was a brawl in the Glenrowan Hotel. Tough Melbournian "down and outs" played extras—and were allowed to drink the real Australian brew. Production costs shot up like the thermometer on a sweltering summer's day as the liquor took control and tempers rose. W. A. Gibson tried to keep order, but a real brawl followed with pieces of the set flying in all directions. Finally, the extras began shooting up the place with blanks and real police arrived at the Glenrowan Hotel. It took a lot of fast talking to persuade the law that it was only "convincing acting." At least, that's how the story goes.

The *Story of the Kelly Gang* continued its triumphant showing at the Athenaeum Hall, Melbourne, and on 9 February had its Sydney premiere at the Palace Theatre, where it was advertised as the biggest and most costly cinematograph work ever undertaken. The *Sydney Morning Herald* critic enthused over the galloping horses and beautiful bush scenes. "The voices behind the screen supplied the realistic dialogue needed to keep the audience in touch with the action of the story."

Melbourne celebrated the end of the year with a most realistic film coverage of the biggest and most sensational fire in Elizabeth Street. Warehouses and shops were reduced to smouldering ashes and even the Post Office was threatened. The estimated damage was £70,000. After that, the arrival of West's Pictures at Wirth's Olympia was rather an anticlimax.

In November the Oxford Theatre in Sydney proudly boasted of the Australian premiere of Charles McMahon's stirring picture drama *Robbery Under Arms,* photographed by C. B. Coates. Nearly 5,000 feet long, it cost £1,000 to produce.

Unfortunately Melbourne stole some of the glory by screening the film a week earlier at the Athenaeum, but the following advertisement by the Oxford shows that the Melbourne premiere did not affect the box office in Sydney. "The ticket office was almost wrecked by patrons in a remarkable crush. In order to prevent a re-occurrence doors will be opened at 6.30 p.m."

During the season a limerick competition was conducted, the prize being a first grade Royal Speedwell bicycle, for the best line completing the following:

> To rob under arms is an art
> In which Starlight took a chief part,
> But between you and me,
> There's a chance, don't you see . . .

Oliver Gordon won the coveted bicycle with, "Of an 'awful suspense' if you start."

On 30 November, Sydney's Novelty Hall in King Street featured the 20-minute picture sensation the *Burns-Squires Fight.* Tommy Burns, the heavyweight panther, stopped the Australian, Squires, in the first round. This was fought in California and filmed by British Biograph.

West's closed the year in Sydney on a rather unspectacular note with *Australian Agricultural and Farming Pursuits.*

West's poses a question connected with the Melbourne scene in 1907. The entry reads "Living Melbourne—T. J. West—1907." This is taken direct from film records. One authority who was responsible for giving early film information proved to be years out in nearly all the details supplied, and "Living Melbourne" proved to be no exception. Considerable research and double-checking has failed to discover any reference to a special T. J. West feature on Melbourne until 11 February 1909, when he screened *Marvellous Melbourne* in Sydney.

In Melbourne by the middle of the year, the excitement created by *The Story of the Kelly Gang* had died down a little, and Cook's Living Pictures were trying to rekindle interest with views of the Barron Falls, the Hawkesbury River, and scenes of Sydney Harbour. The films were taken by Sidney Cook. In August there were visits from Best and Baker, Coward's, Sudholz, and West. A return season of the Kelly film was billed for the Athenaeum Hall on 5 October.

The Athenaeum by now was firmly established as a picture house and on 19 October advertised yet another Australian film, *The Eureka Stockade.*

An old stage adage seemed to have been—"when in doubt, feature *East Lynne.*" Films in this country were to adopt the theme in spirit—but to alter the subject matter—to produce *Ned Kelly* or *The Eureka Stockade.*

The 1907 version of *The Eureka Stockade,* however, has not been included in previous film records. Made by the Australasian Cinematograph Company, it ran for a fortnight. The advertisement promised excitement and action, Eureka Stockade reproduced in every detail, by biograph:

A picture story of the most memorable event in Australian history; throbbing with the pulse and memories of the Roaring Fifties. Gold-seekers leaving London ... On the road to the diggings ... the gold rush ... lost in the bush ... the gold robbery ... diggers chained to logs ... building the Eureka Stockade ... Murder at Bently's Hotel ... and storming Eureka Stockade ... The unveiling of Lalor's Monument with a grand Military March Past. Undoubtedly, the most realistic combination of pictures ever produced in the annals of animated art.

ALLAN T. SUTHERLAND

The Yorkshire Pioneers

It has become so commonplace to look at film production as an activity organised on a national, if not indeed an international scale, that the idea of regional production companies may seem almost a contradiction in terms. But in the early years of this century a great deal of British film production was carried out by such companies, which ranged from minute one-man enterprises serving a handful of local exhibitors to firms such as the Sheffield Photo Company, whose films were exported all over the world. This examination of early production in Yorkshire is thus by no means of purely local interest, but reflects upon the pattern of filmmaking in Britain up to the early years of the 1914–18 war.

This is not to say that Yorkshire can be treated as a simple microcosm of the country as a whole. Undoubtedly the area has an unusually rich cinematic history, as a current research fellowship sponsored by the Yorkshire Arts Association continues to demonstrate. And this history spans a much longer period even than that of the Brighton group of filmmakers (James Williamson, G. A. Smith, etc.). The combination of two important production companies (Bamforth's of Holmfirth and the Sheffield Photo Company) with local exhibitors as independent and forceful as Henry Hibbert and Sydney Carter enabled the area to retain its distinct regional identity until well after other independent producers had either been absorbed by one of the London-based companies or abandoned production altogether (by far the more frequent end).

But to begin at the beginning we must look further back, over a decade before either of the companies mentioned above was founded, to the work of a largely neglected pioner, L. A. A. Le Prince. At a date when many authorities do not admit the motion picture to have been invented at all, Le Prince took a series of films in and around Leeds, using a camera of his own design which incorporated a film strip with sprocket holes (at first with a paper and later a celluloid base) and intermittent motion. He projected these films on a screen using a projector with electric arc illumination and a Maltese Cross intermittent movement.

Le Prince, a Frenchman who spent much of his life in England, was born in August 1842. Daguerre, who was a close friend of Le Prince's father, gave him lessons in photography. After postgraduate study of chemistry and physics at the University of Leipzig, he started working as a photographer and also took up painting and ceramics. In 1866 he moved to Leeds, where he joined the firm of Whitley Partners, brassfounders, as a designer. He married in 1869; with his wife he opened a school of applied art in Park Square, Leeds. Here he carried out colour photography on metal and pottery, fixing the colours in a special kiln. He established a reputation as a photographer, executing commissions for Queen Victoria and W. E. Gladstone among others.

It seems likely that Le Prince became attracted to the idea of attempting to produce motion pictures after seeing Eadweard Muybridge's series of photographs taken with a battery of up to twenty-four cameras, which were published in 1875. A man of Le Prince's background would have been well acquainted with the many forms of optical entertainment (panoramas, dioramas, etc.) that had been popular since the eighteenth century. He was probably equally familiar with the optical toys, such as the Zoetrope and the Praxinoscope, which, using the principle of persistence of vision, brought at least one form of moving picture into people's homes. And he certainly both knew and used the optical ("magic") lantern which, used with various forms of mechanical slide, familiarised the Victorian public with projected two-dimensional movement. (As Kevin Brownlow has pointed out in *The Parade's Gone By*, the uproar created by the Lumière film of a train entering a station was due not to the fact that it was moving, but that it was moving *towards the audience*: "Lumière selected this head-on view in order to get the whole train into the picture; a side angle would have been inadequate. By doing this, he unconsciously added the one element missing from other attempts at simulating movement: dynamism.") For Le Prince, as for other pioneers of cinema, the nature of the problem was clear: how to combine the by now familiar concept of projected movement with the rapidly developing science of photography?

In 1881 Le Prince moved to New York, where he lived until May 1887, when he returned to Leeds. During this period he was permitted to use the facilities of the workshop at the American Institute for the Deaf, where his wife was teaching art. He was at this time faced with difficulties in exposing his pictures in fast enough succession, experimenting with multiple lenses, used in series. In November 1886 he applied for an American patent for a camera having from one to sixteen lenses.[1] (Much confusion has been caused by the fact that when the

---

[1]"Method of, and Apparatus for, Producing Animated Pictures," American patent no. 376,247.

Patent Office issued the patent they cut out the reference to the one- and two-lens versions, claiming an earlier patent was an infringement; it should be made quite clear that there is no evidence that Le Prince was, as has been suggested with monotonous frequency, treating a sixteen-lens camera as his main line of investigation. Such a camera was given prominence in his patents for the excellent reason that it was the most complex of a number of possible versions he had not yet totally ruled out: if that one worked, then so would all the others.) The only evidence I have been able to trace as to whether Le Prince had constructed a camera or projector ("receiver" or "deliverer," to use his own terms) prior to his patent application is a statement by his daughter Marie, whose source I have not been able to locate, but which I reproduce in the fullest version known to me:

> I remember my father when I was a very small child always talking and thinking about this idea. He had little money and his family was large, so it was difficult for him to do anything about it then, but when he went to New York in 1881 he found some facilities for his work. That would be in the early 80s; my mother taught at a deaf and dumb school and he had a little room there fitted up for his experiments. One day, when I was about fourteen, I wanted to call him to tea and I pushed open the door of the little room, and there, on the whitewashed wall, I saw some forms which moved. I did not know what they were and my father shut the door quickly, but I suppose I was the first child ever to see a moving film picture.

Marie was born in 1871, so if this account is correct Le Prince succeeded in projecting a motion picture in 1885—a decade before the Lumières' famous demonstration at the Grand Café.

Soon after his return to England, Le Prince did make a sixteen-lens camera/projector—which is now on display in the Science Museum, London—for use as "proof of working" when he was applying for European patents. This camera took two bands of film, mounted side by side; the eight shutters facing one film were released in quick succession, after which the remaining eight were discharged while the first film was being moved on ready for another set of pictures.

In January 1888 Le Prince applied for a British patent, granted the following November, which was almost identical in specifications to the American patent of 1886, but did not exclude the one-lens version. The significant feature of this camera was the use of a continuous length of pliable film, drawn intermittently between two revolving drums, which was clamped firm during exposure. It is evident that Le Prince had not as yet found a material he regarded as totally satisfactory as a supporting base for the film emulsion.

In 1888 Le Prince built two single-lens cameras and a projector. With these he took a number of series of pictures, some of which are still extant, at least in part. In October 1888 he took a series of pictures, at about 12 per second, using the second one-lens camera. At around the same time, he took another series, at around 20 per second, of traffic on Leeds Bridge. According to Frederic Mason, a woodworker who assisted in building these pieces of equipment, Le Prince found the construction of the projector much more difficult than the camera: it evolved through several stages. Eventually he arrived at a model having a single lens and electric arc illumination in place of the limelight he had used earlier. When, in the autumn of 1889, he obtained some rolls of celluloid film, one of his last difficulties—that of finding a suitable supporting base for his photographic emulsion—was solved.

Le Prince visited his brother in Dijon in September 1890. He caught the train back to Paris on September 16th, but did not arrive at his destination. Neither he nor his baggage was ever seen again. After this mysterious disappearance, Le Prince was eventually presumed dead, and most of the contents of his workshop were put up for sale. Thus, ironically, though Le Prince had developed a camera and projector containing all the features that were to become standard in later years (and which were indeed considerably more sophisticated than many of the early machines that were marketed commercially) he had, so far as one can tell, no influence at all on later researchers; all his discoveries had to be made afresh.

Le Prince's lack of influence was of little matter, since the invention of the cinematograph was by this point a matter of historical inevitability. When the Lumières gave their show at the Grand Café in 1895, it became public property. Lantern operators and fairground showmen quickly recognised the potential for entertainment, and an immediate demand for cinematograph machines, or any working substitute, was created. Among the members of the Lumières' audience to foresee the possibility of commercial exploitation was William Riley, of the Bradford firm of Riley Brothers, lantern slide and equipment manufacturers. With solid Yorkshire pragmatism, Riley returned to Bradford and gave a description of the Lumières' machine to Cecil Wray, a local manufacturing optician, commissioning him to manufacture one. Or so the story goes; I personally have reservations about this version of affairs, in view of the fact that Wray was evidently already experimenting with cinematography, having filed a patent specification the previous January for a device to project the pictures of the kinetoscope (which Edison had neglected to patent in Europe) on to a screen. In August 1896 he submitted a patent application for a more complex device designed to be fitted to any optical lantern.[2] This was marketed by Riley's as the "Kineoptoscope."

Whether or not it was manufactured by Wray, Riley's did possess a camera

[2]"Improvements in or Relating to the Kinetoscope," patent no. 182, 1895; and "Improvements in Apparatus for Exhibiting Kineoptoscope or Zoetrope Pictures," patent no. 19, 181, 1896.

by about 1899, and in cooperation with Bamforth and Co. of Holmfirth, a prominent firm of lantern slide and picture postcard manufacturers, started producing "RAB" films. Bamforth's, founded in 1870 by James Bamforth, pioneered the use of life models in lantern slides, a practice later adopted by other manufacturers, including Riley's. By the 1890s Bamforth's was advertising itself, very probably correctly, as "The Largest Producer of Life Model Slides in the World."

The partnership between the two firms was an obvious one. Riley's possessed a camera, thrusting business acumen and a wide distribution network: in October 1895 they had, beside their thriving British and European business, eight branches in the U.S.A. Bamforth's had, for their lantern slide work, assembled a full studio set-up, including costume, props, and scenery departments.

> The premises in which the business is conducted are curious in the extreme, consisting as they do of a series of successive studios and workshops perched at various points on a precipitous slope between the house, which overlooks the valley and the village of Holmfirth, and the first studio, which is well down towards the valley. This slope, almost impossible of cultivation as a field, has been banked, terraced and dotted with flights of steps, fountains, shady walks, leafy dells and pleasant summer-houses in a variety that might be thought impossible in such a space.... The life-model studio is a room of 31 ft. by 18 ft. with a scene-dock and a property room at each end; and with roof-light and side-light at both sides . . .

Such extensive facilities were then unknown to filmmakers; most of them were working on open-air stages such as that erected by Cecil Hepworth in 1898–99: "It consisted of a wooden floor, about 10 ft. by 6 ft., laid down in the tiny back garden with two or three uprights to prop the flats against. The scenery was painted in the kitchen." And they certainly did not enjoy the degree of cooperation that James Bamforth obtained by virtue of his firm's position in a town the size of Holmfirth. "Policemen can always be borrowed, in their own uniforms 'by arrangement,' but real soldiers and firemen are not so easily obtainable in Holmfirth. . . . Fortunately the railway officials are always willing (subject to the calls of duty) to place a train in any position . . ." (*The Photogram,* February 1899).

Whether these facilities were greatly used in the early films seems doubtful. Riley and Bamforth's first film was *A Snowball Encounter,* a short (probably around 50 feet) comedy about boys throwing snowballs. This seems typical of what followed; the Hepworth 1903 catalogue lists fifteen RAB films of which eleven are comedies, the rest being actualities or scenic films, none longer than about 75 feet. The "schoolboy escapades" type of comedy was evidently a favourite, perhaps because of the saving on wages: the 1903 catalogue lists four such: *Boys Sliding, Pillow Fight, The Schoolmaster's Portrait,* and *Leap Frog,* in which "the numerous collapses cause great amusement." The lack of dramatic subjects indicates that Bamforth's regarded their filmmaking as distinct from, and secondary to, their lantern slide and postcard work. This impression is supported by the fact that no attempt was made to produce filmed equivalents of their slide sets though they were often turned into postcards. Bamforth's did in fact abandon film production in about 1903, and concentrated on lantern slides and postcards for the next ten years. The exact reasons are not clear, but I suspect that Bamforth's simply decided that to keep pace with the (by then) increasing length and complexity of other companies' films would conflict with the lantern slide work which was still their main business.

This attitude contrasts strongly with that of Frank Mottershaw of the Sheffield Photo Co. and his sons, for whom film production was from an early date a much more serious commitment. SPC was started in 1882 as a photographic business. Mottershaw began to give "cinematograph entertainments" in about 1900, and soon ventured into production.

Cinematograph pictures were causing quite a sensation about this time, so the two eldest sons devoted much of their time in this direction. They built a Cine Camera from old camera parts and the first moving picture was quite a success. From this stage a new Cine Camera and Projector were purchased and in a very short time the firm had launched an all out effort to take moving pictures of football matches and topical events, which were developed and shown on the screen the same evening.[3]

Topicals remained a major element of SPC's business. But since these were usually made for "same evening" showing, by prior arrangement with individual cinemas, and hence not advertised, records of them are scarce. One of the most significant early topicals was taken when Edward VII visited Sheffield in 1904; Mottershaw used a number of operators, positioned at vantage points, and the films were shown at two Sheffield halls that night. (This incident indicates the value of Mottershaw's experience in still photography: in 1895 he had used his entire staff of photographers to take pictures of Queen Victoria visiting Sheffield.) Their work in this field was by no means confined to the immediate locality. The *Bioscope* of September 18th 1908 reported that SPC had filmed the St. Leger at Doncaster (as no doubt they did every year) and dispatched copies to reach Nottingham and Doncaster by 8:30 and catch the 7:20 train to London.

In 1902 F. S. Mottershaw, Frank Mottershaw's eldest son, spent a year in London working with R. W. Paul to gain experience. On his return to Sheffield new premises were opened, with an open-air stage and rooms equipped for

---

[3]Personal communication to Robert Benfield by Frank Mottershaw's daughter, Edith Marion Spring.

printing and developing cinematograph film. Apart from the topicals, SPC then started to produce films in almost all the genres current at the time: comedies (*Mixed Babies, Tramps and Washerwomen*), dramas (*Lost in the Snow*), scenics (*A Ride on the Kinver Light Railway*), reversing films (*An Eccentric Burglary*), and even the more unusual genres such as the faked topical (*Russo-Japanese War—Attack on a Japanese Convoy*). In particular, SPC won a reputation for its chase films, a genre it pioneered with *A Daring Daylight Robbery* (early 1903), described in 1929 by F. S. Mottershaw:

> I used the back of a hotel in a valley in Derbyshire as a mansion, and showed a burglar trying to break in.... The burglar was interrupted by a policeman, there was an exciting struggle on the roof, and the policeman was flung to the ground—we stopped the camera and substituted a dummy. Then followed a chase from the mansion by a second policeman—over walls, through a little river, through fields and hedges. Finally there was the capture, an unexpected bit of realism! A real country policeman, then coming off his beat, saw the finish of the chase down a hillside and hurried to the aid of his supposed colleague.... Down he came, full of fight and purpose, and joined in the affair in deadly earnest![4]

Mottershaw stated that the film was shot in three days at a cost of £25, and that between 500 and 600 copies were sold, including an American order for 100 copies.

This film, a copy of which has recently been located in the U.S.A., was the first of several such, with which SPC established an international reputation. They followed it later in the year with *Robbery of the Mail Coach*, a vigorous custume drama. But their most notable work was *The Life of Charles Peace* (1905), which told the story of the notorious local murderer. This film, 870 feet long, was probably the longest work the British cinema had yet produced—slightly over twice the length of *Rescued by Rover*, made at approximately the same time—though it seems from the catalogue synopsis to have lacked the latter's sophistication of narrative technique. From this point SPC's work gradually tailed off, and they ceased to make films for general sale in about 1911. Although their later films tended to be increasingly less enterprising (they included, for example, a remake of *Daring Daylight Robbery: A Daylight Burglary*) they did include a single sound-on-disc film, *They Can't Diddle Me*.

---

[4]*London Evening News*, October 1, 1929. Full synopses of this film, *Robbery of the Mail Coach*, and *The Life of Charles Peace* are to be found in Rachel Low and Roger Manvell, *The History of the British Film*, vol. 1 (London: Allen and Unwin, 1948); pp. 104–7.

PART II

Exhibition and Distribution

Introduction

The flickers' entrance into various exhibition situations (vaudeville was one) differently determined the character of the films. Vaudeville films were another act, sometimes replacing the truncated 10–20–30 little live melodramas usually presented (10–20–30 referring to seat prices at such events). Another extension grew from magic lantern entertainments, a circumstance involving obvious esthetic continuities[1] as well as providing established distribution and exhibition patterns.[2]

Much of the thinking about early film's exhibition, distribution, and financing has been inflected by historical conventions long overdue for reconsideration. The notion that movies served as chasers in vaudeville houses, bustling out a dissatisfied audience for the sake of new ticket holders, figures, for example, in many accountings. In this section, Robert C. Allen's "Contra the Chaser Theory" disputes that proposition, which is not to say that it is altogether disproved. No chapter of new film history is inscribed in stone.

One curiosity of the years immediately preceding the nickelodeon era was Hale's Tours, another step toward "real" experience, here thoroughly researched by Raymond Fielding in "Hale's Tours: Ultrarealism in the Pre-1910 Motion Pictures." William Selig made films for Hale's Tours, and Hale's exhibitions served to link Adolph Zukor's penny arcades to his movie empire. A different pattern of traveling film exhibition is described by Edward Lowry in "Edwin J.

---

[1]This issue is discussed in light of Burnes St. Patrick Hollyman's essay, "Alexander Black's Picture Plays, 1893–1894," in part 3.

[2]Joseph North, in *The Early Development of the Motion Picture, 1887–1909* (New York: Arno, 1973), traces other transitions from magic lantern shows to cinema, as well as discussing vaudeville, theatrical fire hazards, and early steps toward rental systems.

Hadley: Traveling Film Exhibitor." The author argues that storefront movie theaters existed for the most part in major cities. A showman such as Edwin J. Hadley brought the movies to New York towns like Ticonderoga and Glen Falls, and thence to the Midwest. Drawing from the work of Edison, Lubin, Biograph, and Méliès, Hadley may have provided his audiences a greater variety than they might have found in an urban nickelodeon, certainly a less specialized selection of film titles. A New York audience, such as the one at Tony Pastor's Fourteenth Street Theater that Vitagraph served for a while, might have had particular interest in the up-to-date news events, real or faked, that Vitagraph provided; fare for the rural audience was less topical.

A different, though clearly fertile, field of recent inquiry has been the systematic study of film exploitation in contexts of technology and industrial practice; recent theoretical work has amplified and underscored the roles of filmmaking practice and film consumption, all of a piece with the screen image itself.[3] Robert C. Allen, in "Vitascope/Cinématographe: Initial Patterns of American Film Industrial Practice," contrasts the Vitascope with the Lumière Cinématographe in terms of machine design and production patterns, arguing that the Cinématographe incorporated particular advantages that regularized film production and enhanced distribution. Further, Edison's marketing agents thought more limitedly about exhibition possibilities. Alan Williams, in "The Lumière Organization and 'Documentary Realism,'" centers attention on the Lumières' first French introduction of the Cinématographe. He views their success as the consequence of canny accommodations to a scientifically minded, bourgeois audience. Where Allen emphasizes Edison's shunning of vaudeville as a marketplace, Williams cites Edison's vaudeville-derived subject matter as an explanation of its relative failure in France and England.

A final Robert C. Allen essay, "Motion Picture Exhibition in Manhattan, 1906–1912: Beyond the Nickelodeon," contributes even further arguments for reexamining old historical conventions, in this case the description of the nickelodeon as an incommodious proletarian parlor exclusively servicing male, working-class audiences. Examining a Manhattan business directory, demographic descriptions of New York neighborhoods, and period newspapers, Allen demonstrates that questions about film may sometimes be usefully answered through other sources than filmmakers, films, and company records. Jeanne Thomas Allen takes another tack in "Copyright and Early Theater, Vaudeville, and Film Competition." She compares turn-of-the century theater, vaudeville, and film entertainments, all disposed to infiltrate middle-class family audiences,

---

[3]In spirit or reaction, much such work derives from Jean-Luc Comólli and Jean Narboni, "Cinema/Ideology/Criticism," originally printed in *Cahiers du cinéma*, no. 216 (October 1969), translated to English in *Screen* 12 (Spring 1971), and reprinted in Bill Nichols, *Movies and Methods* (Berkeley: University of California Press, 1976); pp. 22–30.

in the way each medium was uniquely affected by special circumstances of copyright protection and by the legal loopholes used to circumvent them.

Burnes St. Patrick Hollyman's article, "The First Picture Shows: Austin, Texas, 1894–1913," focuses on a nonmetropolitan locale, Austin, Texas, and documents the more sluggish introduction of cinema into rural life. His essay encourages us to reflect on the extent to which cultural factors may have affected the movies' receptions under different exhibition circumstances. Elsewhere, one can study the introduction of film theaters in such locations as the English provinces (preceding nickelodeons and including a visit from Hale's Tours)[4] and in distant South Africa (accompanied by conjurers and soon followed by local subject matter on screen as well as by issues of censorship).[5]

Garth S. Jowett's work evidences the current utility of sociology in early film study. In his book *Film the Democractic Art: A Social History of American Film*,[6] Jowett traces this society's efforts to accommodate the new entertainment. Here, in "The First Motion Picture Audiences," Jowett poses ancillary questions about the socioeconomic characteristics of early movie audiences. His study addresses matters of increasing leisure time, patterns of social entertainment, and dispositions toward subject matter (often melodrama) on the part of patrons whose needs were no longer served by live entertainments.[7]

David Levy's essay, "Edison Sales Policy and the Continuous Action Film, 1904–1906," reexamines promotion campaigns while organizing our attention for the kind of film analyses offered in part 3. Edison's approaches to film sales, derived from his use of the Kinetoscope, are contrasted with American Mutoscope and Biograph's new policy of leasing services rather than selling products, which may be seen as a prelude to forthcoming film exchanges; for a few short years, Biograph was the wave of the future.

By situating Edwin S. Porter firmly in Edison's organizational hierarchy, Levy questions older propositions that Porter was a self-consciously innovative artist, a notion that may remain somewhat implicitly at odds with other essays on Porter discussed in part 3. Levy's history of copyright litigation expands on the issue, raised by Jeanne Adams, of whether the value of a film shall be legally determined by its status as an entity or as a sum of the segments with which it is composed. Finally, Levy's investigation of Edison sales records helps us to pinpoint popular interest in longer fictional subjects as early as 1903, a finding

---

[4]G. J. Mellor, *Picture Pioneers* (Newcastle-upon-Tyne: Frank Graham, 1971).

[5]Thelma Gutsche, *The History and Social Significance of Motion Pictures in South Africa, 1895–1940* (Cape Town: Timmins, 1972).

[6]Garth Jowett, *Film the Democratic Art: A Social History of American Film* (Boston: Little, Brown, 1976).

[7]For broader considerations of melodrama's part in American life at the turn of the century, see Daniel C. Gerould, ed., *Melodrama*, New York Literary Forum, vol. 7 (New York: New York Literary Forum, 1980), part 2.

that challenges the customary historical connnections between the rise of the nickelodeons and enthusiasm for movie stories. Jowett's sources estimate about a thousand little movie parlors around 1906 and 10,000 by 1910.[8] Until now, a common assumption has been that the nickelodeon boom carried some causal relation to shifts toward movie story, away from chases, trick films, and actualities.

---

[8]Jowett, *Film the Democratic Art*, pp. 30–31.

ROBERT C. ALLEN

Contra the Chaser Theory

Many aspects of the history of American cinema as an economic institution have not received the scholarly attention they deserve. One of them, certainly, is exhibition before the rise of the nickelodeon in 1906—a time when motion picture exhibition was conducted primarily as part of vaudeville programs.

During this period supposedly there occurred one of the most puzzling phenomena in the history of motion picture exhibition: between roughly 1897 and 1901, most historians maintain, vaudeville audiences so completely lost interest in the motion pictures being shown them that they left the theater rather than sit through an exhibition. Motion pictures acquired the reputation of "chasers," acts which were so poorly received that vaudeville managers used them to clear the theater to make room for a new group of patrons.

This paper examines motion picture exhibition between 1897 and 1901 in light of the "chaser theory." Obviously, from the title of this paper one can see that I disagree with the designation of this era as the chaser period. It is my contention that at the very least the chaser period is a misnomer, at the most a complete misrepresentation of the exhibition situation at that time.

On April 23, 1896, Thomas Armat and Francis Jenkins's Vitascope was featured on the Vaudeville program at Koster and Bial's Music Hall in New York City. While this was not the first commercial use of projected motion pictures nor even the first presentation of films in vaudeville, it was (so far as I can determine) the first successful commercial use of projected motion pictures in vaudeville.

In the wake of the Koster and Bial exhibition, vaudeville managers all over the country attempted to acquire this latest visual novelty for their theaters, and, for the most part, vaudeville audiences greeted the Vitascope, Lumière Cinématographe, American Biograph, and other motion picture devices with tremendous enthusiasm during the first year of widespread commercial use of motion pictures in vaudeville (April 1896–April 1897).

Many film historians hold that after this initial wave of popularity, the motion picture fell into universal disfavor as a vaudeville act—a situation which was not remedied until 1901 at the earliest. In a section of his 1949 dissertation, Joseph North presents a summary of views taken by film historians on the fate of the motion picture in vaudeville after 1896. He cites Gilbert Seldes's observation that "nothing whatever of interest" occurred in the American cinema prior to 1903 and adds:

> And evidence is not wanting that portions of the public who attended the first programs felt pretty much about the motion pictures as Seldes indicates they might. While many people had viewed the showings in 1896 with enthusiasm, it does seem that a good number of them lost interest in the medium shortly thereafter.... Their [the films'] success... was only temporary, for in a little more than a year they were relegated to the position of "chaser." In the latter state the appearance of the pictures on the screen signaled the audience that the show was over, and that it was time to clear the house for the next performance. This condition prevailed in all vaudeville houses which exhibited the motion pictures. And in some houses the films were used only when the crowds awaiting an entrance were overwhelming.[1]

There are two notions of the duration of the chaser era. Seldes maintains that this unpopularity of films persisted until the advent of the narrative film around 1903—until films like *The Great Train Robbery,* as Mast subsequently put it, "pulled the movies from the abyss" of chaser ignominy.[2] According to Grau and Ramsaye, the chaser period lasted only from 1898 to 1901.[3]

By and large, the chaser theory as presented by North still represents the thinking of most film historians who have written on the matter. Mast's view has already been cited. Jowett repeats the statement of the theory intact, drawing directly upon North:

> By 1898 the motion picture had become established as a staple item in vaudeville shows, although there as a low period when films were used as "chasers" to force patrons to leave the theaters to make room for the

---

[1] Joseph H. North, *The Early Development of the Motion Picture: 1887–1909* (New York: Arno, 1973), pp. 184–85.

[2] Ibid., p. 186; Lewis Jacobs, *The Rise of the American Film* (New York: Teacher's College Press, 1939), p. 5; Gilbert Seldes, *An Hour With the Talkies and the Movies* (Philadelphia: Lippincott, 1929), p. 20; Gerald Mast, *A Short History of the Movies* (New York: Pegasus Books, 1971), p. 44.

[3] Robert Grau, *Theatre of Science* (New York: Broadway, 1914), pp. 11–12; Terry Ramsaye, *A Million and One Nights* (New York: Simon and Schuster, 1926), p. 407.

next audience. The relegation of the medium to this lowly status was primarily due to the rather dull nature of the films then being turned out. These consisted mainly of scenic shots or fake reproductions of current and historical events, and audiences soon grew tired of having to watch the same type over and over again.[4]

Jowett concludes, "the exploitation of the movies by the vaudeville houses was the lowest point in motion picture history, and almost succeeded in killing off the young medium before it had completely matured and attained its full commercial potential."[5] Sklar takes a step back from the generally held view, but cites no evidence in support of his own:

> When the seats were filled and patrons were lined up outside waiting to get in, managers sometimes threw movies on the screen before their regular place on the bill, falsely signaling that the program was over. Thus movies earned a reputation as vaudeville "chasers," though in later years this has sometimes been erroneously understood to mean that movies were unpopular. The opposite was, in fact, true.[6]

The problem with the chaser theory begins with the term itself. Most film historians assume the function of the "chaser" in vaudeville to have been to clear the house by virtue of the act's unpopularity. There is evidence, however, that the term had a different meaning.

In 1912, B. F. Keith claimed to have begun the use of chasers during his curio-hall days. The opening act, he said, was stage manager Sam Hodgdon giving a lecture on an arctic expedition. After the first program had been run, Keith told Hodgdon to do his act again, assuming that most of the patrons who had seen it once would not want to sit through it again. The repetition of the act cleared or "chased" out the house, enabling a partial turnover of patronage while still allowing Keith to advertise his entertainment as "continuous": "Come when you please; stay as long as you like."[7]

The purpose of the chaser, as originally used by Keith, was not so much to drive the audience from the theater as it was to announce that the program had run its course. The chaser in this sense was not a particularly bad act, but the repetition of an act. Later, Martin Beck, manager of the Orpheum Circuit, would use the theater orchestra to signal the end of the show, a device he thought better

---

[4]Garth Jowett, *Film: the Democratic Art* (Boston: Little, Brown, 1975), p. 29.

[5]Ibid.

[6]Robert Sklar, *Movie-Made America* (New York: Random House, 1975), p. 14.

[7]Albert McLean, "The Genesis of Vaudeville: Two Letters from B. F. Keith," *Theatre Survey* 1 (1960): 82–94; Joe Laurie, Jr., *Vaudeville: From the Honky Tonks to the Palace* (New York: Henry Holt, 1953), p. 338.

than simply bringing up the lights since "he wanted no one exiting from a suddenly silent, cold theatre."[8] It appears doubtful that a closing act or chaser was ever used primarily as a means of driving an audience from a theater. Why pay for an act to chase customers away, when for nothing the manager could bring up the lights or have the orchestra end the program?

But the chaser issue involves much more than simply a semantic argument over the status of the chaser act in vaudeville. At the heart of this theory is a two-fold assumption: 1) that motion pictures were universally unpopular during this period and 2) that the cause of this public disfavor was probably the repetition of the same types of films—according to Jowett, "scenic shots or fake reproductions of current and historical events."

These two interrelated notions are difficult to maintain in the face of evidence from contemporaneous theatrical trade papers and the weekly reports of local vaudeville managers on the Keith circuit. First, and perhaps most interesting, is what we don't find: a single instance reported in any issue of the *New York Clipper* or the *Dramatic Mirror* between 1897 and 1903 of a vaudeville manager intentionally using a film to clear his/her house, or evidence of this practice in weekly Keith managers' reports.

On the other hand, we do find numerous instances of the popularity of film in vaudeville and, furthermore, the popularity of several quite distinctive types or genres of film. During the first months of motion picture exhibition in vaudeville, the contents of films shown seem to have mattered little. Newspaper advertisements and programs announcing the first appearances of motion pictures in vaudeville often did not mention the specific films to be shown; it was enough merely to proclaim that the Vitascope or Cinématographe would present "moving photographs." It is clear, however, that as regular vaudeville patrons became accustomed to seeing motion pictures on every vaudeville program, the novelty of a machine that gave the illusion of motion quickly dissipated. From the papers of the Vitascope Company, the concern initially given exclusive franchise for the Vitascope projector, we know that a regular supply of new films became a matter of crucial importance at some theaters within several months of the start of regular exhibition of the motion pictures. But to assume that the chaser era emerges as a result of the diminishing success of primitive motion pictures to satisfy vaudeville audiences also assumes that American film companies either did not recognize this problem or did nothing to try and solve it. Neither was the case. The period during which motion picture acts in vaudeville based their appeal merely on the cinema's ability to render highly iconic representations was short-lived; producers quickly began to emphasize the subject matter of their films, producing several types of films, each designed to address a particular vaudeville audience need.

---

[8]John E. DiMeglio, *Vaudeville U.S.A.* (Bowling Green, Ohio: Bowling Green University Popular Press, 1973), p. 36.

A powerful, though frequently overlooked, appeal of some early motion pictures was narcissism: seeing oneself, neighbors, town, firetruck, even vaudeville manager on the screen. Both the Lumière Company and the Biograph Company exploited this function of the motion picture as early as the 1896–97 season by having their operators make films while traveling in the vaudeville circuits. These "local actualities" were shot during the first part of the motion picture act's engagement at a local vaudeville theater, then shown to the patrons at the end of the week. The fascination with seeing one's community on the screen was very strong for several years after 1896, and the Biograph's extensive exploitation of the local actuality made its films the star attractions of a number of vaudeville bills during the 1897–98 season.[9] Even as late as 1900 the local actuality could be counted on to arouse enthusiasm among vaudeville patrons. In October of that year the Biograph Company sent a cameraman to Providence to shoot film to be shown at the Keith vaudeville theater there. The cameraman mounted his camera on the rear platform of the Westminster Street trolley. The *Providence Journal* recorded the enthusiasm generated by the event:

> Crowds were out to see it done, not a few of whom were hoping to see their own figures on the canvas at Keith's. Shrewd advertisers, too, tried to take advantage of every opportunity for prominence, but police prevented any endeavor by individuals to monopolize the foreground. . . . Several prominent city officials had heard that something was doing, and they were waiting to cross the street and smile at the biograph as the car went by.[10]

It is also easy to underestimate the power of what I call Kinesthetic films: those designed to give the illusion either of being in the path of a moving object or of actually moving through space. In 1897 the Biograph company, for example, set up its camera on a flatcar pushed along by a locomotive through the Haverstraw Tunnel in New York. This seemingly simple film was shown in vaudeville theaters across the country in the fall of 1897, prompting notice in at least thirty-seven newspaper articles. An eloquent writer for the *New York Mail and Express* gives us some idea of the impact of the film:

> The way in which the unseen energy swallows up space and flings itself into the distances is as mysterious and impressive almost as an allegory. A sensation is produced akin to that which Poe, in his "Fall of the House of Usher," relates was communicated to him by his doomed

---

[9]Kemp R. Niver, *Biograph Bulletins: 1896–1908* (Los Angeles: Locare Research Group, 1971), p. 6.

[10]*Providence Journal*, October 20, 1900, clipping from Keith-Albee Collection, The University of Iowa Library (hereafter cited as K-A).

companion when he sketched the shaft in the heart of the earth, with an unearthly radience [sic] thrilling through it. One holds his breath instinctively as he is swept along in the rush of the phantom cars. His attention is held almost with the vise of a fate.[11]

In Boston this film drew applause "from the most blasé"; in New York it provoked cheers; in Philadelphia, where it appeared in the forty-first week of the Biograph's run at Keith's Bijou Theatre, it proved that the Biograph remained "as popular as it was on the first day this moving picture device was exhibited."[12]

On February 15, 1898, an event occurred which launched a new role for motion pictures in vaudeville: that of visual newspaper. The event was the sinking of the American battleship *Maine* in Havana harbor—the act which, the American people were led to believe at least, precipitated the Spanish-American War. The war was probably the most propitious event in the early history of the American cinema. War fever escalated the motion picture into new prominence in vaudeville theaters—making motion picture acts stellar attractions throughout 1898.

The actual hostility in Cuba was but the most visible and visually exploitable aspect of a complex of interrelated political issues—issues which were vociferously debated in magazines, newspapers, and electoral campaigns between 1897 and 1900. For months before war was declared on April 25, the Hearst newspapers had whipped up public sentiment against Spain with a series of exposés of supposed Spanish repression in Cuba. Long after the ten-week military adventure was over in Cuba, the real issue of the war, United States expansionism, continued to consume public attention. Even more opportunity for cinematic exploitation of these issues was provided by American military action in the Philippines, which occurred after the war in Cuba had been won. Guerrilla forces had been fighting Spain over independence for the islands for several years. They turned their guns on the Americans when it appeared that annexation would follow victory over Spain. By 1899, 75,000 American troops were fighting in the Philippines, and military action there did not cease until March 1901.[13]

War and its accoutrements have been favored subjects for the motion picture since the beginning of screen projection, and the Cuban and Philippine campaigns had particular visual appeal. The exotic, tropical settings of the battles of the Spanish-American War added an extra dimension to the appeal of their

---

[11]"Where the Past Speaks," *New York Mail and Express*, September 25, 1897, quoted in Niver, *Biograph Bulletins*, p. 28.

[12]*Boston Journal*, September 26, 1897; *New York Mail and Express*, October 2, 1897; *Philadelphia Call*. October 5, 1897; all quoted in Niver, *Biograph Bulletins*, pp. 27–36.

[13]Barbara Tuchman, *The Proud Tower* (New York: Macmillan, 1962), p. 163.

cinematic treatment. Newspapers could describe the events, but the motion picture could show ships steaming toward Cuba and the places where heroes like Teddy Roosevelt and Admiral Dewey were made. Most Americans knew as much about the Philippines as did their president, William McKinley, who "could not have told where those darned islands were within 2,000 miles."[14] The motion picture could give the middle-class patrons of vaudeville theaters visual images to attach to the odd-sounding names of places where American soldiers were fighting and could provide faces for the nameless, dark-skinned enemies, whose alleged atrocities made banner headlines.

By April 1898 war movies were, according to the *Dramatic Mirror,* "the biggest sensation in the program" in vaudeville theaters across the country. Projectors were even given martial names; Edison dubbed his Projecting Kinetoscope the "Wargraph" for the duration.[15] The Edison and Biograph Companies engaged in competitive warfare to obtain pictures of the fighting in Cuba. The former arranged with W. R. Hearst to have a cameraman transported to the island via the *New York Journal's* yacht, while the latter hired its own ship for the purpose. The war-film craze continued unabated through the summer of 1898. By the middle of June, military subjects were featured at vaudeville houses in New York, Chicago, Boston, Philadelphia, Providence, Toronto, Albany, Detroit, Milwaukee, Jackson (Michigan), and Paterson (New Jersey). The return of Admiral Dewey from the Philippines in October signaled another, albeit briefer, round of patriotic enthusiasm to be exploited by the cinema. At the Union Square Theatre in New York, Biograph films of the Dewey parade were prominently featured. Not to be outdone, a Vitagraph cameraman was dispatched to New York harbor for pictures of Dewey's flagship and had them ready in five hours for an evening performance at Tony Pastor's theater.[16]

The success of the Dewey parade films prompted Austin Fynes, manager of three of the Proctor vaudeville theaters in New York, to hire William Paley, a freelance cameraman, and equip a lab for him in Proctor's Pleasure Palace in order that he might shoot, process, and exhibit films of local events on the same day. The *Dramatic Mirror* reported, "A staff of expert photographers will be in constant readiness to 'take' important events as fast as they occur."[17] This seems to me hardly the actions of a vaudeville manager who is using films to drive patrons away from his theaters.

The ability of motion picture acts in vaudeville to serve as visual newspapers, to fulfill, in Harold Lasswell's terms, a "surveillance" function for vaudeville audiences meant that whenever vaudeville managers could present films of, or

[14]Ibid, p. 151.

[15]*Dramatic Mirror* (New York), May 7, 1898, p. 18.

[16]*New York Clipper*, October 7, 1899, p. 652.

[17]*Dramatic Mirror*, November 4, 1899, p. 20.

purported to be of, important news events, they were assured of an enthusiastic reception. Disasters of any kind depicted on the screen aroused interest. In October 1900 one of the worst hurricanes in American history struck Galveston, Texas, and Biograph cameramen were sent to record the destruction. The *Pawtucket* (Rhode Island) *Evening Times* of October 9, 1900, said of the motion picture program at Keith's in Providence, "the biograph pictures are all of marked interest, and that showing a panoramic view in Galveston after the flood affords an idea of its devastation which columns of newspaper reports have not conveyed."[18] Many vaudeville theaters featured films of the Pan-American Exposition in Buffalo during the summer of 1901. The *Dramatic Mirror* called those at Tony Pastor's "so complete a revelation that the people came away with a good idea of the affair and a notion that they might as well save the price of a ticket to Buffalo."[19] In September 1901 President William McKinley was assassinated while visiting the Exposition. While the actual murder was not recorded on motion picture film, the events surrounding McKinley's funeral were, making motion picture acts featured attractions at vaudeville theaters for several weeks.[20] Numerous other examples of the popularity of topical and documentary subjects in vaudeville between 1898 and 1903 could be cited. The success of films depicting the Boer and Russo-Japanese Wars; football games; yacht, auto and horse races, and other news and sporting events is noted in the trade press of the time.[21]

Two other types of films helped to maintain the popularity of motion picture acts in vaudeville: comic vignettes and trick films. Both types of film, but particularly the latter, had special appeal for children and were used to attract a juvenile audience. By 1900 it was estimated that fully one-half of afternoon audiences and one-fourth of evening audiences in vaudeville were made up of children.[22] After a two-week engagement of Méliès's *A Trip to the Moon* at Keith's in Philadelphia in May 1903, the manager remarked in his weekly report of the following week's film program, "a fair selection of views, without our usual spectacle film. We miss it greatly; and should have one every week if for no other reason than to draw the children." The report from M. J. Keating of the Keith Theatre in Boston for the week of June 8 cited Méliès's *Bluebeard* as "a big attraction for the juveniles." Later that month, Keating recommended Méliès's *Cinderella* as appealing "particularly to the children."[23]

---

[18]*Pawtucket Evening Times,* October 9, 1900, clipping (K-A).

[19]*Dramatic Mirror,* June 29, 1901, p. 16.

[20]*Dramatic Mirror,* October 5, 1901, p. 18; October 12, 1901, p. 18.

[21]*Providence Journal,* clipping book (K-A); programs of Keith's Theatre, Boston, September 16, 1901, October 21, 1901; program of Union Square Theatre, October 28, 1901, file MWEZ n.c. 11,906, New York Public Library Theater Collection.

[22]*Providence News,* August 21, 1900, clipping (K-A).

[23]Manager's reports, Keith Theatres, Philadelphia, May 25, 1903; Boston, June 8, 29, 1903 (K-A).

In short, evidence from the period indicates that the use of motion pictures in vaudeville between 1897 and 1904 does not deserve the opprobrium of being called the "chaser" period. While it would be equally erroneous to maintain that movies were regularly used as headline acts, there are numerous instances of motion picture acts being as well received or better than any other act on the bill. Further, filmmakers experimented with several different types of films, each having its own unique appeal to vaudeville audiences. Motion picture producers were businessmen operating in an increasingly competitive market. To expect them to be collectively oblivious to the tastes of the audience they served for a period of five to seven years goes against any model of mercantile behavior.

There is also the matter of the supposed end of the chaser period. A number of historians, among them North, Ramsaye, Grau, Jacobs, and Jowett, use the White Rats Strike of 1901 to indicate an increased interest by vaudeville patrons in the motion picture. Briefly, the strike was called in February 1901 by a vaudeville performers guild, the White Rats, in protest over contractual practices of a syndicate representing the major East Coast vaudeville circuits. Jowett, drawing upon Jacobs and Grau, calls the strike "one of those fateful incidents which historians love so much. . . . The vaudeville managers faced with the alternatives of closing down or finding a substitute, immediately turned to the motion picture as their principal attraction. The response from the public was clear."[24]

There are two major problems with the above interpretation of the strike. First, I can find no evidence of the widespread use of the motion picture as substitute entertainment during the strike in trade or general circulation perodicals or in the records of the Keith-Albee vaudeville circuit. According to Joe Laurie, Jr., what killed the strike was not the motion picture, but the availability of non-White Rat performers and the lack of solidarity among the guild's membership. The *New York Times* of Feb. 23, 1901, supports this interpretation. It reported that non-White Rat talent "flocked" to the offices of the vaudeville managers. No mention is made in the *Times* coverage of the strike of the use of motion pictures to keep houses open.[25]

Secondly, if one assumes a period of extremely low popularity of the motion picture in vaudeville between 1898 and 1900 and then sees an event in 1901 as revealing a high level of popularity, there ought to be some mediating factor which accounts for this dramatic change. Unfortunately, copyright records, the trade and general press, Edison Company records, vaudeville programs, and clipping books from the Keith theaters fail to show any change in motion picture content that could be interpreted as the intervening variable in the chaser/strikebreaker transition.

---

[24]Jowett, *Film: The Democratic Art*, p. 164.

[25]*New York Times*, February 23, 1901, p. 9; March 7, 1901, p. 2.

From the primary sources I have been able to locate and examine, it does not appear that motion pictures in vaudeville sank to the low level of popularity suggested by most film historians. I would be amiss, however, were I not to point out some possible reasons for instances of dissatisfaction with motion picture acts in vaudeville during this period. First, some companies were set up to service vaudeville theaters better than others. The Biograph Company, for example, used a complete service approach—providing theaters with projectors, films, and operator, and making the movies very similar to any other act on the vaudeville circuit. Also, within months of the regular use of motion pictures in vaudeville, a regular change of subjects became of crucial importance.

Again, the Biograph Company seems to have had no problem in providing its clients with weekly changes of innovative films. The minority of vaudeville managers who bought films outright, on the other hand, had reason to try and run their films as long as possible—risking, of course, the boredom of their audiences each time a film was repeated. The heavy reliance of the film producers on topical films naturally meant that the popularity of individual motion picture acts would vary considerably from week to week, since public response was dependent in large measure upon the impact of the news events depicted. The problem was articulated by Thomas Armat in a letter to Thomas Edison in November 1901:

> The problem with the motion picture business was that as things are now business runs by spurts. If there happens to be a yacht race or the assassination of a president there is a good run on films for a few months. Then it drops down to a demand that keeps the large force busy about one-fourth of the time while much money is wasted in experimenting with costly subjects that the public will not buy.[26]

It is my contention that the unpredictability of the success of topical films might well have been responsible first for increased proportion of comic vignettes and finally for the ascension of the dramatic narrative film—these two forms not being dependent for their popularity upon exigencies external to the immediate production situation. The above factors might well have been responsible for some audience dissatisfaction with motion pictures in vaudeville, but there is sufficient evidence to indicate that they did not drag down the motion picture into the "abyss" of chaser ignominy, to use Mast's term.[27]

If the chaser theory is indefensible, then why do we find it in so many histories of early American cinema? The reason is a simple, though distressing

---

[26]Thomas Armat to Thomas Edison, November 15, 1901, Edison Archives, Edison National Historic Site, West Orange, N.J.

[27]Mast, *Short History*. p. 44.

one: little original scholarship into the exhibition situation existing prior to the nickelodeon has been conducted, and film historians like Sklar, Jowett, Jacobs, etc., concerned with the historical development of the American cinema over a forty- or seventy-year period, have seen fit to rely entirely upon other secondary sources for their information in this area. In fact, Jowett, Sklar, Jacobs, and North are heavily reliant upon a single early writer on motion picture history: Robert Grau. Grau was a theatrical agent who between 1909 and 1914 wrote three books of reminiscenses of his many years in show business. His *Theatre of Science* (1914) is the key source for information on the chaser period used by many historians. While it is true that Grau "was there" during the period in question, his account of events fifteen or more years in the past is peppered with inaccuracies, entirely undocumented, and contradictory with aspects of his account of the same events contained in his other writings.

David Bordwell began a recent article on camera movement during the early sound era by saying, "Beginning with a simple, even naive, question may be an advantage, since the study of film history is in such a state that only a naive question has a decent chance of being answered."[28] As a corollary to his assertion I would add that we can allow no historical interpretation, no matter how oft repeated, to go unexamined.[29]

---

[28]David Bordwell, "Camera Movement, the Coming of Sound, and the Classical Hollywood Style," *The 1977 Film Studies Annual*, part 2 (Pleasantville, N.Y.: Redgrove, 1978), p. 27.

[29][Chaser theory might also take account of a *Variety* ad of September 21, 1907, p. 26, by the 20th Century Optiscope Company, Chicago-GP]:

What's the Difference

between our service and that rendered by other concerns? Only this, if you want the crowd to stick the moving pictures, then use our services, while if you want

"A Chaser"

use the other fellow's service. . .

"Viascope Model No. 4 . . . "

RAYMOND FIELDING

Hale's Tours:
Ultrarealism in the Pre–1910 Motion Picture

In the course of its erratic seventy-five-year history, the motion picture has suffered continuous technological experimentation in its owners' attempts to achieve maximum realism in the production and exhibition of its products. Over the years, showmen have moved steadily toward a less stylized, more naturalistic cinema, beginning with the addition of color, then monophonic sound, stereophonic sound, three-dimensional images, and, finally, wide-screen aspect ratios.

Indeed, something of a high point in motion picture realism seemed to have been reached in 1955 when the late Walt Disney introduced his spectacular "Trip to the Moon" show at Disneyland, California. This continuing attraction takes the form of a gigantic rocket, with seating for 150 passengers, complete on the inside with incandescent dials, blinking lights, airplane hostesses, and all the other theatrical accoutrements of a well-appointed flying saucer. Following a dramatic countdown, the seats shake, dials move, the roar of the motors is heard, and—perfectly synchronized—a realistically animated film of travel through outer space is projected onto motion picture screens above and below the audience. All effects combine to produce a theatrically convincing illusion of space travel.

Impressive as this imaginary voyage is, however, there is nothing new about it. As early as 1895, novelist H. G. Wells and British film pioneer Robert Paul applied for a patent on a similar motion picture designed to simulate travel through time and space, along the lines of Wells's science fiction novel *The Time Machine.* The members of the audience were to be seated on platforms which rocked to and fro, and which moved toward and away from a screen onto which still and motion picture scenes were to be projected.[1] It was an ingenious and

---

[1] The film and slide projectors which produced these scenes were to be mounted on

ambitious design for its day. Because of the excessive cost of such a venture, however, Wells and Paul were obliged to abandon their motion picture spacecraft, thereby failing to anticipate the Disney attraction by more than fifty years.

Instead, it was across the Atlantic in the United States, where, as in Great Britain, the turn-of-the-century motion picture still remained a novelty, that the first permanent, ultrarealistic cinema attraction was to make its appearance. It took the form of an artificial railway car whose operation combined auditory, tactile, visual, and ambulatory sensations to provide a remarkably convincing illusion of railway travel. It was called *Hale's Tours and Scenes of the World* [2] and was a product of the fertile, inventive mind of George C. Hale, popular ex-fire chief of Kansas City, Missouri, and freewheeling entrepreneur.

George C. Hale was a mechanical engineer with a flair for show business who spent most of his career as a fireman. By 1882 he had risen to become fire chief of Kansas City, a position he held for twenty years, until his retirement in 1902.[3] He invented and patented many devices employed in fire fighting, including a swinging harness for fire horses, a fireman's cellar pipe, a tin roof cutter, an electric wire cutter, the Hale rotary steam engine, and the Hale improved telephone fire alarm system, the last of which was a rather complicated device—perhaps a little ahead of its time—which coupled the telephone and the gramaphone, by means of which "the knowledge of an incipient fire is immediately announced at headquarters by the human voice."[4]

---

rollers and tracks so that their distance from the screen could be changed during the performance, and the size of the images thereby varied. As a final touch, a current of air was to be directed over the audience to suggest the speed with which they were racing through space. British patent application no. 19984, filed October 24, 1895. See Terry Ramsaye, *A Million and One Nights*, vol. 1 (New York: Simon and Schuster, 1926), pp. 152-61. Paul and Wells did not complete the formalities required for the issuance of the patent.

[2] The titles by which the attraction was known varied, sometimes appearing as *Hale's Tours*, other times as *Hale's Tours and Scenes of the World*, *Hale's Tours Cars of the World*, etc.

[3] Hale was born in the town of Colton, St. Lawrence County, New York, on October 28, 1849; he was a descendent of the American patriot, Nathan Hale. In 1863, at the age of fourteen and in the midst of the Civil War, he came to Kansas City, Missouri, and went to work as shop boy for the manufacturing firm of Lloyd and Leland. From 1866 to 1869 he assumed supervision of the machinery employed in building a bridge that spans the Missouri River at Kansas City. In 1869 he became employed by the Great Western Manufacturing Co. at Leavenworth, Kansas, which he left sometime between 1871 and 1873 to become engineer of John Campbell Engine No. 1, the first fire engine owned by Kansas City. See *Men of Affairs in Greater Kansas City, 1912* (Kansas City, Mo., 1912), p. 57; *Memorial and Biographical Record of Kansas City and Jackson County, Missouri* (Chicago: Lewis, 1896), pp. 183–86; Howard L. Conrad, ed., *Encyclopedia of the History of Missouri*, Vol. 8 (New York, 1901), pp. 148–49; Carrie Westlake Whitney, *Kansas City, Mo., Its History and Its People, 1808–1908* (Chicago: S.J. Clarke 1908), p. 208.

[4] Conrad, ed., *Encylopedia of the History of Missouri*, 3:149.

At some point prior to 1904 Hale turned his attention to the recently introduced motion picture, and conceived of a new application for it.

The cinema at this time was scarcely more than a novelty, momentarily doomed to occasional end-of-the-bill performances at vaudeville houses. The average motion picture program lasted about ten to fifteen minutes, and was made up of several brief "turns" or "bits" of a comic, dramatic, informational, sports, scenic, or novelty sort. The use of film for storytelling purposes had hardly begun. Indeed, up to this time, many films were never seen projected onto screens at all, but were seen in peep shows of the Kinetoscope or Mutoscope variety in penny arcades.

EUROPEAN PRECEDENTS

Whether Hale had ever heard of the 1895 Wells-Paul spaceship design is not known. We do know that Hale and his fire fighters traveled to London to represent the United States at the International Fire Congress held at Agricultural Hall 12–17 June 1893.[5] A few years later, in 1900, he and his men returned to Europe to participate at a similar congress held in Paris.[6]

The appearance of Hale's fire fighters at these two European congresses was a spectacular success, involving, as it did, a dramatic performance of fire-fighting techniques by a complete Kansas City fire company, fully equipped with trained horses, apparatus, and lifesaving devices. Hale's group received many honors, and he blossomed in his new role as a theatrical showman.

Quite possibly, during these trips he may have heard of the Wells-Paul design. More important, while in Paris, he may have seen or heard of the two ultrarealistic film attractions which were exhibited at the 1900 Paris Exposition.

The first of these was called *Cinéorama*, and was presented by Raoul Grimoin-Sanson. Its exhibition simulated the view which one would have had from a basket of a gigantic balloon as it soared upward and over the European countryside. The audience stood on the top of a raised, circular platform, beneath which ten synchronized film projectors threw a 360° motion picture onto a circular screen, 330 feet in circumference and 30 feet high. The hand-colored 70 mm. films which were shown had been photographed from a real airborne balloon.[7]

---

[5] *Memorial and Biographical Record of Kansas City,* pp. 183–86.

[6] *Encyclopedia of the History of Missouri,* 3:149.

[7] *Scientific American,* supplement, no. 1287 (September 1900):20631; Georges Sadoul, *Histoire générale du cinéma,* vol. 2 (Paris: Editions Seghers, 1947), pp. 100–107; Kenneth Macgowan, *Behind the Screen* (New York: Delta, 1965), pp. 465–67; Paul Rabaud, *Promoteurs et réalisateurs du spectacle cinématographique sur écran large* (Paris: privately printed, 1955), pp. 8–11. *Cinéorama* had to close down on the third day because the arc lamps on the projectors overheated the room underneath the spectators.

The second motion picture attraction, presented by the Lumière Brothers, was called *Maréorama* and simulated the view which one would have had from the bridge of a ship as it sailed through the seas.[8]

Hale may also have heard of the so-called Phantom Rides which had achieved great popularity in England, beginning in 1898. These were conventionally projected motion pictures of scenic locales which had been photographed from the cowcatcher of a speeding train.[9]

With this information at hand, we may now begin to reconstruct the events which led Hale into the film business.

It appears that during the period from 1902 to 1904, an inventor named William J. Keefe of St. Louis, Missouri, conceived of an entertainment pavilion, circular in shape, around the periphery of which an open-sided railroad car was made to run on tracks within a dark tunnel. The wall of the tunnel which faced inward toward the center of the pavilion was to be a continuous screen (whether translucent or reflective is not quite clear), onto which could be projected motion pictures or still images from projectors located either at the center of the pavilion or mounted on the railway car itself.

The purpose of this entertainment device was to provide the passengers with a fairly faithful representation of the scenes which they could see if they were to take a real train ride through scenic areas of the world, incorporating motion pictures which were to have been photographed from a real moving train. The

---

[8]According to one description: "It is a voyage in the Mediterranean, a voyage on a ship on which an ingenious mechanism causes the rolling and the pitching which has all the aspects of a true ship; smoking funnel, air ventilator, siren, a voyage, in a word, where one witnesses all the spectacles of the sea and shore; here, the storm with its lightning and thunder; there, the rising of the sun; further, an effect of night...." Sadoul, *Histoire générale du cinéma*, pp. 454–56. See also Macgowan, *Behind the Screen*, p. 468.

[9]According to Cecil Hepworth, the British film pioneer who photographed many of them, the Phantom Rides were supposed to have been first presented by the American Biograph Company at the Palace Theater in London in 1901. See Cecil M. Hepworth, *Came the Dawn* (London: Phoenix House, 1951), pp. 44–45. A reference to an even earlier appearance, however, can be found in the "Music Hall Gossip" column of the April 9, 1898, issue of *The Era*, according to which "the most startling of the series of train pictures taken by Chard's Vitagraph is a phantom ride, 'snapped from' the front of an engine of the S.E.R. The scene depicted is through Chisellhurst Tunnel and station, the surrounding being very distinct, and the pictures remarkably steady." See Anthony Slide, "Extracts from *The Era*, 1898," *Cinema Studies* 4 (June 1966): p. 37. In the United States, too, during the period, numerous films had been photographed from moving railroad trains, trolleys, or subway cars. Of the 141 titles which deal in some fashion with such vehicles in the Library of Congress' pre-1912 film collection, we find that over 50 were shot either from the cowcatchers or rear platforms of moving trains. Most of these date from 1899 to 1906, copyrighted by the Edison and the American Mutoscope and Biograph Companies. See Kemp R. Niver, *Motion Pictures from the Library of Congress Paper Print Collection, 1894–1912* (Berkeley: University of California Press, 1967), pp. 381–82.

illusion of the ride was to be heightened by the use of an unevenly laid track which would cause the car to sway and vibrate, thus suggesting a high rate of speed. Some sort of wind-producing machine was to be used within the tunnel to produce a rush of air throughout the length of the car. The design for this entertainment device was patented by Keefe, application being made on 22 March 1904 and the patent being issued on 9 August of the same year.[10]

Sometime prior to filing application for this patent in March 1904, William Keefe, seeking funds for development of the invention, brought his idea to Judge Fred W. Gifford, a magistrate of Kansas City and a close friend of George Hale. Hale and Gifford decided to provide the financial backing necessary for the exploitation of the invention. Accordingly, when the patent was issued in August of 1904 it called for assignment of two-thirds of the ownership of the patent to George Hale and Fred Gifford, with the remaining one-third assigned to William Keefe.[11] In the end, Hale and Gifford bought all rights to the system from Keefe, and then set out to develop it commercially. Gifford's son, Ward, joined them, contributing both to the system's technical sophistication and to its subsequent marketing.

FIRST APPEARANCE: ST. LOUIS

They introduced their show commercially at the 1904 St. Louis Exposition. This world's fair, which commemorated the Louisiana Purchase, opened on 20 April 1904 and was, from its opening, a grand success. Among the firsts which fair goers saw that year were the first ice cream cones, the first iced tea, and the first hot dogs.[12] The Lee de Forest wireless exhibit was one of the main attractions and received the Grand Prize and Gold Medal,[13] while elsewhere on the fair grounds, the German film pioneer, Oskar Messter, demonstrated his sound motion pictures.[14]

Less impressively, Hale and Gifford opened their motion picture attraction on the "Pike"—the amusement midway which had become a feature of world's fairs since its introduction at the Paris Exposition of 1867.[15] Hale also presented

[10]United States patent no. 767,281.

[11]Our reconstruction of these negotiations is in line with statements communicated to the author in a letter dated April 12, 1967, from Mrs. Mildred J. Gifford of Kansas City, Missouri, daughter-in-law of the late Judge Gifford and widow of his son, Ward.

[12]Robert Paul Gordon, "St. Louis," National Geographic, November 1965, p. 640.

[13]Lee de Forest, Father of Radio (Chicago: Wilcox and Follett, 1950), p. 103.

[14]Albert Narath, "Oskar Messter and His Work," Journal of the Society of Motion Picture and Television Engineers 69 (October 1960): 721.

[15]Joseph Gies, "Shows That Make Dreams Come True," This Week Magazine, March 12, 1961, p. 11.

a fire-fighting show on the midway, in which a fire of some size was set and then extinguished on regular schedule by his firemen. He was also placed in charge of all facilities, planning, and operations for fire fighting and prevention throughout the fair grounds.

Apparently, no photographs of the Hale's Tours show at this exposition survive, nor is there any clear reference to it in any of the surviving publicity and news releases of that day. Were it not for Terry Ramsaye's reference to it in his 1926 film history, *A Million and One Nights*, we would not have been led to expect its presence there.[16]

Apart from Ramsaye's reference, however, we have acquired testimony from two other people who recalled seeing the Hale's tour show at the exposition as children.

The first of these was the late film producer and historian, Professor Kenneth Macgowan of Los Angeles. The other was film producer Reid Ray of Minneapolis. Each clearly recalled attending the show, but could not describe its location on the Pike or the details of its appearance and operation.

The following spring, on 14 March 1905, Hale applied for a new patent for what he called the "Pleasure Railway"—a patent which was granted on 19 September of the same year.[17]

The new design called for two cars on a single, short, straight stretch of track. Customers boarded one of the cars which traveled a short distance within a tunnel and then coupled onto a second car. The second car was stationary and was open on its sides and at its front. It was from this stationary car that the audience was to see the show and experience the sensations of travel. In subsequent commercial practice, most installations of Hale's Tours seem to have employed only a single, stationary railway car, dispensing with the moving car which was intended to transport passengers from the front of the building to the stationary car.

The stationary car provided a number of seats for its passengers, suitably inclined upward toward the rear to provide good sight lines. Through the open front, the audience viewed a motion picture which had been photographed from the cowcatcher of a moving train, and which was thrown onto a slightly inclined screen from a motion picture projector situated in a gallery above and slightly behind the car. The size of the screen, the distance of the screen from the car, and the distance of the projector from the screen were intended to provide an image which covered the entire field of vision of the car's occupants and which was life size. The patent also provided for rear projection of the image, if desired. (As it happened, many, if not most, of the Hale's Tours which were operated commercially did employ rear projection.)

---

[16]Ramsaye, *Million and One Nights*, pp. 428–29.

[17]United States patent no. 800,100.

Beneath the car, an endless belt with projecting lugs moved continuously over rollers and shafts during the performance. The lugs came into contact with a metal piece under the car, thereby creating the typical clickety-clack sound of real railway wheels as they passed over joints in the tracks. The speed of the belt could be regulated at will in order to allow for starts, stops, accelerations, and decelerations which occurred in the motion picture. An artificially produced rush of air was to be provided, and the whole car was to be pivoted on its longitudinal axis so that the operator could, by throwing a lever, sway the car from side to side during the performance. (Later, with gradual sophistication of the design, many of these manual operations were accomplished electrically.[18])

Hale and Gifford set out to exploit their invention. In doing so, they were ultimately to make a considerable profit for themselves. More important for the history of the motion picture, their "Pleasure Railway" was to play a major role in furthering the careers of several then inconspicuous individuals who, once involved, remained in the film business and ended up running a substantial part of the American motion picture industry. These included Sam Warner, cofounder and owner of Warner Brothers Studios; J. D. Williams, founder and president of First National Studios; Adolph Zukor, a founder of Famous-Players-Lasky Productions and president of Paramount Pictures; and Carl Laemmle, founder and head of Universal Pictures Corporation. For Carl Laemmle, Hale's Tours was the first film show he had ever seen—an introduction to the motion picture which convinced him that this was the business in which he ought to invest his modest capital and his enormous energy.[19] For J. D. Williams, an itinerant road-show entrepreneur in 1905, Hale's Tours was the first motion picture show he opened in Vancouver, British Columbia.[20] Sam Warner's first job in the film business was as projectionist for Hale's Tours, first at White City Park in Chicago, then at the Idora Amusement Park in Youngstown, Ohio.[21] For Adolph Zukor, Hale's Tours was the link which bridged his penny arcade operations in New York City and his much more ambitious entrance into conventional operations.[22] Other film pioneers whose first view of a motion picture was a Hale's Tours show

[18]B. S. Brown, "Hale's Tours and Scenes of the World," *The Moving Picture World*, July 15, 1916, p. 372.

[19]Ramsaye, *Million and One Nights*, pp. 449–50, 679–80, 789–90, 793, 826.

[20]E. C. Thomas, "Vancouver, B.C. Started with 'Hale's Tours,'" *The Moving Picture World*, July 15, 1916, p. 373.

[21]Jack Warner, *My First Hundred Years in Hollywood* (New York: Random House, 1964), p. 49.

[22]Adolph Zukor, *The Public Is Never Wrong* (New York: G.P. Putnam's Sons, 1953), pp. 46–48; Will Irwin, *The House That Shadows Built* (New York: Doubleday, 1928), pp. 98–106.

included actress Mary Pickford, actor Ronald Colman, and British nature-film producer Percy Smith.[23]

COMMERCIAL INSTALLATIONS

The first commercial installation of Hale's Tours following the St. Louis Exposition was in 1905 at the Electric Park at Kansas City, Missouri. According to *The Moving Picture World* of 1916,

> It was a two-car "house" with an ornate stucco front and cost $7,000, including the projection equipment. Admission was 10 cents; and each car was more or less filled—about 60 passengers—20 to 75 times a day.[24]

It was not, however, until the press reported the show's debut at 64 Union Square (Fourteenth Street and Broadway) in New York City, and on State Street in Chicago, that Hale's Tours began to attract national attention.

The New York show was opened by film pioneer Adolph Zukor, in association with the American showman William Brady. The latter had acquired the rights for Hale's Tours in ten eastern states. Later, Zukor and Brady opened other Hale's Tours in Pittsburgh, Newark, Coney Island, and Boston. In a letter written to the author in 1957, Zukor recalled that the entire show lasted for 20 to 25 minutes, of which 15 minutes were devoted to the film itself. His railway car held sixty people, for each of whom the admission price was ten cents.[25] Often, the front of the theater was made to look like a railroad depot office. Tickets were taken at the door by a uniformed guard who became the conductor and operated the various controls for the car's machinery once the ride was under way. Zukor's show also included a lecturer who described and elaborated upon the scenic points of interest which were shown.

Except for the lack of color, the illusion was quite convincing; all the more so because of the way in which the moving image of the tracks slipped away under the forward edge of the coach. According to a trade paper account, the illusion was so good that when trolley rides through cities were shown, members of the

---

[23]Leslie Wood, *The Romance of the Movies* (London: W. Heinemann, 1937), p. 66; Charles Allen Oakley, *Where We Came In* (London: G. Allen and Unwin, 1964), p. 54; Edward Wagenknecht, *The Movies in the Age of Innocence* (Norman: University of Oklahoma Press, 1962) p. 144.

[24]Brown, "Hale's Tours," p. 372. See also Homer Croy, *How Motion Pictures are Made* (1918; New York: Arno, 1978), p. 78.

[25]Statement prepared by Adolph Zukor for Raymond Fielding, December 30, 1957. See also Adolph Zukor, "Origins and Growth of the Industry," in Joseph Patrick Kennedy, ed., *The Story of the Films* (1927; New York: J.S. Ozer, 1971), pp. 55–71.

audience frequently yelled at pedestrians to get out of the way or be run down. One demented fellow even kept coming back to the same show, day after day. Sooner or later, he figured, the engineer would make a mistake and he would get to see a train wreck.[26]

A variety of makes of 35 mm. projectors was used in different installations. Zukor used an Edison projecting Kinetoscope, as did Sam Warner. By 1907, the film manufacturer William Selig had a special model of his 35 mm. Polyscope projector on the market which was designed expressly for Hale's Tours. This model incorporated a wide angle lens and was designed for rear-projection installations, which was the prevailing mode for Hale's Tours. That is to say, the screen which was used was translucent, the image of the railroad ride being projected upon it from *behind* the screen rather than from the front, as in conventional practice. The use of rear-projection technique hid the projector from the audience and helped to isolate the noise it made. The use of a wide angle lens allowed the projector to be set fairly close to the screen so that the whole Hale's Tours ride could be operated in rather cramped quarters.

Both calcium light and electric arc lamps were available for Selig's special Hale's Tours model of the Polyscope projector which sold, in 1907, for $150. Selig also manufactured a seamless rear projection screen in 9½' x 12' sizes which sold for $25, or 25¢ a square foot in larger sizes.[27]

Following its East Coast opening, Hale's Tours spread across the United States and Canada, opening in cities in California, and in Denver, Portland, Spokane, Winnipeg, Toronto, and scores of other locales. Eventually, according to one trade paper account, there were 500 such Hale's Tours running at one time in the United States alone![28]

The show was frequently seen at summer amusement parks in the United States from 1905 to 1907. Typical installations could be found at White City Amusement Parks in Syracuse, New York, and Chicago; at the Atlantic Coast Resort in Atlantic City, New Jersey; at the Athletic Park, Montgomery, Alabama; at Ponce de Leon Park, Atlanta, Georgia; at the Luna Parks in Cleveland and Pittsburgh; and at Riverview Park in Chicago.[29] These amusement park settings seemed particularly appropriate for Hale's Tours inasmuch as most of the parks were themselves owned and operated by trolley or railroad companies. For many years, too, such parks had featured so-called scenic railroads, in which customers rode on narrow-gauge trolley or railroad cars through tunnels, enclosures, and garden settings whose decor simulated a variety of exotic locales.

---

[26]E. C. Thomas, "Vancouver, B.C.," p. 373.

[27]*1907 Catalogue of the Selig Polyscope and Library of the Selig Film* (Chicago, 1907), pp. 19–21, 36, from the Charles Clarke Collection.

[28]Brown, "Hale's Tours," p. 373.

[29]*Variety*, July 14, 1906, p. 12; June 23, 1906, p. 13; June 9, 1906, pp. 12–13; April 21, 1906, p. 12; February 17, 1906, p. 11.

The railroad theme also appeared in park attractions such as the "Train Wreckers and Robbers" show, which was a part of the entertainment scene in 1906.[30]

In this first decade of the twentieth century, the railroad train was the only mechanical means for transporting passengers and freight over land that had been extensively developed, the airplane and automobile still being in their infancy. Moreover, for most of the economic lower class, a ride on a railroad train and Pullman car was prohibitively expensive and was, therefore, exotic in appeal.

Eventually, in 1906, Ward C. Gifford took the show to Mexico, South Africa, South America, the European continent, and the British Isles. It even opened in Hong Kong.[31]

In Great Britain, Henry Iles acquired a franchise for Hale's Tours and opened it at 165 Oxford Street, London. It also opened at Hammersmith and in the provinces. In England, as in America, Hale's Tours was the first permanent, widespread, specialized motion picture show to appear, and it played an important role in introducing the British public to the motion picture medium. Interestingly, the Hale's Tours which opened in London broke precedent by abolishing class distinctions and admitting all patrons at the same price of sixpence. Competing penny arcade owners derided the practice, predicting that "first class won't ride with third class." But they were wrong. Silk-hatted gentlemen rode side-by-side with laborers, and the shows played to as many as 1,000 people a day—at least for a while. In time, just as in America, the novelty wore off, and the Tours shows were replaced by the British equivalent of the nickelodeon—the small "Bijou" type of motion picture house which provided a regular change of bill.[32]

PROGRAM MATERIAL

Conventionally, each Hale's Tours film program ran in a particular installation for one week, and was then replaced with another program which showed railroad trips in entirely different locales. In dealing with exhibitors, Hale and

[30]*Variety*, March 10, 1906, p. 11.

[31]Brown, "Hales's Tours," p, 372.

[32]Ibid., pp. 372–73; Oakley, *Where We Came In*, pp. 18, 47–48; Rachel Low, *The History of the British Film*, vol. 2 (London: Allen and Unwin, 1949), p. 12. Low states that Hale's Tours was followed by a Maréorama type of attraction in London called "Scenic Attractions," which was patented by a Mr. Starr; Leslie Wood, *The Miracle of the Movies* (London, 1947), pp. 125–26; Wood, *The Romance of the Movies*, pp. 64–66; In the latter work, Wood states that colored lights were played upon the screen at different times during the London Hale's Tours presentation: Ray Allister, *Friese-Greene: Close-up of an Inventor* (London: Marsland, 1948), p. 97; Croy, *How Motion Pictures Are Made*, p. 78; excerpts of notes written in 1946 by Albany Ward, quoted in Rachel Low and Roger Manvell, *The History of the British Film*, vol. 1 (London: Allen and Unwin, 1948), p. 115.

Gifford sold their completed films for fifteen to twenty-two cents a foot, then bought the films back, after their showing was completed, at a lower figure.[33] This business practice preceded the development of the exchange system in the United States. Once introduced, the exchanges began to function as middlemen between producers and exhibitors, substituting rental-lease arrangements in the booking of films in place of outright sale of prints. Without the development of such exchange systems, the motion picture industry as we know it today could never have come into being. A 1916 trade paper account credited the numerous and widespread Hale's Tours shows with singlehandedly creating so substantial a demand for films that it became necessary to develop the exchange system in the United States.[34]

In the beginning, Hale secured some of his films from the American Edison company and the French firm of Pathé. Later, he contracted with particular cameramen for such footage. Two such cameramen—both of them American— were Norman Dawn[35] and T. K. Peters.[36] Dawn photographed footage for Hale in Switzerland and Mexico, Peters did so in the Orient. Both mounted the cameras on moving trains to achieve the desired effect, sometimes on the cowcatcher of the locomotive or on a flat car pushed in front of it, other times on the rear platform of the last car. Peters recalled that he was paid fifty cents a foot for this material.

Later still, some of the early motion picture studios and exchanges offered films to the general trade which were suitable for Hale's Tours presentations. The William Swanson and George Kleine Companies of Chicago both offered such films. The Kleine list of offerings, as of 20 April 1907, for example, showed fourteen Hales' Tours titles, all of them photographed in foreign locales. These included Tokyo, Canton, Switzerland, Ceylon, Hanoi, Lourdes, Mount Cerrat, Vesuvius, Agra, and Frankfort.[37] These ranged in length from 65 feet to 508 feet, with an average length of 161 feet. Assuming that the 35 mm. film used in Hale's Tours ran at 16 frames a second, or 60 feet a minute, this meant an average running time for each title of only 2.7 minutes. Presumably, several such films were spliced together to make a complete show.

The Selig Polyscope Company of Chicago considered the market for Hale's Tours films substantial enough to issue a catalogue supplement in August 1906

---

[33]Brown, "Hale's Tours," p. 373.

[34]Ibid.

[35]Interviews with Norman Dawn by Raymond Fielding throughout 1963–64. See also Raymond Fielding, "Norman Dawn: Pioneer Worker in Special Effects Cinematography," *Journal of the Society of Motion Picture and Television Engineers,* 72 (January 1963): 15–23.

[36]T. K. Peters to Raymond Fielding, April 3, August, 2, August 11, 1967.

[37]*The Moving Picture World,* April 20, 1907, p. 110.

which was devoted entirely to their description.[38] It listed twenty-five separate films, running from 445 feet to 635 feet, with an average running time of approximately ten minutes per title. Most of the railroad and trolley trips shown in this catalogue are of American locales, and include trips to Red Rock Canyon, Royal Gorge, Pike's Peak, Ute Pass, Denver, the Columbia River, Chicago, Niagara Falls, Chattanooga and Lookout Mountain, Jacksonville, Tampa, Cincinnati, Palm Beach, Utah, Tacoma, Seattle, the Black Hills, and the White River Valley. Also included were some foreign railroad trips, including those of Argentina, Switzerland, Borneo, Ceylon, Ireland, and England. Each of the titles was described separately. Thus:

1825-Ute Pass from Freight Train

This subject also departs from the conventional. The first section shows a locomotive just ahead and gives a wonderful idea of the busy life of the fireman and engineer. The rolling and pitching of the engine and tender are very realistic. The scene starts at Divide on the Colorado Midland and runs down the pass until Pike's Peak, covered with snow, is seen just ahead. Then the camera is taken to the caboose and the freight train is seen ahead winding around the tortuous curves into tunnels and rounding steep crags. The background is sublime. The entire picture is filled with hypnotic views that make the beholder steady himself to catch the motion of rounding curves. It is impossible not to imagine that you are actually on the train. The scene closes at Manitou. Length 600 feet. Price: $72.00.[39]

Note that, according to the description of this particular film, the convention of the continuously moving train ride as photographed from one single position is contradicted at the moment that the camera moves back to the caboose of the train. In other Selig films, abrupt changes of *locale* sometimes occur during the moving shots, from a stretch of track in one part of the country to an entirely different one elsewhere. In still other films, the camera leaves the railroad track for a few moments in order to show scenes of a particular city or locale in conventional static-camera shots. And, finally, in some of these films, the convention of the continuous moving-camera shot is broken entirely in order to tell a simple story

---

[38]1906 catalogue of the Selig Polyscope Co., 43–45 Peck Court, Chicago, Illinois. This is a four-page brochure designated supplement no. 44, August 1906, and entitled *Hale's Tours Films,* from the collection of Charles Clarke.

[39]Ibid. The Clarke copy of this catalogue has numerous handwritten corrections throughout, which were apparently entered during the period of the brochure's circulation and use. These corrections deal with the films' contents, titles, lengths, and costs. The quotation given here is from the original printed text.

in the middle of the railroad trip. This occurs, for example, in Selig's 1907 film entitled *Trip Through the Black Hills:*

> A very fine trip and one that every car show should have. It starts with the train leaving the station, then a panorama with a double leader ahead. Panorama climbing the Mountains, *stopping for a comic scene showing the difficulties of trying to dress in a Pullman berth,* closing the trip by arriving in a station [italics added].[40]

PROFIT AND LOSS

For Hale and Gifford, the sale of territorial rights to the show was immensely profitable. It was reported that the British rights alone sold for $100,000, while Hale's total profit on his Tours was estimated at $500,000—a colossal profit for those days.[41]

For exhibitors who bought the machinery and the territorial rights that went with it, however, Hale's Tours was often less rewarding. In Zukor's case, for example, his show at 41 Union Square ran only for three or four months before he was obliged to close it. At first, long lines of people waited to see the attraction and attendance ran high. Within a few weeks, however, it began to wane, and then fell off precipitously. Finally, with liabilities estimated at $180,000,[42] Zukor hit upon the idea of interrupting the Hale's Tours show midway in its presentation and running the very popular railroad melodrama film, *The Great Train Robbery,* which Edwin S. Porter had made for the Edison Studios in 1903. Attendance at Zukor's show shot up instantly as people turned out to see this exciting melodrama. In the end, Zukor ripped out the expensive Hale's Tours apparatus, converted the area into a conventional nickelodeon theater with a regularly changing program, and christened it The Comedy Theater. The new venture was a great success and launched Zukor on his career as a major motion picture exhibitor and producer.[43]

As Zukor had discovered, there was a point of diminishing returns in the operation of a Hale's Tours show. In the first place, films for the program were hard to come by, despite Hale's efforts to contract with early cameramen such as Norman Dawn and T. K. Peters for exclusively produced footage. Only a limited number of titles were ever available at any one time, and this meant monotony in program fare. Second, as with all technological innovations, once the novelty

---

[40]Ibid.

[41]Ramsaye, *Million and One Nights,* p. 429; Brown, "Hale's Tours," p. 373.

[42]Irwin, *House That Shadows Built,* p. 104.

[43]Zukor to Fielding, see n. 25. Also Zukor, *Public Is Never Wrong,* pp. 46–48.

wore off, the customers tired of the show and turned to other recreations. A 1906 account in *Variety* summed up the decline of Hale's Tours in this manner.

> With the closing of the summer comes what eventually will mean the last of what are known as "Hale's Tours." Little success has followed the car enclosed picture machines. The rocking has caused the women to remain away after the first visit, and the difficulty in securing sufficient scenic views has been another reason. Close confinement also contributes its share of disagreeable features. Some cars made money in the beginning, but lost it later.[44]

No one knows when the last of the Hale's Tours shows finally passed from the international entertainment scene, but it was probably around 1912.[45] As for Hale, he played no further role in the film industry, but enjoyed a secure retirement in Kansas City, Missouri, where he died on 14 July 1923 at the age of seventy-three.[46]

Hale's crude attempts to simulate reality may seem ludicrous to us now, but the influence of his little show on the emerging motion picture should not be underestimated. It served not only to introduce and popularize the early projected motion picture, but also acted as a bridge which linked the primitive arcade peep shows and vaudeville presentations of the day with the makeshift motion picture theaters which spread across the United States between 1905 and 1910.

Because of its widespread distribution and its insatiable demand for films, Hale's Tours played an important role in sustaining the early motion picture exchanges. Without the growth and success of these exchanges the motion picture industry could never have survived.

Finally, it represented one of the earliest examples in a long series of continuing attempts by film producers to duplicate or simulate certain aspects of perceived reality. Half a century after Hale's Tours was first presented at the 1904 St. Louis Exposition, a motion picture called *Impressions of Speed* was introduced at the 1958 Brussels World's Fair. Quite likely, its proprietors had never even heard of Hale's Tours. An article in *Evergreen Review* described it this way:

---

[44]*Variety*, September 22, 1908, p. 11.

[45]Carlos Fernández Cuenca, *Historia del cine*, vol. 2 (Madrid, 1949). Fernández Cuenca states that a Hale's Tours was operating in Madrid as late as 1912 under the name "Metropolitan Cinema Tour." The Irish playwright Denis Johnston told the author in 1968 that he attended a Hale's Tours show as a child in Dublin, around 1910.

[46]Obituary, *The Kansas City Star*, July 14, 1923, p. 2.

Impressions of Speed: in a special pavilion, a thoroughly engrossing experiment, for only 25 spectators at a time: the audience is seated as if in the cab of a simulated railroad engine, with a full view of the landscape not only in front but also on both sides of the train; a continuous, all-encompassing image is projected through the simulated windows; stereophonic sound is used; the landscape flashes by, in perfect synchronization and in color, the total impression so vivid as to approach the actual experience. The jury is stumped: Has film left behind the "illusion of art" and become reality itself?[47]

No doubt, compared to this 1958 offspring, the original Hale's Tours was much less sophisticated; but then, so were its audiences. All things considered, Hale's customers probably enjoyed his show far more.

---

[47]Amos Vogel, "The Angry Young Film Makers," *Evergeen Review* 2 (1958): 175.

EDWARD LOWRY

Edwin J. Hadley:
Traveling Film Exhibitor

We often assume that once Edison presented Thomas Armat's Vitascope at
Koster & Bial's Music Hall in New York on April 23, 1896,[1] motion pictures had
been introduced to America. In fact, the process of bringing projected films to the
American public was a good deal more complex. Those famous storefront
theaters in which the earliest films were projected were for the most part located
in large urban areas.[2] For people outside the cities, the first moving
pictures arrived with traveling shows which moved between the smaller towns,
introducing, for a profit, the new medium to the uninitiated. For a number of
years, these touring exhibitors provided the only contact between rural America
and the moving picture. One such early exhibitor was projectionist Edwin J.
Hadley, who seems to have been involved in this type of traveling motion
picture show since 1897. In advertisements for its 1899–1900 season, the Hadley
Kinetoscope and Concert Company claimed to be making its fifth annual tour,[3]
which would, by conservative calculation, place its first tour well over a year
before the New York premiere of the Vitascope. Not only is it almost impossible
that Hadley could have been projecting films that early, but Hadley himself
contradicts the claim in a later list of credits which places the beginning of his
show in 1897.[4] We are thus warned, almost before we begin, that Hadley's
advertisements are never to be taken at face value and are always to be weighted

---

[1]Kenneth Macgowan, *Behind the Screen: The History and Techniques of the Motion Picture*
(New York: Delta, 1965), p. 84.

[2]Ibid., p. 124.

[3]Hadley Kinetoscope and Concert Company, advertisement for 1899–1900 season.

[4]Edwin J. Hadley, advertisement for appearances at LeRoy, New York, November 9,
1903, and at Wellsville, New York, November 14, 1903.

for probability. Hopefully the reviews of Hadley's show, reprinted as testimonials in his 1899 advertisement, are a little more reliable, since dates of the articles and the names of the newspapers from which they came are quoted. If they are to be trusted, it seems that Hadley toured New York state with his own show as early as August 1897, appearing in Warrensburg, New York (population 2,267—1890 census) on August 24 and 25, and in Ticonderoga, New York (population approximately 2,000—1900 census) on August 31. A year later, on August 26, 1898, his company played Glen Falls, New York, a town of over 10,000 people (1890 census).[5]

A Hadley performance was usually sponsored by a local civic organization which made arrangements for his appearance by providing a place for the show (the local opera house, a YMCA hall, the basement of the library, etc.) and distributing his advertisements prior to the company's arrival. The local group took a cut of the profits, so that the moving picture show was frequently referred to as a "benefit." For example, in Warrensburg, the Hadley company appeared at the local Music Hall sponsored by the Warrensburg Military Band; in Ticonderoga, at the Union Opera House "under the auspices" of the Epworth League; and in Glen Falls, in the courthouse "for the benefit of the Sons of Veterans."[6] By the fall of 1898, the Hadley Kinetoscope Company was touring the midwest, and Hadley had begun to list Chicago as his permanent headquarters. The company appeared on October 24, 1898, in Lincoln, Illinois (population 8,962—1900 census), on October 29 and 31 in Louisiana, Missouri (population 5,131—1900 census), and on February 2 and 3, 1899, in Fort Wayne, Indiana, a city of some 45,000 (1900 census).[7] Obviously the company played many (maybe several hundred) performances of which there is no record, so any speculation based on the limited information available has its pitfalls. But judging from the larger towns and longer engagements played by the company in the Midwest, Hadley seems to have moved his show to the area in order to reach larger towns of people less familiar with moving pictures than those in the vicinity of New York City. Bigger audiences, of course, meant bigger profits, but they also enabled Hadley's company to give more than one performance in a single location, saving him the time, effort, and expense of moving his equipment and personnel more frequently.

Although billed as a "Kinetoscope Company," and despite the enthusiastic comment of one reviewer that "the Kinetoscope is a wonderful machine and all it was represented to be,"[8] Hadley was not using a Kinetoscope (Edison's "peep

---

[5]Edwin J. Hadley Kinetoscope Company, advertisement for appearance at Fort Wayne, Indiana, February 2–3, 1899.

[6]Ibid.

[7]Ibid.

[8]"A Fine Exhibition," *Warrensburg News* (Warrensburg, N.Y.), August 25, 1897, quoted in Hadley Kinetoscope Company advertisement for Fort Wayne.

show" machine) to project his views. His ads claimed only that he used "Edison's Improved 1899 Model Machine,"[9] probably a Vitascope. It is certain that his views were *projected*, as is evident from newspaper references to films being viewed by a packed house and to unanimous applause from an audience obviously responding to a scene they all viewed simultaneously.[10] The projection of "$500.00 worth of animated pictures"[11] was not the only attraction Hadley's show offered. Films were alternated with "Monologue Impersonations, Illustrated Popular Songs, Sleight of Hand Illusions, [and] Edison's Marvelous New Electric Phonograph." The illustrated songs seem to have been played on the phonograph and accompanied by the projection of stereopticon slides.[12] Traveling with the show was Mr. Charles E. Phipps, "the well known Musical Wonder," violin and mandolin virtuoso, who was said to play "America" on "a small pair of bellows" and to perform another selection on "a common nail puller." His specialty, however, was "solo palm whistling," whereby he did "imitations of the cry of different animals and fowls, also of the steamboat whistle, and the buzz of approaching trolley cars."[13] Variety was obviously the keynote of such early film exhibitions, with the moving pictures themselves (doubtless the main attraction) taking their place between the acts of a music hall show.

The films shown by Hadley during this period apparently consisted of those which were available from Edison. A number were "actualities" such as scenes of busy streets, locomotives, and "surf bathers."[14] And, judging from the comments in the *Louisiana* (Mo.) *Daily Press*,[15] at least two of Edison's comic views were shown: *Pie Eating Contest*[16] and *Rainmakers*[17] (a variation on the Lumières' *L'Arroseur arrosé*[18]). The views most commented on in the news articles were those of the military, a subject both popular and inherently spectacular: the troops at Fort Sheridan, the First Chicago Regiment, British Dragoons on the Upper Nile. Loudly proclaimed in the advertisements, and used in the performances as a finale, were the famous Edison War Views of naval engage-

---

[9]Hadley, advertisement for 1899–1900 season.

[10]Hadley, advertisement for Fort Wayne.

[11]Hadley, advertisement for 1899–1900 season.

[12]Hadley, advertisement for Fort Wayne.

[13]Hadley, advertisement for 1899–1900 season.

[14]Hadley, advertisement for Fort Wayne.

[15]"The Hadley Exhibition" *Louisiana Daily Press* (Louisiana, Mo.), October 31, 1898), quoted in Hadley, advertisement for Fort Wayne.

[16]Kemp R. Niver, *Motion Pictures from the Library of Congress Paper Print Collection, 1894–1912* (Berkeley: University of California Press, 1967), p. 327.

[17]Ibid., p. 81.

[18]Gerald Mast, *A Short History of the Movies* (Indianapolis: Bobbs-Merrill, 1971) p, 37.

ments during the Spanish-American War.[19] It seems probable that some of the war scenes faked by Edison[20] were among those shown, but, testifying to the ingenuousness of the audience, an October 31, 1898, article in the Louisiana, Missouri, paper noted, "The pictures of the battleships in action were so real that every time a shot was fired the women would duck their heads to let the 13-inch shells pass over."[21]

According to Hadley, his career began with "the well known firm of J. B. Colt & Co., New York City, manufacturers of electrical apparatus, moving picture machines, etc.,"[22] where he was employed from 1894 to 1896.[23] In his capacity with Colt, he claimed to have been "instrumental in placing the first automatic arc lamps ever used in connection with the famous Lumière Cinématographe when first exhibited in this country at B. F. Keith's theatre, New York City."[24] The only corroborating evidence for this claim is the date of the Lumière Cinématographe's American premiere at Keith's Union Square Theatre in New York on June 29, 1896, while Hadley was working for Colt.[25] In 1896, Hadley joined traveling exhibitor Lyman H. Howe for his "pioneer season."[26] After a single season with Howe, he left to establish his own touring company in 1897. His move to the midwest seems to have been unsuccessful, for, by the end of 1899, Hadley had returned to the East Coast to work once again as Howe's projectionist.[27] After four consecutive seasons together,[28] relations between Hadley and Howe had deteriorated considerably, and, by January 1903, Hadley was ready to leave Howe's company for a second time. Howe did not accompany his show on tour, but placed its supervision in the hands of a tour manager. In early 1903, Howe's company consisted of Hadley as projectionist, the manager— whom Hadley referred to as "Max"—a female pianist, and a man named Mr. Wilson, whom Howe was apparently breaking in on the tour for the position of manager. Howe hoped to initiate a second touring company which Max would manage. Upset at the thought of being left under the supervision of the

[19]Hadley, advertisement for Fort Wayne.

[20]Raymond Fielding, *The American Newsreel, 1911–1967* (Norman: University of Oklahoma Press, 1972), p. 31.

[21]*Louisiana Daily Press.*

[22]"A New Invention," *Wilkes-Barre Daily News* (Wilkes-Barre, Pa.), July 2, 1903, quoted in Hadley, advertisement for LeRoy and Wellsville.

[23]Hadley, advertisement for Leroy and Wellsville.

[24]*Wilkes-Barre Daily News.*

[25]*New York Times,* June 28, 1896, pp. 10–11.

[26]Hadley, advertisement for LeRoy and Wellsville.

[27]Ibid.

[28]Ibid.

inexperienced Wilson and of assuming the added responsibilities he was sure would be expected of him, Hadley wrote to Howe to request a compensating increase in pay "of about seven dollars extra a week."[29] Howe denied his request; Hadley responded on January 18, 1903, in a letter written from Oswego, New York—where the company was apparently on tour—sent to Howe at his home in Wilkes-Barre, Pennsylvania. In it, Hadley stated his opposition to the proposed situation:[30]

> Mr. Wilson is just beginning to realize that his hands will be more than full with work. In some towns, Max does not finish his settlement until after midnight. Mr. Wilson might take a longer time, and then who would pack up his stage outfit? Why I would, and cheerfully at that. At the finish of my proposed tour with Wilson, I would probably be a fit occupant for the Danville Sanitorium.

Hadley went on to say that he did not believe his contract with Howe required him to accompany such a tour, since the contract had been signed at a time when Howe had only one show. He concluded by saying, "If, owing to the contents of this letter being unsatisfactory to you, you wish to give me two weeks notice, you can do so, without incurring any feeling of resentment on my part."[31]

Howe responded in a long and patronizing letter in which he stated that Hadley's letter had revealed "a mutinous and inharmonious state of mind."[32] Reminding Hadley of his previous unsuccessful attempt to make it on his own, Howe continued:[33]

> History is repeating itself. Have you forgotten that you went through this same thing with me once before? Your outlook then was brighter than it possibly can be now and yet you know what happened. You know how you came back to me with tears in your eyes to be taken back and how I finally took you into my employ and into my confidence but lo the same evil spirit is again at work in your heart.

Never attempting to address any of Hadley's specific objections, Howe suggested only,

---

[29]Edwin J. Hadley to Lyman H. Howe, January 18, 1903.

[30]Ibid., pp. 1–2.

[31]Ibid., p. 4.

[32]Lyman H. Howe to Edwin J. Hadley, n.d., circa January 1903, p. 1.

[33]Ibid.

get some sunshine into your heart, think pleasant things . . . and develop a true blue feeling that will strengthen your manhood and my love for you.

Do not let my success worry you, but rather be glad to work for a man that is a winner.[34]

Soon afterward Hadley left Howe's show permanently. The first indication that Hadley was preparing a tour of his own came in an article which he ran in the newspaper of Howe's home town, the *Wilkes-Barre Daily News,* on July 2, 1903.[35] He announced that he had "invented an apparatus which reduces to a minimum the flutter seen in moving pictures." Listing next his credits with Colt and Howe, he stated with regard to the latter, "The public can thank Mr. Hadley for the many fine exhibitions they have witnessed in the past." Claiming he was in the moving picture business at a time when Howe was still "a phonograph exhibitor," Hadley attempted to establish his prior claim to the field.[36] This type of self-promotion to the detriment of his former employer characterized Hadley's advertising during the solo season.which followed, and began the transferal of the hard feelings between Hadley and Howe from the personal to the professional level.

By September 1903 Hadley had established his headquarters in Brooklyn and had begun to tour the same areas he had covered with Howe's show. Around September 24, 1903, the new Hadley company appeared in Gloversville, New York,[37] a town of over 20,000 (1900 census); on November 9, in LeRoy, New York[38] (population 3,144—1900 census); on November 14, in Wellsville, New York[39] (population 3,556—1900 census); on December 1, in Beaver Falls, Pennsylvania[40] (population 10,054–1900 census); on January 23, 1904, in Montpelier, Vermont[41] (population 6,266—1900 census); and around the same time in Burlington, Vermont[42] (population 18,640—1900 census). On at least two

---

[34]Ibid., p. 5.

[35]*Wilkes-Barre Daily News.*

[36]Ibid.

[37]Edwin J. Hadley to Lyman H. Howe, September 24, 1903.

[38]Hadley, advertisement for LeRoy and Wellsville.

[39]Ibid.

[40]Edwin J. Hadley, program for performance at Beaver Falls, Pennsylvania, December 1, 1903.

[41]"The Hadley Exhibit," Montpelier, Vermont, newspaper, n.d., circa January 25, 1904; and Edwin J. Hadley, newspaper advertisement for appearance at Montpelier, Vermont, January 23, 1904.

[42]"Hadley's Moving Pictures," Burlington, Vermont, newspaper, n.d., circa January 1904; and "Edwin J. Hadley Company Gives Fine Moving Picture Exhibition," Burlington, Vermont, newspaper, n.d., circa January 1904.

occasions, in Gloversville[43] and Burlington[44] (the two largest cities Hadley is known to have played that season), his show arrived in town in advance of a scheduled appearance by the Howe company. Fearing Hadley's show would take away the business he hoped to draw a few weeks later, Howe had advertisements distributed in these areas encouraging the public to wait for his, the original show. Angered by Howe's counterattack, Hadley sent a terse letter to Howe from Gloversville on September 24, 1903, which stated: "I am assisting you in advertising that Lyman H. Howe's exhibition will appear *later*. The best advertisement I ever had."[45]

Yet, as independent as he tried to seem, Hadley was still trading on the names of Colt and Howe, his credits with whom he had employed into the logo of his ads, and his advertised record of "2000 Perfect Exhibitions" must have been made almost entirely during his association with Howe. He claimed during this solo season, however, that he was projecting with "the Most Perfect and Costly Machine ever constructed," equipped with "Applied Improvements and Inventions by Mr. Edwin J. Hadley, Expert Operator and Electrician."[46] The ads also promised that "realistic sounds, true to nature, startling in their realism, accompany many of the views," made by a "sound making apparatus" which was "the most elaborate ever constructed."[47] Accompanying Hadley on tour was Mr. E. George Hedden, who, according to the advertisements, had been a member of Howe's company as well.[48] If he had accompanied the 1902–3 Howe tour, however, Hadley had not listed him among its personnel[49] unless Hedden was the man he had referred to as Max. This is possible since, on Hadley's tour, Hedden acted as both entertainer and business manager,[50] the latter position being Max's known function with Howe. It seems likely that Hadley's departure deprived Howe of at least two important members of his company. Also listed with Hadley's show are Clarence S. Weiss, booking agent, and William H. Seibel, pianist,[51] indicating a traveling crew of four, supplying Hadley with the manpower he feared he would lack with Howe.

For prices of 25, 35, and 50 cents,[52] Hadley's show delivered between two and

---

[43]Hadley to Howe, September 24, 1903.

[44]"Hadley's Moving Pictures" and "Hadley Company Gives Fine Moving Picture Exhibition," Burlington newspaper(s).

[45]Hadley to Howe, September 24, 1903.

[46]Hadley, advertisement for LeRoy and Wellsville.

[47]Ibid.

[48]Ibid.

[49]Hadley to Howe, January 18, 1903.

[50]Hadley, advertisement for LeRoy and Wellsville.

[51]Ibid.

[52]Ibid.

two-and-a-half hours of entertainment.[53] But the 1903–4 show offered a good deal less variety than the one of 1897–99. The prestidigitator and palm whistler had been replaced by Hedden, "Society Entertainer and Lecturer,"[54] who made a single appearance during the show. Seibel performed only two piano "overtures" unaccompanied by moving pictures.[55] The stereopticon views, "which elicited the wildest applause" in 1898,[56] had so declined in popularity in comparison with the moving pictures that Hadley's 1903 ad proclaimed: "Positively NO STEREOPTICON views will be shown."[57] Perhaps in response to the disrepute into which certain films had fallen by this time,[58] he also felt compelled to advertise: "Nothing to offend! Everything moral! Fun can be clean and wholesome. That's the kind of fun we present."[59] Instead of a music hall variety show, Hadley presented his audience a program of over sixty moving picture views. The variety occurred in the views themselves, which included scenes of such diverse subjects as a London dog show, a yacht race, an auto race, "broncho busting," American battleships, and a team of acrobats called "Uncle Sam and His Midgets." The views were drawn from a number of companies, including Edison, Biograph, and Lubin. Headlining the show were the famous "Rip Van Winkle" scenes with actor Joseph Jefferson. Military scenes had decreased in number from Hadley's earlier season, while travel views had begun to predominate. One section of the show, entitled "Tour of the World," promised views of England, Paris, Lucerne, Venice, Egypt, Algeria, Tunis, Abyssinia, India, Hanoi, and the Klondike[60] (the last, in fact, a view of the Fraser River Canyon in southeastern British Columbia,[61] no doubt billed by Hadley as the Klondike because of the recent gold strike there). Also shown were several story films of the children's fantasy-fairy tale type, including *The Little Match Seller* and two new Siegmund Lubin productions: *Gulliver's Travels* (c. April 28, 1903)[62]

---

[53]"Moving Pictures Pleased Audience," clipping from unknown newspaper, n.d., circa late 1903-early 1904; and "Edwin J. Hadley Company Gives Moving Picture Exhibition," Burlington newspaper.

[54]Hadley, advertisement for LeRoy and Wellsville.

[55]Hadley, program for Beaver Falls.

[56]"Successful Exhibition," *Lincoln News* (Lincoln, Ill.), October 25, 1898, quoted in Hadley, advertisement for Fort Wayne.

[57]Hadley, advertisement for LeRoy and Wellsville.

[58]Fielding, *American Newsreel*, p. 12.

[59]Hadley, advertisement for LeRoy and Wellsville.

[60]Hadley, program for Beaver Falls.

[61]Niver, *Motion Pictures from the Library of Congress Paper Print Collection*, p. 137.

[62]Howard Lamarr Walls, *Motion Pictures, 1894–1912* (Washington, D.C.: Library of Congress, 1953), p. 24.

and *The Sleeping Beauty* (c. May 1, 1903),[63] consisting of twelve scenes, the last of which was color-tinted.[64] One film called *Life of a London Fireman* may have been J. Williamson's 1901 British production, *Fire!* [65] Comedy scenes were still popular and among the many shown was Edison's *Streetcar Chivalry*.[66] The most popular film seems to have been a swashbuckler, to which Hadley claimed he had "special and exclusive" rights. The scene, entitled *The Great Sword Combat on the Stairs*, was a filmed excerpt from a contemporary play, *A Gentleman of France* by Stanley Weyman, which Hadley claimed was "especially posed for our camera by the Eminent Actor Mr. Kyrle Bellew and his Talented Company of Artists."[67] Once again, Hadley's claim is doubtful, as there is no indication that he was ever involved in the production of moving pictures. Furthermore, a contemporary brochure from the traveling American Vitagraph Company advertised the same scene.[68] Hadley's presentation of the scene was so popular that, at the Burlington performance, "the picture had to be repeated to satisfy the audience."[69]

Judging from the available clippings, Hadley's solo tour was well received. "Naturally the exhibition given by him will be compared with the great many given here by the Howe company, which has long been at the head of organizations of this character," an article in a Burlington paper commented. "And it is praise enough to say that it did not suffer by such comparison."[70] Several articles noted the absence of the flickering in the image, one Hadley claim which apparently bore some truth.[71] But he drew at least one unfavorable response with regard to his advertising. Following Hadley's December 1, 1903, appearance in Beaver Falls, Pennsylvania, J. A. Carroll, a local resident, mailed Lyman Howe a clipping of an article run by Hadley in the December 2 *Beaver Falls Daily Tribune*. In the letter which accompanied the clipping, Carroll commented:

> This is a paid advertisement and it is certainly very mean and cowardly work on the part of the Hadley company. He uses your name in his advertisments to increase his box office receipts and he knows it. . . . I

---

[63]Ibid., p. 56.

[64]Edwin J. Hadley, advertisement, n.d., circa late 1903-early 1904.

[65]Anthony Slide, *Early American Cinema* (New York: A. S. Barnes, 1970), p. 9.

[66]Niver, *Motion Pictures from the Library of Congress Paper Print Collection*, p. 137.

[67]Hadley, advertisement for LeRoy and Wellsville.

[68]American Vitagraph Company, advertisement, n.d., circa late 1903–4.

[69]"Hadley Company Gives Moving Picture Exhibition," Burlington newspaper.

[70]"Hadley's Moving Pictures," Burlington newspaper.

[71]"Moving Pictures Pleased Audience," "Edwin J. Hadley Company Gives Fine Moving Picture Exhibition," Burlington newspaper(s); "The Hadley Exhibit," Montpelier newspaper.

just enclose this clipping so you will be on your guard. I presume he leaves a trail like this in every town he visits.[72]

The article itself was simultaneously a low jab at Howe and an outlandish bit of Hadley self-promotion, which claimed that Howe had possessed "a monopoly on the moving picture business" while Hadley had been associated with him. "Now his monopoly is a shattered idol," the article continued. Hadley claimed the right to use Howe's name in his ads,

> to establish the fact that for many years he [Hadley] was the one upon whose ability the success or failure of satisfactory exhibitions depended. . . . The superior quality of Mr. Hadley's exhibition is so pronounced that he invites, rather than fears, comparison or competition, and he is not compelled to "cry baby" weeks in advance of his public appearance, and appeal to the public to wait for his exhibition to the exclusion of all others. . . .[73]

The next information available on Hadley is a program for a performance of "Mr. Edwin J. Hadley's Elite Moving Pictures," which, judging from the films being shown, appears to be from 1905 or a little later.[74] The films on the program, though not identical, resembled in type those shown by Hadley in his 1903–4 season. Notably, a wrestling scene was included and a film called *An Adventurous Automobile Trip from Paris to Monte Carlo*,[75] which seems almost certainly to have been Méliès's 1905 *An Automobile Chase.*[76] Pianist Seibel still accompanied the scenes, but Hedden was no longer with the company and his spot on the program had been filled by Mr. Harvey Kahler, "Lyric Tenor," who performed "high-class illustrated songs,"[77] indicating, perhaps, that stereopticon views had been returned to the show. Of most interest is the reduction in the number of scenes from the sixty or more shown in 1903–4 to around twenty.

An advertisement for a September 3, 1908, performance of "Edwin J. Hadley's High-Class Moving Pictures" refers to their "Semi-Annual Engagement,"[78] indicating that Hadley's company had probably begun to concentrate on a specific area in which they would make regular appearances. By this time, the emphasis of the show had shifted almost entirely to travel scenes and views

---

[72]J. A. Carroll to Lyman H. Howe, December 4, 1903.

[73]"Asks Comparison," *Beaver Falls Daily Tribune* (Beaver Falls, Pa.), December 2, 1903.

[74]Program of Edwin J. Hadley's Elite Moving Pictures, n.d., circa 1905.

[75]Ibid.

[76]Walls, *Motion Pictures, 1894–1912*, p. 4.

[77]Program of Hadley's Elite Moving Pictures.

[78]Edwin J. Hadley, advertisement for appearance, September 3, 1908.

of notable persons, with a few comic scenes to lighten the show. The number of scenes shown, however, had returned to their 1903–4 volume. At the top of Hadley's ad appear the words "Touring Europe," and the list of films included eight scenes of "Ancient and Modern Rome," five of Venice, four of King Haakon of Norway, seven "on board a modern battleship" (among which was said to be "the finest picture of Kaiser Wilhelm ever presented"), a panoramic railway view of the Riviera, an English fox hunt, King Edward and Queen Alexandra enroute to the Olympics, a German auto race, and a colored sea view.[79] Apparently by this time, the films themselves were thought to be enough for a show, as no mention was made in the advertisement of a singer or monologuist. No longer able to depend on an audience which would attend his show strictly for the novelty of seeing projected films, Hadley had begun to present views of subjects which were exotic and "newsworthy" enough in themselves to draw a crowd. The advertisement was intent on justifying the show's worth, claiming it was "the only attraction which is—Instructive as a Lecture, As Entertaining as a Concert, Realistic as a Theatrical Performance."[80]

The final piece of information discovered is an advertisement for a January 26, 1912, performance at Milton, Pennsylvania, a town of only 7,460 (1910 census). By this time called "Edwin J. Hadley Popular Travel Tours," the show had become entirely specialized in scenes of foreign countries and leaders. The 1912 program featured film of the coronation of George V and Queen Mary of England, and, in accordance with this event, devoted much of its time to views of London, one of which showed the late King Edward "as in life." The remainder of the show consisted of scenes of Paris, Germany, Russia, Switzerland, and a series of five scenes under the title of "What Roosevelt Saw in Egypt."[81] The things which had remained unchanged in the show were the presence of comic scenes and the use of sound effects, "that add so much to the realism of the views."[82] By 1910, some 10,000 motion picture theaters were operating in the United States.[83] With permanent theaters so widespread, the original function of the traveling exhibition had disappeared. To stay in business, Hadley was forced to specialize and he chose to present popular travelogues. Hadley's career provides a kind of mini-history of the traveling film exhibitor in America. Beginning in the early days, when he was literally introducing a new medium, he remained in the business during its waning period, when the success of the medium threatened the very existence of the touring exhibition. The cutthroat

---

[79]Ibid.

[80]Ibid.

[81]Edwin J. Hadley Popular Travel Tours, advertisement for appearance at Milton, Pennsylvania, January 26, 1912.

[82]Ibid.

[83]Macgowen, *Behind the Screen*, p. 129.

antagonism between Hadley and Howe indicates that unscrupulous competition characterized early film exhibition as surely as it did the better known rivalry among film producers. But most important, when films were available in the music halls of the larger cities, it was the traveling exhibitor who provided the only link for the new medium to rural America. For the people in the smaller towns, who must have awaited the moving picture show with much the same anticipation with which they awaited the circus, the exhibitor came to seem more important than those who actually made the films. It is interesting that, throughout Hadley's advertisements, the person responsible for making a film is mentioned only once, and that in the case of Edison and the war views shown during Hadley's first season. Instead, the emphasis was placed on the exhibitor himself and on the skill with which he was able to accomplish the illusion of the moving images. It was the projectionist, like Hadley, who, by actually operating the almost magical equipment, represented to his rural audiences those electrical wizards who had created the motion picture.

CHRONOLOGICAL BIBLIOGRAPHY OF SPECIAL MATERIAL

Available in Hoblitzelle Theater Arts Collection
Harry Ranson Center
University of Texas, Austin

Hadley Kinetoscope and Concert Company. Advertisement for 1899–1900 season.

Edwin J. Hadley Kinetoscope Company. Advertisement for appearance at Fort Wayne, Indiana, 2–3 February 1899.

Edwin J. Hadley. Letter to Lyman H. Howe. 18 January 1903.

Lyman H. Howe. Letter to Edwin J. Hadley. n.d., circa January 1903.

Edwin J. Hadley. Letter to Lyman H. Howe. 24 September 1903.

Edwin J. Hadley. Advertisement for appearances at LeRoy, New York, 9 November 1903, and at Wellsville, New York, 14 November 1903.

Edwin J. Hadley. Program for performance at Beaver Falls, Pennsylvania, 1 December 1903.

"Asks Comparison." *Beaver Falls* (Pennsylvania) *Daily Tribune.* 2 December 1903.

J. A. Carroll. Letter to Lyman H. Howe. 4 December 1903.

Edwin J. Hadley. Advertisement for appearance at Montpelier, Vermont, 23 January 1904.

"The Hadley Exhibit." Monteplier, Vermont newspaper. n.d., circa 25 January 1904.

"Edwin J. Hadley Company Gives Fine Moving Picture Exhibition." Burlington, Vermont newspaper. n.d., circa January 1904.

"Hadley's Moving Pictures." Burlington, Vermont newspaper, n.d., circa January 1904.

"Moving Pictures Pleased Audience." Clippings from unknown newspaper. n.d., circa late 1903–early 1904.

Edwin J. Hadley. Advertisement. n.d., circa late 1903–early 1904.

American Vitagraph Company. Advertisement. n.d., circa late 1903–1904.

Edwin J. Hadley's Elite Moving Pictures. Program n.d., circa 1905.

Edwin J. Hadley. Advertisement for appearance, 3 September 1908.

Edwin J. Hadley Popular Travel Tours. Advertisement for appearance at Milton, Pennsylvania, 26 January 1912.

ROBERT C. ALLEN

Vitascope/Cinématographe:

Initial Patterns of American Film Industrial Practice

The earliest patterns of industrial practice in American film distribution and exhibition have remained obscured by historical inattention. Gordon Hendricks's detailed studies of the invention of the Kinetograph, Kinetoscope, and Biograph leave relatively unexamined the contexts in which these initial cinematic devices were commercially exploited. In most survey histories of the American cinema, discussion of this period focuses on the Koster and Bial exhibition of the Vitascope on 23 April 1896. The reason this event is included in most chronicles of early film history is that it demonstrates the popularity of film as a vaudeville attraction. Yet missing from these histories is the integration of this single event into a systematic analysis of the early film industrial history. What causal factors led up to the Koster and Bial exhibition? What was its full significance as a precedent for the marketing of motion picture technology?

Using data collected from the contemporaneous trade press and the business records of the Vitascope Company (Raff and Gammon) and the Edison Manufacturing Company, this article considers the first year of large-scale commercial exploitation of the cinema as a projected medium: 1896–97. The two principal companies involved, the Vitascope Company (licensees of Edison) and the Lumière Company, represent divergent marketing strategies for the American cinema. The success of the Lumières and the concomitant lack of it by the Vitascope Company attest to the determining influence exerted upon early motion picture industrial practices by vaudeville.

The history of American commercial screen exhibition begins with the invention of the Kinetograph camera in the laboratories of Thomas Edison. Developed between 1887 and 1891, the Kinetograph was the camera with which "every subject known to us up to May 1896" in the United States was shot. The Kinetograph films were not projected, however, but viewed by means of a peep-show device, the Kinetoscope, which was first marketed in April 1894. During the spring and summer of that year, Kinetoscopes were installed in penny arcades, hotel lobbies, summer amusement resorts, and phonograph parlors.[1] By 1895, the Edison Company had 1) demonstrated the practicability of motion photography, 2) begun regular production of films for use in the Kinetoscope, and 3) established the commercial usefulness of the motion picture as a popular entertainment novelty.

It was not until five years after Edison had patented the Kinetograph in 1891 that his laboratory produced its own movie projector. Journalist Terry Ramsaye's widely quoted explanation for Edison's delay was that the Wizard reasoned, "If we put out a screen machine, there will be use for maybe about ten of them in the whole United States. . . . Let's not kill the goose that lays the golden egg."[2] There is reason to doubt that Edison thought in terms of the Kinetoscope as his magic goose and thus discounted the profitability of opening up motion picture exhibition to group audiences. It is much more likely that the Kinetoscope scheme was perceived as a *turkey* rather than a magic goose; records of the Edison Manufacturing Company show that its supply of golden eggs lasted but a few months. Edison probably doubted the commercial value of the Kinetoscope from the beginning, and when returns from the device began to dwindle after a brief success, he turned his attention to the myriad other projects he was working on. Even before the first Kinetoscope had been placed into commercial service, Edison wrote Eadweard Muybridge, "I have constructed a little instrument which I call a kinetograph with a nickel slot attachment and some twenty-five have been made out. I am very doubtful if there is any commercial feature in it and fear that they will not earn their cost."[3]

Ohio businessmen Norman Raff and Frank C. Gammon became exclusive American marketing agents for the Kinetoscope on 1 September 1894.[4] The following May, Raff wrote, "The demand for Kinetoscopes (during 1895) has not been enough to even pay expenses of our company. . . . In fact our candid opinion is that the Kinetoscope business—at least as far as the regular company is concerned—will be a 'dead duck' after this season."[5] Public interest in the peep show was waning, and the owners were selling their machines, further depressing the

[1]Gordon Hendricks, *The Kinetoscope* (New York: privately printed, 1966), p. 3; memo, "Kinetograph Case: 1900," Edison National Historic Site, West Orange, New Jersey (hereafter referred to as ENHS).

[2]Terry Ramsaye, *A Million and One Nights* (New York: Simon and Schuster, 1926), p. 119.

[3]Thomas Edison to Eadweard Muybridge, February 8, 1894 (ENHS).

[4]Hendricks, *Kinetoscope,* p. 79.

[5]Norman Raff to Thomas R. Lombard, May 31, 1895, Raff and Gammon Collection, Baker Library, Harvard University (R-G).

market for new Kinetoscopes.[6] To make matters worse, by May 1895, news had reached Raff and Gammon that Frenchmen Louis and Auguste Lumière had patented and publicly exhibited a camera/projector, the Cinématographe.[7]

Their Kinetoscope business a bust and the prospects of a successful commercial projector imminent, Raff and Gammon pleaded with the Edison Company to develop its own projector during the summer and fall of 1895, but to no avail. Just when the partners were trying to sell their business and cut their losses, they learned of a projector, the Vitascope, invented by two Washington, D.C., men, Thomas Armat and Francis Jenkins. In January, 1896, they concluded negotiations by which Raff and Gammon received the license to market the device on a territorial rights basis. To avoid potential patent litigation and to assure a supply of films, they also contracted for the Edison Company to manufacture the projector and provide films.[8] The marketing plan devised by Raff and Gammon for the Vitascope was based upon that initially used for the Edison phonograph. In June 1888, the North American Phonograph Company was formed for the purpose of exploiting the Edison phonograph and a competing machine, the graphophone. This company was authorized by Edison to grant exclusive territorial licenses for the lease of the phonograph and the purchase of recording cylinders. Within two years, North American had issued franchises to thirty-three state or regional companies. This territorial-rights marketing scheme was based on the assumption that the phonograph would be used primarily as a piece of office machinery: a stenographic aid. Within a short time, however, it was discovered that the phonograph, as then designed, was not particularly useful as a dictating machine. Rights holders resorted to attaching coin-in-the-slot devices to their phonographs in an effort to recoup their investment. By 1892, most phonographs were being used not in offices, but in saloons and penny arcades, a development which made the territorial rights plan outmoded.[9] Rights-holders discovered that as the demand for phonographs increased with their popularity as entertainment devices, their clients began purchasing cheap copies of the Edison machine rather than leasing the original from them.

There is no discussion of the merits of the territorial-rights marketing scheme among the Raff and Gammon correspondence; its dubious usefulness in marketing entertainment devices did not deter them from resorting to it. The scheme devised for marketing the Vitascope called for the selling of franchises in the United States and Canada. For an initial advance payment, an agent could purchase the exclusive rights to the Vitascope for a state or group of states, giving this

---

[6]Ibid.

[7]Georges Sadoul, *Louis Lumière* (Paris: Editions Seghers, 1964), p. 148.

[8]Norman Raff to Mssrs. Daniel and Armat, January 17, 1896 (R-G).

[9]Oliver Read and Walter L. Welch, *From Tin Foil to Stereo* (New York: Bobbs-Merrill, 1959), p. 110.

person the right to lease projectors (for $25–$50 monthly per machine) and buy Edison films. The manner and location of the exhibitions were left entirely to the franchise holder. The agents could exploit the Vitascope themselves, or, as Raff and Gammon repeatedly pointed out in their correspondence, the territories could be further divided and sub-franchised.[10]

The exhibition context Raff and Gammon had in mind for the Vitascope is unclear from their correspondence with prospective rights purchasers. In their initial catalogue, they suggest that a twenty-five or fifty cent admission charge could be made for a brief program of Vitascope subjects.[11] What they do not seem to have had in mind was the use of films in vaudeville theatres on a regular basis. The films were to be sold, not rented. Raff and Gammon told prospective customers that the films could be used "for a long time." With a stock of only fifteen to twenty films at the beginning of their marketing campaign, Raff and Gammon were not in a position to supply vaudeville managers with the regular change of program their audiences had come to expect. The two types of exhibition outlets Raff and Gammon envisioned for the motion picture seem to have been the penny arcade or phonograph parlor and presentations by itinerant showmen. Several people who bought territorial rights were operators of phonograph parlors. A. F. Reiser, the Vitascope agent for Pennsylvania (exclusive of Philadelphia and Pittsburgh), operated a publishing company that specialized in providing books for public libraries. If the community did not have the funds, Reiser would help them raise the money by sponsoring musical concerts. He wanted to use the Vitascope in rural Pennsylvania to assist him in these fund-raising efforts.[12]

Raff and Gammon did not aspire to a relationship with vaudeville; it was thrust upon them. The public and commercial debut of the Vitascope at Koster and Bial's Music Hall in New York on 23 April 1896 was a result of a hurriedly-made decision, arrived at in the face of news that several vaudeville managers were attempting to secure the Lumière Cinématographe for their theaters.[13] Realizing the adverse publicity value of having another machine open in New York ahead of the Vitascope, and, no doubt, the potential economic advantages of a combination between vaudeville and foreign motion picture interests, Raff on 7 April wrote to Abraham Bial, offering him the use of the Vitascope "at a largely reduced compensation," out of consideration for "a certain benefit to us from your advertising, etc."[14]

[10]Norman Raff and Frank C. Gammon to M. Hendersholt, April 4, 1896 (R-G).

[11]Vitascope Company Catalogue, 1896, Crawford Collection, Museum of Modern Art.

[12]A. F. Reiser to Edison Kinetoscope Company, February 29, 1896 (R-G).

[13]Norman Raff and Frank C. Gammon to Thomas Armat, March 21, 1896 (R-G).

[14]Norman Raff and Frank C. Gammon to Abraham Bial, April 7, 1896, (R-G).

The interest of vaudeville managers in the movies was by no means coinci-
dental. For decades, vaudeville, with its modular program of brief, self-contained
acts, had featured visual novelties of all sorts: pantomime, shadowgraphy, pup-
petry, *tableaux vivants*, and lanternry, among others. By 1896, vaudeville was
rapidly becoming the preeminent American popular entertainment form, with
competition among theaters growing intense—especially in New York. Two seasons before (1894–95), New York vaudeville managers had begun an all-out
battle for patronage. F. F. Proctor presented opera stars at his Twenty-Third
Street Theater. B. F. Keith countered by securing the stage luminaries to appear in
condensed dramatic vehicles at his Union Square Theater. The warfare intensified when Oscar Hammerstein opened his Olympia Theater in the fall of 1895,
importing French chanteuse Yvette Guilbert at a cost of $3,000 per week.[15] By
April 1896, the five major New York vaudeville entrepreneurs were frantically
trying to surpass each other with more lavish theater environments, more acts on
the bills, and especially, novel attractions. It was perhaps the most auspicious
moment in the history of vaudeville for the introduction of a new visual curiosity.

Raff and Gammon, however, were much less interested in providing vaudeville with its latest sensation than in generating publicity on the eve of distributing
the first Vitascopes to the state-rights holders. The Koster and Bial exhibition was
preceded by three weeks of press coverage, beginning with a press screening at
the West Orange Laboratory of Thomas Edison on 3 April.[16]

The only thing Edison had contributed to the development of the Vitascope
was the imprimatur of his name, yet Raff and Gammon promoted the projector as
the latest marvel from the Wizard's workshop—a ruse which, no doubt, was
largely responsible for the generous publicity given the Vitascope.

The second purpose of the Koster and Bial exhibition was to attempt to
preempt foreign competition. In this, Raff and Gammon failed for several reasons:
1) it was already too late; 2) by demonstrating that the motion picture could be
adapted successfully to form a vaudeville act, they helped to spawn a demand
from vaudeville managers which benefitted not only them but also the exploiters
of other machines; and 3) the tremendous demand for motion picture demonstrations which arose after the Koster and Bial exhibition was premature for Raff
and Gammon—they were not able to satisfy it, leaving a growing market ripe for
competition.

Despite Raff and Gammon's assurances to actual and prospective franchise
holders that they would be protected from competing projectors entering the
market, competition with the Vitascope developed almost immediately. In May,
the Lumière Cinématographe opened at Keith's Union Square Theater, where for
several weeks each performance was "wildly applauded."[17] Even with New York

---

[15]Maxwell F. Marcuse, *This Was New York* (New York: Carlton Press, 1965), p. 199.

[16]*New York Journal*, April 4, 1896, clipping (R-G).

[17]*Dramatic Mirror*, July 4, 1896, p. 17; July 11, p. 17; July 18, p. 17.

sweltering in a June heat wave, the Cinématographe enabled the Union Square to double its weekly box office receipts.[18]

During the summer and fall of 1896, Raff and Gammon's Vitascope Company fared badly. Their first problem was that their marketing strategy militated against a strong connection between vaudeville and the Vitascope in that their state-based franchise plan conflicted with the institutional structure of vaudeville. By 1896, vaudeville was in a period of inter-state circuit building—growth which ignored the political boundaries at the very basis of the Raff and Gammon scheme. Unlike other vaudeville acts, the Vitascope could be booked only into a circuit of theatres with great difficulty. Separate deals had to be negotiated with rights holders in each state. The state-rights arrangements explains why no franchises were sold to vaudeville circuits. The Lumières, on the other hand, used no such territorial plan. All engagements for the Cinématographe in the United States were booked through a single New York office.

Secondly, even before the Koster and Bial exhibition, Raff and Gammon had begun making commitments to their agents on delivery of Vitascopes. But Raff and Gammon could not control the manufacture of the machines at the Edison factory, and late deliveries were a problem almost from the start.[19]

Even prompt delivery of the projector did not assure that the Vitascope would be able to debut as advertised. The Vitascope arrived at Ford's Theater in Baltimore the day of its scheduled opening. The manager had sold out his house long in advance. But when the electrician sent along to set up the Vitascope saw that the house electricity operated on alternating current and the projector on direct, he refused to install the machine. The franchise-holder, who had arranged the exhibition with the theater manager, blamed the problem on the ineptitude of the electrician, but the problem was in the design of the Vitascope:[20] all the early Vitascopes were made to work only on direct current, and in 1896, municipal lighting systems were a hodge-podge of incompatible currents and voltages. Throughout the summer and fall, exasperated Vitascope agents complained to Raff and Gammon about the situation, the agent for the Maritime Provinces writing, "If the small towns of the continent are to be worked, a radical change will have to be made in the construction of the machines so that exhibitions can be utterly independent of electric power companies." Otherwise, he said, "It is simply working for nothing."[21] The Cinématographe needed no electrical current, being hand-cranked and illuminated by limelight or another nonelectrical source.[22]

---

[18]Robert Grau, *Theatre of Science* (New York: Broadway, 1914), p. 9.

[19]A. F. Reiser to Norman Raff and Frank C. Gammon, May 8, 1896 (R-G).

[20]P. T. Kiefaber to Norman Raff, June 11, 1896 (R-G).

[21]A. Holland to Norman Raff, September 9, 1896 (R-G).

[22]Sadoul, *Lumière*, p. 67.

While Raff and Gammon provided a trained projectionist to set up and operate the Vitascope for early exhibitions at Koster and Bial's, they offered no such assistance to their agents, only "detailed instructions" on the operation of the machine. In many instances, the success of a Vitascope exhibition depended far less on the projector itself than on the skill of its operator.[23] The most serious obstacle facing the Vitascope agents, and, in turn, Raff and Gammon, was obtaining a regular supply of new films. The franchise holders needed to be able to count on regular shipments of new films whose contents were as appealing as those of the Lumière films. Raff and Gammon's inability to meet this demand resulted in a rising chorus of frustration and anger from their agents. The Pennsylvania franchise holder chided them, "the museum people were so much disappointed that they stopped the Vitascope. They expected eight new subjects and I only had three and they were poor."[24] The Wisconsin agents wrote in August, "It seems singular to us that our orders are so long about being filled. We are not safe in promising anything.... With ... the cinématographe and others menacing us, we ought to be accomodated [sic] promptly."[25]

The design of the Cinématographe gave it a considerably wider range of subject matter than the Edison camera. The latter, still called the Kinetograph, was a bulky, electrically driven apparatus weighing several hundred pounds.[26] The production situation devised for its operation was the famous Black Maria open-air studio behind the Edison works in West Orange. The principal components of the Edison repertoire were condensations of vaudeville turns, circus acts, and minute extracts from popular plays. These reenactments had limited popular appeal, however, and there is evidence that their popularity as Kinetoscope peep-show subjects had begun to decline even before the Vitascope appeared.[27]

The Lumière Cinématographe was both camera and projector, hand-cranked, and weighed slightly over sixteen pounds. The Lumières sent cameramen all over the world and could offer their patrons scenes of the Czar's coronation, Venice as seen from a moving gondola, and Trafalgar Square. These travel films were so popular that in August 1896, Raff and Gammon resorted to having the English agents for the Vitascope surreptitiously purchase Lumière films shot in Russia, Italy, and France for use with the Vitascope in the United States.[28] Also with camera/projector/printer in one, the Lumière operator could take, develop, and show films while on tour. The ability to take these "local actualities," as they were

---

[23]Hixom and Wollam to Norman Raff and Frank C. Gammon, June 23, 1896 (R-G).

[24]A. F. Reiser to Norman Raff and Frank C. Gammon, undated but filed with 1896 letters (R-G).

[25]Hixom and Wollam to the Vitascope Company, August 28, 1896 (R-G).

[26]Sadoul, *Lumière*, p. 41.

[27]Hendricks, *Kinetoscope*, p. 140.

[28]Norman Raff and Frank C. Gammon to Maguire and Baucus, August 25, 1896 (R-G).

called, was of no small benefit to the Lumières. It also speaks to fundamental differences in business organization between the Lumières and the Vitascope Company—differences that gave the Lumières significant advantage in the vaudeville market.

Raff and Gammon had control over only one part of the Vitascope operation. The Edison factory manufactured the machines and films; these were distributed by Raff and Gammon, who did not engage themselves in exhibition, but often sold off parts of their territory to others. As the Raff and Gammon correspondence shows, the route from source of supply to its final destination could be, and too often was, a long and uncertain one. Exhibition was separated from production by distance, business and legal arrangements, and technology—the Vitascope was not able (without substantial and illegal modifications) to serve as a camera.

With the Cinématographe, although the distance from the Lyons factory to the exhibition site in the United States was certainly greater, this problem was alleviated to a large extent by the collapsing of some of the functions of filmmaker, distributor, exhibitor, and projectionist into a single individual: the "operator" sent out from Lyons to tour in the United States. Felix Mesguisch, the first Lumière operator to arrive in the United States, stated that in the first six months of exploitation there were some twenty-one projectionists/cameramen/developers on tour with the Cinématographe.[29] The Lumière representative in New York was an employee of the Lumière Company, not a rights speculator. He arranged for exhibitions, scheduled tours, and distributed films to the operators, acting very much like the booking agent for a vaudeville act. The operator with his Cinématographe and films was not *like* a vaudeville act, he *was* one—a self-contained unit which could travel an interstate circuit as easily as an acrobat or trained dog act.

The marketing scheme for the Vitascope failed because it did not anticipate the use of the motion picture as a popular entertainment device exhibited in a theatrical setting. Moreover, the territorial rights plan could not be easily adapted to the institutional structure of vaudeville. All the blame for the demise of the Vitascope Company cannot be attributed to the unsuitability of its marketing plan, however. Certainly design limitations of the Vitascope itself contributed to Raff and Gammon's troubles. Another part of the problem was Raff and Gammon's desire to reap short-term profits through rights speculation rather than engaging in exhibition themselves. Edison's lack of foresight regarding the motion picture is well known, and the Edison Manufacturing Company did its share toward placing the Vitascope in an impossible position within the vaudeville exhibition market. Films were slow in being delivered, and the subjects prepared at West Orange were unsuitable for urban vaudeville performances. Clearly Edison did not anticipate the relationship between vaudeville and film.

---

[29]Sadoul, *Lumière*, p. 134.

He did see, however, that Raff and Gammon's attempt to market the Vitascope was a failure. Thus, when the Edison laboratory developed its own projector, the Projecting Kinetoscope, Edison sold the machine outright with no territorial restrictions. He further undercut Raff and Gammon by selling films for the Projecting Kinetoscope at a lower price than Raff and Gammon were offering to their Vitascope customers.[30] Raff and Gammon's agreement with Edison and Armat prohibited their selling the Vitascope, and they had sold the rights to it for most of the United States for five years. By the end of 1896, the Vitascope enterprise was no more.

Clearly, the Lumière operation was better adapted to servicing the American vaudeville market, but their victory was short-lived. In the spring of 1897, the Lumières left the American market, presumably under the threat of patent litigation from Edison.[31] But they left behind them a pattern of industrial practice that survived for the next decade: the providing of vaudeville theaters with a complete "act" consisting of projector, films, and operator. This marketing plan formed the basis for much of the success by the Edison and Vitagraph film companies prior to 1905.

The Lumière approach to marketing we might call "pre-industrial." The Lumières, Biograph, and Vitagraph were providing a service to vaudeville. This dependency upon vaudeville temporarily obviated the need for the American cinema to develop its own exhibition outlets, but it also prevented film from achieving industrial autonomy. The industrial structure of vaudeville did not call for a division of labor in the usual sense. Rather, the division came within the vaudeville presentation itself: each act was merely one of eight or more functional units, one cog in the vaudeville machine. Hence it is not surprising that a machine would quite literally replace the acrobat, animal act, or magician on vaudeville bills. Neither did the use of films in vaudeville require a division of the industry into distinct production, distribution, and exhibition units. In fact, it favored the collapsing of these functions into the "operator," who, with his projector, became the self-contained vaudeville act. It was not until the American cinema achieved industrial autonomy with the advent of storefront movie theatres that a clear separation of functions becomes the dominant mode of industrial organization, and film enters its early industrial phase.

---

[30]A. F. Reiser to Vitascope Company, November 24, 1896; Hixom and Wollam to Norman Raff and Frank C. Gammon, December 9, 1896 (both R-G).

[31]Sadoul, *Lumière*, pp. 135-36.

ALAN WILLIAMS

The Lumière Organization and "Documentary Realism"

The work of the Lumière organization occupies an important but as yet underdefined position in the history of cinema in general and that of documentary film in particular. In cinema history, the Lumières' work is generally taken to mark the beginnings of the medium as we now define it, its "prehistory" ending with the Edison Kinetoscope. In documentary film, their work marks another beginning; Eric Barnouw entitles his treatment of this topic "Prophet."[1] And yet, the Lumières' priority in purely technical or chronological terms is difficult to establish and has been the subject of vituperative, generally pointless debate. For example, it is clear that they were *not* the first to exhibit animated photographic images projected from strips of celluloid upon a screen before a paying audience. (The cumbersomeness of this formulation speaks volumes for the difficulties involved in such a judgment.) This distinction probably belongs to Max Skladanowsky, who exhibited his Bioskop to much acclaim in Berlin beginning November 1, 1895—almost two months before the commercial debut of the Cinématographe in Paris at the Grand Café.[2] Nor had the Lumières satisfactorily solved all or even the most important of the complex mechanical difficulties involved in projecting animated photographs. Many contemporary reports

---

[1] Eric Barnouw, *Documentary* (New York: Oxford University Press, 1974).

[2] Unless otherwise noted, such details as these are based on vol. 1 of Jacques Deslandes's remarkable *Histoire comparée du cinéma*, 5 vols. (vols. 3–5 in process; Tournai, Belgium: Casterman, 1966). [Firm evidence indicates that the Eidoloscope screened motion picture film at the Olympic Theatre in Chicago the week of August 26, 1895. See Marshall A. Deutelbaum, ed., *"Image": On the Art and Evolution of the Film* (New York: Dover, 1979), p. 21, col. 1—GP.]

reveal that the machine's lack of precise registration was apparent even to relatively untutored eyes.[3]

Thus there is the possibility of all sorts of arguments about who "invented the cinema." Nonetheless, the Lumières do have a clear position in film history, but it seems likely that this is best defined in financial and organizational terms, rather than technological ones. More precisely, technical competence was necessary but not sufficient to their success. Even if some sort of priority could be established for the Cinématographe, it was far from the only apparatus of its kind under development in 1894–95. But the Lumières clearly *are* the fitting successors to Edison in that they, unlike Skladanowsky, William Paul, or Armat and Jenkins, had sufficient capital, contacts, and entrepreneurial skills to market their machinery with success. Beaumont Newhall's compact formulation seems the best judgment: that the Cinématographe was "the first projector to meet with instant success."[4] But entrepreneurial skill and adequate capital do not exist as pure essences. The Lumière organization's resources (in the broadest sense of the term, including contacts with the press and the scientific establishment of their day) occupied a specific historical position; not all options were open to them in launching the commercial career of their machine. How this was so, I will maintain, has a great deal to do with their other distinction in film history, that of being the "prophets" of documentary cinema.

Success breeds imitation. Edison's film subjects (with the notable exception of *Fred Ott's Sneeze*, which was not intended for commercial exploitation)[5] were, generally speaking, vaudeville numbers. Skladanowsky followed suit with his Berlin program (among the films: *Italian Peasant Dance, The Juggler*, etc.), as did William Paul in his post-Grand Café programs in London. Paul's greatest critical success, however, was a view of the ocean, doubtless inspired by the already celebrated and clearly financially viable Lumière works.[6] Lumière influences can likewise be seen in the programs of subsequent exhibitors, mixed in seemingly indiscriminate fashion with Edison-style vaudeville turns. The Lumière organization had "created" (if one can use the term in this manner) a filmic genre. In the midst of theatre, there was "real life"—or, rather, there was *photography*, in the

---

[3]In at least one case this has been deliberately obscured. It is altogether characteristic that Georges Sadoul omits with no indication whatever (!) the comments on registration difficulties of the apparatus from his seemingly complete citation of Janssen's famous comments at Lyon in praise of the Cinématographe. Compare Sadoul, *Louis Lumière* (Paris: Seghers, 1964), pp. 116–17, with Deslandes's citation, *Histoire comparée* 1:227.

[4]Beaumont Newhall, *History of Photography*, rev. ed. (New York: Museum of Modern Art, 1964), p. 91.

[5]Gordon Hendricks, *The Edison Motion Picture Myth* (Berkeley: University of California Press, 1961).

[6]John Barnes, *The Beginnings of the Cinema in England* (London: David and Charles, 1976), pp. 94–99.

sense that their subjects were recognizably those of nineteenth-century "amateur" photography. Many years later, John Grierson saw this state of affairs as perfectly "natural":

> When Lumière turned his first historic strip of film, he did so with the fine careless rapture which attends the amateur effort today. The new moving camera was still, for him, a camera and an instrument to focus on the life about him. He shot his own workmen filing out of the factory and this first film was a "documentary." He went on naturally to shoot the Lumière family, child complete. The cinema, it seemed for a moment, was about to fulfill its natural destiny of discovering mankind.[7]

In treating his camera as if it were "still, for him, a camera," Louis Lumière used it as would a manufacturer in a major French city of the late nineteenth century—that is, he made an industrial publicity photograph. And so Grierson is more right than he admits in labeling the film a "documentary." *Workers Leaving the Lumière Factory* not only records life, it does so with a purpose, and the film is the first example of a notable nonfiction subgenre, the industrial publicity film.

The other early Lumière works, even when incorporating protofictional elements (*Watering the Gardener, The Chess Game*) were similarly prophetic in their choice of settings and themes. There is an entire thematics of the Lumière *oeuvre* that prefigures much in later nonfiction film. One task that awaits serious Lumière criticism is the categorization of subjects and filmic strategies. For example, three large categories would be (1) work and related activities (*Tearing Down a Wall*, but also *Watering the Gardener* and even in a sense *Feeding the Baby*); (2) ritual/ceremony (the countless military or governmental displays but also *The Sack Race* and other "happy worker" films, as well as the early film of debarking congress members); and (3) travel, most frequently with emphasis on physical transport (*Gondola Party, Arrival of a Train*, etc.). There would be other shorter lived (for the Lumières) groupings, such as "family portraits," perhaps a subcategory of ceremonials.

One thing any such breakdown would help to illustrate would be the debt the films owe to the subjects and styles of nineteenth-century still photography.[8] This is a characteristic the Lumière works most definitely do not share with those of the Edison organization, and it is probably the sense in which Grierson finds the Lumière approach to be "natural." And yet, if this was so "natural" then why does the Lumière films' very *uniqueness* seem tied up so inextricably with this choice of subjects and approach? And might it not be "natural" that there be some

---

[7]John Grierson, *Grierson on Documentary*, ed. Forsyth Hardy (New York: Praeger, 1971), p. 199.

[8]Though it seems murky to me, Sadoul's discussion of Louis Lumière as filmmaker offers helpful comments on the matter.

connection between the "documentary" subjects of the Lumières and their extraordinary commercial success? Papa Lumière, of course, had been a modestly successful portrait photographer, exploiting the newly created market for bourgeois family memorabilia. The family wealth came from success in the mass manufacture of photographic supplies. But what is mass manufactured must be mass marketed, and the diffusion of Lumière products was dependent on, among other factors, an entire publicity machine tied into the newly created publications such as the *Moniteur de la photographie*, as well as the flourishing "popular science" press of the day. Not only was there a family tradition of still photography that would have influenced Louis Lumière in his first filmmaking essays, there was, more to the point, a ready-made publicity apparatus that he must have already known how to exploit. The Lumière organization seems to have been as aware as Edison was of the value of publicity in launching a new commercial enterprise.

In order to understand the Lumière strategy, we must keep in mind its probable goals. The cinema was one invention among many at the end of the nineteenth century. The principal problem of any publicity campaign for such a device must certainly have been obtaining sufficient media coverage. Jacques Deslandes has pointed out that, for example, the industrial amusements journal *L'Industriel du forain* paid cinema almost no attention in its first years but saw, on the other hand, great potential in x rays. These and other "wonders of science" (like the phonograph, launched some years before but still marketable at fairgrounds and the like) made the cinema seem almost tame by comparison— particularly since animated *drawings* projected on a screen had been exhibited for some time, and toys like the zoetrope were well known. On the other hand, the specialized scientific and photographic press presented a different sort of problem. The cinema was not an "invention" as the phonograph or x rays were; rather it was a matter of bringing together existing mechanisms in a workable fashion.[9] That this could be done had already been demonstrated by Muybridge and Marey (who both had developed early projection systems). So it is not surprising that serious contemporary assessments were sometimes harsh. Thus the English journal *Photographic Work* responded to the Kinetoscope:

> The exhibition of Mr. Edison's kinetoscope in London is disappointing, as when it is announced that Mr. Edison has "invented" something, we at least expect that he will carry refinement, completeness and perfection of construction a long way beyond what has previously been

---

[9]Louis Lumière's great innovation was to borrow an industrial analogue to solve the problem of intermittent motion. Not surprisingly, given the relative sophistication of the European garment industry of the day, he found the mechanism he needed in a common sewing-machine design. The problems of moving cloth and film, he saw, were similar in the two machines. This is certainly one of the high-water marks of nineteenth-century bricolage.

done. Mr. Edison should, perhaps, rather rank as a careful and laborious constructor than as inventor.[10]

What is crucial in all of this for the Lumières is that it was precisely this sort of publication to which they had most immediate access for publicity purposes. It would have clearly been necessary to procede carefully and methodically (to insure positive reactions); it would also have seemed beneficial to test the machine in "sneak previews" (the equivalent of trying out a play in New Haven). And this, in fact, is what they did.

Between the first known public showing of the Cinématographe in Paris on March 22, 1895, at the *Société d'Encouragement à l'Industrie Nationale* and the beginnings of commercial exploitation at the Grand Café on December 28, 1895, there is a gap of over nine months. Although technical problems, specifically a shortage of film stock, account for some of this delay—but no more than two-and-a-half months, since by June 10 they could show eight films and produce two more "on the spot"—the bulk of this period must be ascribed to a well-known capitalist dictum: to launch a new product it is crucial to create a *demand* for it. Jacques Deslandes appears to be the only writer on the subject to have classified what the Lumières did as a marketing strategy; the chapter of his book on the Lumières' first efforts makes worthwhile reading for anyone tempted to see the Cinématographe's success as solely the result of its technical merits (though these are obviously not negligible). Because Deslandes's work is not as well known as it deserves, and because he is reluctant to go much beyond his carefully documented facts, it is worth retelling and commenting upon this, the first truly inspired hype job in the history of cinema, most particularly since this will shed much light on the types of films that were required.

The Lumières took their machine on what can easily be described as the scientific equivalent of the talk-show circuit of their day—photographic congresses in Lyon and Brussels, a demonstration for the popular science monthly *La Revue Générale des Sciences*, conferences of learned societies. They chose, in other words, the "wonder of science" option for marketing their appartus. Did they have any choice in the matter? Possibly, but it is hard to imagine their abandoning such a familiar and clearly workable set of tactics. But the "scientific" status of the Cinématographe, even in a very restricted sense, was not at all certain. Thus, not at all coincidentally, the machine made its debuts as one-half of a double bill benefiting from a clever and doubtless planned sort of prestige-by-association. In the fixed, standardized (to judge by reports)[11] presentation that they had established from the very first show in March, the Cinématographe shared the

---

[10]Quoted in Barnes, *Beginnings of the Cinema in England,* p. 14.

[11]I base this judgment on accounts quoted by Deslandes, *Histoire comparée,* and (with some trepidation) Sadoul, *Louis Lumière,* and Maurice Bessy and Giuseppi Lo Duca, *Louis*

stage—shared the same *screen*—with another Lumière project, color photography (still images). It is easy enough to assume that the desired result of this juxtaposition was exactly that provided by Leon Vidal in—where else?—*Le Moniteur de la Photographie:* "The prestige of movement triumphs over that of color."[12] The double billing of movement with color doubtless also had the effect of planting the suggestion that if color was lacking in the Cinématographe's moving images, the Lumières were working on the problem. These early shows might therefore account for the otherwise bizarre report cited by Deslandes that the Lumière views at the Grand Café were projected "life size, in color."[13]

Needless to say, the Lumières' experiments with color photography were little advanced in 1895; they clearly provided, however, a most useful complement for the ruminations provoked by the Cinématographe, placing it squarely within the larger, implied project of "reproducing life." They also serve to underline what is probably most important for the question of the Lumière "documentary" impulse—that the audience to whom these early demonstrations were directed would scarcely have been impressed by Edison-style vaudeville turns. These were images fit to make the apparatus suitable for contemplation by a bourgeois, *sérieux*, technically informed public. This public was presumed to be interested in the question of the "realism" of the images, though certainly *not for the sake of the subjects represented* but for the demonstration they afforded of "scientific" interest and technical virtuosity. In choosing to publicize their machine through channels already available to them as manufacturers of photographic products and as technocratically-inclined, "scientific" industrialists, the Lumières could have little choice, in retrospect, but so-called "documentary" images. But what was documented was the work of the apparatus itself.

At the Lyon Congress (in June, when the full complement of films first was screened) the Lumières inaugurated another practice later to be associated with nonfiction filmmaking. They made what Deslandes and others have called the first "newsreels" (*actualités*). Here, the connection between subject matter and publicity project is, if one wishes to see it, completely clear. It is, in fact, deliciously crass. Louis Lumière filmed congress members disembarking from an excursion boat (non-workers leaving an anti-factory) and also the celebrated scientist (and, not at all coincidently, inspirer of Marey's early researches into motion photography) Pierre-Jules-César Janssen in conversation with a colleague. These two films they projected the next evening at the final session of the congress, thus impressing on the delegates the extraordinary capabilities of their machine—

Lumière, Inventeur (Paris: Prisma, 1948). The color slides came first, followed by a spoken bridge to the new topic, then the films (always, apparently, in the same order after the Lyon conference).

[12]Deslandes, *Histoire comparée* 1:225.

[13]Ibid., p. 277.

doubly extraordinary, doubtless, thanks to the implicit flattery of being made subjects of one of its first films. It is somehow remarkable that film historians have reported this clever publicity coup solely as "documentary" event. It would indeed be interesting to check provincial newspapers and magazines for the participants' reports of the congress (standard practice in the press of the day). We do know of the biggest payoff of this gimmick, however. Pierre-Jules-César Janssen gave an impressive boost to the Cinématographe's public career in remarks made after seeing his own noble image on the screen, calling the Lumière demonstrations the "big event of this session." These remarks were reprinted in the widely read *Bulletin de la Société Française de Photographie*.

And so on. This elaborate and admirable publicity campaign, the first in the history of the medium (Edison's efforts, outlined in Gordon Hendricks's book, seem crude and unsystematic by comparison) is important for a number of reasons. First, it goes a long way to explaining the Lumières' success, both financially and in film histories (which are written, of course, largely from journalistic sources such as those exploited by the Lumières with such virtuosity). Second, the films used for the publicity buildup were those exhibited at the Grand Café. The subjects, although certainly well received by the Parisian spectators who finally paid to see them, were first employed to impress a quite specific audience, one that the Lumières already knew well, and to impress them in a manner that largely dictated the films' content and style. Third, any successful marketing and publicity endeavor rests on a certain crucial measure of continuity. The style and subject matter of the first Lumière programs was inevitably carried over into later ones. The importance of an exploitable "brand loyalty" to the Lumières' project may be seen already in the fact that their "first" film, *Workers Leaving the Lumière Factory*, was also the first "remake" in the history of cinema. When the first negative was no longer usable, this subject was reshot, as literally as possible—clearly for the continued exploitation of its established publicity value. Later subjects were likewise duplicated, though not so slavishly (hence the agonizingly endless series of military horsemen, etc.) and doubtless for the more general purpose of conserving a "Lumière look" in programs that nonetheless had to show a certain measure of renewal. (There is also the well known maxim that one does not tamper with success!)

But I do not mean in these remarks to dismiss the Lumière project or solely to begin its "demystification." It strikes me that the Lumières are more interesting and certainly more historically accessible figures when viewed as talented entrepreneurs rather than as minor gods or "prophets." After all, when all this is said, they are still prophets, though what they prophesy must be evaluated in a different fashion than has been done up to now. It was, in a sense, "natural" that the Lumières made the films that they made—but only if one takes "natural" to mean an inspired and appropriate (hence financially viable) response to real historical circumstances. It also seems to me that conceiving of the Lumière project in the manner I have suggested here might eventually allow a consideration of their "realistic" images in the context of a larger problematic of mimesis. Perhaps Roland Barthes's celebrated dictum is appropriate:

> Thus, realism (badly named, at any rate often badly interpreted) consists not in copying the real but in copying a (depicted) copy of the real: This famous *reality,* as though suffering from a fearfulness which keeps it from being touched directly, is *set farther away,* postponed.[14]

A POSTSCRIPT ON TECHNOLOGICAL DETERMINISM

This paper was originally delivered at the Spring 1980 meeting of the Society for Cinema Studies. In the discussion that followed, a problem of cinema history emerged that deserves some examination here. Briefly put: aren't the subjects of the early Lumière films more economically and forcefully explained by the very nature of the portable Lumière camera than by the argument presented above? Certainly the differences between the Lumière equipment and that of the Edison organization are striking. The Lumière camera was light and mounted on a tripod; the Edison machinery was bulky and too heavy for a single operator to move. And so the argument can be made that a sort of technological pressure is exerted by these two physical configurations, and that the Lumière organization could more readily adapt to "documentary" subjects. The Edison "Black Maria" was, in fact, designed with limited stage-show subjects in mind—as a glance at any photograph of it will confirm.

This point is clearly relevant to my argument. But technological factors do not exist in a historical vacuum. We know from film history that the Lumière camera quickly became the model for equipment used in *fiction* filmmaking. Its portability and flexibility, while necessary to the kind of "documentary" subjects discussed here, is for this reason obviously not sufficient to guarantee the emergence of these subjects. The Lumières themselves made fiction films (dismal commercial failures, it should be stressed) a few years after the works discussed here. Equally important, the Edison equipment, cumbersome as it initially was (though this was quickly changed, presumably with the Lumière equipment as one influence), was on occasion taken out of its studio shell for "outdoor" subjects.

And so the argument I have outlined in these pages is at the least a necessary supplement to any thesis about the equipment of early cinema and what it was best adapted to record. Furthermore, it can be argued that the equipment design of the Edison and Lumière companies was itself a logical outgrowth of material,

---

[14]Roland Barthes, *S/Z* (New York: Hill and Wang, 1974), p. 55.

historical factors. The two organizations existed in radically different economic climates. Edison, to make the most important point first, had little trouble getting bank financing for any extensive mass distribution scheme. The obvious model for the kinetoscope was the phonograph, and the Edison marketing effort in both was directed (initially) at the mass marketing of equipment, both hardware and software. This was only possible with ready access to adequate capital, as it involved factories to produce the goods, channels of distribution for them, advertising, etc. The Lumières, on the contrary, worked in what is generally considered an economically "primitive" environment. Banks in nineteenth-century France made few loans to industrial concerns, and charged high interest rates for what little capital they did advance for product development and marketing.[15] The Lumières, like most of their French contemporaries in business, were limited to autofinancing of an effort handled almost completely within a small family business.[16]

The French firm's celebrated decision not to sell or license their equipment but to exploit it themselves with the limited means at their disposal—thus emphasizing exhibition as opposed to Edison's focus on profits from sales—is thus a response to this socioeconomic imperative. With this in mind, the differences in equipment make perfect sense. Louis Lumière designed a machine that would take, print, and also project films (with only a slight adjustment of the shutter mechanism). The machine was in all ways, of which portability was only one aspect, adapted to the needs of an organization with limited capital and manpower. Papa Lumière's comment that the cinema was an invention with "no future" was apt, from the perspective of the family business. The Lumières created and, within a few years, then dismantled an organizational structure for the intensive exploitation of their product. The machine itself was part and parcel of this effort. It was left to the Americans and to the next generation of French industrial firms, operating as they did on a largely new financial basis (in France), to use Lumière-inspired machinery while abandoning the "documentary impulse" that made it known, for a time, as the very model of Cinema.

---

[15]See Theodore Zeldin, *France, 1848–1945,* 2 vols., (Oxford: Oxford University Press, 1973 and 1977), for an overview and references.

[16]Even so, they did have to form one significant alliance with another French firm to assure access to film stock. Their difficulties in this, as recounted by Deslandes, are symptomatic of the prevailing industrial climate.

ROBERT C. ALLEN

Motion Picture Exhibition in Manhattan, 1906–1912:

Beyond the Nickelodeon

On June 19, 1905, on Smithfield Street in Pittsburgh, a vaudeville entrepreneur, Harry Davis, and his partner, John P. Harris, opened a theatre devoted to the showing of motion pictures. Audiences on that opening night sat in seats salvaged from a defunct opera house and, for their five-cent admission charge, watched *The Great Train Robbery* unroll on the screen to piano accompaniment.[1] There was little more to the performance. The Nickelodeon, as the theatre was called, could boast only ninety-six chairs, a piano, projector, and screen. Yet, with the possible exception of Koster and Bial's Music Hall, the Nickelodeon Theatre is the most famous theatre in which motion pictures were shown prior to 1914. It was here, according to most film historians, that movies in America entered a new era. Inside this dingy little storefront and the thousands like it which, we are told, sprang up in the wake of its success, the motion picture found its own exclusive exhibition outlet and a new audience of working-class Americans. The movies had outgrown their role as minor adjuncts to vaudeville performances, and, while the middle-class patrons of variety snubbed their noses at this upstart amusement, the nickelodeon proceeded to revolutionize American mass entertainment in only a few years' time.[2]

Most students of American film history are familiar with the descriptions of nickelodeons in secondary sources. "Concentrated largely in poorer shopping

---

[1]Eugene L. Connelly, "The Life Story of Harry Davis," *Pittsburgh Sun-Telegraph,* January 3, 1940; Alexander Parker, "Fifty Years Ago," *Box Office,* June 4, 1955, pp. 20–21.

[2]See Benjamin Hampton, *A History of the Movies* (New York: Covici, Friede, 1931), pp. 44–48; Lewis Jacobs, *The Rise of the American Film* (New York: Harcourt, Brace, 1939), pp. 55–57; Robert Sklar, *Movie-Made America* (New York: Random House, 1975), pp. 14–20, 30–32; Garth Jowett, *Film: The Democratic Art* (Boston: Little, Brown, 1975), pp. 31–42.

districts and slum neighborhoods," writes Jacobs, "nickelodeons were disdained by the well-to-do. But the workmen and their families who patronized the movies did not mind the crowded, unsanitary, and hazardous accommodations most of the nickelodeons offered."[3] Sklar locates the nickelodeons ("crowded, dark, and smelly rooms") in working-class neighborhoods and says their programs of films and illustrated songs "lasted no more than fifteen or twenty minutes."[4] Hampton also describes nickelodeons as "crowded, poorly ventilated" places in which film programs lasting approximately twenty minutes were given.[5] North places the nickelodeons mostly "in big industrial cities with large foreign populations of poorly paid laborers."[6] Sklar and other film historians maintain that a large portion of the nickelodeon audience was made up of newly-arrived immigrants. He notes, "what was distinctive about the movies as they entered their second decade . . . was their success in providing entertainment and information to an audience that did not need English or even literacy to gain access to urban popular culture for the first time."[7]

While both Sklar and Jowett go into more detail on the nature of early film exhibition than previous historians, we still know relatively little about this crucial stage in the development of the American film industry. As Russell Merritt has put it, "The nickelodeon era, for the most part, has been ignored in the current literature of film history."[8] We have yet to answer the following questions: Were nickelodeons located exclusively in working-class neighborhoods? Did immigrants form a large portion of the nickelodeon's audience? How long was the nickelodeon the primary form of motion picture exhibition? Did exhibition patterns vary from city to city and/or between urban and rural areas? How do we explain the alleged nickelodeon "explosion": the establishment of as many as 7,000–10,000 nickelodeons in a two or three year period?

Recent studies by Merritt and Gomery have cast doubt upon the characterization of early motion picture exhibitions as taking place in "crowded, dark, and smelly rooms." Merritt found that in Boston nickelodeons were located along busy commercial thoroughfares, rather than in working-class residential areas. He also found that Boston exhibitors were much more interested in attracting middle-class patrons than in serving working-class moviegoers.[9] Gomery

[3]Jacobs, *Rise of American Film*, p. 56.

[4]Sklar, *Movie-Made America*, pp. 14–17.

[5]Hampton, *History of the Movies*, pp. 45, 47.

[6]Joseph H. North, *The Early Development of the Motion Picture: 1887–1909* (New York: Arno, 1973), p. 239.

[7]Sklar, *Movie-Made America*, p. 30.

[8]Russell Merritt, "Nickelodeon Theatres, 1905–1914: Building an Audience for the Movies," in *The American Film Industry*, ed. Tino Balio (Madison: University of Wisconsin Press, 1976), p. 60.

[9]Russell Merritt, "Nickelodeon Theaters," *AFI Reports*, May 1975, p. 4.

discovered the location of Milwaukee nickelodeons to be determined not so much by the socioeconomic status of particular neighborhoods as by proximity to mass transit lines and previously established shopping areas.[10]

Remarkably, there has been no study of early motion picture exhibition in New York City, the popular entertainment capital of America during the early years of this century. This paper examines the conditions of exhibition in Manhattan between 1906 and 1912, attempting to answer two questions: 1) does the usual characterization of nickelodeons offered in secondary sources apply to those in New York City?; and 2) what were the determinants of location for nickelodeons during this period? In addition to the fact that New York was then the hub of the motion picture industry, it was selected for this study for several other reasons: 1) it was the largest American urban center; 2) there is considerable demographic and other data on New York to aid in determining possible factors responsible for the location of nickelodeons; 3) in the words of one urban historian, "New York represented the Immigrant City *sui generis*," so that it is here of all cities that the relationship between immigrant neighborhoods and motion picture exhibition should be revealed most clearly;[11] and 4) much of our mythology of early American exhibition originates in New York, due in large measure to the fact that theater magnates William Fox and Adolph Zukor were products of the city's Lower East Side Jewish ghetto. (This latter, "great man" emphasis in early exhibition history hardly gives us an accurate indication of the economic, social, and demographic forces which shaped their first business ventures and those of the myriad other New York exhibitors as well.[12])

On the basis of this study, I will argue that: 1) our picture of the nickelodeon is at best sketchy, at worst misrepresentative; 2) several factors might account for the location of nickelodeons; and 3) the "nickelodeon era," as usually conceived, was much briefer than generally believed—important changes in exhibition format after 1908 radically altered the nature of moviegoing in New York City, if not the entire country.

---

[10]J. Douglas Gomery, "A History of Milwaukee's Movie Theatres," unpublished paper, pp. 3–5.

[11]Thomas Kessner, *The Golden Door: Italian and Jewish Immigrant Mobility in New York City, 1880–1915* (New York: Oxford University Press, 1977), p. 51.

[12]The principal sources of data for this study were the listings of "Moving Picture Exhibitions" of *Trow's Business Directory of Greater New York* for the years 1906–12, inclusive, and theatrical and motion picture trade journals from the period. It is, of course, possible that these listings are not exhaustive. However, the 1908 Trow's list was compared with a similar one prepared by Edison employee Joseph McCoy in July 1908 and found to correlate highly. The McCoy list is contained at the Edison Archives, West Orange, New Jersey.

THE LOWER EAST SIDE

While storefront motion picture theatres date back to 1896, it does not appear that they were established in any numbers until around 1906. The first trade press notice of the nickelodeon phenomenon comes in the March 17, 1906, issue of *Variety*. The paper notes that several storefront theatres, giving fifteen-minute shows, had recently opened "along the main thoroughfares" in New York City. Early·in 1907 a "conservative estimate" of the number of nickelodeons in the United States was 2,500, "but," *Variety* pointed out, "they are increasing so rapidly that positive figures are unobtainable."[13]

The 1908 *Trow's Business Directory* lists 123 motion picture exhibitions in Manhattan, exclusive of vaudeville theatres. Of this number, forty-two were located in the Lower East Side, an area bounded roughly by the East River, Catherine Street on the south, the Bowery on the west, and Fourteenth Street on the north. It is here that we find the nickelodeons so beloved of film historians: they were almost certainly proletarian and immigrant oriented.

In 1908 the Lower East Side was heavily populated by recent Jewish immigrants. By 1900 there were already 654 persons per acre, the highest population density in the city, and crowding did not peak until 1910. Living conditions ranged from bad to intolerable; ninety-five percent of the families lived three or more to a room.[14] But, as urban historian Thomas Kessner has pointed out, "congestion also produced economic dividends" for peddlers and small shopkeepers, whose potential market numbered in the hundreds of thousands.[15] It is difficult to prove whether the nickelodeons located along Delancey or Rivington Streets were dingy or crowded, but it is fairly certain they were small. Detailed fire insurance maps from the period reveal that the size of most nickelodeons on the Lower East Side did not exceed twenty-five by one hundred feet.[16]

Of the Lower East Side nickelodeons, nearly one-third (thirteen of forty-two) were not located in the residential blocks per se, but were strung along the Bowery. For decades the Bowery had been a center of popular entertainment. Before 1875 it was the locus of New York's legitimate theatres; thereafter it became a prime location for cheaper amusements: vaudeville, burlesque, dime museums, shooting galleries, and approximately six saloons per block.[17] A civic reformer wrote of the street a few years before the nickelodeon boom:

---

[13]*Variety*, January 26, 1907, p. 12.

[14]Kessner, *Golden Door*, p. 131; Thomas M. Henderson, *Tammany Hall and the New Immigrants* (New York: Arno Press, 1976), pp. 17–19.

[15]Kessner, *Golden Door*, p. 136.

[16]*Insurance Maps of the City of New York Borough of Manhattan* (New York: Sanford Map Co., 1905).

[17]Alvin F. Harlow, *Old Bowery Days* (New York: D. Appleton, 1931), pp. 367–401.

The Bowery is the main artery of night life on the East Side. At night it is a blaze of light from one end to the other. It is a center for saloons of every order, from gin-palaces to bucket-shops; theatres, concert-halls, 'free-and-easys,' and dime museums abound, all of them profusely ornamented with every device of colored light. . . . In and out of these resorts pours a constant crowd.[18]

Although not a part of the Lower East Side proper, the Union Square area at Fourteenth Street and Broadway was nearly adjacent to it. Like the Bowery, Union Square had been a major New York entertainment center for years. Seven movie theatres were crowded around the square, cheek-by-jowl with two important vaudeville theatres (Tony Pastor's and Keith's), several legitimate and burlesque theatres, and a number of penny arcades. Union Square was but a short walk from the tenements of the Lower East Side, but several of the movie theatres there bore little resemblance to those in the heart of the Jewish ghetto. William Fox's Dewey Theatre, a former legitimate house acquired by him in 1908, seated nearly one thousand persons. Fox gave a show lasting almost two hours, including five reels of film and five vaudeville acts. Twelve uniformed ushers were among the fifty employees at the Dewey.[19]

To repeat, of 123 New York movie theatres in 1908, only forty-two were located in the heavily immigrant-populated Lower East Side. The sites of the thirteen theatres along the Bowery were probably due as much to the traditional entertainment orientation of the boulevard as to its proximity to the nearby tenements. The same might be said of the seven other theatres clustered around Union Square.

OTHER NEIGHBORHOODS

Proximity to public tranportation lines helps to explain the location of some movie theatres, especially along the east side of the island. Some nineteen theatres were scattered along Second and Third Avenues between Twenty-Third Street and their termination at 129th and 130th Streets. It was along Second and Third Avenues that major East Side streetcar lines ran. Interestingly, however, we do not find a high correlation between subway or streetcar lines and movie theatres elsewhere on the island, leading to the speculation that most New York theatres were probably patronized by those who lived or worked in the immediate area. This neighborhood orientation is supported by the fact that large numbers of movie theatres were centered around four easily identifiable ethnic

---

[18]Helen Campbell, Thomas W. Know, and Thomas Byrnes, *Daylight and Darkness: Or Lights and Shadows of New York* (Hartford: The Hartford Pub. Co., 1895), p. 211.

[19]*Variety*, December 19, 1908, p. 13.

and/or socioeconomic areas of the city: Yorkville, 125th Street, Jewish Harlem, and Little Italy.

Nine theatres were located in the Yorkville section of the East Side. This neighborhood, bounded by Seventy-Fourth and Eighty-Ninth Streets, Third Avenue and the East River, was in 1909 a German and Irish enclave where "many of the residents were small merchants or tradesmen."[20]

There were also concentrations of nickelodeons in two other clearly defined ethnic communities on the Upper East Side: Jewish Harlem and Little Italy. The first of the so-called New Immigrant groups (non-Northern European) to move into Harlem was the Italians. During the 1890s Italians began congregating in an area bordered by Ninety-Ninth and 119th Streets, Third Avenue and the East River. In this area in 1910 there were 60,897 Italians out of a total population of 113,920. The heart of Little Italy was between 114th and 119th Streets, and First and Third Avenues, where Italians were seventy-two percent of the population.[21] E. Idell Ziesloft, writing in *The New Metropolis* in 1899, described this neighborhood as "one of the most flourishing and picturesque Italian colonies in New York.... The tenements that line these streets are not much to look at in themselves, but the quaintly furnished rooms in them ... the gay lines of wash, the small shops and street scenes make up a picture that never loses interest.... These are the peaceful Italians from the north of Italy, and the stiletto is rarely brought into play here."[22] Although clearly an ethnic community, Little Italy seems to have been much more affluent than the immigrant ghettoes of Lower Manhattan. There were thirteen movie theatres here in 1908.

Ten more nickelodeons were located in nearby Jewish Harlem. This neighborhood of first and second generation Jews was bounded by Ninety-Eighth and 118th Streets, Park Avenue, the northeast shoulder of Central Park, and Lenox Avenue. Its residents were the more prosperous and Americanized Jews who had been able to escape from the Lower East Side. The illiteracy rate among males in Jewish Harlem was less than one quarter of that on the Lower East Side.[23]

North of these two areas was Harlem proper, in 1908 still a middle and lower-middle class neighborhood, although the transformation of the area into a black community had just begun.[24] As late as 1902 in the East Harlem Twelfth Ward, only 10,786 families out of 103,570 were New Immigrants.[25] For over a

---

[20]Henderson, *Tammany Hall and the New Immigrants*, p. 78.

[21]Ibid., p. 49.

[22]Quoted in Grace Mayer, *Once Upon a City* (New York: Macmillan, 1958), p. 58.

[23]Henderson, *Tammany Hall and the New Immigrants*, p. 20.

[24]Charles Lockwood, *Manhattan Moves Uptown: An Illustrated History* (Boston: Houghton-Mifflin, 1976), p. 306; Gilbert Osofsky, *Harlem: The Making of a Ghetto* (New York: Harper and Row, 1963), p. 89.

[25]Osofsky, *Harlem*, p. 79.

decade the principal crosstown street of Harlem had been 125th Street—a street which also formed the community's primary entertainment district.[26] By 1908 twelve movie theatres had pushed in among the Harlem Opera House, the Gotham Theatre, Hurtig and Seamon's Music Hall, and Keith and Proctor's 125th Street Theatre.

In all, some forty-four movie theatres were located in Yorkville, Little Italy, Jewish Harlem, and on 125th—two more than were located on the Lower East Side in 1908.

SMALLER CONCENTRATIONS OF THEATRES

The major groupings of movie theatres discussed above (lower East Side, Union Square, Second and Third Avenues, Yorkville, Little Italy, Jewish Harlem, 125th Street) account for 102 or eighty-three percent, of the 123 movie theatres listed in the 1908 *Trow's Business Directory*. The remaining theatres were scattered around the island in smaller clusters. There were a few along Twenty-Third Street between the subway stops at Seventh Avenue and Broadway. Three were established a few blocks northwest, in the area of Miner's Eighth Avenue (vaudeville) Theatre. Four more theatres were further up Eighth Avenue, between Thirty-Eighth and Forty-Ninth Streets. All of these movie theatres were located in or adjacent to traditional entertainment districts.

But in addition to accounting for the location of nickelodeon concentrations, we must also account for areas where nickelodeons were not to be found. We do not, for example, find a single movie theatre along Fifth or Madison Avenues, from Union Square to 100th Street, a fact not difficult to explain given the character of these two streets. French novelist Paul Bourget wrote of Manhattan in 1894, "It is but too evident that money cannot have much value here. There is too much of it. The interminable succession of luxurious mansions which line Fifth Avenue proclaim its mad abundance. No shops—unless of articles of luxury . . . only independent dwellings, each of which including the ground on which it stands, implies a value which one dares not calculate. . . . This avenue has visibly been willed and created by sheer force of millions."[27] Madison Avenue was "second only to Fifth as a residential thoroughfare," and was also termed "the Avenue to the Gods."[28]

The absence of movie theatres on the Upper West Side might be due to two factors. First, this area was much slower to develop than the Upper East Side. It was not until the completion of the Ninth Avenue "El" in the 1880s that large scale residential building began. Secondly, by 1900 the social character of the Upper West Side was set: mansions along Riverside Drive, handsome houses along

---

[26]*New York Clipper*, April 29, 1889.

[27]Quoted in Mayer, *Once Upon a City*, p. 29.

[28]Mayer, *Once Upon a City*, p. 50.

West End Avenue, and fashionable apartment buildings spreading westward from Central Park: in other words, the area was solidly middle and upper class.[29]

The large concentration of movie theatres in the Lower East Side is not surprising; however, it is somewhat puzzling not to find significant numbers of nickelodeons in the equally dense and immigrant-dominated Middle West Side (roughly marked by Thirty-Fourth and Fifty-Eighth Streets, Eighth Avenue and the Hudson River) and the neighborhood immediately west of the Lower East Side (bounded by Canal and Houston, the Bowery and Sullivan). Both areas housed newly arrived immigrants—mostly Italians—of the poorest means. In the former we find but one movie theatre, in the latter only three. The combined area of these two neighborhoods makes them nearly equal in size to the Lower East Side, but, omitting those theatres located along the Bowery, there were seven times more movie theatres in the Jewish area than in the Italian. Yet, the more affluent Italian and Jewish neighborhoods on the Upper East Side are roughly equal in the number of movie theatres in each. This seeming paradox might be explained by differences in immigration patterns between the two ethnic groups during this period.

Many Italians who came to the United States around the turn of the century did not come to stay; they earned what money they could and returned to Italy. Between 1907 and 1911, seventy-three out of one hundred Italians landing at Ellis Island repatriated. That most Italian immigrants in New York City were either working toward building a personal nest egg or supporting families in the old country is indicated by the fact that between 1880 and 1910 eighty percent of Italian immigrants to the city were male, most between the ages of fourteen and forty-four. Children made up an insignificant portion of the immigrant population.[30] It is plausible, therefore, that many of the Italians who lived in the Middle West Side or Lower Manhattan were unlikely to spend part of their paltry earnings on something so frivolous as the movies.

On the other hand, as Thomas Kessner has pointed out in a recent study, "statistics on the Eastern European Jewish immigrants show no comparable repatriation." The average repatriation for all New Immigrants was forty-two percent, but among Jews only seven percent. Among 295,000 Russian Jews who entered the United States between 1908 and 1912, only 21,000 re-emigrated to another country. Further, Jewish immigration was a movement of families. Between 1899 and 1910, forty-three percent of arriving Jewish immigrants were female and nearly one-third were under the age of sixteen.[31] Other factors need to be investigated—child-rearing practices, possible religious sanctions against certain forms of entertainment—but it does appear that the family-oriented,

---

[29]Lockwood, *Manhattan Moves Uptown*, p. 319.

[30]Kessner, *Golden Door*, pp. 28–31.

[31]Ibid., pp. 30–31.

American-minded Jewish community was a more lucrative location for a nickelodeon than the transient, predominately male Italian neighborhoods. We do not find this to be the case in Little Italy, probably because it was the most prosperous and hence most stable Italian enclave in the city.

SMALL-TIME VAUDEVILLE

Comparing the listings under "moving picture exhibitions" in the extant *Trow's Business Directories* between 1906 and 1912 reveals that the patterns established by 1908 do not substantially change. The total number of movie theatres increased only slightly (to 138), and the proportional distribution among geographical areas generally remained stable. The increase in the total number of theatres was due largely to their establishment in the upper reaches of Harlem. In 1908 only six theatres were located north of 125th Street; in 1912 there were nineteen.

What these data do not show, however, is an important qualitative change in motion picture exhibition between 1908 and 1912—a change wrought by the growth of what came to be called small-time vaudeville. As we have seen, just as all movie threatres were not located in immigrant ghettoes, not all of them were the small, sawdust-floored dives of historical legend. As early as 1907 enterprising entrepreneurs saw that huge profits could be made by converting large-capacity theatres into movie houses, where audiences enjoyed not only movies but the trappings of theatrical entertainment. Moreover, as Russell Merritt found in Boston, improvements in theatre decor and comfort led to increased patronage by middle-class citizens.

By early 1908 several New York theatres had been converted into movie houses. In November 1907, William A. Brady took over the 1,200-seat Alhambra Theatre on Union Square and renamed it the Unique, making it, according to *Variety,* "the newest and easily the handsomest popular priced vaudeville theatre in the city." The Unique offered movies and vaudeville acts for ten to twenty-five cents.[32] A few weeks later, a group of investors, led by Philadelphia theatre entrepreneur Felix Isman, rented the Manhattan Theatre for $25,000 annually. Its transformation into a movie theatre was an immediate success; on opening night "a capacity attendance took up all the available space."[33] Almost simultaneous with the above, the New York entertainment industry was shocked to learn that Keith's Union Square Theatre and Proctor's Twenty-Third Street Theatre, two of the premier vaudeville houses in the city, were to be made into movie theatres. By February 1908, the Twenty-Third Street Theatre, renamed the Bijou Dream, was attracting 2,000 people daily.[34] Of motion picture exhibition in New York *Variety*

---

[32]*Variety,* November 9, 1907, p. 5; December 15, 1907, p. 33.

[33]*Variety,* December 14, 1907, p. 13.

[34]*Variety,* February 15, 1908, p. 4; February 29, p. 6.

commented, "the tendency is clearly toward fewer, bigger, cleaner five-cent theatres and more expensive shows."[35]

What evolved from this movement toward spacious, middle-class oriented theatres and away from the converted storefront was small-time vaudeville: the showing of a mixed program of film and vaudeville acts in large capacity theatres for between ten and thirty-five cents. Several film historians have mentioned attempts by some exhibitors to upgrade the quality of nickelodeon presentations and surroundings between 1906 and 1912.[36] Almost no attention, however, has been given to the growth of small-time vaudeville as an autonomous entertainment form, despite the fact that by 1910 it was a major factor in motion picture exhibition in New York and in the country as a whole. As early as August 1909, *Moving Picture World* predicted that the "store-room" shows would shortly disappear, their place being taken "by especially built theatres, seating five hundred to a thousand, most of them giving a mixed bill of vaudeville and motion pictures."[37]

The mixing of vaudeville and film in large, often ornate theatres was a result of three factors: 1) the saturation of large cities (including New York) with nickelodeons, leading to a highly competitive exhibition market; 2) a scarcity of new film product; and 3) a desire on the part of some exhibitors to attract more middle-class customers.

The clustering of movie theatres in residential neighborhoods, along commercial thoroughfares, and in traditional entertainment districts led to fierce competition among them. Early in 1907 *Variety* correspondents from around the country began commenting on the battles for movie patronage raging in large cities. Managers employed many gimmicks to differentiate their house from the one across the street. Some gave longer bills or promised daily changes of movies; some even tried lowering admission to three cents. One of the most popular ploys was the addition of a few vaudeville acts to the nickelodeon program. In November 1907, *Moving Picture World* acknowledged that "a vaudeville act or two interspersed between the changes of reels has been a means of doubling the receipts of many moving picture theatres."[38]

The use of vaudeville on movie theatre programs was also spurred by a shortage of new films, resulting from the tremendously increased demand for them by the thousands of nickelodeons established between 1906 and 1908. Since 1896 motion picture producers had been supplying each of several hundred vaudeville theatres with approximately 1800 feet of film each week. By

---

[35]*Variety*, December 14, 1907, p. 33.

[36]Hampton, *History of the Movies*, p. 116; Jacobs, p. 167; Jowett, *Film: The Democratic Art*, p. 31.

[37]*Moving Picture World*, August 28, 1909, p. 280.

[38]*Moving Picture World*, November 16, 1907, p. 593.

1908 the number of exhibition outlets had increased to several thousand, each using two or three reels and changing programs three or more times each week. Although the amount of new film placed on the American market weekly increased from 10,000 feet in November 1907 to 28,000 feet in March 1908, there was still not enough product to satisfy exhibitor demand at the established price level.[39]

The addition of vaudeville acts to the nickelodeon program meant that the exhibitor could expand the length of his/her show without increasing the number of reels of film required. The acts could also be used to bolster a weak film program: if, for some reason, an exhibitor's films were not particularly attractive one week, he/she could attempt to attract patronage on the basis of the variety portion of the bill.

Vaudeville acts also made movie theatres more palatable to middle-class audiences, offering them a version of what they went to Keith's, Proctor's and other vaudeville theatres to see. In August 1908, *Moving Picture World* noted that theatres presenting more than "the average nickelodeon" were able to raise their prices to ten cents, "and are in addition blessed with a better and cleaner patronage."[40]

Presenting vaudeville acts in movie theatres did present some problems for the exhibitor, however. Additional salaries had to be paid. In some cases ticket sales per day declined as the vaudeville acts lengthened each show presented. Because of municipal theatre licensing laws, nickelodeons in New York and other cities were limited in seating capacity (in New York to 199 seats). With costs up and performances per day down, nickelodeon managers who could not expand their seating capacity were hard pressed to keep their houses profitable. In the face of stiff competition, they were reluctant to increase ticket prices. Some managers found that by moving into larger buildings or leasing former vaudeville or legitimate theatres, they could cover increased costs with larger capacity, and even raise the price of admission to ten cents or more.

New York quickly became a major center of small-time vaudeville activity, due largely to the growth of two theatre circuits: those belonging to William Fox and Marcus Loew. Fox became an exhibitor in 1906, when he purchased a failing nickelodeon in Brooklyn. By 1908 he had joined the trend toward the use of vaudeville and film in large-capacity theatres. As noted previously, he leased the Dewey Theatre on Union Square and turned it into "the best run and most profitable" movie theatre in New York.[41] On Thanksgiving Day, 1908, the Dewey sold 12,000 tickets, a feat believed by *Variety* to be the largest business ever done

---

[39]*Moving Picture World*, May 4, 1907, p. 124.

[40]*Moving Picture World*, August 29, 1908, p. 152.

[41]*Variety*, December 19, 1908, p. 13.

by a movie theatre.[42] By the end of 1910, Fox owned a circuit of fourteen in the New York area. The Fox theatres offered long programs, often including as many as seven or eight vaudeville acts, comfort, and low prices (ten and twenty-five cents). The Fox audiences included many middle-class patrons. When Fox's Nemo Theatre opened in October 1910, *Variety* remarked, "The audience was one of real 'class' . . . dinner coats were in evidence in the auditorium."[43]

In 1903, Marcus Loew, a New York furrier, was persuaded by fellow businessmen Adolph Zukor and Morris Kohn to invest in their penny arcade business. In 1904, Loew opened arcades in New York and Cincinnati and later operated several nickelodeons. As Bosley Crowther tells the story in *The Lion's Share,* Loew made the discovery of many nickelodeon managers, that theatres which offered vaudeville acts as well as pictures had a competitive edge. "Loew went along with this fashion, but he soon saw that the small size of the 'stores' limited the attraction and the variety of such tabloid vaudeville. He sensed that he might get a jump on his competitors if he could do it on a somewhat larger scale."[44] In the summer of 1907, Loew saw an opportunity to move his style of entertainment into more pretentious quarters. He leased Watson's Cozy Corner burlesque theatre in Brooklyn, and, after redecorating it, opened it as the Royal Theatre in January 1908 as a small-time vaudeville theatre. By the summer of 1909, Loew's People's Vaudeville Company operated "one of the largest of the big small-time circuits," with twelve houses in New York City alone.[45]

The locations of small-time vaudeville theatres in Manhattan are significant in that they demonstrate an increasing movement toward a middle-class audience. Small-time theatres were located where earlier movie theatres had been (Union Square, 125th Street, Yorkville), but also at Columbus Circle, Riverside and 96th Street, 145th Street and Amsterdam Avenue, 110th Street and Broadway, and 165th Street and Broadway—previously unbreached middle-class bastions. The extent to which small-time vaudeville attracted middle-class patronage is indicated by the fact that as early as 1910, New York theatres on the Loew circuit were actively competing with those belonging to members of the United Booking Office, the "high-class" vaudeville syndicate.[46]

Small-time vaudeville theatres also attracted patronage away from smaller movie theatres. The old nickelodeons, restricted to a few hundred seats by the size

---

[42]*Variety,* December 12, 1908, p. 12.

[43]*Variety,* October 1, 1910, p. 10.

[44]Bosley Crowther, *The Lion's Share* (New York: Dutton, 1957), pp. 23–39.

[45]*Moving Picture World,* September 11, 1927, p. 2.

[46]*Variety,* August 28, 1909, p. 8. Fuller discussion of the rise of small-time vaudeville and its interaction with "high class" vaudeville and legitimate theatre is contained in Robert C. Allen, "Vaudeville and Film, 1895–1915: A Study in Media Interaction," Ph.D. dissertation, University of Iowa, 1977.

of the building or municipal fire regulations, simply could not compete in many cases with the huge, luxurious small-time theatres. *Variety* noted in December 1909, "anyone who overlooks this 'small time' is falling into a great error.... It has driven out the 'picture palace' and how."[47]

CONCLUSIONS

In light of the findings of this study, as well as those of Gomery and Merritt, it is obvious that accounts of early motion picture exhibition contained in secondary sources are grossly inadequate. As is too often the case in motion picture history, easy generalizations serve to hide complex historical issues. In Manhattan moviegoing between 1906 and 1912 was by no means an exclusive activity of the poor or the immigrant. Our one-dimensional image of early exhibition taking place in the dingy, converted cigar store does not hold in Manhattan. Some patterns do, however, emerge. Most movie theatres were located near large working-class and middle-class populations. Few theatres were found in exclusively middle- and upper-class neighborhoods. Like vaudeville theatres, burlesque houses, and dime museums before them, many movie theatres were located in traditional entertainment districts. It is difficult to generalize about the relationship between movie theatres and public transportation. Major shopping areas, such as Union Square and 125th Street, were of course serviced by transit lines. The low correlation between transit lines and nickelodeons outside of established retail and entertainment districts seems to indicate that these movie houses drew their patronage from the immediate area. Small-time vaudeville theatres show a higher correlation with subway and streetcar lines, indicating, perhaps, that these larger theatres drew from a wider area than the nickelodeons. While the heavy concentration of nickelodeons on the Lower East Side indicates that moviegoing was popular among the immigrant population there, the sparsity of theatres in other immigrant neighborhoods suggests differences among ethnic groups in their moviegoing behavior.

The growth of small-time vaudeville indicates that the middle-class embraced the movies much earlier than is generally believed—several years before the advent of the feature film. The nature of small-time vaudeville, with its large, often ornate theatres, uniformed attendants, and long programs, makes it an important link between the storefront shows of 1906 and the picture palaces of the late teens.

The extent to which the findings of this study can be generalized beyond Manhattan is a moot question. New York might well turn out to be typical only of New York; factors quite alien to the situation there might prove to be decisive

---

[47]*Variety*, December 11, 1909, p. 7.

elsewhere. What is needed are studies of exhibition in other cities—large and small, polyglot and homogeneous, in all parts of the country. Only when this task has been accomplished can we safely make generalizations about the nickelodeon era.

JEANNE THOMAS ALLEN

Copyright and Early Theater, Vaudeville, and Film Competition

The emergence of film in late nineteenth-century America was closely tied to the mass theatrical entertainments from which it was launched as a business and as a mass art. Film's incorporation into the vaudeville program and eventual eclipse of vaudeville by the 1920s presents an instance of inter-media symbiosis and competition.[1] These inter-media relationships in the decades around the turn of the century should be viewed within the greater context of the nineteenth-century revolution in industrial production and business management.[2] It is that larger context of changes within American business as an institution that can amplify our understanding of film's supremacy by the end of the 1920s beyond current explanations of idiosyncratic shifts in public taste.[3] From this perspective, the central question becomes, "What factors enabled certain businesses to survive and succeed in the era of 'big business' competition?" This study will briefly sketch the nature of inter-media competition, survey aspects of business organization that account for film's superior competitive abilities, and focus on one tool of competitive strategy employed during this period of industrial centralization—the

[1]Robert C. Allen, "Vaudeville and Film, 1895–1915: A Study in Media Interaction," Ph.D. dissertation, University of Iowa, 1977.

[2]Alfred D. Chandler, Jr., *The Visible Hand* (Cambridge: Harvard University Press, 1977) and *Strategy and Structure* (Cambridge: MIT Press, 1962), are excellent secondary sources on nineteenth- and twentieth-century American business history.

[3]Kenneth Macgowan, *Behind the Screen* (New York: Dell, 1965), pp. 121–29. Jerry Stagg, *The Brothers Shubert* (New York: Ballantine, 1968), pp. 102 ff. The suggestion is not uncommon that vaudeville's constant emphasis on variation and originality to sustain its appeal made film an attractive "act." [For an earlier date than is suggested here respecting film's introduction to vaudeville, see Alan Williams "The Lumière Organization and 'Documentary Realism,' " n. 2—GP.]

176

protection of an industrial product by copyright—in order to more fully account for the relative ability of theater, vaudeville, and film to respond to inter-media competition.

It can be argued that the differing prices and locations of theater, vaudeville, and film entertainments suggest a division of the consumer market (to appeal to various classes). But in the early decades of the twentieth century, all three attempted to expand by seeking to attract the growing middle-class family trade. Sharing this goal, all three competitors entered each other's territory, suggesting that each perceived the other's audience as a potential market.

Even before film was introduced into the vaudeville program (1896), the rivalry between legitimate theater and vaudeville set the stage for competition among all three forms. Vaudeville's attempt to extend its audience to the middle class by acquiring a family audience of women and children took the form of borrowing an image of respectability from the legitimate theater. Vaudeville's condensed, modular format of autonomous but interrelated acts included plays in abbreviated form. The playlet, a twenty- to-thirty-minute condensation of legitimate theater, appeared in the early 1890s, bridging the more expensive legitimate theater and the 10¢–30¢ vaudeville performance.

After film became a staple of the vaudeville program, inter-media competition among the three entertainments grew more intense. Many businessmen abandoned vaudeville entirely, sensing film's potential for rapid expansion, while others attempted to diversify into film and keep their original holdings intact. J. Austin Fynes left vaudeville for film in 1906. Harry Davis and others followed in 1907, the same year that the Shuberts teamed up with the Klaw and Erlanger Syndicate to enter advanced vaudeville as the U.S. Amusement Company, while retaining their theater holdings. Although U.S. Amusement withdrew from vaudeville in 1908, John Murdock of the United Booking Office (UBO), the vaudeville managers association, picked up their cue the following year and formed the short-lived International Projecting and Producing Company. A few years later, in 1913, the UBO formed the United Feature Film Company, the Shuberts contracted with Lubin to create the Shubert Film Service, and Klaw and Erlanger entered film distribution as the Protective Amusement Company (offering two features per week to 100 Syndicate-affiliated theaters[4]), all of them seeking diversification.

Despite these potential competitors, Zukor's Paramount Distributing Company, organized the same year, proved more successful. Zukor discovered that B films were more widely popular than any of vaudeville's legitimate theater attempts at the film market, including Klaw and Erlanger's ill-starred venture with Biograph manager Joseph P. Kennedy to make films of scripts and actors' performances supplied by Klaw and Erlanger.

---

[4]*Variety,* March 14, 1913, p. 7.

Although entrepreneurial strategy and the suitability of the product for its intended audience help to explain the relative success or failure of these enterprises, theatrical businessmen realized that the single most important factor behind film's competitive superiority was its massive expansion of the market audience for a single performance.[5] The low-cost and almost limitless duplication of a single print allowed film to participate in the broader pattern of production and marketing which characterized American business at the turn of the century. The creation of a national market in the nineteenth century, supported by the communications-transportation infrastructure of telegraphy and railroads, facilitated and stimulated methods of mass production and distribution.

Theater and vaudeville had developed a system of mass distribution in the second half of the nineteenth century which included national circuits and a "combination system" of traveling stars and their nucleus of supporting staff, and film could utilize that distribution system and add the component of mass production much more feasibly than its theatrical competitors. In 1884, George Eastman had innovated continuous assembly in photography, placing photographic supplies in a category with matches, soap, and grains as commodities that could be produced rapidly and in large enough quantities to supply the entire national market. The machinery of the motion picture camera and projector could also be mass produced, benefiting from the techniques of interchangeable parts and job specialization developed in other machine tool industries.[6]

The reduced costs of presenting photographic entertainment simultaneously to a national audience was a major factor in giving film such economies of scale that entrepreneurs could easily undersell their theatrical and vaudevillian competitors. Nicholas Vardac has further pointed out the theater's propensity toward "realistic spectacle" which conditioned audience expectations, fulfilled better and less expensively by film.[7] Indeed, the two-dollar admission for D.W. Griffith's *The Birth of a Nation* is viewed by film scholars more as a strategy of filmic aspirations to theatrical art and an upper-class audience than as a necessity of high production costs.[8]

The film industry was able to adopt successful patterns of late nineteenth-century business organizations because its mechanized nature facilitated vertical integration of production, distribution, and exhibition. The technical and

---

[5]Some controversy arises about what is meant by the *performance* of a film, since there is a legal basis for arguing that the projecting or exhibiting of a film is its performance. What is meant here is what film theorists have termed the pro-filmic event or the event transpiring in front of the camera.

[6]Jeanne Allen, "The Industrial Context of Film Technology: Standardization and Patents," scheduled for an as yet untitled book edited by Stephen Heath and Teresa de Lauretis (New York: Macmillan, forthcoming).

[7]Nicholas Vardac, *Stage to Screen* (Cambridge: Harvard University Press, 1949).

[8]Robert Sklar, *Movie-Made America* (New York: Random House, 1975), p. 58.

mechanical complexities of film production enabled the industry to move from the ready-made theatrical distribution system to its own marketing network and thus to gain more control. Since they were not generally selling the means to produce a film to the public nor contracting to distribute a product which could be produced independently (e.g., a vaudeville act), or exhibited without access to complicated machines, the film industry was encouraged, and able, to exert control at all levels.

Theater and vaudeville sought to control competition within their businesses primarily in the areas of distribution and exhibition, but the film industry rapidly sought to control production as well. The financial effects of the lack of control over production of theater and vaudeville are evidenced by their continual negotiations with major stars. While theater and vaudeville presented the star as a kind of interchangeable part within a larger theatrical performance (theater's combination system or vaudeville's headliner in a modular format), the importance of stars to box-office success and the lack of long-term binding contracts made each production subject to disparate production costs. The lack of identifiable stars in film's early history and the status of actors as company employees rather than as talent contracted at high salaries gave film the advantage of lower and more consistent production costs, affording greater market stability. By 1908, Edison, through the Motion Picture Patents Company, standardized the price of film at 8½ cents per foot regardless of varying production costs.

All of the above factors suggest a greater adaptability on the part of film to the business demands of reducing per unit costs through mass production and distribution. The high rate of inflation accompanying an overall rise in wages and decrease in the length of the work day and work week in this period further enhances the importance of lowering the costs of family entertainment in order to expand market size vertically (through the various classes in society) as well as horizontally (geographically).

A further tool of competition in manufacturing industries of this era was patent and copyright law, which provided barriers to potential competitors. The late nineteenth century saw the transformation of invention from an operation of a single individual to a sector of corporate organization, which both defended current innovations from incursions and searched for new ones, placing science and invention increasingly in the service of corporate objectives. Patent law was a far more significant factor for film than for theater or vaudeville, which were basically preindustrial in their production process. But copyright as a form of protection for industrial property was pertinent to all three of these entertainment forms, and it was sought by all of them. The relative degree to which these three forms lent themselves to copyright protection suggests again the relative superiority of film as a commodity in the context of inter-media competition at the turn of the twentieth century.

Patent and copyright law protects intellectual property: discoveries or inventions. Despite national laws forbidding the operation of business monopolies in the United States, these two natural forms of monopoly were allowed as designated by Article 1, Section 8, of the U.S. Constitution, which gave Congress the power "to promote the progress of science and useful arts by securing for limited times (17 years for patent, 28 for copyright) to authors and inventors the exclusive right to their respective writings and discoveries." The patentee enjoys "the exclusive right to make, use and vend the invention or discovery," and the holder of copyright has the sole liberty of "printing, reprinting, completing, copying, executing, finishing and vending" the work.

Patent and copyright laws with their explicit reference to discoveries and inventions, a domain of property which includes the arts as well as science and engineering, became a fulcrum for the growing businesses of the popular arts and entertainment of the nineteenth century. Art, as original ideas, underwent a transition to machine production like the rest of the economy and similarly became a battleground for the laws which sought to protect artistic creation as property.[9]

The very scale of production practiced in this era argued the urgency of determining the status of a work of art as a commercial property and the conditions that obtain for the protection and exploitation of that property. In the competition for business success, mass culture industries sought and responded to legal decisions which determined what aspects of their property could be controlled and defended and hence what pursuits might reward the considerable financial investment that national distribution required. Did one form of mass entertainment offer greater control? greater opportunity for monopoly protection? Did the law, in responding to mechanization and the possibilities of reproduction and pirating, grant the same benefits to each culture industry? The competition between three coexistent dramatic entertainments—theater, vaudeville, and film—demonstrates in fairly gross terms the triumph of that mass culture industry which was most suitably adapted to the practices of turn-of-the-century business and to the legal structures which governed it.

Copyright protection generally lagged behind the business exploitation of intellectual property in the nineteenth and early twentieth centuries. The first copyright law of 1790 included maps and charts as well as books and was extended to engravings, etchings, and prints in 1802. In 1856, dramatic compositions and the right of publicly performing the same were protected by copyright. Paintings, drawings, chromos, statues, models, designs, photographs and their negatives were not protected until 1870, considerably after all these forms had begun to be merchandized in a competitive market. This gap in time

---

[9]Mechanical reproduction of material copyrighted in another form constituted a particularly controversial issue as each form of mechanization borrowed from materials in a preexistent form: engraving, lithography, photography, player piano, phonograph, radio.

between artistic products as marketable commodities and their protection by copyright allowed those businessmen who built the largest scale of distribution to maximize the exploitation of the artist's work commercially with minimal, if any, remuneration to the artist. Only social value granting unique status to "the original" protected the commercial value of the artist's property.

While copyright law generally manifested a lag in response to commercial exploitation arising from mechanical reproduction, vaudeville or variety acts were never able to qualify for strong protection. Vaudeville was not tied to print or to publishing, to a centuries-long tradition of artistically respectable entertainment, nor to a mode of notational representation which was capable of making subtle discriminations. Its domain was effervescent, nonliterary, too close to personal style and modes of behavior belonging to public domain rather than to private property. Originality lay in execution and subtle variation. As a kind of folk art derived from traditions of public entertainment, vaudeville was not well adapted to legally-supported conceptions of respectable art, private property, or originality tied to material form which protected other artistic entertainments.[10]

Frederick E. Snyder argues that while the vaudeville act itself was a non-mechanized popular art, the format for assembling the acts into a unified performance bore a resemblance to machine structure, as the photoplay for film continuity would a decade or so later.[11] The vaudeville act was a discrete interchangeable unit in a system of eight or nine acts. Resembling a specialized machine component, it was performed three times a day, six days a week for as many weeks as the circuit lasted. Indeed, by changing circuits and achieving popular success, some vaudeville performers could present a single act for as many as twenty years, again not unlike those actors and actresses who entered the touring circuit of legitimate theater and played *The Count of Monte Cristo* or *Rip Van Winkle* for decades. The vaudeville performer presented entertainment of a pre-industrial nature but in an industrialized format.

The fact that a performer could potentially become completely identified with a single act suggests that the ability to possess or own an original act as a means of one's livelihood would be essential to the performer and to the employer, who would compete with other entertainment forms in seeking the audience's patronage. Yet there seems to be little indication that a vaudeville act

---

[10]Vaudeville's derivation from popular folk entertainments such as the circus or traveling singers, jugglers, and acrobats had few pretensions to the patronage afforded art forms first associated with the aristocracy before they became sponsored by masses of the public.

[11]Frederick E. Snyder, "American Vaudeville: Theater in a Package," Ph.D. dissertation, Yale University, 1970, p. 21. See also Janet Staiger, "Dividing Labor for Production Control," *Cinema Journal* 18 (Spring 1979): 16–26, for a discussion of the continuity script as a form of management control particularly at Ince studios, 1911–16.

as an original idea or intellectual property enjoyed extensive protection of law at any period in its history.

The trade papers of the period not infrequently offered ads or statements of outraged performers who claimed that someone had "stolen" their act, which they first performed on 'such and such a date.[12] And the pattern of big-time vaudeville breaking an act that was copied or duplicated by numerous small-time vaudeville competitors in major urban areas suggests a very limited ability of performer and entrepreneur to gain legal protection.[13] One might argue that the lack of union power or perhaps the lack of sustained dependence on individual performers or acts by owners of vaudeville houses and chains precluded a forceful lobby for legal protection. The transiency of the performers, the lack of vertical integration in the business which would involve the vested interest of owner in performer, may have shifted the problem of theft to labor, unorganized at least until the "White Rat" strike of 1901, which was broken by nonunion performers and "special offers" to union members from owners.

Vaudeville acts could and did seek copyright protection at both state and federal levels, but the protection provided was not strong enough to restrict competition for several reasons: the lack of a notational system which could delineate an act's originality; the brevity and public or folk quality of the behaviors that made up the vaudeville routine; the element of personal style which frequently constituted the appeal of a performance; and the informal or preinstitutionalized quality of the business of vaudeville (performers relying more on the machinery of social pressure than contractual law as the means of regulating each other's behavior).

Copyright protection operated at two levels: state and federal. State protection is referred to as "common law copyright" and offers protection to an artistic creation until it is published, at which point it is regarded as public domain. The case of *Ferris vs. Frohman* in 1909 determined that performance was not the equivalent of publication under U.S. law (although it was so considered in Great Britain). Under this ruling, nationally circuited performance qualified for some property protection at the state level; but the laws varied from state to state, they were not spelled out in the state statute books, and in the absence of decided

---

[12]Fred Allen refers to a form of industry self-regulation for copyright protection which argues by its very existence for the lack of effective federal legal protection in his autobiography, *Much Ado About Me* (Boston: Little, Brown, 1956), p. 248.

[13]"Keith's Big Small Timer Cleaning Up in Boston," *Variety*, October 7, 1911, p. 10; "Big Managers Desperately After Big Small Time," *Variety,* July 12, 1912, p. 5; "Observations," *Moving Picture World,* August 23, 1913, p. 834; September 20, 1913, p. 1271; April 11, 1914, p. 203.

cases in most states, lawbook writers attempted to forecast judicial reaction to particular controversies.[14]

Federal copyright could be acquired only through the registration of a description of the act with the Office of Copyrights and afforded more comprehensive and widespread protection. Until 1909, when the law offered protection to dramatico-musical compositions (e.g., a sketch consisting of a series of recitations and songs but containing little action or dialogue), vaudeville acts had to qualify under the provisions for dramatic or musical copyright.[15] In these cases a notational system which bore a direct relation to the performance was necessary. *White-Smith vs. Apollo* had established that the performance of a piece of music by a player piano did not infringe the copyright for the music because the piano roll bore no visual resemblance to the notational system of the musical composition.[16] A vaudeville act had to have enough dramatic substance to qualify for copyright protection. As late as 1914, the courts ruled that the voice, motions, and postures of an actor and mere "stage business" possessed no *literary* quality and could not be protected by dramatic copyright. Consequently, the vaudeville act could be protected only if it used an original piece of music delineated by a published notational system or if it depended upon a script sufficiently to qualify it as a dramatic composition.

While vaudeville was both musical and dramatic in broad terms, the array of qualities the courts used to define drama and to tie musical performance to published compositions made it very difficult for vaudeville performers to qualify for federal protection. While musical copyright did protect the composer from having others publish and perform a particular song, the variety act which used music, dancing, some dialogue, and action of various kinds generally had to qualify for dramatic copyright, and the problems of defining a drama were indeed complex. The courts used a diverse and shifting criteria of sufficient plot and dialogue, the arousal of distinctive audience emotions, morally uplifting content, and narrative structure.

The requirement of sufficient plot and dialogue was effectively brought to bear on nonlegitimate theater performance (burlesque, revue, variety), which sometimes excerpted production numbers from other theatrical performances.

---

[14]Stanley Rothenberg, *Legal Protection of Literature, Art and Music,* (New York: Clark Boardman, 1960), p. 203. Ferris v. Frohman, 223 U.S. Reporter 424.

[15]Categories listed which include vaudeville act cases as listed in *American Digest,* 1907–1916, 2nd decennial ed., vol. 5, *Chattel Mortgages to Corporation Courts,* and *Federal Digest,* 1754 to date, vol. 18 (St. Paul, Minn.: West, 1940.).

[16]In the case of White-Smith Music Publishing Co. v. Apollo Co. in 1908, the court decided a perforated piano roll was not an infringing copy of the musical composition embodied in the roll, because the roll was not a written or printed record of the musical composition in intelligible notation.

The Black Crook, cited as the beginning of burlesque in the United States, was denied copyright protection both because it lacked originality and because, as a spectacle, it depended on action and had little dialogue.[17] The attempt to discriminate between infringing and noninfringing performances on the basis of whether they aroused identical emotional responses in the audiences was another criteria. Invoked in 1868, in *Daly vs. Palmer,* the factor of "conveying substantially the same impressions to and exciting the same emotions in the mind, in the same sequence or order as the original" was the basis of the infringement decision.[18] A 1903 decision declared a vaudeville act noninfringing because identical emotions of arousal had been engendered but in audiences of different sexes.[19] Another 1903 decision determined that mimicry of the performance of a song was not subject to infringement because lyric music which "sounds the note of personal emotion" had nothing dramatic in its words or music.[20]

The courts used the goal of the copyright law "to promote the progress of science or the useful arts"—to deny copyright protection to theatrical representations which were immoral or indecent and hence implicitly not useful. In both *Martinetti vs. Maguire* and *Barnes vs. Miner,* protection was denied not on the basis of whether or not the originality of a theatrical representation had been duplicated and a copyright infringed but on whether or not the performance was morally deserving of copyright protection.

Finally, the criterion of whether or not an act told a story was invoked in *Fuller vs. Bemis* to deny Marie Louis Fuller copyright protection for her "Serpentine Dance." The dance consisted of lights and shadows, stage settings, draperies in a striking tableau, but according to Judge Lacombe, it did not constitute a dramatic composition.

> It is essential to such a composition that it should tell some story.... An examination of the description of compliant's dance, as field for copyright, shows that the end sought for and accomplished was solely the devising of a series of graceful movements, combined with an attractive arrangement of drapery, lights and shadows, telling no story, portraying no character, depicting no emotion. The merely mechanical movements by which effects are produced on the stage are not subjects of copyright where they convey no ideas whose arrangement makes up a dramatic composition.[21]

---

[17]Edward S. Rogers, "The Law of Dramatic Copyright," *Michigan Law Review,* vol. 1 (1902), p. 112.

[18]"Dramatic Copyright," *The Law Journal,* vol. 4 (May 14, 1869) p. 267.

[19]Barnes v. Miner, et al., 122 Fed. Reporter 490.

[20]Bloom and Hamlin v. Nixon, et al., 125 Fed. Reporter 978.

[21]Rogers, "Law of Dramatic Copyright," p. 114.

While skits and playlets which figured on the vaudeville bill did tell a story, it is questionable whether a comic dialogue, a series of jokes, and the action of juggling, acrobatics, dancing, etc., would constitute storytelling any more than the "Serpentine Dance" did.

Had the vaudeville act been the property of a significant industry rather than the property of an individual performer who could be replaced by any number of other acts or features, pressure might have built to remove these obstacles to copyright protection. Theater had a long and sometimes aristocratic tradition which lent it respectability and an institutional claim for legal protection. In addition, the resources of sizeable businesses (the Syndicate, the Shuberts, etc.), which sometimes contracted to secure all the scripts of a certain playwright—a "house" playwright—tied the fate of the play and its legal protection to considerable financial power. Despite this difference in status, infringement of dramatic copyright, although frequently invoked, could not be clearly predicted in advance of a court decision. Consequently the degree to which it operated as a competitive tool would probably have to be determined by an examination of the power of various theatrical producers.

Introduced to the theatergoing public in the period shortly after 1897, in vaudeville houses all over the country, film was much more a child of the industrial century than either vaudeville or theater. Its material base was closely related to the electrical and chemical industries of that era as well as to mechanical engineering. As the result of mechanical innovations discovered and patented in the nineteenth century, film was one of those industries for which patents were a central property if not commodity. In addition to patents on machinery of production and exhibition, film copyright offered business entrepreneurs protection of their property and restraint on competition that was intensified by piracy and theft.[22]

Film enjoyed distinct advantages as a copyrightable entity: its materiality could be closely scrutinized for evidence of duplication; the relation between the performance and its notational system achieved visual intelligibility *par excellence;* and as a result of being regarded as an extension of the copyright for photographs, film did not have to qualify as a dramatic composition. Indeed, at least theoretically, it would seem that films could have vaudeville acts as their subject matter and receive better copyright protection, at least in principle, than the touring act itself.

In 1903 the case of *Edison vs. Lubin,* which extended the 1870 copyright law's protection of photographs to film, ruled that the film as a whole, rather than its individual frames, could be copyrighted. The rationale for this status again rested on a quality of *visual intelligibility*—that the difference between successive pictures is not distinguishable—and *economic value*—that its status as a commodity

---

[22]"Films Pirated and Duped," *Moving Picture World,* September 21, 1907, p. 451; "Who is Pirating films?" *Moving Picture World,* July 6, 1907, p. 275; July 13, 1907, p. 291.

depended upon its being considered a single entity.[23] It would seem to follow then that infringement of copyright protection would consist in appropriating the film in its entirety (does this open the door to the piracy of particular segments?).

Despite film's seeming congruence with the law's premises about the relation between originals and copies, the case of *Harper and Bros., et al., vs. Kalem Co.*, over Kalem's film based upon *Ben Hur*, introduced a categorical distinction between film as material artifact and film as performance. In this case the court ruled that the film of *Ben Hur* as a series of photographs did not infringe Section 4952, *Revised Statutes, United States*, of 1901, which gives the author of a book not only the sole right of printing but also the sole right of dramatizing. Invoking the case of *White-Smith vs. Apollo*, which discriminated between sheet music and perforated music rolls, the court maintained the distinction between infringing the copyright of a book and performing rights. It ruled that as a photograph Kalem's film did not infringe a copyrighted book or drama (the material artifact is not a copy because the pictures only represent the artist's idea of what the author has expressed in words [see *Parton vs. Prang*]; the narrative idea is not copyrighted but only the concept as expressed by printed words).

But when the film is put on an exhibiting machine, it was argued, it becomes a dramatization and infringes the exclusive right of the owner of the copyrighted book to dramatize it as well as the right to publicly produce it.[24] One year after *White-Smith*, the courts rejected the parallel between sheet music versus perforated piano rolls and theatrical dramatization versus film passing through a motion picture projector, although both mediated similar conceptions by mechanical reproduction. Film's photographic resemblance to the dramatized play was regarded as categorically different from the piano roll's relation to the sheet music. The principle of visual intelligibility caused the courts to recognize filmic representation as a *copy* of theatrical dramatization.

Despite this limitation on films based on plays, the two competitive weapons of patent law (protecting production and exhibition) and copyright law (protecting the film commodity) were united in the film industry in the early part of the twentieth century when film gained national and even international dominance in mass entertainment. Such pairing was not matched by either legitimate theater or vaudeville. I am not arguing that this was the sole factor that enabled film to gain hegemony over both of its theatrical competitors by the end of the 1920s. I do think that the coincidence of the Motion Picture Patents Company and the Berlin Convention in 1908 granting film international copyright recognition argues for an extended examination of the importance of the legal structure's support for certain entertainment commodities. Explanations of financial success based on popular preference or a drive towards realism

---

[23]Edison v. Lubin, 122 Fed. Reporter 240 (C.C.A. 3d 1903).

[24]Harper and Bros. v. Kalem Co., 169 Fed. Reporter 61 (C.C.A. 2d 1909).

ignore both the degree to which laws protecting private property supported the success of particular commodities and the financial arrangements marketing them.

Although many of the copyright infringement suits reveal competition *within* the businesses of vaudeville, theater, and film, the facts that small-time vaudeville served as a launching vehicle for film and that legitimate theaters converted to film theaters indicate that difficulties in copyright protection added a further argument for conversion. The national distribution orientation of theatrical circuit owners (e.g., the United Booking Office) demonstrates the emphasis on developing a commodity best suited to that structure of marketing. If film reduced the costs of distribution and exhibition, standardized production, achieved greater economies of scale, and in addition, offered greater protection from reproduction and theft than vaudeville or theater, then it was certainly better suited to the structure of business in the twentieth century.

BURNES ST. PATRICK HOLLYMAN

The First Picture Shows:

Austin, Texas, 1894–1913

While the Kinetoscope parlor (and later, the "nickelodeon") became immediately popular in large cities where it was introduced, little is known about the introduction of the motionized image in smaller communities like Austin, Texas.[1] Austin had its first experience with the machine on November 10, 1894 when the first Kinetoscope parlor went into operation on Congress Avenue.[2] The encounter was typical of most other places where the Kinetoscope was introduced.[3] Although the opening was quite well-publicized, no mention was made in subsequent advertisements and announcements.[4]

Many people did not take the Kinetoscope parlor as anything more than a novelty. According to W. E. Simpson, who worked as a projectionist in Austin from 1915 until his retirement in 1975, the products were "bad technically," simplistic narratives that usually "showed" a single action: dancing ladies, boxing sequences, horseshoeing, and domestic scenes.[5] J. W. Carpenter, who worked as

---

[1]The census of 1890 in Austin, Texas, placed the population at 14,575. By 1900, when the first *projected screen image* was shown in Austin, the population had grown to 22,258. Figures available from the Department of Planning, City Hall, Austin, Texas.

[2]*Austin Statesman,* November 10, 1894, p. 6. Gordon Hendricks confirms this date in his *The Kinetoscope* (New York: Graus, 1966), p. 64.

[3]Both Hendricks and Robert Sklar point out that at the national level, the Kinetoscope enjoyed a relatively short life. Sklar comments that "The Wizard (Edison) seemed to know that they would be a nine-day wonder," *Movie-Made America* (New York: Random House, 1976), p. 13.

[4]*Austin Statesman* from November 10–24, 1894, and through all issues until January 11, 1900.

[5]In conversations with W. E. Simpson recorded on March 26–28, 1976, Austin, Texas. Simpson was a motion picture projectionist in International Association of Theatrical Stage

an Austin projectionist from 1911 until 1972, remarked that many people did not consider the "moving pictures in those parlors to be respectable," and "average fellows didn't want to be seen there.... The show... wasn't a *'show'* as we conceive of the motion picture today."[6] There was no audience except the individual viewer, who, in full daylight, bent over and placed his or her eye over a small viewing port to observe a "small reproduction of reality."[7] With all of these drawbacks (lack of darkness in the room, small image size, and awkward viewer position in relation to the image), the total "magical" effect of the viewing experience was considerably reduced.

With the coming of the Vitascope, the projected motion picture medium had an inauspicious beginning in Austin, on January 10, 1900.[8] The cinema's great debut took place upon a screen under the rain-soaked canvas tents of the Omaha Exposition Midway, located just north of the town. The local paper, the *Austin Statesman,* eagerly anticipated the opening.

On Thursday, January 11, 1900, the *Statesman* reported that "the Midway opened under the most trying of circumstances. The opening had been delayed for two days as a result of inclement weather, and last night it took place in a perfect torrent of rain."[9]

The rain was the least of the Midway's problems, however. Until the January 1900 Midway, Austin had never really had a "legitimate" exposition: gypsies and dog and pony shows had "stolen the money of the citizenry" in previous years. As a result, the promoters went to great lengths to assure the public that the "Exposition" was safe and respectable. In this way, movies were "respectably introduced" to Austin's middle class. Mrs. Hattie McCall Travis, a well-known and respected Austin resident, organized the Midway and personally vouched for its credibility:

> My Midway is not the ordinary common Midway one reads about or sees at inferior fairs and carnivals. I have a thoroughly up-to-date and refined amusement enterprise put together by myself, personally, and it

---

Employees and Moving Picture Machine Operators (I.A.T.S.E.) Local 205, Austin, from 1915–75. He is one of the two oldest living projectionists in the city.

[6]In conversation with J. W. Carpenter recorded on March 30, 1976, in Austin, Texas. Carpenter, like Simpson, was a motion picture projectionist in I.A.T.S.E. Local 205. He is the oldest living projectionist in the Austin area and started his career with the introduction of the motion picture medium, working from 1911–72. Carpenter helped install many of the first motion picture projectors in Austin's vaudeville and nickelodeon houses. His statements support the general view that the Kinetoscope parlors were places that were frequented by the working class. The remarks are from recorded conversations with both Simpson and Carpenter.

[7]Ibid.

[8]*Austin Statesman,* January 11, 1900, p. 3.

[9]Ibid.

is therefore a Midway that can be visited with safety by every man, woman and child in Austin. I have secured only the best shows from the Omaha Exposition. I have only the best men in the Exposition line in this or any other country at the front of my show. Not showmen mind you— exposition men. Men who know their business and are perfect gentlemen; who can walk in the best element of society in the land. Come and see my new venture, and I know that you will enjoy it. It will act as a salad and increase your appetite for more amusement in your city.[10]

Despite the Omaha Exposition Midway's billing as "respectable," its origins were in the carnival. Mrs. Travis's Midway had a snake show, an "Oriental Theater," the "Happy Holiness Dancing Girls," a baby incubator, an "Electric Theater," the "Moulin Rouge," a "Gypsy Camp," an illusion called "Darkness and Dawn," an electric fountain and most importantly, the "Warograph" and the "Cinémato-graphe." These last two attractions were the most remarked upon in the pages of the *Austin Statesman* since they were the very first examples that Austin saw of projected motion pictures.[11]

Although the "Warograph" and the "Cinématographe" were identical to each other in their workings (both machines were manufactured by the Lumière Brothers), the Exposition exhibited them separately.[12] The subject matter to be shown determined the choice of machine. The "Warograph" showed pictures of the Spanish American War—hence its title—and seems to have created quite a stir among viewers: it provided motionized pictures of an actual war which viewers had read about in the pages of the *Austin Statesman*,[13] even though the original footage had probably been staged at the Edison studios in 1898–99.

The Warograph attracts large crowds illustrating as it does our recent military achievements. In the operation of this wonderful piece of mechanism, photography and electricity join hands and grim visaged war is portrayed while you wait. The American Infantry rush by

---

[10]Ibid.

[11]Ibid., p. 2. In fact, Austin's mayor attended with a party that included a justice of the Texas Supreme Court, the Austin chief of police, and the Texas secretary of state. The mayor said that "the Cinématographe was first visited and the wonderful pictures enjoyed to the fullest extent."

[12]Ibid., p. 3.

[13]*Austin Statesman,* January 1, 1900, p. 1; January 5, 1900, p. 5; and January 11, 1900, p. 3. Edison was partly responsible for the production of the staged film footage of battles from the Spanish-American War. His studios produced several films, in particular, *Spanish American War* (1898) and *Raising Old Glory over Morro Castle* (1899).

platoons up the height of San Juan. Roosevelt's Rough Riders make one of the impetuous charges; Dewey sails into Manila Bay and sinks Spanish war ships right and left while the dynamite cruiser "Vesuvius" hurls whole bales of gun-cotton into Morro Castle. Some idea of the intricacy of the mechanism that produces such effects may be gained from the fact that Charles Hodges, the inventor and operator of the machine has as many as 3000 successive photographs of a scene to give it life and motion.[14]

If Charles Hodges falsely claimed to be the inventor of the "Warograph," then the second motion-picture attraction at the Exhibition was also a case of mistaken identity. J. B. Morris used the Lumière Brothers' Cinématographe to show some of the films made by Méliès.

J. B. Morris' show of wonders, including the CIEMTOGRAPH [sic] and "Lunette," the flying lady is an amusement that appeals to everyone, particularly to women and children. The Cinematographe portrays all the famous moving pictures of Lueniere the Parisian artist."Lunette" after being put under hypnotic control by Mr. Morris, floats through the air without the aid of any conceivable device. "Lunette" is a handsome woman and very graceful in all of her actions.[15]

In both accounts in the *Austin Statesman*, the two technologies (The "Warograph" and the "Lunette") created viewer confusion. The "Warograph" was partially accepted as "producing " the "effects." And although the "Lunette" was a magic illusion, it too was accepted as the creation of J. B. Morris; the viewers assumed that Morris had performed the illusion, when in fact, he was probably merely projecting a print of a film like Georges Méliès' *Séance de Prestidigitation* (1896).[16]

In 1900, Austin had quite a lively cultural life. The most widely attended was the traveling theater. Each week as many as four or more attractions would appear at theaters such as the Hancock Opera House. Vaudeville was quite popular and large touring companies would appear with their shows which sometimes included as many as ten different acts.[17] Because Austin had so many entertain-

---

[14]*Austin Statesman,* January 11, 1900, p. 3.

[15]Ibid.

[16]Many exhibitors traveled with Cinématographes that had been purchased in the East (or Europe). They could obtain prints of Méliès's work, which were fairly available in the United States. One large outlet was the Eden Musee in New York City.

[17]Ibid., January 6, 1910, p. 8.

ment sources (theater, vaudeville, and later burlesque), the cinema had a difficult time capturing its own audience during the first decade of the century.[18]

By 1910, the moving picture show was on almost equal footing with vaudeville shows in Austin.[19] Nationally, movies had been alternated with theater and vaudeville through the first decade, but it was vaudeville and theater which seem to have attracted audiences in Austin.[20] In 1910, the Hancock Opera House installed its first movie projector to alternate presentations of films with vaudeville acts. A large advertisement appeared in the *Austin Statesman* on Tuesday, January 4, 1910.

> Manager Walker of Hancock Opera House desires to announce that on Wed., Thurs., Fri., and Sat. matinee and night the attraction will be two hours of moving pictures. 6000 feet of film will be run at each performance. In connection with the moving picture shows Manager Walker has secured well-known blackfaced comic Mr. Billy Van Allen in a new and up-to-date blackface act. The price of admission is 5¢ for children and 10¢ for adults.[21]

The Hancock Opera House was the first theater in Austin to permanently install and show motion pictures for the main attraction.[22] Vaudeville, it was hoped, would begin to take the back seat to the main attraction, with the "movies" or "flickers" cutting cost on the more expensive acts.[23] However, by Wednesday of that week, the Hancock Opera House realized that its Friday and weekend performance sales were suffering. In the Thursday edition of the newspaper, Manager Walker entered a newly-revised advertisement that emphasized vaudeville and barely even mentioned the moving pictures.[24]

---

[18]F. H. Richardson's *Motion Picture Handbook* (New York: Moving Picture World, 1910), p. 186, stated that "vaudeville acts may be had from $25 a week for a single or $50 a week for a double, to as high as you want to go. Acts vary in length from usually ten to twenty minutes. As a rule, the house is obliged to stand traveling expenses one way. By traveling expenses, railway fare only."

[19]Ibid., January 5, 1910, p. 6.

[20]Conversation with J. W. Carpenter, supported by playbills and reviews in the *Austin Statesman*, January 3, 1910 to December 16, 1910.

[21]Ibid., January 4, 1910, p. 5.

[22]J. W. Carpenter helped install the equipment at the Hancock Opera House, which was located off Congress Avenue. The projectors were mounted in a small loft over the ticket booth.

[23]Recorded conversation with Carpenter.

[24]*Austin Statesman*, January 6, 1910, p. 8.

HANCOCK OPERA HOUSE

Tonight
Friday & Saturday — **10 Big Vaudeville Acts**
Dixieville Polite Vaudeville Co.

Mr. and Mrs. Van
Alice Belmer
Lawrence P. Wall and the Dancing Kid
Clytre Markley
Billie Van Allen
Jimmie Van
3000 Feet of Moving Pictures

The advertisement graphically illustrates the problems that moving pictures encountered in the 1900–1910 period in Austin. The number of feet of film to be exhibited was reduced by half (from 6000 feet to 3000 feet) and by Sunday, the advertisement made no mention of the film footage whatsoever. Subsequent reviews made scant reference to the films.

This sluggish introduction of the cinema into Austin proved to be the rule, rather than the exception. In the February 11, 1910 issue of the *Austin Statesman* a number of vaudeville theaters advertised acts, making no large notice of showing films. No attention was given to the content of the "moving pictures" either. Exhibitors were content merely to advertise "2000 feet of moving pictures." The mere fact that moving pictures were on the program suggested to the prospective customers that they wouldn't be bored between major vaudeville acts. It was during this period that films were referred to as "chasers." Usually shown between the end of one show and the beginning of the next, moving pictures were used in much the same way that recorded music is today between shows.[25]

The 1910–1913 period is the most historically significant period for the introduction of film to Austin. In four short years film moved from its part-time position in vaudeville shows to a full-time entertainment medium, one that could hold its own with the vaudeville stage. The moving picture theater or "nickelodeon" in this period became a social institution.

---

[25]Recorded conversations with Carpenter and Simpson.

Projectionist J. W. Carpenter stated: "You want to know why people first went to the movies? I'll tell you why: 5¢. It only cost you 5¢ and you saw one reel of film. It was entertaining. You saw shots of many different places. Film that would show you many different places around the world."[26] Edward Van Zile went further when he wrote that because of film's capacity for portraying the world, "The New Yorker has learned that what happens in Peking or Canton may affect him more vitally than anything which may occur in Mott or Pell Street. Against his own volition he has become, perforce, a citizen of the world."[27] Films of this period were one reel in length, lasting ten to fifteen minutes, depending on how fast the projectionist turned the crank of the projector.

By 1913, the cinema had become predominently a feature-length medium. A new institution had emerged: the Sunday, September 7, 1913, edition of the *Austin Statesman* announced the opening of Austin's first "movie house":

MacCormack and Company have acquired the theater at 920 Congress Avenue formerly known as the "Unique" and re-christened it THE CRESCENT. We have contracted for the best picture service and will give our first high-class program Monday afternoon and night. Repairs will be made on the theater immediately and it will run to please the most refined and critical audience.[28]

There were other factors at work to justify the move of films from vaudeville into theaters of their own. The harsh economic realities of the entertainment world were reported in the *Statesman* and confirmed by J. W. Carpenter:

See, stage shows in the theaters got to be fewer and fewer as time went on. And the stage shows were not continuous the way that movies were. With stage shows, the most turnover we ever had come to one theater in a week was three shows a week. Then the shows went down to one a week, and then down to one a month, by 1913. A theater manager couldn't make a living at it (the shows being so sporadic) so they had to go with something steady (the movies). The stage shows disappeared for one reason: transportation on the railroads started going up, up, up and up . . . . Expenses got so high that theatrical companies just couldn't travel and make it financially. Rent, food—everything—was getting high. They just cut down the number of stage shows. The movies simply took up the vacuum of the stage shows.[29]

---

[26]Ibid.

[27]Edward Van Zile, *That Marvel the Movie* (New York: Putnam, 1923), p. 65.

[28]*Austin Statesman*, September 7, 1913, p. 6.

[29]Recorded conversation with Carpenter.

By late 1913, the moving picture show had become a major, storytelling medium, "feature-length," capable of "making an artistic appeal sufficient to stir our emotions."[30] By 1914, Austin was exhibiting films by Ince, Griffith, Sennett, Arbuckle, and others. Dorothy Gish, Irene Hunt, Charles Chaplin, Sarah Bernhardt, "Broncho Billy" Anderson, William S. Hart, Tom Mix, and others regularly appeared on a daily basis in the newly created nickelodeons of Austin. The Queen, the Yale, the Casino, the Aerodome, the Princess, the Crescent, the Besmar, Littlefield's, the Cactus, the Texan, the Paramount, the State, the Orpheum, the Majestic, and the Hancock Opera House: many came and went and had various names as the cinema became a major American social institution in Austin, Texas.[31]

---

[30]Henry Albert Philips, "A New Medium for Artistic Expression," *Motion Picture Magazine* 8, no. 10, p. 111.

[31]Department of Planning, City Hall, Austin Texas.

GARTH S. JOWETT

The First Motion Picture Audiences

The exact composition and nature of the first motion picture audiences has always been something of an historical mystery. While the classic histories of the movies all attempt to describe the initial devotees of the new entertainment, they are seldom able to go beyond a cursory analysis of the type found in Benjamin Hampton's *A History of the Movies* (1931), where the author noted that "a new class of amusement buyer sprang into existence as quickly and apparently as magically as screen pictures themselves appeared."[1] Only Lewis Jacobs in his seminal work, *The Rise of the American Film* (1939), goes into the kind of detail useful to film and social historians.[2]

The question remains—who was this audience, and where did they come from? And why were they attracted to this new entertainment form in such vast numbers in such a short period of time? Only now are some of these answers beginning to appear as film and social historians start to piece together the early years of the motion picture industry. It is becoming more and more obvious that the movies were no idle innovation, arriving at a propitious time, but that they answered a deep social and cultural need of the American people. The work in this area has just begun, and only by continuing such research can we hope to reconstruct the dimensions of the social impact of the motion picture on American society in the last seventy years.

---

[1]Benjamin Hampton, *A History of the Movies* (New York: Covici-Friede, 1931), p. 17.

[2]While very little work has been done in this area of film studies in recent years, an important article on this topic has recently been published. See Russell Meritt, "Nickelodeon Theaters: Building an Audience for the Movies," *AFI Report*, May 1973, pp. 4–8. For a more extended examination of the factors surrounding the introduction of the motion picture into America see Garth Jowett, "Media Power and Social Control: The Motion Picture in America, 1896–1936," Ph.D. dissertation, University of Pennsylvania, 1972.

RECREATION AND ENTERTAINMENT AT THE
TURN OF THE CENTURY

A major aspect of the immense social and cultural changes taking place in America in the period after the Civil War was a growing interest and participation in new forms of recreation and entertainment. Eventually these new "mass" recreational forms would alter the pattern of American social and cultural life away from an emphasis on local interests and activities to a more national level of participation, with which we are so familiar today. The rapid influx of immigrants and rural Americans into the burgeoning urban centers provided the raw population base, but this alone did not account for the tremendous increase in newspaper and periodical literature readership. The circulation of daily newspapers increased 400 percent between 1870 and 1900, while the population grew only by 95 percent.[3] This discrepancy is partly accounted for by the decrease in illiteracy, and by a general raising of educational standards. The aggressive tactics of the publishers, who became much more expert in gauging the tastes of their readers, was also a major factor.

However, the single most important reason favoring the growth of all recreational activity was the increase in available leisure time. The decline in the work week of American workers meant more time for reading and other forms of self-improvement, which in turn led to greater efficiency and productivity and more available leisure hours. Thus in nonagricultural industries, the work week declined by about 10 hours between 1850 and 1900—from 66 to 56 hours. In the next four decades reductions were even sharper than in the previous half century. Between 1900 and 1940 the work week in nonagricultural industries declined from 56 to 41 hours, with the sharpest declines occurring between 1900 and 1920, when the average work week in nonagricultural industries dropped about 5 hours every 10 years.[4] An examination of the decrease in the work week of certain types of workers between 1890 and 1928 indicates the amount of extra leisure time available. The increase in available leisure time would encourage the creation and usage of all recreational forms, especially commercial amusements such as the motion picture, which required a more definite and specific commitment of free time, unlike books, newspapers, or periodicals, which could be read in the home with greater ease.

Recreation of all forms took a firm hold in America in the 1890s, and the newspapers of the time were also full of advertisements for summer resorts or for fashionable tours of Europe or to the American West. However, the old American ethic which praised the virtues and rewards of 'hard work' taught so assiduously

---

[3]Edward Emery, *The Press in America* (Englewood Cliffs, N.J.: Prentice-Hall, 1962), p. 346.

[4]This summary is taken from Joseph S. Zeisel, "The Workweek in American Industry, 1850–1956," in *Mass Leisure*, ed. Eric Larrabee and Rolf Meyersohn (Glencoe: The Free Press, 1958), pp. 145–53.

Table 1. Average Hours of Labor Per Week in Eleven Industries, 1890–1928

INDUSTRY	AVERAGE HOURS PER WEEK		PERCENT DECREASE DURING PERIOD
	1890	1928	
Bakeries	64.7	47.4	26.7
Boot and shoe	59.5	49.1	17.5
Building	52.0	43.5	16.3
Cotton goods	62.8	53.4	14.9
Foundry and machine shops	59.8	50.4	15.7
Blast furnaces	84.6	59.8	29.3
Marble and stone	54.7	44.0	19.6
Millwork	52.0	44.8	13.8
Book and job printing	56.4	44.3	21.5
Newspaper printing	48.2	45.1	6.5
Woolen goods	58.9	49.3	16.3

SOURCE: *Recent Social Trends in the United States* (New York: McGraw-Hill, 1933), p. 828.

in the famous McGuffey Readers was still much in evidence, and the increased leisure time made available by the shorter work week was seen by some as a frivolous waste of human resources. It was especially in the city that this traditional view would meet its strongest opposition, while in the rural sectors the old prejudices against amusement would continue to hold fast for some time to come. City children found outlets for their pent-up energies in the various activities created specifically for them by well-meaning social organizations conscious of their needs. The Boy Scouts, the Girl Scouts, and Camp Fire Girls were all created to supply city children with some knowledge and understanding of the outdoors. Towards the end of the century urban needs led to larger-scale planning of public parks, reaching a peak in the 1890s and resulting in such achievements as Chicago's beautiful Lincoln Park along the lake front and the metropolitan park systems of Boston, Cleveland, and other cities. Old favorites such as the circus, the theater, burlesque, vaudeville, and the melodrama continued to thrive in the growing urban environment.

These entertainment forms sometimes had a social significance which was not immediately apparent but which went deep into the social fabric of the newly emerging urban culture. Albert F. McLean, in a provocative study, *American Vaudeville as Ritual*, examined this entertainment form and suggested that vaudeville was "for at least four decades, not only a significant social institution but also a mythic enactment, through ritual, of the underlying aspirations of the American people."[5] Much of what McLean claims for vaudeville could be said for the movies, with the added factor that movies had a much greater audience, and appealed to a wider range of immigrant groups, especially to those in the lower socio-economic groups. In the final analysis the two entertainments were essentially different, in that vaudeville was a highly stylized, artificial, and ritualistic form, with recognized and repetitive actions which were expected by the audience, while the film medium relied more on elements of surprise and visual effects in an attempt to be as realistic as possible. (In time the film audience would also come to expect certain forms of "ritual.")

The demand for urban recreational activities seemed insatiable, and sharp-witted entrepreneurs were not slow to exploit this need by supplying a myriad of entertainment forms such as the dime museum, dance halls (which were extremely popular, but also a great source of consternation to many city authorities), shooting galleries, beer gardens, bowling alleys, billiard parlors, saloons, and other more questionable social activities. Thus entertainment in the cities was available in many different forms, but there were still many segments of the population which were unable to partake of these amusements on a regular basis because of economic considerations, long working hours, or problems with the language. It was from this group that most of the initial adherents to the motion picture would come, for the movies could satisfy all of these problems in one way or another—they were cheap, available for the whole family, easily accessible and needed no proficiency in the English language.

THE NEW AUDIENCE

But what was the nature of this "new" audience that so eagerly embraced this welcomed digression in their lives? Part of this answer can be found in a brief examination of the religious, social and economic conditions of the era. The motion picture's first audience seemed to have been made up from three groups: first, those from the middle class who had never previously attended the theater or other amusements because of religious beliefs, and who were now free to explore new entertainments. Benjamin Hampton, in his *A History of the Movies*, noted that the motion picture was perfected at a time when "more and more people, mainly the young, broader-minded and more daring than their forebears, crept through the barriers which had been erected by religious prejudice."[6] Once freed from religious strictures this group began to enjoy theatrical presentations of local or professional repertoire groups. Amongst the plays which helped break

[5]Albert F. McLean, *American Vaudeville as Ritual* (Lexington: University of Kentucky Press, 1965), p. 2.

[6]Hampton, *History of the Movies*, p. 15.

down the religious objections to this type of entertainment were *Uncle Tom's Cabin* and *Ten Nights in a Bar Room*.[7] As church restrictions were relaxed, informally at first, then later by popular assent, more and more Americans began seeking new diversions, with the major criteria being moral acceptability and low cost. It was many of these same people who also welcomed the phonograph, kinetoscope parlors and arcades, and then later the dime museums, trolley rides, and amusement parks. However, most of them turned to the movies as a principal source of entertainment, slowly at first and then with an increasing fervor which caught the whole country by surprise.

The second group of early movie adherents came from those middle- and upper-working-class patrons of the live theater, especially the fans of the popular melodramas. They grabbed hold of the movies as a new source of theatrical experience because the live theater was unable to fill the entertainment void created by the alteration in social and cultural conditions. Nicholas Vardac in book *From Stage to Screen* has shown how the audience's desire for "pictorial realism" had created a demand favorable to the introduction of the motion picture, for the theater was not capable of providing the extension to the realism already indicated on the stages of that period. The dramatic improvement in theatric lighting with the introduction of electricity also helped to destroy many illusionary effects. Only the movies, with their realistic illusion of depth, could continue the evolutionary process begun with the increasing attempts at realism in the melodrama.[8]

Then too, as a commercial offering, the theater suffered from the many serious deficiencies found in the majority of provincial theaters, which were not technically equipped to handle the very complex machinery used for the realistic productions in New York or other large Eastern cities. Most towns with a population of below 10,000 possessed inadequate equipment for the presentation of road shows which might have competed with the realism and sensationalism available in the motion picture melodrama. In *Middletown*, the Lynds point out how meager were the offerings of the provincial theaters in the 1890s:

> Like the automobile, the motion picture is more to Middletown than simply a new way of doing an old thing; it has added new dimensions to the city's leisure. To be sure, the spectacle-watching habit was strong

---

[7]"Uncle Tom's Cabin" was one of the many theatrical presentations which found its way into film scripts, thus creating a further bond of continuity. For a detailed examination of the career of this play as a motion picture, see William L. Slout, " 'Uncle Tom's Cabin' in American Film History," *The Journal of Popular Film*, 2 (Spring 1973): 137–53.

[8]The best treatments of the melodrama are Frank Rahill, *The World of Melodrama* (University Park, Pa.: Pennsylvania State University Press, 1967); and Nicholas Vardac, *From Stage to Screen* (Cambridge: Harvard University Press, 1949). See also John L. Fell, "Dissolves by Gaslight," *Film Quarterly* 23 (1970) pp. 22–34.

upon Middletown in the nineties. Whenever they had a chance people turned out to a "show," but chances were relatively fewer. Fourteen times during January, 1890, for instance, the Opera House was opened by performances ranging from *Uncle Tom's Cabin* to the *Black Crook*, before the paper announced that "there will not be any more attractions at the Opera House for nearly two weeks." In July there were no "attractions"; a half dozen were scattered through August and September; there were twelve in October. [In a footnote, Lynd adds that there were less than 125 performances, including matinees, for the entire year.][9]

By 1923, however, there were nine motion picture theaters in Middletown, (the city of Muncie, Indiana), operating from 1 to 11 p.m. seven days a week, summer and winter, with a total of over 300 cinematic performances available to the residents every week of the year. It is clear therefore that by the time of the introduction of the film as a commercial entertainment, the extensive provincial audiences were being offered nothing more than conventional staging, while the more "realistic" productions were limited in circulation to a few large Eastern cities. This is further evidenced by the remarkable growth in the number of motion picture houses in those outlying areas once they had been spawned and had found acceptance in their urban birthplace.

In the cities the live theater, although a very popular and well-publicized entertainment, was still not capable of reaching all the people. Benjamin Hampton estimated that "perhaps a million, possibly two million people were regular patrons of the various forms of theater entertainment—opera, spoken drama, musical comedy, vaudeville and burlesque—and perhaps another million enjoyed the stage occasionally. . . . However ninety percent of the American population was not reached by any method of story-telling and character delineation by play-acting."[10]

A special study commissioned by the Twentieth Century Club of Boston on "The Amusement Situation in the City of Boston" in 1909 supported Hampton's contention that the live theater did not reach as many people as the movies later did.[11] The exhaustive survey indicated that in 1909 the weekly seating capacity (calculated by multiplying the theater's seating capacity by the number of weekly performances) of the various segments of the entertainment industry was as shown in table 2.

---

[9]Robert S. Lynd and Helen Merrell Lynd, *Middletown* (New York: Harcourt, Brace, and World, 1929), p. 263.

[10]Hampton, *History of the Movies*, p. 14.

[11]*The Amusement Situation in the City of Boston*, a report prepared by the Drama Committee of the Twentieth Century Club, Boston, 1910, pp. 10–11.

Table 2. Seating in Boston Places of Amusement, 1909

Amusement	Weekly Seating Capacity
Opera	13,590
First-Class Theaters	111,568
Popular Theater	17,811
Stock House	21,756
Vaudeville Houses	45,744
Burlesque Houses	80,700
Vaudeville and Moving Pictures	79,362
Moving-Picture Theaters	402,428

The population of metropolitan Boston at this time was estimated at 625,000. The study noted that of the entertainment seating total, vaudeville and moving picture shows accounted for 85.4 percent; legitimate performances, 13.5 percent; and grand opera, 1.1 percent. The average attendance prices were as follows:

Moving-picture shows   .10
Vaudeville and moving pictures   .15
Vaudeville   .50
Regular theater $1.00
The Boston Opera $2.00

The authors of this study noted with some alarm the "overwhelming preponderance of cheaper and less desireable forms of entertainment," but realistically commented that "these theaters evidently appeal more and more strongly to their habitues. The great growth of new houses of this type indicates not only a rapidly increasing following, but also a tremendous and growing tendency toward a lower and less desireable form of recreative amusement."[12]

The relatively high cost of the theater also proved to be prohibitive to its wide acceptance and use, especially amongst the lower, working classes. The price of tickets ranged from $1.50 to $2.00 for orchestra seats, to 50¢ for the gallery in metropolitan areas, and $1.50 to 25¢ in smaller areas.[13] At this time the average workman's pay was approximately $2 a day, and the relatively high cost of the gallery seats could not have been a great inducement considering the noise of the gallery mob. However, after 1880, the presentation of drama and melodrama at "popular prices" in second-class theaters in the larger cities had achieved some success in attracting new groups of entertainment buyers. Many of these

---

[12]Ibid., pp. 6–7.
[13]Hampton, *History of the Movies*, p. 14.

same companies also later toured country seats and larger provincial towns, appearing in opera houses, which we have seen remained dark between these infrequent engagements. Nevertheless, all the live theatrical entertainment available could not satisfy the special and growing needs of a very large segment of the American population.

As the moving picture evolved from its early exposure in arcades, vaudeville, and "store-front" theaters it passed into the mainstream of American life. For the price of 5¢ to 10¢ a patron could partake of an entertainment experience that was demonstrably more realistic than anything he would find on the stage. Initially at least, this low cost was a great inducement to sampling the new entertainment, and was an important reason for its quick success. However, once established as a permanent and highly desirable attraction, the price of filmgoing increased commensurate with the increasing length and improved quality of the product being offered.

The third and most important group which made up the first movie audiences came from members of the large urban working class, who seldom went anywhere near live theatrical entertainment. For them the movies were the ideal form of recreation. Especially for the immigrant worker, the movies provided more than just a way of filling in time, but also acted as a guide to the newcomer on the manners and customs of his new environment. It is somewhat ironic that while the workers formed by far the largest segment of the nickelodeon audience in the early years, the owners of these establishments very quickly coveted the more prestigious middle class.[14] Russell Merritt has demonstrated that from the first, the nickelodeon "catered to him [the worker] through necessity, not through choice. The blue-collar worker and his family may have supported the nickelodeon. The scandal was that no one connected with the movies much wanted his support—least of all the immigrant film exhibitors who were working their way out the slums."[15] However, whether he liked it or not, the exhibitor had to contend with the worker, and especially the immigrant, as the backbone of his support.

There is no doubt that the movies were indeed an important factor in the social life of the urban working class, and this is graphically confirmed in the following extracts taken from one of the studies forming the *Pittsburgh Survey*, an in-depth social study of the workers in that city done in 1907–9. One researcher reported:

> I shall not soon forget a Saturday evening when I stood among the crowd of pleasure-seekers on Fifth Avenue, and watched the men and

---

[14]Merritt cites a Russell Sage study which indicates that 78 percent of the audience in New York City nickelodeons were members of the "working class." See Merritt, "Nickelodeon Theaters," p. 5.

[15]Ibid., p. 5.

women packed thick at the entrance of every picture show. My companion and I bought tickets for one of the five cent shows. Our way was barred by a sign, "Performance now going on." As we stood near the door, the crowd of people waiting to enter filled the long vestibule and even part of the sidewalk. They were determined to be amused, and this was one of the things labeled, "Amusement." They were hot and tired and irritable, but willing to wait until long after our enthusiasm was dampened, and we had left them standing in line for their chance to go in.

It was an incident not without significance, this eagerness with which they turned toward leisure after a working week of unmeaning hours. . . .[16]

The lack of available recreational opportunities for many workers is amply demonstrated in the findings of the *Pittsburgh Survey*. Discussing the role of recreation in the lives of working women the *Survey* pointed out that of the 22,185 working women surveyed in Pittsburgh in 1907, only 258, less than 2 percent were in touch with a center for social development and recreation.[17] While the importance of the motion picture in filling this "leisure gap" was obvious even then to the social workers involved in doing the survey, they were still somewhat sceptical about its ultimate value. The report continued: "Nickelodeons and dance halls and skating rinks are in no sense inherently bad, but so long as those maintained for profit are the only relief for nervous weariness and the desire for stimulation, we may well reckon leisure a thing spent, not used."[18]

A few of the reasons for the immense popularity of the "movies" have already been suggested, but the extra relief they provided in a dreary, work-laden life must be emphasized. The *Survey* research only alluded to this when it continued: "In so far as hours of work tend to dull and stupefy the worker, they are longer than the community can afford. Dulled senses demand powerful stimuli; exhaustion of the vital forces leads to a desire for crude, for violent excitation. . . . Craving for excitement is the last symptom of a starved imagination. . . ."[19] However, the fact that some forms of recreational stimuli were needed was not lost on the social workers; their only doubts concerned the medium's social utility. The report continued: "Any excitation, destructive or not, is acceptable, if only it be strong; the effect of it is to create a desire for stronger stimulation. Roller skating rinks, dance halls, questionable cafes, may figure only temporarily in the worker's life or by increasing the demand for excitement, may

---

[16]Elizabeth Beardsley Butler, *Women and the Trades: Pittsburgh, 1907–08* (New York: Charities Publication Committee, 1909), p. 333.

[17]Ibid., p. 332.

[18]Ibid., p. 333.

[19]Ibid., p. 356.

lead to sexual license."[20] It was becoming ominously clear: the motion picture, although a major source of entertainment and recreation for a large portion of the working class, was already being classified as "destructive," "unsocial," "wasteful," and the cause of "sexual license."

The whole problem of leisure and recreation was of great concern to the newly emerging professional social workers, who were anxious that all Americans made maximum use of their spare time in constructive ways. Unfortunately, the movies' origins as an adjunct of both vaudeville and the rather "seamy" arcades had saddled it with an unsavory reputation. While there certainly were unscrupulous motion picture house operators, and storefront theaters that were both unsanitary and morally unsafe, by far the majority of nickelodeons provided their ever-increasing clientele with a form of recreation and entertainment which was vastly superior in "moral tone" and low cost to that available in many other urban leisure activities such as saloons, vaudeville, or burlesque.

In many working-class districts the motion picture was the only source of amusement available, and certainly the only form of public amusement which many working-class families could afford to attend together as a family unit. In a survey of the mill town of Homestead one researcher reported:

> Practically the only public amusements in Homestead during my stay there, were the nickelodeons and skating rinks. Six of the former, all on Eighth Avenue, sent out their penetrating music all evening and most of the afternoon. There was one ten-cent vaudeville house, but others charge five cents for a show consisting of songs, moving pictures, etc., which lasts fifteen minutes or so.
>
> The part these shows play in the life of the community is really surprising. Not only were no other theatrical performances given in Homestead, but even those in Pittsburgh, because of the time and expense involved in getting there, were often out of the reach of the workingmen and their families. . . . Many people, therefore find in the nickelodeons their only relaxation. Men on their way from work stop for a few minutes to see something of life outside the alteration of mill and home: the shopper rests while she enjoys the music, poor though it be, and the children are always begging for five cents to go to the nickelodeon. In the evening the family often go together for a little treat. . . . In many ways this form of amusement is desireable. What it ordinarily offers does not educate but does give pleasure. . . . As the nickelodeon seems to have met a real need in the mill towns, one must wish that it might offer them a better quality of entertainment.[21]

---

[20]Ibid., p. 356.

[21]Margaret F. Byington, *Homestead: The Households of a Milltown* (New York: Charities Publications Committee, 1910), pp. 110–11.

The expense of entertainment was therefore a major consideration for most working-class families, and the study indicated that with a weekly budget of between $12 and $15, the average allowed for "sundries" was $1.23. The social worker commented, "we see how small an amount can be free at this and lower levels for what could be called amusements. Ten cents a week for the nickelodeon or for candy, a car ride to the country once in a while—these are the possibilities which seem open to mothers and children depending on a day laborer's pay."[22]

It was, however, the lack of alternative recreational opportunities which was the major factor accounting for the popularity of the motion picture amongst the entire urban working-class population, of which the immigrants were, of course, a significant segment. We have already noted the relatively high cost of other forms of commercial amusements, and the expense and other difficulties encountered in attending the live theater. Alternative forms of recreation were either too expensive or not widely available in the working-class districts of cities. Very few public playgrounds were in existence at this time, and by 1910 the playground movement had just begun to make a little headway.[23] The report on "Recreation" in the U.S. government study *Recent Social Trends* noted that in 1910 only 17.6 percent of the playgrounds reported were operating on a year-round schedule, and that organized playground activities formed only a small part of the regular recreational program of the urban community.[24] It is little wonder therefore that the motion picture appealed to the working class, and especially to the children with time on their hands. The new medium of entertainment had no difficulty in finding a ready-made and eager audience amongst this segment of the urban population.

---

[22]Ibid., p. 89.

[23]*Recent Social Trends in the United States* (New York: McGraw-Hill, 1933), p. 916.

[24]Ibid., p. 917.

DAVID LEVY

Edison Sales Policy and the Continuous Action Film, 1904–1906

It has been an axiom of the pre-Griffith cinema that in 1903 Edwin S. Porter, working for Thomas Edison's Kinetographic Department, launched a great editing revolution that consequently transformed the American film industry and world motion picture art. But if such a thing ever occurred, neither Porter nor his employer was even vaguely aware of it. The fact of the matter is that there could not have been a more unlikely organization from which to expect, let alone get, a radical movie concept either before or after 1903. Indeed, a study of primary documents, including copyright registrations, court depositions, film catalogues, and sales records, mostly reveals Edison productions in the grip of an obsolete marketing strategy, one firmly stacked against the sort of continuous action subject Porter was supposed to have pioneered.

ONE JOKE, TWO FILMS

What seems the earliest explicit statement of how filmmakers in that period in fact perceived narrative continuity, as it involved a changing relation of the individual shot to the whole film, is contained in the legal-industrial discourse of a copyright infringement suit brought against the Edison company in the fall of 1904. At issue was a subject turned out in August of that year by Edwin Porter, *How a French Nobleman Got a Wife Through the New York Herald "Personal" Columns.* The American Mutoscope and Biograph Company alleged that the Porter film was a transparent steal of their own vaudeville house hit, *Personal,* released a couple of months previously.

Detecting the obvious similarities required no sharp legal mind. The story was a simple one. A French gentleman in the Biograph version—a nobleman in the Edison remake—places an ad in the *New York Herald* personal columns stating his desire to meet and marry an American woman—handsome in the

Biograph version, wealthy in Edison's. When a crowd of "Gibson girls" show up for the rendezvous at Grant's Tomb, the fellow flees, triggering a brief "chase" through city and country that culminates in his capture by one of the pursuants. The wording of the ad in the *Biograph Bulletin* no. 28 of August 15, 1904, read:

> PERSONAL—Young French gentleman recently arrived in this country, desires to meet handsome American girl; object matrimony. Will be at Grant's Tomb at 10 this morning, wearing boutonnière of violets.[1]

Edison Films, September Supplement, 1904 had it this way:

> Young French Nobleman recently arrived, desires to meet wealthy American girl; object matrimony; will be at Grant's Tomb at 10 this morning, wearing boutonnière of violets.[2]

Edison being Edison, their catalogue description added the hype that the "ad" had actually appeared in the *New York Herald* on August 25, 1904. They even went as far as to back the claim with a press quote from an unnamed newspaper piece chastizing the *Herald* for carrying the "bogus advertisement of a moving picture concern." All in all, it amounted to a crude attempt at representing their remake as part of a "yellow journalism" exposé about improvident foreign noblemen preying upon affluent American women whose less well-off sisters posed as "marriage-mad heiresses."[3]

In a court deposition, Porter, preoccupied with the differences between his film and the Biograph original, made no reference to any of this.

> My photograph is not a copy but an original. It carries out my own idea of how the French Nobleman should appear, as to costume, appearance, expression, figure, bearing, posing, gestures, postures and action. Complainant's Frenchman is short, mine is tall; theirs dresses in poor taste, mine dresses in good taste; theirs presents an undignified appearance, mine is of gracious and gentlemanly bearing. Theirs looks and behaves like a monkey—mine like a gentleman. These differences I believe I have made apparent in every picture of the series, by means of the said costume, poses, postures, actions, etc.[4]

---

[1] *Biograph Bulletin* no. 28, (August 15, 1904) in *Biograph Bulletins, 1896–1908*, ed. Kemp Niver (Los Angeles: Locare Research Group, 1971), p. 121.

[2] *Edison Films*, September supplement (1904), pp. 11–12.

[3] Ibid.

[4] Defendant's affidavits in opposition to complainant's December 4, 1904, motion for preliminary injunction, *American Mutoscope and Biograph Company vs. Edison Manufacturing Company*, United States Circuit Court, District of New Jersey.

Biograph was inclined to keep its eyes on the business end of the action. In outlining the *Personal* chase structure, the *Bulletin* gave this preview of what audiences could expect:

> At one time down a steep embankment where several of the girls slip and "bump the bumps." The professor in the orchestra plays a solo on the bass drum when this happens.[5]

The legal wrangle that ensued is important for several reasons. First there is the light it sheds on the way the leading obsessions of the Edison company, the protection of investment and its dollar rewards, determined their production concepts. The legal arguments, advanced by Porter, together with sales records for the period that followed, make it clear that Edison executives had little interest in furthering the cause of the continuous action film narrative along the lines of the alleged breakthrough cinema historians have claimed for *Life of an American Fireman* and *The Great Train Robbery*.

Secondly, the formulation of the Edison legal strategy and what it revealed about the general policy of the Kinetographic Department point to the extremely limited authority Porter wielded there and the even greater unlikelihood of his having possessed the scope to work even by inadvertence such miracles as have been attributed to him.

BIOGRAPH MOVES AHEAD

Between the completion of *The Great Train Robbery* in December 1903 and the release of *How a French Nobleman* in August 1904 Porter's output consisted mainly of short comic and trick films and a handful of actualities, very much the sort of thing he had been assigned before *The Great Train Robbery*.[6] The longest films he produced in that interim period included the *Buster Brown Series*, based on a comic strip, the news reproduction *Skirmish Between Russian and Japanese Advance Guards, Fire and Flames at Luna Park, Coney Island,* based on a live show and two actualities, *Inter-Collegiate Regatta, Poughkeepsie, N.Y.,* and *Scenes in an Orphan Asylum.* For the most part, Edison officials appear to have drawn their 1904 inspiration for longer films, *not* from Porter's classic train robbery subject, but from the work of Biograph directors. On February 20, 1904, an anonymous *New York Dramatic Mirror* reviewer hailed Biograph's "long film of scenes in the life of Kit Carson" on view at Keith's as "by all odds the best that has been shown at this house."[7]

---

[5]*Biograph Bulletin* no. 8.

[6]Motion picture copyright records, Edison National Historic Site, West Orange, N.J. (hereafter referred to as ENHS).

[7]*New York Dramatic Mirror*, February 20, 1904, p. 18.

The pictures are beautifully colored and splendidly taken, and reflect
the utmost credit on the man who posed them and selected the scenes in
which they were photographed. It would be hard to imagine anything
finer in the line of animated pictures.[8]

The publication was equally lavish in its praise for *The Escaped Lunatic* at Keith's
the following month.[9] And in November the *Mirror* applauded *The Lost Child* as "a
remarkable picture."[10]

Formed in 1895 by magic merchant Bernard Koopman, Henry Marvin,
Herman Cassler, and former Edison employee W. K. L. Dickson, the American
Mutoscope Company, originally called simply the KMCD Company, had been
set up to produce flipcard movies for mutoscope machines. In 1897, the company
decided to get into the production of films for theatrical projection on their
Biograph apparatus.[11] Edison officials moved quickly to tie them up in a patent
suit, which they succeeded in doing until March 2, 1902. On that date, a Circuit
Court of Appeals judge overturned the Edison company's major patent claims.

In the interim the Biograph company had tried to compensate through
innovation in short novelty subjects. The company's first long production dated
from October 1903, when they completed *The American Soldier in Love and War*, in
three parts, *Kit Carson*, in thirteen parts, and *The Pioneers*, in six parts. But at that
point, Biograph was simply endeavoring to keep up, taking its cue in part from the
popular Buffalo Bill Wild West Show historical spectaculars, but mostly from
Edison's longer 1902–3 subjects like *Jack and the Beanstalk*, *Life of an American
Fireman* and *Uncle Tom's Cabin*.

By the summer of 1904 the tide had turned. In January, a mere month, that is,
following the completion of *The Great Train Robbery*, Biograph had released *The
Escaped Lunatic*, one of the earliest American "chase" subjects. They followed it up
with *Battle of the Yalu* in March, *Personal* in June, *The Moonshiner* in August, *The Hero
of Liao Yang* in September and *The Lost Child* in October. The Edison company
suddenly found itself having to struggle to keep up with remakes. Porter
completed *Maniac Chase*, the Edison version of *The Escaped Lunatic* in October
1904 and *Stolen by Gypsies*, Edison's remake of *The Lost Child*, in July 1905. In April
1904, the company had Porter hurry out a static rehash of Biograph's *Yalu*, called
Skirmish Between Russian and Japanese Advance Guards.

As early as the March 1904 release of *Battle of the Yalu* it was clear that
Biograph had begun offering serious competition in the longer film field. And so

[8]Ibid.

[9]*New York Dramatic Mirror*, March 12, 1904, p. 17.

[10]*New York Dramatic Mirror*, November 5, 1904, p. 17.

[11]Paul Spehr, "Film Making at the American Mutoscope and Biograph Company, 1900-
1906," *The Quarterly Journal of the Library of Congress* 37 (Summer–Fall 1980) 413–21.

when Edison officials in the late summer of 1904 assigned Edwin Porter the task of turning out a remake of *Personal*, it was as good as an admission that they had fallen behind Biograph in the "chase" for motion picture profits.

One possible explanation for Biograph's ability to outdistance Edison productions by mid-1904 was their "complete service" method. It involved supplying vaudeville houses with machines, operators, and films and, according to research on the period, constituted the most common vaudeville-motion picture connection.[12] The Edison Company, apparently, offered no such service. Their marketing strategy was simply to sell their subjects mostly to two jobbers, George Kleine in Chicago and Percy Waters in New York. Kleine did not offer a complete service but sold films to others like George Spoor who did through his Kinodrome service. Waters was involved in film exhibition in addition to his film sales and projector rental business. Biograph's "complete service" approach, one that gave them control over exhibition, would have enabled the company to rapidly gauge vaudeville house reaction and work refinements into their productions.

As for Edwin Porter's role in all this, one must, of course, concede that there is no evidence to show that he had superior ideas that were rejected by his employers. There are, as far as anyone has been able to determine, no written accounts of active studio resistance either among Edison records or in the form of personal correspondence. If there is any sort of conclusion to be drawn from an examination of Edison company documents it is that the company treated him as an employee whose job it was to follow instructions; he was rarely consulted on business policy or on decisions that would affect motion picture production. In other words, a minor company figure whose input into the formulation of legal and marketing strategy, the pivotal Edison concerns in the period, was quite limited. To put it another way, if in 1904 Edison had lost significant ground to Biograph, Porter could be assigned the task of helping them play catch-up, but really little of the blame.

TOWARD A LEGAL DEFINITION OF THE "CONTINUOUS INCIDENT"

In August 1904, Edison general manager W. E. Gilmore wrote to George Kleine, Edison's western jobber since 1898, complaining about ads Kleine's company had placed in *The New York Clipper* on August 6, 1904, and August 13, 1904, for Biograph and Pathé subjects:

> From a purely commercial standpoint I do not see how we can continue
> to give you every advantage to the detriment of all other dealers, and

---

[12]Robert C. Allen "Vaudeville and Film, 1895–1915: A Study in Media Interaction," Ph.D dissertation, University of Iowa, 1977, pp. 160–61, 179.

from a legal standpoint we do not consider it good policy that a jobber like your concern should take up and push the goods of other manufacturers. . . .[13]

On August 18, 1904, Kleine wrote back protesting his loyalty and affirming his usefulness to the company. Gilmore replied six days later, in effect reiterating his charge that Kleine was not holding up his end of the deal between them, and insisting that Edison subjects were at least on a par with Biograph's.[14]

That Gilmore could get few people, including himself, to agree with the claim is testified to by the company's release of the Edison remake of *Personal*, a film that went into production a mere five days after Gilmore's self-serving assertion. In a published letter dated August 31, 1904, the Biograph company advised their customers that *Personal* had just completed a four-week run at Keith's Union Square in New York City. A caveat was added against the Porter-Edison remake which, the letter went on,

deliberately appropriated our original idea changing the advertisement upon which the story is founded . . . for the purpose of avoiding our copyrights, and reproducing the action of our film as nearly as they could.[15]

In early September, John C. Kerr, an attorney acting for Biograph, formally advised Edison counsel Frank Dyer of his client's displeasure.[16] Dyer, in a letter dated September 17, 1904, told Kerr that he didn't think Biograph had much of a copyright infringement case. "I have," he noted, "serious doubts if a copyright can legitimately cover a moving picture film, comprising many scenes and incidents in widely different localities."[17]

What precisely Dyer had in mind was an April 20, 1903 ruling that granted the Edison company an injunction to prevent Sigmund Lubin from duping and selling portions of an actuality Edison had copyrighted on March 1, 1902, *Kaiser Wilhelm's Yacht Meteor Entering the Water*. The legal argument had been over whether the Edison company, in order to comply with an 1870 copyright law for photographs, ought to have registered *each* of the 4,500 pictures in the 300-foot length of film individually. Overruling a lower court decision in Lubin's favour, the appellate court judge declared that: (i) since the series had been taken from one camera at one operation; (ii) since there was no distinguishable difference

[13]File "Motion Pictures—1904" (ENHS).

[14]Ibid.

[15]*Biograph Bulletins, 1896–1904*, p. 125.

[16]John C. Kerr to F. L. Dyer, September 16, 1904, ENHS.

[17]F. L. Dyer to John C. Kerr, September 17, 1904, ENHS.

detectable by the naked eye between the separate pictures; and (iii) since the economic or commodity value of the footage depended on its status as a single entity, the series was practically one picture. By duping even a portion, Lubin had been infringing on the Edison copyright.[18]

On November 28, 1904, Melville Church, another Edison attorney, wrote to Delos Holden at the Edison laboratory requesting that he obtain an affidavit from Edwin Porter stating that the *Personal* footage "must have been taken from different standpoints, at different times, and, probably upon different films."[19] Church did not refer to the late-September completion of another Edison remake of a Biograph success, Porter's *Maniac Chase*, essentially a copy of *The Escaped Lunatic*. He mentioned that he had been reading the judgment in the Edison-Lubin case which, he noted, was based on the finding that "all of the pictures appear to be taken from a single standpoint, by the same camera, as a continuous performance." The key tactic in Edison's legal strategy would be to demonstrate that since Biograph's *Personal* consisted of a number of negatives and not one continuous strip taken from a single camera position, it was not protected by their single copyright.

But the extent to which that move was a blend of confidence and bluff is revealed by the Edison side's eagerness to dig up a comic strip that Porter claimed contained the original idea. He had seen it, he said, in a newspaper lying around the office of Wallace McCutcheon, the director of *Personal*, several months before the film had been undertaken.[20] On November 29, 1904, the same day that Holden wrote to Church about his failure to uncover the strip, he received a letter from the City Editor of *The New York World*, Horace Thurlow, informing him that he, Thurlow, had been unable to track the strip down. Thurlow, apparently unaware of the circumstance that had honed Holden's interest, added: "exactly (the) scene as, you describe is on exhibition in a moving picture series. I have seen it at Keith's."[21]

CONTINUOUS AND NATURAL: RECIPE FOR AN ILLUSION

Sent in to carry the ball for the Edison side, Porter's task was twofold: to persuade the court, in Dyer's terms, that Biograph had not properly copyrighted

---

[18]119 Fed. Reporter, 993-94; 122 Fed Reporter, 240–43.

[19]Melville Church to Delos Holden, November 28, 1904, ENHS.

[20]Defendant's affadavits in opposition to complainant's motion for preliminary injunction, December 4, 1904, *American Mutoscope and Biograph Company vs. Edison Manufacturing Company*. An earlier version of this had Porter getting the story from a "woman who saw the comic page in McCutcheon's office"; Delos Holden to Melville Church, November 30, 1904, ENHS.

[21]Horace Thurlow to Delos Holden, November 29, 1904, ENHS.

their picture, and in the event that the *Personal* copyright did stand up, to convince the judge the Edison film was an original and not a plagiaristic infringement.

Much of Porter's December 3, 1904, deposition was devoted to defining the technical, commercial, spatial, and temporal unities of movie production in the period to show that *Personal* comprised a discontinuous "aggregation" of separate sequences rather than a single "continuous" photograph that could be covered by a single copyright registration. He began by describing what he called the two "common" motion picture production practices. The first involved

> a camera placed in a single position, in order to depict a single event, such as the launching of a vessel or the run of a fire department. In this class of pictures all the exposures are taken upon a single sensitized film ... and the background of each picture of the film is exactly the same except when the camera is turned on a pivot to a different point on the compass.

The other method was "to build up long series of moving pictures" with each "scene or set of pictures entirely different from that of another set or scene." A film of this type, Porter stated, might require several weeks to complete and include "six or eight different acts or scenes taken from as many different view points."[22]

By way of emphasizing the time element, Porter observed that widely separated views were "seldom taken the same day." And more, that "the different scenes were almost invariably taken on different films," which Porter and his employer apparently believed was an additional argument, from a technical standpoint, in deciding whether *Personal* could be considered a single photograph.

> I have been informed and believe that the taking of the pictures occupied three different days. My opinion is that four or five separate sensitized films were used, and that these films contain as many as five or six different series of impressions, each portraying a different scene.

And those different scenes, Porter added, depicted settings at distances too great to have been managed "even with a camera pivoted so as to take a panorama." *Personal* was thus "in no sense a single photograph, since the view points are not the same in all the views."

In attempting to adhere as closely as possible to the legal precedents of the Edison-Lubin case, Porter didn't forget commercial argument:

---

[22]Defendant's affidavits in opposition to complainant's motion for preliminary injunction, December 4, 1904, *American Mutoscope and Biograph Company vs. Edison Manufacturing Company.*

the photographer generally aims to take more exposures than are necessary, in order that he may trim off some of the pictures from both ends of the film and thereby produce what he considered a fitting and attractive beginning and end to the scene.[23]

The Edison people believed that the integrity of the continuous action film was a matter of commercial option. As Porter described it, the long film was merely a "series of scenes" or "really an aggregation of several series of negative impressions" that were used "to produce a positive film upon a single long continuous strip." Each series deliberately constituted one independent photograph, and for a very good reason:

each scene is generally sold separately so that a purchaser or exhibitor may obtain one scene or two scenes or the entire series, as he wishes.

To counter *Personal*'s claim to originality, Porter simply repeated the groundless allegation that the Biograph film was based on a newspaper comic strip and even went as far as to insist that Wallace McCutcheon had admitted as much to him in a conversation. Though a common enough practice, there was no evidence that *Personal* had been taken from such a source. And perhaps aware of the weakness in the assertion, Porter switched horses. He had, he recalled, seen *Personal* "probably" a short time after it was completed and had immediately associated it with the British genre of "chase pictures," a large number of which had been turned out prior to the June 29, 1904, copyright of *Personal*.

I remember one entitled "A Day Light Burglary" in which a thief or burglar is pursued by persons endeavoring to capture him. I remember another film in which a pickpocket is pursued, another in which poachers are pursued and another in which train robbers are pursued.

Porter did not mention that it was the sort of film Biograph had begun importing from England for their American business. Nor did he say when and in what circumstances he had viewed those works. But it does appear to be his first and perhaps sole reference to his familiarity with the work of the so-called Brighton school that Georges Sadoul and others have claimed as a major source of his own ideas. In the context of his observations on Edison sales policy, however, we can understand why the Edison company would have chosen to avoid the Brighton production model.

Porter's deposition offers a reasonably complete picture of his multiple

---

[23]In the case of *How a French Nobleman . . . ,* 822 feet were trimmed to a 658½-foot complete version.

functions as Edison studio chief. In addition to participating in Edison's running legal wars, they included film casting, "engaging the pantomimic performers"; directing, "instructing them as to the scenes which I wished to have enacted"; as well as camerawork, choosing the locations and processing the negatives. Editing was a minor procedure in the Edison motion picture processing operation and not, as Edison lawyers would argue, a feature of authorship.[24]

Wallace McCutcheon led off his deposition for Biograph by refuting the claim that *Personal* was derived from a comic strip, stating that the idea had been developed by another Biograph employee, Frank Marion.[25] But of much greater import was a document he appended to his statement called "Descriptions of Positions of Camera in Taking Views for Complainant's 'Personal' Photograph." McCutcheon listed eight separate camera positions or scenes and, conceding their physical noncontiguity, concluded with this:

> These positions were carefully chosen so that when the impressions were joined in one photograph, the action would appear continuous and natural.

The principle of the trick film, in other words, applied to filmed action in real-life settings. Here we have the rudiments of an editing scheme of sorts in which the key role of the cameraman creating independent tableau shots, as Porter saw it, was subordinated to a larger conception that determined the selection of the settings in which the "pantomime" was to be photographed. The illusion of continuous screen action, a merger of actuality framing and trompe l'oeil effect, was based on a sort of temporal stop-motion technique, in which the perceived spatial unity of a "continuous exterior setting" was a necessary condition for an impression of "continuous and natural action." The structure of the Biograph subject and the Edison remake, and in fact the larger chase picture genre, did little more than satisfy that condition: action emerging from the frame depth, with the chasers and the chased heading toward the camera-viewer, always in the frame together, before they left the frame out of one of the bottom corners, the empty scene then bringing on a cut to a comparable piece of action, and the procedure repeated a half-dozen times until the "capture."

To substantiate McCutcheon's claim on technical grounds, Harry Marvin, a Biograph executive, stated that the "successive views" in *Personal* "were taken on one negative consisting of a strip of film about 370 feet long." As for the

---

[24]Certainly nothing like the sort of thing Karel Reisz, in *The Technique of Film Editing*, (New York: Farrar, Strauss and Young, 1953), p. 19, claimed that Porter had demonstrated in *Life of an American Fireman*, viz., "that the single shot, recording an incomplete piece of action, is the unit of which films must be constructed." If anything, Porter, by his own admission, strove to do the reverse, i.e., to record actions in a form as complete as possible.

[25]Deposition of Wallace McCutcheon, September 17, 1904.

commercial aspect of the case, Marvin maintained that "each view [was] not sold or rented by itself, but . . . in one strip of film."[26] (Curiously in their August 15, 1904 bulletin Biograph announced that *Personal* and their "other great productions" were "restricted to our own use and not for sale," adding that they were "the only concern in America prepared to supply an exclusive service.") And to further counter Edison claims, Frank Marion brought forward the fact that *How a French Nobleman* had been advertised for sale in *The New York Clipper* in a complete version on September 17, 1904, but in parts on October 10, 1904.[27] (Hoping perhaps to capitalize on the confusion, Lubin on November 5, 1904, offered for sale a straight dupe of *Personal* in the *Clipper* which he even went as far as to copyright on the same day as *A New Version of "Personal."*)[28]

To press the brief that *Personal* was "a single photograph of a whole" Biograph attorneys pointed to the continuity of performance—"actors the same"—and the continuity of action—"motion continuous from beginning to end"—while conceding that "only the background is changed as the scene progresses from point to point." Moreover, they contended that there was a similarity of method in the production of Edison's *Meteor* footage and in that of *Personal.* In the former the angle of view had been altered by the movement of a camera on its pivot; in *Personal,* the change was the result of the movement of the camera and tripod from one position to another. And there was, they reasoned, "no difference in principle between the minutes, or seconds it may be, in the one case, and days in the other, between the taking of several views." The very method of *Personal,* they argued, signified progress in motion picture art which they said had gone from the showing of "single scenes of objects and persons in motion" to "continuous action of objects and persons in the portrayal of episodes, public functions and events."[29]

But the Edison side held its ground. Biograph's projected positive was, they insisted, a mere mechanical print, since "the negative alone require(d) the work of authorship."[30] The Edison studio's championing of the independence of the individual shot or "series of impressions" was not simply a clever legal dodge but as I will show a very real and overriding aspect of their marketing policy, one which appeared to have the support of the 1903 Edison-Lubin judgment.

[26]Affidavit of Harry Marvin, November 11, 1904, complainant's motion papers and rebutting affidavits, *American Mutoscope and Biograph Company vs. Edison Manufacturing Company.*

[27]Frank Marion, November 11, 1904.

[28]Ibid. [Within two weeks, Lubin had altered the title from *A New Version of "Personal"* to *Meet Me at the Fountain.* The film survives, and Eastman House has it–GP.]

[29]Complainant's brief in reply, December 22, 1904, *American Mutoscope and Biograph Company vs. Edison Manufacturing Company.*

[30]Defendant's rejoinder to complainant's brief in reply, December 24, 1904, *American Mutoscope and Biograph Company vs. Edison Manufacturing Company.*

On May 6, 1905, Judge Lanning, in denying Biograph's application for a preliminary injunction, accepted the argument that a positive film containing "a series of pictures that may be thrown in rapid succession upon a screen telling a single connected story of a man fleeing from a crowd of women," even though it had been taken from different positions, could be copyrighted as a photograph. Biograph, he concluded, did hold a valid copyright, but whether in producing its remake Edison had infringed upon it was another matter.[31]

Here it would be unwise to leap to the conclusion that the Biograph company was bravely attempting to lead the American film industry out of the feudal darkness of tableau production in the face of an ill-tempered onslaught of churchy Edison obduracy. Each of the parties was simply trying to make the best of their respective positions in what was really a battle between two opposing sales philosophies, a battle Edison executives lacked the wit to see they had lost. Fittingly, the major impact of the case at the Edison studio was a new copyright registration scheme. On May 9, 1905, Dyer wrote to Kinetograph Department Manager, Alex Moore, about the desirability of registering their longer films in separate parts or scenes and wondering about the additional expense.[32] Six months later he had apparently found a way to reduce that expense. On October 6, 1905, he wrote to the Registrar of Copyrights in Washington, D.C., requesting seven separate copyrights for Edwin Porter's *Poor Algy*. But instead of forwarding paper rolls of the material, Dyer enclosed seven "single pictures from successive scenes of the film."

> In Edison vs Lubin . . . it was held by the Court of Appeals, Third Circuit, 'that a series of pictures of such a character that the difference between successive pictures is not distinguishable by the eye' may be regarded as a single photograph, and therefore, the subject of a valid copyright.[33]

As Dyer explained, he was sending a "representative picture from each scene, limiting the copyright to that picture, but depending in case of infringement upon the substantial identity of all the pictures of any scene with the copyrighted picture." It was a practice designed to permit the Edison company to play both sides of the street; to turn out longer fictional pictures but to market them in parts as well as complete versions.

CONTINUOUS INCIDENTS AND EDISON SALES POLICY, 1904–6

According to one film historian, Porter's *Life of an American Policeman* (1905) "was so loosely connected that later editions of the film were able to rearrange its

---

[31]137 Fed. Reporter, pp. 262–68.

[32]Frank L. Dyer to Alex T. Moore, May 9, 1905.

[33]Frank L. Dyer to Registrar of Copyrights, Washington, D.C., October 6, 1905.

scenes quite drastically without in any way harming its continuity!"[34] Shot in November 1905, the film was copyrighted on December 6, 1905, in eighteen separate scenes, numbered H69527–44, although the catalogue listed a maximum of eight scenes. How to explain?

In a preamble to the December 1905 catalogue description, prospective buyers were informed that they could choose between two 1,000-foot versions, each containing only one of the production's two "most thrilling and realistic scenes," "River Tragedy" and "Desperate Encounter Between Burglar and Police." The film, shot with the cooperation of the New York City (Metropolitan) Police Department and screened at a benefit for the Police Relief Fund on December 5, 1905, was further described as "absolutely perfect as to detail, action and surroundings, and depict[s] in the most realistic manner actual daily life and happenings." In other words, very much the sort of reenactment of an institutional routine Porter had attempted in *Life of an America Fireman*. The catalogue went on to explain the two versions this way:

> In order to give our customers a selection between these two scenes [River Tragedy and Desperate Encounter Between Burglar and Police], as well as to keep the production within a reasonable length, we have decided to furnish this picture complete with either of the above scenes, as the customer may select, the length in each case for the entire production being 1,000 feet.[35]

Records for the years 1904–6 show that sales of the version with "River Tragedy" totaled six copies in 1905 and twenty-two copies in 1906.[36] A mere five copies of the version with the "Desperate Encounter" scene were sold in 1906, and none in 1905. In 1906, the company also sold or was prepared to sell the film in separate parts. The same records show that two copies of the 300-foot "River Tragedy" scene were sold separately, as were seven copies of the 260-foot "Desperate Encounter." Scene 7, "Runaway in the Park," and scene 8, "Joke on the Roundsman," were also offered for sale separately, each with its own separate catalogue number, but no sales were recorded. (Note: an apparently related 240-foot scene also dating from the same December 1905 period, "Bicycle Police Chasing Auto," earned sales of five copies in 1905 and three copies in 1906, as did a 380-foot subject listed as *Spect. Scenes N.Y. City Fire* [sic], with three copies sold in 1905 and seven in 1906.)

---

[34]William K. Everson, *American Silent Film* (New York: Oxford, University Press 1978), p. 36.

[35]"Life of an American Policeman," in *Edison Film* (publicity flyer), form no. 276, December 1905.

[36]All sales figures come from an eight-page document titled simply "Film Sales" found in a file, "M.P.—Sales" (ENHS).

The company's January 1, 1907 catalogue listed the two versions of the complete film and the separate scenes, "Desperate Encounter," "Runaway in the Park" and "River Tragedy," as well as "Two Little Waifs," which seems to be the film's third scene, "Lost Child." In 1905, each full-length version would cost a buyer $150. The July 1906 catalogue listed both versions at $150. In 1907, the version with "Desperate Encounter" was still being offered at that price while the more popular one with "River Tragedy" had been discounted down to $146.25!

The case of Porter's two 1904 Yeggman films was a little different. Originally filmed in two full-length parts, the first, *Rounding up of the Yeggman*, was shot between August 15 and September 10, 1904, and a 952-foot length registered for copyright on September 16, 1904. The second part, *Capture of the Yegg Bank Burglars*, was filmed in the same period, but copyrighted in four separate parts on September 28, 1904.(Note: the parts were, however, registered, perhaps by a clerk in the copyright office, out of the sequence presumably intended by Porter—"Tracked," "Dive Scene," "Cellar Scene," and "Capture." Niver, following Walls, then transferred the material out of that sequence, which Walls gave as "Capture and Death," "Cellar Scene," "Tracked," and "Dive Scene." Edison sales records for the period do not show sales for two separate films. Rather, there is one title, *Capture of 'Yegg' Bank Burglars* with sales of forty-two copies in 1904, twenty-one in 1905, and twenty-three in 1906 of a 960-foot length. Also, the records show the separate sales of an 80-foot *Locomotive Head-on Collision*, apparently the concluding scene from *Rounding up of the Yeggmen*, as a separate subject. The complete version the company offered for sale, a fifteen-scene subject called *Capture of 'Yegg' Bank Burglars*, combined both parts, but excluded the two-shot actuality railroad collision sequence Porter had apparently added to *Rounding up of the Yeggmen* to supply a spectacular finish. As far as the records indicate, the railroad smash-up sequence was never offered for sale as part of the complete version but only as the separate subject, *Locomotive Head-on Collision*.

Porter's 1,000-foot, eleven-scene *Honeymoon at Niagara Falls*, filmed between August 7 and August 14, 1906, and copyrighted on October 16, 1906, in eleven separate parts, numbered H83903–13, had what seems a typical sales history. Seventy-five copies of the complete 1000-foot release print were sold in 1906. But the company was prepared to sell eight of the parts separately, each of them representing a portion of actuality footage of the Niagara site: "American Falls," "Horseshoe Falls," "Maid of the Mist," "Horseshoe Falls" (in a shorter length), "American Falls" (in a longer length), "Trip on Chippewa," "Whirlpool Rapids," and "Cave of the Winds."

Other Porter films given the same sales treatment were *How a French Nobleman*, etc., *The Whole Dam Family*, *The Kleptomaniac*, *The Seven Ages*, *Stolen by Gypsies*, *On a Good Old Five Cent Trolley*, *The Burglar's Slide for Life*, and *Boarding School Girls*. An exhibitor or exchange operator could purchase the complete 675-foot release print of *How a French Nobleman* or any of nine separate parts. Four parts of the 300-foot *The Whole Dam Family* were available that way; "Sneezing,"

"Cigarette Fiend," "Cry Baby," and "Chewing Gum." A 150-foot section of the 670-foot *The Kleptomaniac* titled "Scenes in a Police Court" was offered as a separate subject, but in 1906 still had *no* takers. Three of the tableau-scenes from *The Seven Ages* were sold as separate subjects: "Engagement Ring," "Old Sweethearts," and "Old Maid & Pet Cat." Two of the scenes from the 845-foot *Stolen by Gypsies,* "Dressing the Baby" and "Fortune Telling Gypsies," were offered in separate parts with little response from prospective buyers. Two sections of the 265-foot *Burglar's Slide for Life,* "Burglar & Vapor Bath" and "Burglar and Bull Dog" were offered in separate parts with better but far from spectacular sales success; a total of one copy of the former and nine copies of the latter were sold in 1905 and 1906. One copy of a section of the 545-foot *On a Good Old Five Cent Trolley,* titled "Always a Gentleman," was sold in 1905 and again in 1906. Six sections of the 965-foot *Boarding School Girls* were offered for separate sale with equally tepid results.

Curiously, the records in fact tend to show that the company was more successful at selling complete release prints: a total of ninety-one copies of *How a French Nobleman* between 1904 and 1906; seventy-five copies of *Honeymoon at Niagara Falls* in 1906; 136 copies of *The Whole Dam Family* in 1905 and 1906; forty-three copies of *The Kleptomaniac* between 1904 and 1906; fifty-nine copies of *Stolen by Gypsies* in 1905 and 1906; ninety-two copies of *Burglar's Slide for Life* in 1905 and 1906; seventy-one copies of *Good Old Five Cent Trolley Ride* in 1905 and 1906; and forty-six prints of *Boarding School Girls* in the same period.

Moreover, the figures suggest that extended film length was not per se a problem in the years 1905–6. And more, that sales for the longer films turned out in that period were superior to those for the shorter production offered in 1904, which began to fall off significantly in 1905 and 1906. In 1904, for example, the company sold forty-two prints of the 240-foot trick film *Dog Factory,* but only nine in 1905 and 1906. Short actuality footage from at home and abroad, which had enjoyed reasonable sales in 1904, likewise dropped considerably in 1905–6: *Russian Infantry, Warsaw,* at forty-five feet, had sales of twenty-five copies in 1904, eleven in 1905, and three in 1906; twenty-five copies of the sixty-five-foot *Baby and Puppies* were sold in 1904, eight in 1905, and only two in 1906.

On the other hand, the sales fate of actuality material, upon which the practice of selling longer films in parts was based, was a different one. The Edison company sold as many complete copies of the 750-foot *Inter-Collegiate Regatta* (1904) as parts, and fewer copies of the 1,000-foot *President Roosevelt's Inauguration* (1905) than 155-foot, 170-foot, 90-foot, and 110-foot sections. Sales of the complete 800-foot *Russian-Japanese Peace Conference* (1904), however, were better than part sales. *Scenes and Incidents Hawaiian Islands* (1906) was only sold in parts as was the footage of *San Francisco Earthquake* (1906). But sales of the complete 735-foot *A Trip Through the Yellowstone Park* (1906) were superior to part sales.

Among the company's top commercial successes in the period 1904–6 were: *Capture of Yegg Bank Burglars,* eighty-six copies of a 940-foot print; eighty-two copies of *Locomotive Head-on Collision* (80 feet); seventy-four prints of *The Ex-Convict* (660 feet); seventy-three prints of *How Jones Lost His Roll* (575 feet); seventy-six prints of *"Raffles" the Dog* (635 feet); thirty prints of *The Little Train Robbery* (725 feet); thirty-eight prints of *White Caps* (835 feet); fifty-seven prints of *Poor Algy* (315 feet); thirty-eight prints of *The Miller's Daughter* (975 feet); forty-two prints of *Watermelon Patch* (725 feet); fifty-nine prints of *Stolen by Gypsies* (845 feet); seventy-five prints of *Down on the Farm* (440 feet); 157 prints of *The Train Wreckers* (815 feet); 192 prints of the 470-foot *Dream of a Rarebit Fiend*.

Until 1908 actuality subjects dominated the work of American film producers. But the bits-and-pieces actuality sales approach did not suit the trend to longer fictional subjects that dated from late 1903. The Edison Company's own records made it clear that by 1906, certainly, the demand for complete versions of those films had outstripped part sales. And yet, immobilized in the straightjacket of that obsolete Kinetoscope marketing structure, the concept of the longer film as an aggregation of independent scenes and trick effects persisted as an Edison production principle.

PART III

The Films

Introduction

Turning to the early films themselves—fleeting, flickering images oddly intact these many years—our final section again demonstrates a richness of approaches. While the movies were once touted as a twentieth-century novelty, the newest, liveliest art, increasing emphasis falls now on their conceptual and narrative continuities with the past. The present author has proposed elsewhere that traditions of "filmic" narrative continuity and exposition nest deep in the prose, theater, art, photography, stereoscopes, dioramas, and comic strips that were all products of the preceding popular culture.[1] Keith Cohen, Bruce Kawin, Frank McConnell, Alan Spiegel, and others have discussed relationships between nineteenth- and twentieth-century film and literature.[2] In this collection John Hagan argues, in "Cinema and the Romantic Tradition," that early films appeared in a moment of heightened visual consciousness that developed in the nineteenth century among Romantic, Symbolist, and Aesthete writers, inflected too by optical phenomena such as the diorama.

Burnes St. Patrick Hollyman's "Alexander Black's Picture Plays, 1893–1894" underlines traditions of storytelling, projected, glass-slide imagery, which included such "cinematic" optical effects as the dissolve. The material supports an argument by Charles Musser that early film ought really to be investigated in the

---

[1]John L. Fell, *Film and the Narrative Tradition* (Norman: University of Oklahoma Press, 1974).

[2]Keith Cohen, *Film and Fiction: The Dynamics of Exchange* (New Haven: Yale University Press, 1979); Bruce Kawin, *Telling It Again and Again* (Ithaca: Cornell University Press, 1972; Richard McConnell, *The Spoken Seen* (Baltimore: Johns Hopkins Press, 1975); Alan Spiegel, *Fiction and the Camera Eye* (Charlottesville: University of Virginia Press, 1976).

context of a history of the screen, of the projected image and its sound accompaniments.[3]

But for the work of Kemp R. Niver, film study would be greatly diminished. "Paper Prints of Early Motion Pictures" describes the conversion of Library of Congress copyright materials back to the mode of projectable images. Of special interest are Niver's descriptions of unexpected and incompatible film gauges, frame lines, and picture/sprocket placements; these underscore the competitive, legal entanglements among the pioneer entrepreneurs.

Katherine Singer Kovács's article "George Méliès and the *Féerie*" traces the sources of many Méliès titles in theatrical traditions of the *féerie*, a kind of gallic melodramatic spectacle emphasizing music, mime, and acrobatics. An altogether different sort of reading will be found in Elizabeth Grottle Strebel's "Imperialist Iconography of Anglo-Boer War Film Footage," which presents image analyses both of actuality material as it was produced for propaganda and of staged "recreations" that were clearly taken as fact by many viewers, like the simulations of contemporary newspaper artists and even the advertised "realism" of enactments like *The Great Train Robbery*. Strebel's work reminds us how every silent film communicates to its audience through a complex layering of coded systems.

John L. Fell's "Motive, Mischief, and Melodrama" undertakes a summary of staged entertainment films extant from 1907, seeking ways to organize the thicket of titles and conjecturing about the more complicated lines that "story" films had begun to assume. In "Toward Narrative, 1907: *The Mill Girl*," Eileen Bowser expands upon one generic mode of 1907, the melodrama, and concentrates on a single film text. In the light of history, her study is especially illuminating because Griffith was soon to produce his avalanche of Biograph shorts from the same mold. We may estimate many characteristics of the pre-Griffith narrative by way of Bowser's study.

Elsewhere, Barry Salt has brought to film study an unprecedented concern for quantifying procedures, measuring shot durations, effects of lighting setups, camera angles, and other characteristics in sufficient quantity to warrant careful generalizations about a given period.[4] In "The Early Development of Film Form," Salt explores staged film before and after 1907, pointing out technical innovations (such as interior lighting), staging patterns, and narrative juxtapositions. Because his study extends beyond the usual time frame of articles in this anthology, it demonstrates certain logical extensions of the first decade's expository dispositions.

---

[3]Charles Musser, "The Early Cinema of Edwin Porter," *Cinema Journal* 19 (Fall 1979): 1–38.

[4]See, for example, Barry Salt, "Film Style and Technology in the Forties," *Film Quarterly* 31 (Fall 1977): 46–57.

More theoretically inclined, Marshall Deutelbaum, in "Structural Patterning in the Lumière Films," argues that various early Lumière titles, customarily consigned to "unstaged" categories, in fact operate through either linear or circular narrative processes. André Gaudreault's "Temporality and Narrativity in Early Cinema, 1895–1908," centers on alternate approaches to time-space continuities and ellipses, tracing forms of overlap that contradict simple notions of coherent evolution in expository method. In Gaudreault's view, space and time wage a running skirmish in cinema in which a relative emphasis on either has its effects on camera placement, editing patterns, and viewer empathy. What the modern eye may view as narrative mismatches were, in fact, alternative ways to think about story.

Contemporary perspectives expropriated from psychoanalysis and social anthropology are invoked by Lucy Fischer, "The Lady Vanishes: Women, Magic, and the Movies," the better to reconsider Méliès's trick films in terms of sexual envy and psychic compensation, these in turn originating in earlier traditions of stage magic translated in Méliès's films into equations between film imagery and illusion. Fischer's article demonstrates and emphasizes the usefulness of early film to support current interest in the relation between feminism and psychoanalysis. These themes, plus treatment of additional sociopolitical frames of reference, may be found in Noël Burch's film *Correction Please,* itself a critique of early film history, and in his article on Edwin S. Porter.[5]

Tom Gunning, in "An Unseen Energy Swallows Space," guardedly compares early films with American avant-garde work in terms of space, spectator-screen relationships, and camera movements. Méliès, for example, develops ambiguous, often contradictory juxtapositions of untypical images operating within a kind of self-contained metaphor; a film like Stan Brakhage's *Dog Star Man* uses multiple, overlaid images that sometimes accomplish similar spatial contradictions while operating with very different esthetic intentions. (A literal meeting between past and present may be found in Ken Jacobs's *Tom, Tom the Piper's Son,* a film made by repeatedly rephotographing the projected images of an American Mutoscope and Biograph title from 1905.)

In conclusion Eileen Bowser in, "Griffith's Film Career Before *The Adventures of Dolly,*" introduces the famous director, prophetically first seen mounting a sheet-screen on the rear wall of a courthouse scene in *Falsely Accused!* Like that of Gaudreault, Bowser's study firmly locates Griffith among operative, ongoing conventions of period filmmaking. There is little question that the growing

---

[5]Noël Burch, "Porter or Ambivalence" Screen 19 (Winter 1978–79). For more detailed examination of Porter's early work see Charles Musser, "Early Cinema of Edwin Porter." Equally close considerations of another filmmaker will be found in Martin Sopocy, "A Narrated Cinema: The Pioneer Story Films of James A. Williamson," *Cinema Journal* 18 (Fall 1978): 1–28. Gaudreault's *Fireman* argument is expanded in "Detours in Film Narrative: The Development of Cross Cutting," *Cinema Journal* 19 (Fall 1979):39–59.

evidence and influence of early film history will amplify this vision of the movies' first years. In truth, all film study ultimately rests on extrapolations from film history, the security of its foundations dependent on work such as exists in the present volume.

JOHN HAGAN

Cinema and the Romantic Tradition

While a proliferation of material, much of it superficial or otherwise undistinguished, exists on the subject of film and Surrealism, there has been a relative paucity of writing on cinema's relationship to an earlier, in some ways anticipatory, artistic movement: Romanticism. The French Romantic movement had begun early in the nineteenth century as a revolt against classicism's stance of objectivity and its consequent restriction of the imagination. "Romanticism," as Edmund Wilson has noted, "was a revolt of the individual." Originally, Romanticism was also a revolt against the rational and mechanistic attitudes which had arisen from the important mathematical and scientific discoveries of the prior two centuries. Around 1830, however, the Industrial Revolution began to effect a noticeable change in the Romantic movement. The technological apparatus necessary for the production of a mass literature became available, and many Romanticists began to write for general audiences through that mélange of art and news known as the *feuilleton:* the daily newspaper supplement in which serialized novels and other literary material now appeared, along with varied bits of cultural and social information.

Despite Romanticism's attack on materialism, industry came to be used as a descriptive element in the poetry of that period. The controversy resulting from the publication of Maxime Du Camp's *Les Chants modernes* in 1855 illustrated the disagreement which occurred among French writers on this matter of industrialization. Du Camp had observed a decline in the quality of literature and blamed this decline on what he saw as a prevalent concern with art for art's sake. He proposed that, in place of *l'art pour l'art,* artists should open their eyes to the miracles that industry had accomplished: the discoveries of electricity, gas, chloroform, and photography. Among the writers who were opposed to *Les Chants modernes* was Charles Baudelaire. In his essays on Edgar Allan Poe, Baudelaire condemned this concern with incessant progress and offered, as an alternative, Poe's world of the imagination. In Poe's oeuvre, states Baudelaire, "the backgrounds and the accessories are always appropriate to the feelings of the characters. The solitude of nature, the bustle of great cities, are all evoked tensely and fantastically . . . So-called inanimate nature participates in the nature of the living beings." For Poe, says Baudelaire, the progress of the outer world is important only in so far as it mirrors and affects the inner one; emphasis is placed on the individual's contemplation and perception of the world in which he exists. Baudelaire sees Poe's work as centering around this act of apprehension so that, in effect, there is only one character throughout his stories: "the man with heightened faculties." According to Baudelaire, in Poe's writing imagination was the queen of these faculties. By "imagination," Baudelaire meant "a virtually divine faculty that apprehends immediately, by means lying outside philosophical methods, the intimate and sacred relation of things, the correspondences and analogies."

Poe knew the effect on literature of technological advances in publishing: "Whatever may be the merits or demerits, generally, of the Magazine Literature in America, there can be no question as to its extent or influence." He felt that the problem with quarterly reviews was that they "discuss only topics which are *caviare* to the many . . . In a word, their ponderosity is quite out of keeping with the *rush* of the age." The daily newspaper reflected this "rush" through its "imperative necessity of catching, *currente calamo,* each topic as it flits before the eye of the public." He claimed that men at present "have more facts, more to think about. For this reason, they are disposed to put the greatest amount of thought in the smallest compass and disperse it with the utmost attainable rapidity. Hence the journalism of the age." As will be seen, points dealt with by Poe in his discussion of this "new literature"—the compression and dispersal of information; the catching of an image "as it flits before the eye"—recur in his fiction, most conspicuously in his story "The Man of the Crowd." They also recur when one considers the influence of his work on "cinematic" proclivities within Romantic aesthetics.

The admiration for Poe of Baudelaire, and of the Romanticists in general, can be seen as part of a heightened visual consciousness which developed in the latter half of the nineteenth century and which both drew upon, and offered itself as an alternative to, scientific and industrial progress. Walter Benjamin offers a particularly intriguing interpretation of this development. Benjamin argues that the appearance of the diorama in France foreshadowed the motion picture, while also signaling a revolution in the relation of art to technology and expressing a new attitude to life.

The diorama was invented by Daguerre and was first exhibited, in a specially designed building, in Paris in 1822. Although its format varied, the diorama generally consisted of gigantic transparent paintings which were displayed under changing lights. Three-dimensional foregrounds sometimes were used to heighten the realistic effect. In many instances, the auditorium was fitted with a large aperture and slowly revolved in order to move the spectators from one part of the picture to another. Benjamin sees as analogous to the diorama, and arising from similar impulses and social circumstances, a dioramic or panoramic literature which consisted of books of individual sketches dealing with various aspects of Parisian life. Among these works were *Le Livre des cent-et-un, Les Français peints par eux-mêmes, Le Diable à Paris,* and *La Grande Ville.* Benjamin sees these books, as well as the feuilletons, as resembling the dioramas in the sense that the anecdotal, expository form of this literature reproduced, as it were, the plastic, detailed foreground of the diorama while the literature's wealth of documentary information on city life corresponded to the diorama's extensive, continually changing background.

One might say that, in both the diorama and dioramic literature, a constant transformation of perspective and an intimacy of detail coexist; one both stands outside of events and is a part of them. The outer and inner strata of reality merge. Exteriority and interiority, objectivity and subjectivity, coalesce; in Benjamin's words, "the street became an *intérieur.*" Benjamin suggests a parallel between this dioramic effect and the contemporaneous writings of Poe and Baudelaire, in which the individual is constantly transforming reality through his contemplation of it. Rather than simply praise industrial civilization, Poe and Baudelaire searched for the mysterious "correspondences and analogies" which it engendered. In doing so, they were drawn toward what would become an archetypal figure of the Romantic age: the *flâneur* or "stroller," moving through the everchanging vistas of bustling life in industrial France.

Baudelaire's conception of the "dandy"—the "artist, man of the world, man of crowds"—obviously resembles Poe's "man with heightened faculties" who moves through "the bustle of great cities." Both art and the bustle of industrial life must be approached with the heightened faculty of imagination. Baudelaire argued that, in the ideal art, the artist must restore truth by triumphing over nature and must show us not only his own visions but those of others also. For this reason, he attacks "the badly applied advances of photography, [which] like all purely material progress for that matter, have greatly contributed to the impoverishment of French artistic genius." In his search for an art which would involve an active use of the imagination, Baudelaire turned not only toward draftsmanship and toward certain painters—among them, Delacroix—but also toward certain devices and conceptions which might be called "protocinematic." Among these devices— toys, really—was the *joujou scientifique.* Examples of this are the stereoscope, or phenakistoscope, which creates the illusion of movement by almost magically transforming many still figures into one moving figure so that, in a sense, stillness and motion exist simultaneously. Baudelaire found in the *joujou* that combination of continuity and transformation which was so important to the Romanticists.

Baudelaire saw the *joujou* as a device which provided immediate gratification of a child's desire *voir l'âme,* "to see the soul." He himself evidently also found pleasure in this instant satisfaction. As if not content with such devices, he created what might be called his own full-scale cinema. It was done with drugs and it was done through the theater. I refer to Baudelaire's empathetic account of the gentleman who, under the influence of hashish, attends a theater performance. He feels as if he is "entering a world of darkness" in which "the stage ... alone was brightly lit, and seemed infinitely small and far, far away, as if at the end of an immense stereoscope." He finds it impossible to listen to the players but occasionally his stream of thought seizes upon a sentence fragment, which "springs his mind to distant dreams." Although the figures on stage seem extremely small, he can distinctly perceive the minutest details of their attire; they "seem cloaked in a cold and magic light, much like the kind that a very clear pane of glass will add to an oil painting." The gentleman concludes: "When at last I was able to emerge from this pit of frozen darkness; when the internal phantasmagoria had disappeared, and I was myself once again, I felt a lassitude far greater than any that sustained hard work had ever caused me."

In recounting this drug activity, Baudelaire in effect is proposing that one's experience of an art work must ultimately be a phenomenological act of imagination. Certain reactions which he describes, in his complete account of the incident, as being caused by drugs—an unusual keenness of the senses; a feeling of unity with external objects; the assumption of strange appearances by these objects; synesthesia—are the same experiences which he and other Romanticists, and Poe before them, sought from the work of art.

Baudelaire stressed the use of analogy in describing these experiences. This reliance upon the analogue or symbol was an essential characteristic of Symbolism, a mid-nineteenth-century aesthetic movement which was largely a reaction to Naturalism and a counterpart to the Romantic reaction at the end of the eighteenth century. One of the crucial events of the early Symbolist movement in France was the publication in 1852 of Poe's tales as translated by Baudelaire, a writer who served as a bridge between Romanticism and Symbolism. In Poe's stories and critical essays, the Symbolists found a substantiation of many of their own emerging tenets, such as a confusion of the perceptions of the various senses and a desire to approximate the indefiniteness of music. As Wilson has remarked, "what is so special, so fleeting and so vague cannot be conveyed by direct statement or description, but only by a succession of words, of images, which will serve to suggest it to the reader. The Symbolists themselves, full of the idea of producing with poetry effects like those of music, tended to think of these images as possessing an abstract value like musical notes and chords."

The images of which Wilson speaks constituted what might be termed a "visionary experience." The Symbolists saw these experiences as eliminating normal time and space. Stéphane Mallarmé, a central Symbolist figure, maintained that everything that claims existence in the absolute must try to free itself of movement and temporality. Just as Mallarmé finds in *minuit absolu* a time which has disappeared, so too does Baudelaire discover in the *joujou* an immobile image infinitely repeating the same movement and, in the hallucinatory experience of the stage, a "frozen darkness" in which "one's eyes focus on infinity."

There is one particular Poe story in which the qualities of the visionary experience enumerated above are found in a protocinematic device of the imagination, comparable to the *joujou* and to the stage as described by Baudelaire. That story is "The Man of the Crowd" (1840), in which the narrator speaks of a time when he found himself in one of those happy "moods of the keenest appetency, when the film from the mental vision departs." While in this mood, he peers through a window into the street. At the same time that the film departs from his mental vision, the window provides him with what might be called another "film" of sorts. He becomes "absorbed in contemplation of the scene without," and this contemplation alters his perception: "I looked at the passengers in masses, and thought of them in their aggregate relations. Soon, however, I descended to details, and regarded with minute interest the innumerable varieties of figure, dress, air, gait, visage and expression of countenance." As the night deepens, so too does his interest in the scene, for the rays of the gas-lamps on the street throw "over every thing a fitful and garish lustre":

> The wild effects of the light enchained me to an examination of individual faces; and although the rapidity with which the world of light flitted before the window, prevented me from casting more than a glance upon each visage, still it seemed that, in my peculiar mental state, I could frequently read, even in that brief interval of a glance, the history of long years.

In order to follow one of these passers-by, the narrator leaves his house and enters into the world which he has watched on the "screen" provided by his window. In doing so, he too becomes a "man of the crowd" or what Benjamin calls a *flâneur*. Referring to this story, Benjamin observes that, since the invention of photography, there has been no end of efforts to capture a man in his speech and actions. He recalls that Baudelaire spoke of a man who plunges into the crowd as into a reservoir of electric energy. Circumscribing the experience of this "plunge," Baudelaire refers to this man as "a kaleidoscope equipped with consciousness." If industrial development turned Man into a kaleidoscope, it also transformed the forms in which the artist worked and consequently the manner in which he approached his subject. Benjamin finds, for instance, in the feuilleton poetry submitting to the exigencies of montage. He sees Surrealism as an ultimate result of this liberation of forms of creation through nineteenth-century technological progress.

Benjamin is apparently referring to the Surrealist notion of the autonomous work of art, freed from the conscious intervention of the artist. He felt that this autonomy liberated the work of art, and the public's response to it, from the reactionary aspects of tradition and the veneration of the artist. One may question Benjamin's reasoning here and instead tend to agree with Theodor Adorno's thesis, advanced in his essay "Culture Industry Reconsidered," that the loss of the aura of tradition did not in fact result in a revolutionary consciousness on the part of the mass public. Even Benjamin conceded that the Hollywood movie industry had managed to substitute a cult of personality for this now extinct aura.

If, however, Surrealism *was* the ultimate result of this "liberation," for Benjamin it was cinema, in which "perception in the form of shocks was established as a formal principle," which eventually met the need created by this release from traditional modes of living: the new and urgent need for stimuli remarked upon by Baudelaire. What Benjamin does not consider, however, is the way in which this need for stimuli was met for Baudelaire through protocinematic devices, either actual or envisioned; or the way in which Poe's window, before which the world of light flitted rapidly in "The Man of the Crowd," is itself protocinematic in the manner in which, while showing a constant movement, it reveals minute details and provides changing configurations.

In his 1924 "Manifesto of Surrealism," André Breton claims that the mind grasps reality unconsciously so that "it is, as it were, from the fortuitous juxtaposition of the two terms that a particular light has sprung, *the light of the image*, to which we are infinitely sensitive." This is essentially a paraphrase of a sentence in Lautréamont's 1869 novel *Les Chants de Maldoror*, in which the shock of the realization of beauty is likened to "the chance meeting on a dissecting table of a sewing machine and an umbrella." Alain Resnais has compared Lautréamont's conception to Eisenstein's theory of a cinematic "montage of attractions," in which emotional shocks are produced through an arbitrary combination of shots. The Surrealists' enthusiasm for both Lautréamont and *Potemkin* would seem to validate this comparison. Although Lautréamont rejected certain aspects of Romanticism, his work was shaped by Romantic style and thought. It should therefore not come as a surprise that the cinematic mode envisioned in his "chance meeting," in which disparate images gain new meaning through their startling and fortuitous conjunction, can also be found in Poe, in Romanticism and Symbolism and, as will be seen, in the comparable work of such writers as Walter Pater during the late nineteenth-century Aesthetic movement in England.

In "The Fall of the House of Usher," Poe has the narrator state "that while, beyond doubt, there *are* combinations of very simple natural objects which have the power of thus effecting us [as if we were experiencing 'the afterdream of the reveller upon opium'], still the analysis of this power lies among considerations beyond our depth." For Roderick Usher, these arrangements and juxtapositions of objects endow them with a mysterious sentience. For the Romanticists, Symbolists, and Aesthetes, the juxtaposition of images provided a visionary experience which could not be attained through specific description. As Mallarmé, also a translator of Poe, stated, "It is not *description* which can unveil the efficacy and beauty of monuments, seas, or the human face in all their maturity and native state, but rather evocation, allusion, suggestion." For Mallarmé, this evocation could be achieved through the combination of elements. In "Crisis in Poetry" and "Music and Literature," he declares that the poet needs to establish a careful relationship between two images from which a third element will be distilled. "Out of a number of words, poetry fashions a single new word which is total in itself and foreign to the language—a kind of incantation." Mallarmé felt that the artists of his time were precisely at the moment of seeking in literature

> an art which shall complete the transposition, into the Book, of the symphony, or simply recapture our own: for, it is not in elementary sonorities of brass, strings, wood, unquestionably, but in the intellectual word at its utmost, that, fully and evidently, we should find, drawing to itself all the correspondences of the universe, the supreme Music.

Like Poe, who advocated "the union of Poetry and Music," and Mallarmé, who saw images as having a musical correspondence, Walter Pater believed that "all art constantly aspires toward the condition of music." Writing of the objects which comprise and decorate a house, he says:

> It was the old way of true *Renaissance*—being indeed the way of nature with her roses, the divine way with the body of a man, perhaps with his soul—conceiving the new organism by no sudden and abrupt creation, but rather by the action of a new principle upon elements all of which had in truth lived and died many times. The fragments of older architecture, the mosaics, the spiral columns, the precious cornerstones of immemorial building, had put on, by such juxtaposition, a new and singular expressiveness. . .

In this passage from *Marius the Epicurean*, that classic study of the self and consciousness, one again senses the Romantic attitude toward mysterious correspondences among objects or images, as if they were musical elements. It was an attitude which later would underlie certain concepts and strategies of the cinema, as was evidenced during the 1920s in the work of France's Impressionist filmmakers.

BURNES ST. PATRICK HOLLYMAN

Alexander Black's Picture Plays, 1893–1894

But if a paleontological botanist came upon a fossil apple in the apparently more ancient strata of the club-mosses he would dig deeper and eventually find the tree, revising the evolutionary time table as he dug. There are no accidents in evolution, no apples before the tree.—Terry Ramsaye, *A Million and One Nights*

The few texts available today that describe the "picture plays" produced by Alexander Black in the years 1893–94 seem to indicate that many of the cinematic devices, both narrative and technical, that we commonly assume "originated" with Porter, Mélies, and Griffith were nothing more than carry-overs from other media that were in their heyday in the last half of the nineteenth century. As John Fell has pointed out in *Film and the Narrative Tradition*,[1] the dime novel with its Western and detective heroes, the stage melodrama, the vaudeville theater, the comic strip, and the magic lantern show are but a few of the myriad sources that went to make up what was to be labeled later as the "cinematic language" of the American narrative film. Black's photoplays predate many of film history's classic landmarks: Porter's technique of cross-cutting to reveal simultaneous action, Griffith's flashback, and Eisenstein's use of montage editing. This article will examine the work of Alexander Black and show how early cinema was, for the most part, a carry-over from the above-mentioned media. Black's work is unique

---

[1] John L. Fell, *Film and the Narrative Tradition* (Norman: University of Oklahoma Press, 1974).

in that it spans the gap in film history between the precinematic period of 1860–96 and what we presently regard as the beginning of modern narrative film.

Alexander Black was born in 1859 and had a career as a journalist, a novelist, a photographer, and a producer of two photoplays. He became an editor for Hearst's Newspaper Feature Service until his retirement. Black died in 1940. His development of the photoplay (or "picture play" as he called it) began with an interest in photography. Several years before Black's first picture play, the hand camera (or "camera without legs" as it was commonly known) was just beginning to come into popularity with the general public. The Kodak camera, found in many households of the early 1890s, was well on its way to creating a new, major American hobby. Alexander Black became a general authority on the new technology, publishing articles in newspapers and magazines and giving lectures as a "Kodak fiend."[2]

Terry Ramsaye reported that Black "addressed marvelling audiences of the time from the lyceum stages of the East, under the auspices of Major Pond, with a lecture entitled 'Ourselves as Others See Us.' It was, naturally, illustrated with stereopticon lantern slides of snapshots made by Black and other amateurs. He went gunning with his camera up and down the highways and byways of New York and spread the pictorial pelts of his prey upon the limelight screen."[3] The "pictorial pelts" were nothing more than snapshots Black had taken of common street scenes in and about New York City of the late 1880s and early 1890s. These "snapshots," however, were quite significant in the development of the motion picture as a major narrative form for several reasons.

Black took images that were normally viewed as prints by the general public and projected them onto a screen for a large audience. There had been much earlier attempts at this: Father Athanasius Kircher, author of *Ars Magna Lucis et Umbrae* (1646), had projected engravings in the first half of the seventeenth century using a primitive magic lantern.[4] The long tradition of images projected upon a screen culminated with the widespread popularity of the magic lantern and stereopticon of the late nineteenth century. Seen as an after-dinner diversion in sitting rooms and parlors, the projected image thrown onto a plain wall or sheet

---

[2]The term "Kodak fiend" was coined in the late 1920s when Eastman Kodak had completed its saturation of the photographic market with the "box" camera of the 1890s. The "box" camera was the precursor to the Kodak "Instamatic" that enjoys current popularity. This widespread use of cameras in the 1890s led to a democratization of "image," the seeds of which we are still experiencing today.

[3]Terry Ramsaye, *A Million and One Nights: A History of the Cinema* (New York: Simon and Schuster, 1926), pp. 92–93.

[4]C. W. Ceram, *Archaeology of the Cinema* (New York: Harcourt, Brace and World, 1965), p. 33.

[5]There are some fine examples of these devices in the H. H. Glanz Collection at the Humanities Research Center, University of Texas, Austin. [Slides of photographs were projected publicly at least as early as June 27, 1864, in New York—GP.].

had become a widely accepted form of popular entertainment, long before Black's public shows. The colored images of the magic lantern were usually painted on glass, depicting scenes that varied from Biblical themes to *Uncle Tom's Cabin*.[5] The glass slides were projected in sequence with relatively elaborate narratives that accompanied the "views"; the story text supplied on a separate sheet compensated for the lack of motion or sound.

Black's slide show, "Ourselves as Others See Us," was innovative in that he projected a photographic image rather than the conventional painted-glass image. The images of a photographed world were pictures of human activity, "frozen moments of action." In them were Wall Street magnates and Fifth Avenue belles, as well as tramps and Bowery bums. Initially presented as a slide show, "Ourselves as Others See Us" began to develop narrative strands. With repeated showings, Black would rearrange the slide sequence to provide fictional narration to accompany his pictures. He became aware of the rich mimetic possibilities of mingling the everyday "realistic living characters" with the fictional. In his "Photography in Fiction," written in 1895, Black said that

> primarily my purpose was to illustrate art with life. Five or six years ago, when my plan was first made [circa 1889], I discovered several instances in which photographs from life were used to illustrate fiction, and many other instances *in which fiction evidently had been adjusted to photographs from life*. [My emphasis.] Neither of these phases offered any practical hint toward the picture play. The suggestion definitely came through a group of photographic studies from living characters, which were tossed together in a "picture talk" that I called "Ourselves as Others See Us." After outlining *a combination of fiction and photography*, each devised with regard for the demands and limitations of each other, it began to be clear that pictures must do more than illustrate.[6]

By the time that Black became aware "that pictures must do more than illustrate," Edison had perfected his Kinetoscope, the peep-show machine powered by an electric motor that ran a looped, 50-foot roll of motion picture images that continuously repeated themselves. Edison claimed that these images were taken out of the peep-show format and were crudely projected in private as early as 1889, but because the picture image was so unsteady the Kinetoscope was returned to the peep-show presentation. It wasn't until 1895 that the first fully successful projection of a motion picture image took place at the Lumière Brothers' factory in France.

Black had been interested in the possibilities of photography and motion since 1889, when he heard Eadweard Muybridge address the Oxford Club of

---

[6]Alexander Black, "Photography in Fiction," *Scribner's* M18 (Summer 1895), p. 348.

[7]Ramsaye, *A Million and One Nights*, p. 94.

Brooklyn.[7] He saw Muybridge's exhibition of moving horses and scientific studies of motion as well as the "Zoopraxiscope," which included a picture of a dancing girl in costume. Conscious of the photograph's ability for motionized storytelling, and feeling constricted by the obvious drawbacks of the single viewer peep-show audience of Edison's Kinetoscope, Black decided to approach the problem from another perspective. He assigned himself the task of taking a long series of individual photographs that would tell a fictional story in sequence. This extended set of photographs was projected with a stereopticon upon a large screen before a large audience as spoken dialogue was delivered from the stage. Black said that

> if it is the function of art to translate nature, it is the privilege of photography to transmit nature. But in this case the "tableaux vivants" must be progressive, that *the effect of reality may arise not from the suspended action of isolated pictures, but from the blending of many.* [My emphasis.] Here the stereopticon came to my aid. By carefully "registering" the backgrounds of the successive pictures in a scene, the figures alone are made to appear to move, thus slowly producing the effect which Mr. Edison has wrought, in a different way, with his kinetoscope.[8]

By motionizing his picture sequence, Black produced his first picture play, "Miss Jerry," on the night of October 9, 1894, at the Carbon Studio at 5 West 16th Street in New York City. The cast included William Courtenay, Ernest Hastings, and Blanche Bayliss as "Miss Jerry." The picture play was a full evening's entertainment, approximately two hours in length, with 480 separate images that were shown at the average rate of one image every 15 seconds. On the margin of the manuscript Black made notes for the pictures representing every 50 or 60 words of story.[9] Using a technical device common to the stereopticon shows of the nineteenth century known as a "fan dissolver," the images would dissolve from one to another, preventing what Black felt would be an "abrupt jump."

Standard film histories report that Méliès "discovered" the secret behind the filmic dissolve technique one day when his camera jammed, causing him to rewind the film in the camera and reexpose it by accident. The development of this effect, it is stated, led to the standard cinematic dissolve which Méliès typically exploited in his 1903 production *L'Enchanteur Alcofrisbas*. Although the dissolve was used in many stereopticon shows throughout the late nineteenth century (that is, a proper dissolve with a steadily controlled fade-out of the first image while the second image was evenly faded in and superimposed over the first image), Alexander Black was one of the first to use the dissolve in conjunction with a semi-motionized photographic narrative projected upon a screen. Méliès,

---

[8]Black "Photography in Fiction," p. 348.

[9]Alexander Black, "Making the First Picture Play," *Harper's Weekly* 38, (October 13, 1894): 988–90.

it must be remembered, did not even see a motionized image until December of 1895, when he attended the Lumière Brothers' showing at the Grand Café.[10]

Alexander Black's projected, dissolving images were accompanied by an elaborate musical score and dialogue spoken from the stage. The premiere was attended by such notables as William Dean Howells, Frank R. Stockton, Brander Matthews, Edmund Clarence Steedman, Dr. Seth Low, as well as other celebrities in literature and the arts.[11] "Miss Jerry" received excellent reviews in *Harper's Weekly, Critic, Scribner's,* and was referred to in several articles by Steedman in his column in the influential *The Dial.* Although "Miss Jerry" was billed as a "comedy" it was received by the audience as a serious art piece in a medium that was to be accepted with all due respect. The popular flavor of Edison's peep-show Kinetoscope had given way to a fully conceived "picture play." Black himself foresaw how the multiple elements contributing to the overall narrative structure of his photoplay could become the motion picture as it exists in its present form. In his "The Camera and the Comedy," he stated that

> indeed, so far as the "picture play" is concerned, I find it hard to fancy the elements of the text, the stage management (that is the purely dramatic element), the artistic work (so far as this might be separable from the dramatic element), and the pure photography as being represented each by a separate person. Certainly my own attempt to be all of these things at the same time has given to me a capacity for sympathy toward each member of such a combination, should it ever be so harmoniously formed.[12]

Black was also cognizant that his picture play was nothing more than a transitional medium, a pleasant blend of fiction and reality. He argued, however, that, "pending the perfection of the vitascope, the cinematograph, and kindred devices, the ordinary camera, in partnership with the rapidly dissolving stereopticon, gives the freest expression to the processes of the picture play, not only for a greater clearness and steadiness in pictorial result, but because of the wider range possible to the portable camera." Black went on to state that, "with whatever medium, we find, as I have suggested, problems in the story-telling function would be imposed upon the pictures."[13]

It is interesting to note that although the critics who reviewed "Miss Jerry" saw the newly created medium as nothing more than a "halfway house" between

---

[10]Georges Sadoul, *Georges Méliès* (Paris: Editions Seghers, 1961), p. 168.

[11]Ramsaye, *A Million and One Nights,* p. 98.

[12]Alexander Black, "The Camera and the Comedy." *Scribner's* M20 (November 1896), p. 606.

[13]Ibid.

the slide show and the cinema, they were unanimous in their praise of it and went even further than Black in predicting what was to come in the future. In the October 13, 1894, edition of *Harper's Weekly*, a reviewer writing about Black's "Miss Jerry" said that

> no one doubts that something in the direction of the picture play will ultimately become a familiar means of entertainment. Already it has been made quite clear that in this scientific millenium the public will not have to betake itself to exhibition halls to see and hear a novellette, but will sit at home and take the novellette over the wires, seeing and hearing with the aid of electricity. In the meantime, however, we must be content at the half-way house. Certainly, the half-way house has proved to be a very interesting place.[14]

Although most of the reviews of "Miss Jerry" centered around the serious technical accomplishments carried out in the new medium of the picture play, a certain amount of attention was directed toward the text of "Miss Jerry." Black wrote the story in the popular vein, combining elements from the stage melodrama that was at its height in the New York theater, the Western novelette, as well as the literary realism of the widely read stories published in magazines and journals of the period.

The heroine of the story is Jerry, a thoroughly American girl brought up among the mines and cow-camps of Colorado by her miner-prospector father, who in her young womanhood faces modern life in New York. She gratifies a life-long ambition to go into journalism. A glimpse of her adventures as a reporter afforded Black an opportunity for various "camera sketches" as Jerry travels about to document the New York City that was seen in Black's earlier "Ourselves as Others See Us." She interviews a prominent railroad president in an office atop Grand Central Station. (Depew, who worked for Vanderbilt, actually played himself in his real office overlooking the station.) Eventually she falls in love with her newspaper boss, Hamilton, who edits *The Daily Dynamo*. There is a happy ending as Hamilton and Jerry marry and decide to move to London, where he will take a high position on an English newspaper staff. There are a number of intricate subplots that unfold in the slum neighborhoods of New York, as well as the appearance of a long-haired buckskinned cowboy from Colorado, a figure from Jerry's past who tells her that she will always be remembered in her home town as the "Princess of the Panther Mine."[15]

---

[14]Black, "Making the First Picture Play," p. 987.

[15]For a full synopsis of "Miss Jerry" consult the original texts: Alexander Black's "Photography in Fiction 'Miss Jerry,' the First Picture Play," in *Scribner's* (see n.6 above), and Black, "The Camera and the Comedy," *Scribner's* (see n. 12 above).

Black structured the narrative of "Miss Jerry" to reflect what he considered the "flexible possibilities of the picture play." It is for this reason that "Miss Jerry" was a highly episodic narrative with multiple locations; it exploited the opportunity to show a photographed "real" world that went beyond the constraints of the stage melodrama with the aid of the portable camera. By the end of the nineteenth century the stage melodrama had become obsessed with verisimilitude; the development of Black's picture play (and the subsequent silent film) provided a vehicle with which to exploit this strong mimetic impulse. John Fell has observed that "sensation scenes in the last half of the century grew so ambitious (with smashing locomotives, military battles, sinking ships) that their execution often became the main point of the performance."[16]

It is in this spirit that Black had his Miss Jerry go to Grand Central Station, through the rush hour bustle of the trains, in an apparently purely gratuitous sequence that did nothing more than place her in an interesting realistic setting. Black felt that "the picture story, that is, the story in pictures, will be most impressive, and consequently more artistic, when it produces, so far as possible, the illusion of reality."[17] Realizing the value of "location shooting," Black exploited the tall buildings of New York City for shots that predated Griffith's high angle frames and used a number of varied settings: the tenements of Cherry Hill, well-known restaurants, large ballroom dances, as well as the streets of the city.

Taking his cue from the sequential cartoon pictures (comic strips) that dominated the pages of the most popular magazines of the period, Black presented action with an ingenious technique that anticipated Eisenstein's theory of montage. As there was no hope of conveying rapid motion, Black chose to depict the moments before and after the swift action involved, a device that comic strip frames had utilized to portray action from frame to following frame. In this way, a violent scene would first show a villain reaching for a knife and the next picture would reveal the victim lying on the ground in a heap. This rapid juxtaposition, while essentially a feature of what we today refer to as continuity editing, further increased the illusion of sequential movement. Because the effect was so innovative, reviewers commented that the technique enhanced the rapid action flow of the narrative, thus making it "sufficiently quick to preserve a naturalistic order in the story."[18] It wasn't until years later that Eisenstein exhausted the variations of this method of juxtaposition.

The portrayal of simultaneous action in the linear narrative ("cross-cutting" as it was later called) was a standard feature in Black's production of "Miss Jerry." Numerous incidents were related in parallel fashion throughout the picture play:

---

[16]Fell, *Film and the Narrative Tradition*, p. 24.

[17]Black, "The Camera and the Comedy," p. 608.

[18]Black, "Making the First Picture Play," p. 989.

Miss Jerry's editor, Hamilton, has a confrontation with Ward, who offers him a bribe at the "Monastery Restaurant," while we see Miss Jerry elsewhere; Hamilton is shown in his office while Miss Jerry is portrayed conducting an interview in a tenement in lower Manhattan, the narrative jumping back and forth between the two locations. Evidence indicates that the public had been more than well-prepared for Porter's cross-cutting technique by the time *The Great Train Robbery* appeared on the screen in 1903.[19]

Alexander Black's innovations in the field of the precinematic development of the motion picture are too numerous to discuss in this limited space. He foresaw the problems inherent in the relationship between sound and picture, screen direction, dramatic or "mood lighting," camera direction, pictorial space, montage, dramatic structure, *mise en scène*, as well as the implications involved in the fictional representation of reality in the photographic image.

The main intention of this article has been to dispel the film history myth of "spontaneous generation": the notion that the narrative techniques and devices introduced in the early days of the silent cinema were "invented" by the early innovators of the cinema. Nothing is further from the truth. It should also be noted that Black was no more the "originator" of these devices than Homer, Cervantes, Méliès, or Griffith were the "inventors" of the techniques for which they were best known. Film history, like history and language in general, is a grey and overlapping domain of contradictory facts that defy absolute classification.

A basic question remains, however: why was Alexander Black's work in 1893–94 so well received and hailed as a great innovation? Weren't all of the elements present in Black's "Miss Jerry" already present in the culture of the late nineteenth century in various forms—the photograph, the Western and detective novelette, the stage melodrama, the cartoon strip, and Edison's Kinetoscope? The answer is yes. But it is precisely because Black was a great synthesizer, a man able to foresee the potential for a motionized storytelling medium, that his work is historically significant. He was a person who, at a critical moment, provided the public with a brief transitional medium, one that allowed them to dissolve from the slow-paced frozen action of the nineteenth century into the rapid, motionized action of the twentieth century.

---

[19]Although Porter is generally credited with this innovative cinematic technique, Black used it to its fullest in "Miss Jerry" in 1894. See Black's "Photography in Fiction" for evidence to support this view.

KATHERINE SINGER KOVÁCS

Georges Méliès and the *Féerie*

Soon after the motion picture was invented, two opposing tendencies became apparent. While the Lumière brothers used the camera to record events and incidents from everyday life, George Méliès eschewed the realism of street scenes in favor of artificially arranged tableaux. Méliès prided himself on the fact that his scenes were invented and that he used theatrical forms and techniques.[1] For his films he borrowed from spectacle shows such as operas, melodramas, historical mimodramas, and especially *féeries*. That George Méliès looked to the *féerie* should not surprise us. Although it has vanished into almost complete oblivion, during its heyday in the nineteenth century, the *féerie* attracted the attention of such men as Théophile Gautier, Charles Baudelaire, and Gustave Flaubert.[2] As the following description will reveal, this genre was the single most important theatrical influence in the development of Méliès's film style.

The *féerie* was born shortly after the French Revolution, when a new theatergoing public composed primarily of uneducated spectators began to attend spectacle shows. This new public which sought thrills, excitement, and surprises in the theater enjoyed melodramas as much as *féeries*. In fact, in its earliest form the *féerie* was a type of melodrama in which acrobatics, music, and

---

[1]As Méliès wrote in an advertisement, "these fantastic and artistic films reproduce stage scenes and create a new genre entirely different from the ordinary cinematographic views of real people and real streets." See Georges Sadoul, *Georges Méliès* (Paris: Editions Seghers, 1970), p. 14.

[2]As a theater reviewer Gautier often wrote about *féeries* (see n. 5). Baudelaire's poem "L'Irréparable" was inspired by a *féerie* called *La Belle aux cheveux d'or*. Its heroine was played by Marie Daubrun, a woman Baudelaire loved. See "L'Irréparable," *Les Fleurs du Mal*, ed. Jacques Crépet and Georges Blin (Paris, 1942), p. 60. Flaubert actually completed one *féerie* entitled *Le Château des coeurs* in 1863. It was never performed on stage.

mime were the main elements.[3] Like melodramas, the plots of most *féeries* pivoted upon a struggle between forces of good and evil. But while these forces remained invisible in melodramas, in *féeries* they were incarnated onstage by gnomes and witches. The plots of *féeries* were usually adapted from fairy tales in which supernatural creatures intervened in the lives of men. These creatures used magical talismans to effectuate the sudden metamorphosis of persons or things and the rapid replacement of one decor by another before the spectator's eyes ("les changements à vue").[4]

The appearances, disappearances, and transformations which were standard fairy play practices delighted and surprised audiences who were unfamiliar with the battery of theatrical machines facilitating these changes. To them the actions which they witnessed were a sort of magic. Gautier compared them to dreams.[5]

In addition to the supernatural creatures, the same four human beings reappear in all *féeries:* the ingenue, the handsome young man whom she loves, his valet (a lazy fellow who loves to eat), and a rival (who is usually grotesque and comic.) With the support or hindrance of extraterrestrial forces, these characters pursue one another through different fabulous lands which are presented in a series of independent tableaux. At the end, the hero and heroine are reunited in a grand finale called the apotheosis scene. As the music swells, beautiful girls in diaphanous costumes either descend onstage from the "heavens" or hang in the air on invisible wires.[6]

---

[3]Many early *féeries* were actually called *mélodrame-féeries*. Between 1800 and 1820, when approximately 60 *féeries* were presented, nearly 20 of them were described in this way. (These figures are based on entries in Charles Beaumont Wicks's four-volume bibliography of the theater entitled *The Parisian Stage*, 4 vols. [University: University of Alabama Press, 1950–64]).

[4]The most widely used method for effectuating an instantaneous scene change from one scene to another was by means of falling flaps. The scenery flat was divided into a certain number of rectangles which moved on hinges like folding doors. On one side of the rectangles set designers painted one scene, and on the other they painted a second. They then attached ropes or strings to each flap along the length of the flat and joined the strings together. At the appropriate moment the stagehands pulled the strings and made all of the flaps pivot to the reverse side, thereby changing the scene.

[5]Théophile Gautier, *Histoire de l'art dramatique en France depuis 25 ans*, vol. 3, *Octobre 1844* (Paris: Edition Heztel, 1859), pp. 281–82.

[6]These wires were painted black so as to be invisible. They ran up to pulleys attached to a carriage and through the carriage to points on the grill. The carriage rested either on a taut rope or on a special railway which could move from side to side above the stage. To begin the "flight," one of the stagehands would draw the carriage across the stage. The pulleys in the carriage would press against the wheels, thus forcing them sideways. In this way, it was possible to raise an object. A movement in the opposite direction would effectuate a descent. See A. de Vaulabelle and Charles Hemardinquer, *La Science au théâtre* (Paris: H. Paulin, 1908), pp. 243–44.

Such finales had been the obligatory ending of all *féeries* since the beginning of the century when *Le Pied de mouton,* the first modern *féerie,* was presented.[7] The plot of this work also became the prototype for subsequent *féeries.* As the curtain rises, the young protagonist, Gusman, is wandering through a thick forest with a cavern in the back (the conventional melodramatic setting). Because the woman he loves is betrothed to another man, Gusman has come to the woods to commit suicide. But when he brings the pistols up to his temple, they fly out of his hands and explode in the air. It is Gusman's guardian angel who intervenes at this propitious moment. With a crackle of thunder a rock opens, flames shoot out, and the genie appears, accompanied by devils and serpents (act 1, scene 2). Like other characters in early melodramas and *féeries,* Gusman's angel pronounces maxims on love, virtue, duty, etc. He reminds the young man that human life is precious and insists that he has no right to contemplate suicide. Heartened by the genie's words and by his gift of a magical mutton foot, Gusman embarks upon an energetic campaign to rescue his beloved Leonora. In subsequent tableaux her chaperones change into guitarists; a cart becomes a cage;[8] portraits yawn and move; his rival is carried aloft in the air; and food is whisked from tables. At the end love triumphs and Gusman and Leonora are married.

The power of love was often the moral of these early plays. It appears in one of Guilbert de Pixérecourt's most famous *féeries, Ondine* or *La Nymphe des eaux* (1830). This work began a vogue of plays about supernatural creatures who fall in love with mortals. *Ondine* is the daughter of an underwater prince. When she falls in love with a mortal being, she acquires the most precious of all gifts: a soul. As befits a play about a water sprite, *Ondine* contains many aquatic scenes.[9] The cabin where she resides at the beginning of the play changes into a rich underwater palace illuminated by brilliant lights. The finale takes place in a crystal grotto,

---

[7] *Le Pied de mouton* was written by a famous pamphleteer named Martainville and presented for the first time on December 6, 1906.

[8] To effectuate changes of objects such as chairs and carts, rather than entire sets, painted set pieces with hinged flaps usually were employed. By means of a simple trick line a flap could be swung over part of the set piece like the leaf of a page. The object could thereby be increased or diminished in size. It was also in this manner that small props would be made to disappear. (See J. Moynet, *L'Envers du Théâtre* [Paris: Hachette, 1875], p. 89.) In a number of films Méliès used set pieces with hinged flaps.

[9] Scenes with water and with ships sailing on the high seas were common in *féeries.* The sea was depicted by means of a carpet that was moved by hoops. Stagehands placed under the carpet would alternately raise and lower the hoops. At different points on the stage they also placed jointed girders cut in the form of crests which increased the illusion of moving waves. Other trusses placed further back in a stationary position simulated the high seas. When it was necessary to present boats, they were usually set on rollers along two curved wooden "railways" (called "les chemins de mer"). The curves along the path of the railway created the illusion of a boat listing. (See Vaulabelle and Hemardinquer, *La Science au théâtre,* p. 212.)

where all of the great rivers of Europe perform a graceful ballet to celebrate the marriage of Ondine and her prince. In such scenes not only machines but also music and dance contributed to create tableaux of charm and beauty.

Mime and dance were key elements in all *féeries*. In fact, over the years *opéra-féeries* and *pantomime-féeries* eventually replaced *mélodrame-féeries* in popularity.[10] The main attraction of these works came from their ballets and the interludes of music and mime interspersed with the action.[11] Plays of this kind remained popular until around the middle of the century when vaudeville intervened and modified the form of the *féerie*.

After around 1840 *pantomime-féeries* and *opéra-féeries* were hardly ever presented. *Vaudeville-féeries* came to dominate the theatrical scene to the extent that by the late 1840s distinctions no longer were made between *vaudeville-féeries* and *féeries*: all *féeries* would henceforth be vaudeville shows.[12] The vaudeville writers who turned to *féeries* altered their tone by introducing more songs, jokes, and puns than ever before. They relied less upon ballet and song and more upon elaborate decors and startling scene changes to hold the interest of the audience.

Technical innovations made during those years considerably facilitated their task. By the late 1830s gas had been installed in most of the important Parisian theaters. Gas was one of the first powerful sources of light for the stage. It enabled scenic artists to present more realistic as well as more fantastic scenes. With the installation of gas in many theaters, set designers could exploit not only its strength and brilliance but also its potential for creating special atmospheric

---

[10]Between 1800 and 1810, fourteen *mélodrame-féeries* were presented in Paris—half of the total number of *féeries*. In the next decade the number of *mélodrame-féeries* fell to four. Between 1821 and 1830 only two were presented in Paris, even though the total number of *féeries* almost doubled. (These figures are based on Wicks's entries in *The Parisian Stage*.) During the same period, and especially between 1818 and 1825, there was a dramatic increase in the number of *opéra-féerie* plays. At the Paris Opera alone, eight such works were presented. After 1830, when romantic ballet reached its apogee, the interest in *opéra-féeries* declined, and only two of these plays appeared. At the same time Deburau, the renowned mime at the Funambules theater, began to present *pantomime-féeries* which enthralled all of Paris. Under his auspices this form became extremely popular and replaced both *mélodrame-féeries* and *opéra-féeries* in importance. In fact, in the decade 1841 to 1850 the number of *pantomime-féeries* performed in Paris equalled the entire production over the preceding 40 years. Upon Deburau's death in 1848 interest in *pantomime-féeries* waned.

[11]All *féeries* had songs. Usually new words were devised for familiar tunes.

[12]Again I am basing this conclusion upon entries in Wicks, *The Parisian Stage*. Before 1840 all *féeries* contained some descriptive term along with the title. One finds *folie-féeries, comédie-féeries* or *vaudeville-féeries*. During the decade 1821 to 1830 more than one-fourth were designed as *vaudeville-féeries*. Between 1841 and 1850, out of a total of 64 plays, only six were identified as *vaudeville-féeries*. This does not suggest that the latter was becoming less popular; on the contrary, it was such a common form that it was a redundancy to use the word vaudeville in the title.

effects. The development of limelight further aided in the creation of special effects by enabling set designers to cross the rays of different lamps and to create a radiant yet mellow light which perfectly imitated the beams of the sun or moon. Once stage lighting could be modified and controlled, it became an important aspect of stage production, and lighting instructions were written directly into the script as an integral element of the story.

Another important advance in theatrical techniques resulted from Louis Daguerre's invention of the diorama. In 1823 it was first exhibited in a specially constructed circular room in which the audience was transported on a platform past a series of tableaux hung from the ceiling. As the spectators moved past, the illumination of each tableau was imperceptibly modified, thereby creating certain magical effects. Later Daguerre perfected double dioramas, the effect of which also depended upon lighting. On each side of a translucent canvas a different scene was painted. When light was shone on one side of the canvas, the scene on that side emerged. When light was shone from behind, the one on the back appeared.[13] In this way, one scene would melt into another. In later *féeries,* the double diorama was utilized not only to effectuate instantaneous scene changes but also to achieve special effects such as fires or sunsets. It was yet another tool enabling playwrights to dazzle and surprise the spectators.

All of these technical advances contributed to the development of the *féerie,* which attained its greatest popularity during the 1850s.[14] Although stage effects were more spectacular during this decade, *féerie* plots did not substantially change. That is to say, new techniques enhanced time-worn *féerie* tricks. We find an example of this new-old style in a work written for the Cirque-Olympique by the well-known vaudeville writer Anicet Bourgeois and two circus writers, Laurent and Laloue. Revived and imitated innumerable times, *Les Pilules du diable* demonstrates the way in which *féerie* writers combined sophisticated stage machinery with acrobatic and dancing skills inherited from the circus.

The plot of *Les Pilules du diable* is a fairly conventional one in which an impoverished artist named Albert wishes to marry Isabelle. His principal rival is a wealthy hidalgo named Sottinez, who pursues the lovers relentlessly. In one famous scene a locomotive in which Sottinez was chasing Isabelle and Albert explodes. Pieces of Sottinez's body fall strewn upon the stage. These precious remains are gathered in a basket. After some searching, the characters locate the hidalgo's head. Before the audience's eyes, they begin to piece him together. When they have finished, Sottinez renews his furious pursuit as if nothing had happened.

---

[13]See Louis Daguerre, "Mémoire de l'Académie des Beaux Arts," cited by Germain Bapst in his *Essai sur l'histoire des panoramas et des dioramas* (Paris: Imprimerie Nationale, 1891) pp. 20–21.

[14]Sadoul mentions a somewhat later period. According to him the genre peaked between 1860 and 1880. (*Georges Méliès,* p. 33).

This scene is achieved in a simple and ingenious manner. At the moment when the locomotive explodes, the actor playing the part of Sottinez hides behind it, while different parts of a mannequin drop from the flies above the stage. They then begin to reassemble him in front of part of the set which is cut out in the shape of a man. All of the parts of the cut-out correspond exactly to the parts of the mannequin's body. When they adjust his leg, for example, they fit it into that part of the set. Meanwhile the real actor, who is located behind the set, surreptitiously places both the false limb and the appropriate part of the set in the wings, substituting his own real leg and then all of the other parts of his body. Since this reconstruction obliged the actor to assume awkward positions in which he could not always maintain his balance, two stagehands held him until he had passed his head through the final cut-out in the set.[15]

Although severed heads and bodies hacked to pieces were frequent sights in *féeries*, these scenes are never alarming. In all *féeries* the victims of violent action are immune to serious disability. Characters in fairy plays resemble dream figures. As they pursue never-ending endeavors, they change clothes, transform, or fall down and break, only to be put back together again in the next scene. Like puppets or machines, they are comic in the Bergsonian sense.[16] Even the devil, a frequent participant in *féeries*, performs evil acts with cheerful good humor.

As the century progressed and vaudeville writers fixed the form and the conventions of the *féerie*, comedy became more important than poetry, and tableaux were more burlesque than beautiful. Authors began to devise more outlandish and elaborate settings for the *féerie*.[17] The number of tableaux increased. By the end of the Second Empire in 1870, *féeries* contained as many as

---

[15]Vaulabelle and Hemardinquer, *La Science au théâtre*, pp. 216–17.

[16]Bergson's definition of comic was "le mécanique plaqué sur le vivant." He thought that all comic situations (ranging from slapstick scenes to word plays) originated when human beings acted like machines. That is to say, when an individual was unable to adjust his responses to changes in his environment, when his movements and actions did not conform to reality, that person would seem comic. One of the examples which he used was that of a man who does not see a step and who continues to walk until he falls on his face. He seems funny because at the moment of his fall he has lost his humanity and becomes like a machine or a puppet.

[17]An extremely successful *féerie* called *La Biche au bois* contributed to this trend. In this work by the Cogniard brothers grotesque and comic forms were introduced on a large scale. Prior to this time (1845) characters in *féeries* had confined their travels to allegorical or mythological lands, in the heavens or beneath the seas. This all changed with *La Biche*. In addition to investigating these conventional locales, characters in *La Biche au bois* explore new domains such as the kingdom of bells, the kingdom of fish, and the kingdom of vegetables, where they talk with fruits and vegetables of colossal dimensions. Each of these tableaux contains a grotesque ballet in which men dress as animals and the intention is comic. It is interesting to note that the subtitle of this work, *Le Royaume des fées*, is the same as the title of one of Méliès's filmed *féeries*, but there is no similarity in terms of the plot.

20 different sets. In addition to the palaces, huts, underground caves, and moving forests which the *féerie* inherited from melodrama, it acquired some new locales such as the sun, the moon, India, China, and Turkey.

One of the theater directors most responsible for this trend was Marc Fournier, who ran the Porte Saint-Martin theater during most of the Second Empire. It was the extravagant stage sets which made his theater thrive. For each production he assembled the most elaborate decors, scenes, and tricks ever imagined. Every few weeks he changed the settings of three or four tableaux. Although eventually he went bankrupt, his grandiose shows enthralled all of Paris for many years. Partly as a result of Fournier's example, a veritable frenzy for spectacle shows gripped Parisian theaters. As other directors followed his lead, the scenes in *féeries* became more extravagant, and the number of tableaux increased. *Rothomago,* a work first presented in 1862, boasted 25 different decors. The Goncourt brothers, who attended the opening night performance, described the *féerie* in deprecating terms, considering it to be a plebeian form of entertainment.[18] Nevertheless, the people they saw in the audience that evening were among the most fashionable in Parisian society. For, to a remarkable extent, the pomp and splendor of *féeries* coincided with the tastes of the Second Empire. This was an extravagant epoch, when the emperor and empress gave lavish dances and masked balls, when ceremonies and parades were very much in style.

Georges Méliès was born in 1863. Even into adulthood the glitter of the Second Empire shaped his tastes. He marveled at the spectacular effects achieved in *féeries* and sought to recreate them in his magic shows at the Robert-Houdin theater. When he began to make motion pictures, it was only natural for him to use the *féerie* as a source of techniques, plots, and themes. It was also an important force in shaping Méliès's film aesthetic. For even when he substituted photo-graphic illusions for the flaps, traps, scrims, and mirrors of the stage, Méliès's point of view remained essentially theatrical.

That Méliès's frame of reference was the stage can be seen in the sets which he designed for his films. In all of them the camera occupies the position of a spectator in the orchestra of a theater.[19] It remains in a stationary position, at a constant distance from the actors who are always shown full-length; there is no such thing as a close-up. The actors enter and exit either from the side wings or through vampire traps in the floor of the stage.[20] All of their movements are

---

[18]Edmund and Jules de Goncourt, *Journal littéraire,* March 1, 1862, p. 1026: "The spectacle shows of the Boulevard (du Crime) are a modern paradise for the people. They have the same importance in the dreams of today's masses as did Gothic cathedrals in man's imagination during the Middle Ages."

[19]Sadoul, *Méliès,* pp. 36–38.

[20]A vampire trap is a two-leaved trap with springs constructed either on the stage floor or in the flats. It permitted a supernatural creature to disappear more rapidly than was possible with older traps without springs.

executed on one plane along the center of the stage, behind an invisible line of demarcation (corresponding to the stage apron) at a considerable distance from the flats at the back of the stage. The latter consists of backdrops painted exclusively in shades of gray.[21] To give an illusion of depth to this two-dimensional playing area, set pieces were placed in a series of grooves between the apron and the backdrop.

In one of his most elaborate filmed *féeries*, *Le Palais des 1001 nuits* (1905), one scene is set in a thick forest where trees fill the entire stage. When the protagonist appears, the successive rows of foliage part to reveal a crystal grotto painted on the backdrop. After the protagonist passes through, the trees slide back to their original position along grooves in the floor. As Méliès noted in his catalogue: "This decoration, which was made only after considerable labor, is a veritable marvel of achievement. It possesses a great artistic beauty."[22]

Other decors found in this film include the exotic settings of palaces, caves, temples, and throne rooms which Marc Fournier and other stage directors had popularized. The plot is also a familiar one: a poor but noble young man arrives at the rajah's court to ask for the hand of his daughter. The rajah refuses, preferring to see her marry a rich usurer named Holdfast. The desperate prince arouses the sympathy of the fairy of gold who leads him to a fabulous treasure. The prince must prove himself worthy of the fortune by fighting the skeletons, toads, and dragon who guard the vault.

The trials which the protagonist must undergo occasion such tricks as the disappearance of objects and people as well as their instantaneous transformation. Méliès employs certain *féerie* effects which had been popular since the Italian Renaissance: statues become animated;[23] strange monsters built of wood and papier mâché dance and cavort onstage;[24] gnomes and witches of frightening aspect weave wicked schemes;[25] and men play the roles of animals.[26] Special effects such as fires, snowfalls, volcanic eruptions, and explosions are accom-

---

[21]As Méliès noted, the shades of gray ran the gamut from almost white to almost black. The painting was much neater than for plays. (See Sadoul, *Méliès*, p. 100.)

[22]Méliès, *Complete Catalogue of "Star" Films* (New York, 1905), p. 76. For distribution of his films in the U.S. Méliès opened an office in New York which was run by his brother Gaston. This *Catalogue* contains detailed descriptions of all of Méliès's films, their prices, lengths, etc.

[23]Statues also became animated in other Méliès films such as *La Statue animée, L'Enchanteur Alcofrisbas,* and *Sightseeing Through Whiskey.*

[24]Monsters appear in *A Trip to the Moon* (the Selenites), *Sightseeing Through Whiskey, À la conquête du pôle, The Merry Frolics of Satan,* and *The Magic Lantern,* to name only a few. These creatures are all created by theatrical means (costumes, makeup, etc.).

[25]Of all of Méliès's evildoers, the devil was his favorite. Méliès himself usually played the part.

[26]Men dress as lions and tigers in *Le Palais des 1001 nuits.* In *The Enchanted Well,* a human horse walks across the stage, and giant frogs assail the protagonist.

plished by the time-tested methods of the theater. *Le Palais des 1001 nuits* is theatrical in inspiration as well as in execution: its changes depend upon costume and stage machinery rather than upon innovative photographic techniques. And yet the film seems richer than descriptions of contemporary theater *féeries*. Perhaps this is because the camera allowed Méliès to link single illusions together in rapid succession. At the end of the film, when the prince defeats the monsters and a series of stage transformations culminate in an endless cortege of women bearing gold and silver, the number of scene changes and the rapidity with which they are executed intensify the magical experience.

Méliès did not restrict his use of *féerie* techniques to those films which were meant to be *féeries*. They recur in nearly all of his works. For example, even in some of his comic films such as *The Terrible Turkish Executioner* (1904), *Delirium in a Studio* (1907), and *The Doctor's Secret* (1910) we find the decapitation scenes which were favored by nineteenth-century *féerie* playwrights. In *The Doctor's Secret* (also known as *Hydrothérapie Fantastique*), a corpulent man who visits a doctor in order to reduce shares the fate of Sottinez in *Les Pilules du diable*. When he is placed inside a steam cabinet which explodes, parts of his body (or rather parts of a mannequin) drop from the flies and land in different locations around the stage. The head of the real actor appears in a clock painted on the backdrop of the stage. One of the doctor's assistants removes the head from the clock while a second one carries a high-backed chair to the center of the stage. They then reassemble the patient by placing the torso, arms, legs, and head against the chair. This prop serves the same function as did the backdrop in *Les Pilules du diable*—it gives the actor a place to hide while he substitutes the appropriate parts of his body through cut-outs in the chair.[27]

The traps, flaps, and dummies employed in *The Doctor's Secret* are used with equal effectiveness in a number of Méliès's films. The plot of one of his most elaborate *féeries*, *The Merry Frolics of Satan* (1906), pivots almost entirely upon these devices. In this work a young engineer named Crackford unwittingly signs a pact with Satan in return for some magic pills.[28] For the remainder of the film he is pursued by Satan who delights in playing tricks upon him: a train in which he travels falls through a bridge; the meal he sits down to eat and the table upon which it is placed disappear;[29] the inn where he hopes to find repose is invaded by apes and demons who pursue him, traversing walls, buffets, staircases, mantle-pieces, etc. In this scene the stage set is a veritable web of traps, flaps, and

---

[27]The doctor places all of the parts of the body against the chair nearly simultaneously. Then Méliès stopped the camera so that the real actor could take the place of the mannequin. Thus the performer never had to place different parts of his body through the flaps, as his stage counterpart was obliged to do.

[28]The idea of magic pills was a common one in *féeries*. It was first used onstage in *Les Pilules du diable*.

[29]Disappearing food was the most common trick in all *féeries*.

peepholes, through which the devils "tumble over every obstacle in their way while performing astonishing acrobatic feats. All these imps finally disappear beneath the floor. . . ."[30] When the engineer attempts to flee, his carriage is transformed into a ghostly vehicle driven by a skeleton-horse which takes him on a vertiginous ride through space. His escape attempt fails. Satan eventually whisks him away to hell where he is burned at the stake.[31]

The most spectacular scene in the film is that of the engineer's aerial voyage in the carriage. Flights through the air or the simple suspension of objects such as spaceships (*A Trip to the Moon*), balloons and helicopters (*A La Conquête du Pôle*), and chariots (*The Kingdom of the Fairies, Jupiter's Thunderbolts*) were frequent effects in Méliès's films. To show vehicles in the air, he often relied upon conventional stage techniques in which life-sized vehicles bearing the actors aloft were suspended from invisible wires hung from the flies. As they rose in the air, they disappeared out of the camera's range.

But in some of these "flights" Méliès went further than stage set designers and substituted photographic processes for the conventional wires and panoramas of *féeries*. In certain scenes, shots of the standard-size object taking off were juxtaposed with views of miniature models whirling through the heavens.[32] These models, which were superimposed upon views of the stars and the sky, rendered flights through the air with greater realism than was possible on the stage.[33]

As these examples suggest, it was quite common for Méliès to join the conventional techniques of the stage to methods of still photography. The motion picture camera, by its very nature, rendered certain stage effects and practices superfluous. Often the camera could effectuate a trick more easily and less expensively. This was certainly so in the case of instantaneous scene changes. The movable stages, elevators, and falling flaps which had evolved over the years to effectuate the rapid change of scene from one decor to the next were replaced by camera dissolves, fade-outs, and fade-ins. The simple process of opening and closing the iris of the camera also outmoded the stage practice of using layers of gauze and of dimming the lights before a scene change and of bringing them up afterward.[34]

The way in which Méliès showed vision scenes also changed from theatrical practice. Instead of presenting spectres behind gauze at the rear of the stage or

---

[30]Méliès, *Complete Catalogue of "Star" Films*, p. 110.

[31]Here Méliès used the stop-action technique to substitute a dummy for the actor.

[32]Méliès used models in *À la conquête du pôle, A Trip to the Moon, The Astronomer's Dream*, and *The Merry Frolics of Satan*.

[33]Méliès also used superimpositions to film scenes beneath the seas.

[34]The most effective use of fade-outs, fade-ins, and dissolves is found in Méliès's *The Kingdom of the Fairies*.

throwing them above the actors with magic lanterns, Méliès would film the apparition before or after shooting the scene on a white background, stop the camera, wind the film back, and reshoot in order to obtain superimposition. Sometimes he would place a piece of muslin gauze over the lens to give a hazy, indistinct appearance to the image.[35] Thus in *L'Enchanteur Alcofrisbas* (1903) we see ghostly creatures shrouded in sheets dance in the air; in *Le Chaudron Infernal* (1903) the barely visible forms go up in flames.

The camera also eliminated the need for trick costumes, falling flaps, dioramas, and doubles, because it was possible to stop filming at any point and to "arrange" a scene. Méliès fully exploited the possibilities inherent in the stop-action technique. This was the single most important cinematic element in his films.[36] It enabled him to effectuate instantaneous transformations by photographing an object, substituting another one in exactly the same position, and resuming the action. When the film was run, it was as if the first object instantly transformed into the second.

Méliès used stop-actions in his films not only to transform men into women and paintings into people, but also to make characters appear and disappear. The technique replaced the leap through flaps which stage actors would make for sudden appearances. It also facilitated more rapid changes of clothing than were possible with the old theatrical methods.[37] In *Knight of Black Art* (1908), the

---

[35] Albert A. Hopkins, ed., *Magic, Stage Illusions and Scientific Diversions Including Trick Photography* (New York, 1897; reprint ed., New York: Benjamin Blom, 1967), p. 434.

[36] In *Georges Méliès*, Sadoul includes Méliès's own description of how he accidentally discovered that the stop-action technique could be used for transformations: "One day early in my career as I was casually photographing the Place de l'Opéra, my camera jammed . . . with unexpected results. It took me a minute to release the film and to start cranking the camera again. During that minute, the passersby, the buses, and the cars had of course moved. Later when I projected the filmstrip . . . I saw a 'Madeleine-Bastille' bus suddenly change into a hearse and some men become women. In this way the substitution trick, the so-called 'stop-action technique' was discovered, and two days later I filmed the first metamorphoses of men into women and the first instantaneous disappearances . . ." (*Georges Méliès*, pp. 106–7).

[37] On the stage changes of clothing were executed in the following manner: when the artist came onstage he was already dressed in the costume which he would change into before the spectators. Over it went another one ("le costume à boyau") in which he would make his entrance. All the parts of this costume were sewn together; there were no seams; it was all one piece. The costume was cut from top to bottom and on each side so that it consisted of two pieces held together by a cord. The cord was passed through rings. At the moment of transformation, the actor placed himself above a trap in the stage. A stagehand reached up and pulled on the ends of the cord so that the costume was no longer around the actor, but resting on him. At the next signal, the stagehand pulled the costume into the trap. (See Paul Ginisty, *La Féerie* [Paris: Michaud, 1910], p. 228, n.1).

magician throws four gowns at his assistants who are immediately seen to be wearing them; in *The Mermaid* (1904), the well-dressed magician is transmogrified into an old and seedy begger.

The stop-action technique enabled Méliès to employ other methods of trick photography in his films. In addition to using fast motion, slow motion, and reverse action photography, Méliès achieved startling effects with composite pictures.[38] These were made by covering parts of the lens, so that one or several areas of the frame would not be exposed, and photographing a scene with a black background. Méliès would then also place a blackened piece of cardboard next to the camera aperture. This cardboard was in a shape corresponding to the black backdrop where the second part of the scene would be photographed after the film had been rewound. In one tableau of *The Kingdom of Fairies* (1903) Méliès made dramatic use of this process of duplex photography by dividing the screen into two distinct pictures. A group of people stand on the balcony of a palace watching as demons carry a princess away in the air. The flight of the creatures is really a separate scene which has been superimposed upon the sky.

With the same methods Méliès achieved other new tricks,[39] including interesting variations on scenes with severed heads. In *Le Mélomane* (1903), the conductor seems to reproduce his own head six times because Méliès photographed the same head in six different positions in the same frame. In *L'Homme à la Tête de Caoutchouc* (1902), the protagonist expands the size of his own head until it explodes.[40]

It is interesting to note that in spite of the new techniques Méliès employed in his films, he did not alter the conventions of the *féerie* but remained within the genre's traditional thematic and structural limits. In all of his films stock characters such as the scientist and the devil reappear, as do familiar scenes such as dream sequences and voyages. Méliès was not interested in revitalizing the *féerie*. His use of stop-actions, superimpositions, and illusionary photography merely offered new ways of effectuating old familiar tricks. Depending upon the illusion which he wished to create, Méliès alternated between filmic and theatrical means. Each film therefore contains a mixture of scenic and photographic devices.[41]

---

[38]Méliès used fast motion in an ingenious way in *The Astronomer's Dream*.

[39]He often juxtaposed different, sometimes incongruous objects and scenes, achieving such effects as that of a woman emerging from a hoop (*Knight of Black Art*), a figure appearing inside an enormous box (*The Mysterious Box*), and two ballerinas dancing upon the curtains of a bed (*The Ballet Master's Dream*).

[40]To make the head expand in size the actor's body was shrouded in black, and he was seated upon a chair which was attached to a "railway," by means of which he could be moved closer or further away from the camera, thereby enlarging or shrinking the size of his head.

[41]Certain general trends can nevertheless be perceived. To a certain extent, the tricks

We see the extent to which Méliès mixed traditional techniques of the *féerie* with those of the film in one of his last elaborate works, *A La Conquête du Pôle* (1912). Although this is not a *féerie* in the conventional sense, by the time the motion picture was invented playwrights were using science-fiction stories rather than fairy tales as a source for *féeries*.[42] Such machines as the car, the helicopter, and the submarine, and such locales as the moon and the North Pole had been presented on stage years before Méliès's *Conquête du Pôle*. At the beginning of the film the titles explain that Dr. Maboul has just invented an "aerobus" which will reach the North Pole. After seeing a miniature model of the vehicle (which will be used in flight later on in the picture) and the "laboratory" where it is being constructed, we witness its take-off, effectuated by means of wires hanging from the flies.

As the aerobus travels through the air, women playing the role of constellations salute it in passage in a scene created by superimpositions. When the explorers arrive at the North Pole they land in a traditional two-dimensional decor which contains cardboard icicles and painted icebergs. As they investigate the terrain they encounter the "Géant des neiges," a giant monster made of papier mâché who smokes a pipe, rolls his eyes, and swallows one of the scientists. When the others attack him, the monster spits his victim out (the latter jumps through the flap in the monster's mouth and lands onstage). The "rescue" of Maboul's party is achieved by another vehicle which first appears in miniature against the backdrop. A set piece corresponding to the central portion of the vehicle replaces the model and descends by means of wires to where the men are located. As the scientists disappear in the air, penguins and seals appear by means of the stop-

---

which Méliès chose to present depended upon the genre in which he worked. Méliès's films ranged from simple magic shows, to burlesque scenes, to historical reenactments, to science-fiction stories, to *féeries*. While he was devising films such as *féeries* which had a narrative structure, he was inclined to adapt more conventional techniques as well as themes and subjects. When, on the other hand, he presented simple magic shows in one tableau, his tendency was to rely exclusively upon such photographic tricks as superimpositions and stop-actions. That is to say, Méliès's *féeries* contain more theatrical techniques than do his magic shows. In the latter category would be included the following films: *Knight of Black Art, Mysterious Box, Bewitched Trunk, L'Enchanteur Alcofrisbas, The Infernal Cauldron, The Mermaid, The Magic Lantern, The Magician, The Enchanted Basket.*

[42]Paul Ginisty considers 1875 to be the year when the evolution of the *féerie* toward science-fiction began. It was in that year that *Le Voyage à la lune*, the first adaptation of Jules Verne, was presented. (Offenbach wrote the music for this work.) See Ginisty, *La Féerie*, p. 214. Between 1875 and the end of the century, when the *féerie* became virtually moribund, a number of other science-fiction *féeries* appeared, including another adaptation of Jules Verne's stories entitled *Le Voyage à travers l'impossible*. Written by an old *féerie* playwright, Adolphe D'Ennery, this work was first presented at the Porte Saint-Martin in November of 1885.

action technique. This is one of the few effects achieved by photographic means in the film. Most of the others are ones which could have been realized on the stage. Thus, even among his last films, on the eve of World War I, Méliès's point of reference remained the world of the nineteenth-century spectacle show.

In the same spirit with which his nineteenth-century predecessors had adapted scientific advances such as gaslight, limelight, and dioramas for use in the theater, Méliès turned to the film; it was but another technique in the service of his first love—magic. By means of film, Méliès sought to render men's dreams and imaginings with greater reality. Ultimately, when one speaks of his films the question should not be whether they are filmic or theatrical. Above all they are magical. They were designed to appeal to that same public of the poor and the uneducated who initially had flocked to the *féeries,* to the masses who were liberated by the French Revolution. This group, which first saw its dreams incarnated onstage in *féeries,* found its full form of expression in the twentieth century with film.

KEMP R. NIVER

Paper Prints of Early Motion Pictures

Undoubtedly all the teachers of film history and the subject of motion pictures are aware of the Library of Congress Paper Print Restoration Program that was started more than ten years ago by the Academy of Motion Picture Arts and Sciences, but few if any have ever seen the paper product itself or know exactly why it was used.

We have just completed a cross-referenced index with synopses of all of the 3,000 films restored during this program, and it occurred to us that something about the paper rolls themselves might be of interest before the book is published by the University of California Press.

Why was it necessary to make a paper print from the original negative of a motion picture and how was it done? Until 1907 there was no motion picture copyright law so there was no legal way a film producer could protect himself from usurpers, plagiarizers, and outright thieves other than to send a paper copy of his work to a government agency like the Library of Congress which would provide unimpeachable evidence as to date and subject of his production.

From the Copyright Office of the Library of Congress we have learned that the earliest picture made from a negative of a motion picture and sent in for copyright as a still picture, on January 7, 1894, was "Kinetoscopic Record of a Sneeze," made by Thomas A. Edison's co-worker William K. Laurie Dickson.

The practice of sending paper copies made from the original negative of a moving picture continued until about 1916, many years after the motion picture law went into effect.

EARLY PRINT PAPERS NON-STANDARD

Producers of motion picture films obtained the paper to make the copies of their negatives from various sources. The type that had the best photographic

258

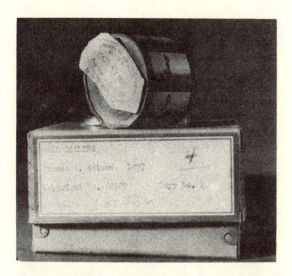

Thomas A. Edison roll of paper from a film, used in a Kinetoscope, stamped October 25, 1897, in the Register of Copyrights. This is the way material was received for reclamation from the archives of the paper print collection.

propensities was normal bromide paper cut into strips the same width as the negative and perforated so that a contact print could be made on the same equipment as was used to make the nitrate prints. However, for lack of source or for whatever reason, some examples arrived at the Copyright Office printed on what was not much better than brown wrapping paper to which photographic emulsion had been applied. Needless to say, the photographic results from this type of paper were not very good, but usually it was possible to follow the theme of the motion picture.

During the period that the rolls of paper came from the Library of Congress for us to restore, we came to enjoy, dislike, or even fear them because there was no way of knowing what problems we might have to face. By the time the program was completed, we had discovered that in order to transfer a photograph from paper to motion picture film, we might encounter any or all of the twenty-seven distinct problems that were associated with the paper rolls.

For instance, some rolls were exactly 35 mm. wide, some were less than 35 mm., while still others were as wide as 70 mm. Some had round or square sprocket holes on the edges. Others had no sprocket holes at all or just one in the center of the paper roll on the frame line.

A 75 mm. paper print. Note location and shape of sprocket holes. Film from which this print was made was displayed in a flipcard device called the "Mutoscope." It is possibly one of the first "commercials"—advertising a cleansing powder (1903).

Made from a Biograph negative, the paper on the left is a good example of frameline width differences—another problem that had to be surmounted in recovering paper prints.

The paper on the right, made from Biograph negatives, shows different widths as well as the single-frame perforation. The camera that made this picture also made its own perforations.

A 35 mm. paper from an early African adventure film. Note relationship of sprocket hole to frame line and the unique method of splicing with thread.

MOST IMPORTANT REPRODUCTION PROBLEM

Of the twenty-seven problems that arose during the restoration program, the one that gave us the most trouble at first was inadvertently built in by the original producer who had sent the paper roll to the Library of Congress half a century earlier. By looking at the wrinkles in the palm of your own hand and then causing the skin to tighten, you can easily understand why emulsion held in a curved position for over half a century would resent being laid out flat to be photographed.

THE EXCITEMENT OF DISCOVERY

We found that by soaking the paper rolls in a chemical and then applying pressure and heat with a drum dryer enough resiliency was returned to the paper to allow restoration procedures to follow.

The inspiration and delight of the program came from knowing that as we looked at the product of our efforts we were seeing projected for the first time the beginning of movement in photography.

The program of restoration became more interesting as the years went by because we who were doing the restoring realized that with a little luck it would now be possible for people to see many films long since believed to have been lost and which our research showed had been written about by authors who could not possibly have seen the films but could only have heard or read about them.

Another exciting aspect of the program for us was the possibility that the next shipment from the Library of Congress might contain still more film considered to be nonexistent produced by such early master filmmakers as the French Méliès, the British Hepworth, a Scandinavian producer, or even the film of some obscure American photographer who was just interested in a local disaster or a horse race that took place in his own home town.

ELIZABETH GROTTLE STREBEL

Imperialist Iconography of
Anglo-Boer War Film Footage

It was the Anglo-Boer War of 1899–1901 that provided the cinematographer with one of his first opportunities to serve as a war correspondent and propagandist.[1] A number of cinematographers actually traveled to South Africa to gain on-the-spot documentation, while others contented themselves with producing rather authentic looking "fakes" and obviously staged propaganda vignettes. The films which ensued, shot exclusively from the British point of view, as the Boers had photographers but no cinematographers, are remarkable documents of the times, undoubtedly more revealing of Victorian England than of South Africa, full of the myths and symbols of British imperialist iconography.

The Gordon Highlanders Leave for the War, Entry of the Scots' Guards into Bloemfontein, Cronje's Surrender to Lord Roberts, Bombardment of Mafeking, Set-To Between John Bull and Paul Kruger, Kruger's Dream of Empire are a few of the hundreds of one-reelers which abound from this period. Unfortunately, relatively little Anglo-Boer War film footage has survived to the present. Some of the raw negative shot in South Africa never even reached England. Some 5,000 feet, or fifty to eighty films, were lost when the Boer general, Christiaan De Wet, exposed tins of captured negative on the veld at Roodeval.[2] More films were lost when a ship transporting them sank off the Cape.[3]

---

[1] For an introduction to this topic see Thelma Gutsche, "The Boer War Period—Development in Production and Exhibition, 1899–1902," chap. 3 of *The History and Social Significance of Motion Pictures in South Africa, 1895–1940* (Cape Town: Howard Timmins, 1972). There is also a brief section on Anglo-Boer War films in Rachel Low and Roger Manvell, *The History of the British Film, 1896–1906* (London: Allen and Unwin, 1948), pp. 65–69.

[2] *Warwick Trading Company Catalogue* (London, 1901).

[3] Ibid.

Many films of course did reach England and ultimately the rest of the Empire to whet the imperial appetite. Anglo-Boer War films were shown regularly at the Palace Theater of Varieties in London, and the Warwick Trading Company Catalogue of July-August 1902 listed no fewer than 111 films pertaining to the "Transvaal War."

Merely a handful of these films can be found in film archives today, but image analysis of these alone is highly revealing.[4] Moreover, it is possible to examine the content of those films which have disappeared using the very detailed descriptions of films available in the distributors' catalogues of the period.

There were three major British companies, British Mutoscope and Biograph Co., Robert W. Paul Co., and the Warwick Trading Company, which launched a full scale effort regarding the production of Anglo-Boer War films. A number of other companies can be said to have dabbled in Anglo-Boer War films, among them, Pathé, Hepworth and Co., Gaumont, Gibbons, John Wrench and Son, and Edison in the U.S.A. The competition amongst these companies was fierce. In advertising its films, the Warwick Trading Company celebrated its representatives Joe Rosenthal and Edgar Hyman as the unique "official" cinematographic war correspondents in South Africa and admonished:

Do not discredit your exhibits and the general animated picture business by trying to fool the public with faked films. You will be the loser in the long run if you do. The Warwick war films of topical events from all parts of the world are taken on the spot and are not made on Hampstead Heath, New Jersey, France or in somebody's back garden.[5]

There was a definite obsession with veracity regarding these early films. Even the "fakes" were painstakingly executed to give the aura of authenticity, which undoubtedly accounted for the elaborate counterpropaganda by the Warwick Trading Company. Thomas Edison, shooting all of his Anglo-Boer War series in the Orange Mountains of New Jersey, was particularly adept in this regard. Once while Edison was filming a scene of the Battle of Spion Kop, one of the cannons was accidentally fired prematurely, and two of the star actors were seriously hurt. In the *British Journal of Photography* it was concluded that the incident would "doubtless, add unexpected realism to the scene."[6]

---

[4]The author is grateful to Mr. De Lange of the S.A. National Film Board in Pretoria for arranging screenings of the Anglo-Boer War films.

[5]*Warwick Catalogue* (1901). Page 52 of this catalogue provided a facsimile of the official list of war correspondents, in which Rosenthal and Hyman featured as the sole cinematographers.

[6]*British Journal of Photography*, April 20, 1900.

To heighten the sense of realistic participation, one enthusiastic London showman projecting Anglo-Boer War and Chinese Boxer Rebellion films even went so far as to set off blank cartridges in the theater. The cartridges cost him a half a crown for a hundred, but he argued that the smell of powder and the natural haze which ensued made it well worth the effort.[7]

Most celebrated of course were the cinematographers who followed the troops into battle. One of the more colorful of these was William Kennedy Laurie Dickson of the Mutoscope and Biograph Co., whose diary *Biograph in Battle* (1901) is a fascinating account of the vicissitudes faced by the wartime filmmaker in those early days. Dickson, who had previously been Edison's assistant for seventeen years in America, left for South Africa just after the outbreak of war. He sailed on the *Dunottar Castle* along with General Buller, his troops, and, incidentally, correspondent for the *Morning Post* Winston Churchill. Dickson's departure was heralded in the popular magazine *Today:*

> In both the Graeco-Turkish and the recent Soudan Wars the camera played an important part in recording the episodes of battle. But no photograph can boast the realism of the biograph.... The biograph will reveal bravery as no dispatch may do, and will tell the truth in all things, owing neither loyalty to chief nor submission to esprit de corps. How far this truthfulness will please the authorities remains to be seen.[8]

Indeed, Dickson complains bitterly in his autobiographical account about certain higher-ups, who go unnamed, who hampered his efforts to shoot footage, despite General Buller's written approval.[9]

Dickson accompanied General Buller on the assault on Ladysmith, participating fully in the life of the troops, pitching tents, braving the elements, eating tinned bully meat or sometimes nothing at all, dodging shell fire, transporting the wounded by stretcher after the Battle of Spion Kop, ultimately contracting the ubiquitous enteric fever. In addition he had to lug around by Cape Cart all his biograph equipment, which was particularly heavy, weighing over a ton.[10] Needless to say the business of picture taking was often trying at best. As Dickson himself describes:

---

[7]"Music and 'Effects' in Cinematography," *The Showman,* September 6, 1901, pp. 574–75.

[8]"A Novel War Correspondent," *Today,* October 26, 1899, pp. 402–3.

[9]W. K. L. Dickson, *Biograph in Battle* (London: Fisher Unwin, 1901), pp. 64–65.

[10]Rosenthal; of the Warwick Trading Company, had an easier time of it than Dickson in that his camera equipment weighed less than ¾ of a ton and could be transported on the back of a single mule.

Just then I heard the 6-inch Boer guns roar, but having previously timed the landing of the shells I knew I had two or three seconds to get a snap—which I did, then dived behind the rock followed by a sound so terrible that it is enough to make one's blood curdle—the bursting of a six-inch melinite shell at close range. The moment I heard the explosion I was up and snapped it. This I repeated several times; then, as the shells were bursting within two hundred yards of our rock and things were getting altogether too hot to be pleasant, I crawled back—not, however, before I had snapped the position I was in, for the sake of the unbeliever.[11]

There were essentially two types of Anglo-Boer War films, the raw documentaries and the staged propaganda films. Of course even the raw documentaries served as propaganda through selection, omission, and emphasis. Revealing lacunae in visual documentation, to take up on Marc Ferro,[12] in this case included the absence of film footage on the concentration camps or the razing of farms and crops, etc. The actual choice of subject matter is equally as illuminating.

One is struck by the proliferation of films of troop movements—embarking at Southampton, disembarking at Cape Town, marching out to the front.[13] To us, a stationary camera fixed on a line of helmeted troops striding single file up a gang plank appears to have little interest at first glance. But for the Victorian public this subject matter held a deep attraction. The succession of various colonial regiments underscored the solidarity of the Empire. The uniforms, generals, the very physical bearing of the men served as an expression of imperial confidence. Often the camera was positioned close enough to the troops to achieve true portraits, and the Victorian public flocked to the theaters hoping to catch a glimpse of a friend or loved one who had just left for South Africa. Dickson, for one, grasped the expressive potential of the medium close-up. Although none of his films remain, reproductions of some of his embarkation frames have survived, showing, for example, the development of a smile on the face of a "Tommy" as "an interesting study in expression."[14]

---

[11]Dickson, *Biograph in Battle*, p. 145.

[12]In his article, "1917: History and Cinema," *Journal of Contemporary History*, no. 4 (1968), pp. 45–62, Ferro raises the whole problem of distortion through gaps in visual documentation.

[13]Sample film titles are *Troops Boarding the SS. Braemer Castle* (*Warwick Catalogue*, #5469), *New Zealand Mounted Rifles from the Docks* (*Warwick Catalogue*, #5548), *The Australian Mounted Rifles Marching Through Capetown* (*Warwick Catalogue*, #5526), and *Embarkation of the Scot's Guards* (Robert W. Paul).

[14]"Cinematograph and Biograph Pictures," *Today*, supplement, November 23, 1899, p. 3.

There was a marked scarcity of actual battle scenes in Anglo-Boer War film footage. Paul's *Bombardment of Mafeking* and *Wrecking an Armoured Train* were reproductions staged under the supervision of a military officer from the front. Warwick's *A Skirmish with the Boers near Kimberley by a Troop of Cavalry Scouts Attached to General French's Column* (Warwick 5545) is then a rare example of an actual military confrontation. This film is described in the Warwick Catalogue of April 1901:

> These pictures produce a stereoscopic effect and the clear atmosphere gives a tremendous depth, enabling one to see thousands of troops in the distance, fighting at the base of a Kopje, while the dust arising from the galloping cavalry lends further realism to this spendid subject.

Logistically, filming of battle scenes was extremely difficult, as we have seen from Dickson's diary. Then too, the nature of warfare did not lend itself to cinematography, as the Boers with their guerilla tactics tended to hide in the hills. Conveniently enough, however, the cinematographer's logistical difficulties spared the Victorian public from most of the true horrors of war and served to preserve traditional notions of heroism, chivalry, and honor with regard to warfare.

Films of non-battle work scenes, like *The Fifth Northumberland Fusiliers Digging Trenches at the Orange River* (Warwick 5507b) and *Wash Day in Camp* (Warwick 5647) contributed to the notion of doing one's duty in a civilized fashion. Even the films of river crossings, a number of which have survived, designed to show the difficulties of the terrain, were no doubt chiefly appreciated for their graphic appeal, especially when the Royal Engineers War Balloon was present. In a river crossing sequence preserved in the South African film archives (the river is most likely the Vaal), we see a succession of wagons drawn by struggling teams of oxen, up to their necks in water, spurred on by Zulu drivers with enormous long whips, all seemingly very romantic for an urbane London audience.

Naturally, one of the very popular subjects for the British cinematographers was the surrender scene—Bloemfontein, Kroonstad, and the dramatic flag raising ceremony at Pretoria. Documentary footage of the Boers themselves was relatively scanty and consisted essentially of captured Boer prisoners. One remarkable film which has survived to today is *Cronje's Surrender to Lord Roberts.* This documentary of the capture of the famous Boer general was made by an officer working for Paul and Co., a complete amateur. In the film, the camera is trained on an open piece of veld. Three C.I.V.'s cross to the left, followed by a horse-drawn cart. There the general sits, peering out at the camera in amazement. The cart is followed by an escort of C.I.V.'s.

Other footage of Boer prisoners, which has since been lost, was of the transport of Boer prisoners to India. One such film was *A Detachment of Boer*

Prisoners Arriving and Detraining at Attamadagar. According to the description in the Warwick catalogue, one saw "a special train with heavily barred windows drawing up at the station. The armed guards then open the carriage doors, taking the precaution to only open one at a time, in order to prevent all chances of an attempted escape. The prisoners are seen detraining, some looking very dilapidated, and having no shoes on their feet. . . ."[15] Here is a rare bit of tarnish on the imperial image.

Documentary footage on the Anglo-Boer War wounded could at first glance be evidence of further tarnishing. A description of a film of a hospital ship refers to the "dark sides of war."[16] Yet most filming of the wounded tended to emphasize the heroic element rather than the tragic. The Warwick catalogue description of its film *Ambulance Corps at Work* (5524b) clearly illustrates this point: "After the Modder River engagement, the many wounded lying on the battlefield were picked up by this splendid ambulance corps who dash from one to the other, carrying and depositing the men in the ten-mule team."

If through selection, omission, and emphasis the Anglo-Boer War raw documentaries constituted a certain form of propaganda to boost the morale of the home population, so much more blatant was the propaganda of the staged films which were made far from the veld. A look at the various images and symbols of these crude propaganda films is highly revealing of the whole imperialist ethos.

As seen in these films, the British Tommy was intended to be fighting for a trinity of God, Motherhood, and Country. In a typical overly sentimental film by Paul, *His Mother's Portrait on the Soldier's Vision,* a C.I.V. is seen parting from his aged mother. She gives him, as a momento, a framed portrait of herself, which he kisses and puts in his breast pocket. The scene switches to the open veld where we find the soldier wounded and staggering for help. He faints and has a vision of his mother praying on bended knee. Discovered by Red Cross attendants, it is found that the soldier's wound is not serious, the bullet having been deflected by the mother's portrait.[17]

If the British are ever heroic and duty-bound, the Boers are portrayed as complete villains. A film of a bombing of a Red Cross tent, which has survived, seeks to promote the idea of the Boer atrocity. This very authentic looking "fake" shows a tent pitched on the veld, the Red Cross flag fluttering prominently to the left of the screen. A hurled bomb lands right outside the tent but fails to go off. A second bomb, underscoring the Boer treachery by intimating that it was no

---

[15]*Warwick Catalogue Supplement No. 1* (London, August 1901), film #6191a.

[16]*Arrival of Wounded at Hospital Ship,* (*Warwick Catalogue* #5551b).

[17]From a description of the film in the Robert W. Paul catalogue *Animated Photograph Films* (London, 1900).

accident, reaches the mark and goes off. Wounded and Red Cross nurses stagger out of the tent in disarray.

Paul Kruger, president of the Boer Republics, is the embodiment of evil in these films, completely lacking in morals or a sense of justice. In the film *Set-To Between John Bull and Paul Kruger,* which can be seen in the archives, Kruger and Bull are seen in two rounds of a boxing match. In round two Kruger begins to engage in foul play. He kicks John Bull, waves a white flag, and hits Bull from behind when his back is turned.

In a number of films Kruger is made out to be an imperialist with insatiable aspirations, in a classic example of psychological projection. In a Robert W. Paul film *Kruger's Dream of Empire,*[18] Kruger appears in a room with a large canvas with the inscription "On Majuba Day the British were Defeated."[19] Rubbing his hands and chuckling, he settles in a chair for a nap. He then dreams that his enemy Joseph Chamberlain offers him the crown of England, but as he jumps up to grab the crown it vanishes in a puff of smoke. Chamberlain then points to the canvas whose inscription now reads "On Majuba Day Cronje Surrendered." Kruger lunges at his tormenter, but the latter vanishes as mysteriously as the crown. Kruger then turns to find that a pedestal which formerly bore a bust of himself now boasts one of the queen of England. He attempts to knock it down but is restrained by four men in khaki who envelop him in a large Union Jack, lift him on a stand, and fire a volley. The flag falls and Kruger has been transformed into Britannia.

This elaborate little film illustrates a number of characteristics common to many of the anti-Boer propaganda films. First is the physical obliteration, transformation, and ultimate transcendence of the enemy. Just as the early cinema audience marveled to see the physical preservation of real objects, so too was it fascinated with the cinema's seemingly magical ability to make images, particularly of villains, disappear. A second characteristic of these films is the all-encompassing, mystical power of the Union Jack, symbol of the all-powerful British Empire.

Another film in which Kruger is purely physically rather than cinematically obliterated is Paul's *Snowballing Oom Paul.*[20] Here some schoolchildren have made a snowman effigy of Kruger. They then vie with each other to knock its block off. Eventually, the snow effigy is completely trampled under foot. Similarly, in a Warwick film (5880b) called *Guy Fawkes Day Incident,* a group of men and boys

---

[18]The film has not survived but an extremely detailed description of it can be found in the Robert W. Paul catalogue of 1900.

[19]The Battle of Majuba Hill, in which the British were completely routed by the Boers in the First Anglo-Boer War of 1881, is alluded to in a number of films as a sore point, a day to be avenged.

[20]Description in the Robert W. Paul catalogue of 1900.

stabs at an effigy of Kruger before igniting it and watching it become consumed by the flames.

In a Hepworth and Co. film, *The Conjuror and the Boer,* described as a new patriotic trick film, a "typical Boer," much to his disgust, is enveloped in a large Union Jack.[21] He is thus transformed into a figure of Britannia, who hangs up the flag on her trident and waves it back and forth. The camera then closes in on the flag so that it fills the entire screen, looming larger than life. The words "Rule Brittania" appear in large letters at the bottom of the picture.

Just as the Union Jack is hallowed, so are other flags reviled. In a Hepworth animated cartoon, *Wiping Something off the Slate,* a Boer flag is seen waving over a slate on which the word "Majuba" is written.[22] A British soldier tears down the flag, tramples it in disgust, and drenches it in water so that he can wipe the objectionable word from the slate.

These Anglo-Boer War propaganda films seem crude and primitive, especially when compared with the sophistication and visual power of latter-day propaganda films, particularly those of the Nazis. Lacking in a highly developed visual language, the early propagandist had to content himself with camera trickery and with the power of the dramatization, as in a morality play. However, the cinema was in its infancy, and the films aptly corresponded to the lack of sophistication in the viewing audience.

Anglo-Boer War films do exhibit the dual preoccupations of the cinema at its birth, the realism of Lumière and the magic of Méliès. There is both the obsession with recording true events, albeit from a certain perspective, and the desire to make the cinema perform feats, through editing and double exposure, to dramatize the "cause."

Even though the Boer War ultimately troubled many a conscience and generally shook imperial confidence, the cinema only served to gloss over that which was disturbing, perpetuating the myths of the Empire and satisfying the emotional needs of a populace at war. And the myths of Anglo-Boer War cinematography aptly conform to the function of all myths, which in the view of Lévi-Strauss are adopted to make coherent that which is basically self-contradictory.

---

[21]Description in *Hepwix Films for the Cinematograph* (London: Hepworth, 1903).
[22]Ibid.

JOHN L. FELL

Motive, Mischief, and Melodrama:

The State of Film Narrative in 1907

Viewing the earliest surviving movies in rough chronological order, year-by-year at least, is to witness film exposition pull itself out of the mudbanks and evolve into a semblance of narrative shape. Its progress is erratic, with false starts and paths untaken, but seems to evidence a kind of inexorable logic; run-on time and space bow to predesigned complications with increasing regularity.

This is not the place to recapitulate what has been discussed elsewhere in substantial detail,[1] but it is useful to note that by 1906, consolidation with respect to organized, predelineated narrative design begins to assume consistent visibility. Some techniques (like motivating a subjective view by a glance, then following it with a matted shot to simulate perspective through a viewing glass or telescope) translate comfortably from one story mode to another: *Grandma's Reading Glass* (G. A. Smith, 1898), *Tour du monde d'un policier* (Pathé, 1905).

Other devices, such as shot-to-shot continuities facilitated through un-matched movement, seem to derive more directly out of a particular kind of narrative, like the chase. Pursued and pursuer contained in one shot give way to pursued/pursuer/pursued/pursuer checkerboarding, what Christian Metz chose to term an "alternate syntagma." In *The Hundred-to-One Shot* (Vitagraph 1904), we

---

[1]See, for example, Noël Burch, "Porter or Ambivalence," *Screen* 19 (Winter 1978–79); John L. Fell, "The Evolution of Narrative," chapter 2 of *A History of Films* (New York: Holt, Rinehart and Winston, 1979), pp. 28–53; André Gaudreault, "Detours in Film Narrative: The Development of Cross-Cutting" in *Cinema Journal* 19 (Fall 1979):39–59; Charles Musser, "The Early Cinema of Edwin Porter," *Cinema Journal* 19 (Fall 1979):1–38; Barry Salt, "Film Form, 1900–1906," *Sight and Sound* 47 (Summer 1978):148–53; Martin Sopocy, "A Narrated Cinema: The Pioneer Story Films of James A. Williamson," *Cinema Journal* 10 (Fall 1978):1–28; and the special issue of *Les Cahiers de la cinémathèque* 29 (Fall 1979) devoted to the subject.

shift from a racing car to incidents at the spot toward which the car is bound.

With this background, 1907 becomes a year of curious interest. It is poised just before Griffith's appearance as a writer/director, and stands, too, at a sort of midpoint: a decade beyond the very appearance of movies, about equally distant from a regular cycle of "features."

Film output accelerates year to year in this period, and more is preserved. We have to qualify our understandings in terms of particular material that has survived, but as the years pass, we may undoubtedly tread with greater confidence on a groundwork of archive holdings. The titles under consideration come from Denmark (Nordisk), Italy (Rossi and Co.), France (Gaumont, Pathé, Eclipse, Méliès), and England (Sheffield, Hepworth, Urban Trading, Warwick Trading, Cricks and Martin, Clarendon). More often than elsewhere, film is American (Belcher and Waterson, Biograph, Edison, Kalem, Lubin, Miles Brothers, Selig, Vitagraph, Winthrop).[2]

Film lengths vary. Occasionally a single-setup, one-shot title evokes earlier history. More often, stories involve several locations, commonly both interior and exterior. Continuity blends (like matching action and screen direction, tempo and position to join exits and entrances) register as increasingly smooth. Much of the output falls within a 300' to 700' range, roughly five to twelve minutes running time. Very occasionally the viewer finds himself startled by an unexpectedly motivated shot-to-shot congruence. In *Francesca di Rimini: Or The Two Brothers* (Vitagraph, National Film Archive), which derives from a passage in Dante, the hunchbacked nobleman Francesca raises his gaze as if cued by some distinct sound. Cutaway to a point-of-view shot detailing the approach of a messenger. Cut back to Francesca, messenger entering screen left. The same film contains

---

[2]This article stems from a research project pursued January 2–4, 1980, through the agency of the Film Department, Museum of Modern Art, New York City. Staged, i.e., "fiction" films dating from 1907 were studied by a collection of interested parties, with supporting information supplied by Eileen Bowser, who coordinated the undertaking. I am also indebted to Professor Daniel C. Gerould of the CUNY Graduate Center for additional references and insights.

Sources of films cited are included with other relevant information at their first appearance. The Museum of Modern Art, the Library of Congress, Archives of the American Film Institute, George Eastman House, the National Film Archive, Cinémathèque Royale de Belgique, Det Danske Filmmuseum, and Stiftung Deutsche Kinemathek are gratefully acknowledged for making this material available for study.

Opportunity for such close examination of early film originated in Fall 1977 when relevant material from the Library of Congress, the Museum of Modern Art, the National Film Archive of Great Britain, and Eastman House was organized at the Museum of Modern Art in preparation for a Spring Conference of the International Federation of Film Archives (FIAF). Some papers resulting from this meeting appear in the *Les Cahiers de la cinémathèque* issue cited above. At the time of this writing, a full collection of papers with other supporting data is scheduled for publication by the British Film Institute.

two additional motivated pairings: Francesca looks fondly at an insert of his wife's miniature in a locket. Overall, such moments are infrequent, and film in 1907 appears little characterized by formal innovation.

Our intention here is to center on the year's output, as far as it has been reviewed, in terms of its kinds of stories, to investigate whether such formulas, as with the chase, may begin to inflect expository techniques. By categorizing the film product, we can also more concisely describe its character, a worthwhile undertaking because so much "new" material has become available through archive cooperation in the last few years. A rough sort of categorization can group the year into eight sorts of storytelling:

ADAPTATIONS

Francesca di Rimini is an example. *"Teddy" Bears* (Edison, Edwin S. Porter, director, Museum of Modern Art) enacts *Goldilocks* with costumed teddies to capitalize on the new doll. Chased by the animal family, Goldilocks comes upon a hunter who shoots Papa Bear and Mama Bear dead and enslaves Baby Bear on a chain, apparently to provide the girl with a new toy.

Water Babies: Or the Little Chimney Sweep (Clarendon, Percy Stow, director, National Film Archive) reproduces the Victorian Charles Kingsley children's story. It contains another motivated continuity when Ellie, the little girl, stands at water's edge. Her glance precipitates a camera pan left, far enough to exclude the human figure, then back.

REENACTMENTS

Staged actualities take several forms. *Daniel Boone* (Edison, Wallace McCutcheon, director, Museum of Modern Art) has the frontiersman and a companion rescue two girls from Indian capture. It draws on stage convention (a horse unties the other man, shackled to a burning stake) and popular stereotype (Indians fight dirty, but always lose to their white brothers). *The Hooligans of the West* (also *Hooligans of the Far West*) (Pathé, National Film Archive) begins as a staged documentary (cowboys capturing wild horses), then reverts to fiction.[3] Again a horse comes through, this time carrying a captured man's scarf to a cavalry camp and leading the unit to the rescue. Actuality merges with show-staging in *Attack on an Emigrant Train* (Biograph, Museum of Modern Art) which films a Wild West performance that includes a painted mountain backdrop.

Another sort of reneactment appears in *The Unwritten Law* (Lubin, Museum of Modern Art), based on the Harry Thaw/Stanford White New York City murder.

---

[3]Alternate titles or titles deriving from other than a country of origin are enclosed in parentheses.

Here the film requires a viewer's precedent understanding of the contemporary scandal; otherwise one could never make sense of motives and characters. Intertitles ("The Red Velvet Swing") capitalize on journalistic versions of key incidents. Ceilinged sets appear twice (as painted flats): a boudoir equipped with overhead mirrors, a courtroom. Alone in his cell, the murderer relives his crime and a jailhouse visit from his mother and Evelyn Nesbit by way of a dream balloon.

TRICK FILM

These productions maintain but do not expand upon Méliès's magic traditions. *Sister Mary Jane's Top Note* (Hepworth, Lewin Fitzhamon, director, National Film Archive) shows the disastrous consequences of a singer's upper range, with furniture and pictures dashed to the ground. *Tryllesaekken (The Magic Bed)* (Nordisk, Viggo Larsen, director, Det Danske Filmmuseum) begins with a comic stage tumbling act, evolving into stop-motion antics. One or both of two acrobats disappear-reappear inside a mattress bag. [*The Roses*] (Gaumont, George Eastman House) and [*Chrysanthemums*] (Pathé, George Eastman House) are hand-colored, short ventures playing on transformations, the first using butterfly motifs, the second Japanese costume and stage-derived use of mirrors to magic effect.

When the Devil Drives (Urban, W. R. Booth, director, National Film Archive) is an elaborate fantasy in which the devil takes command of a passenger train. Its journey across the heavens and under water strongly suggests Méliès's *Le Voyage à travers l'impossible* of 1904. Booth's film includes an interesting effort to match the crazed revolution of a train car (shot "live" by revolving a camera while photographing the panicked passengers) with a model set in which detached cars revolve one-by-one while ascending a ravine and reassembling on a mountain ledge track. The film ends with cars formed in a revolving circle, the composition matched to a round matte with the devil's laughing face inside.

DREAMS

A very few films continue altogether to construct themselves in dream format, although the framing narrative varies. Fuzzing over the dream "entry" serves to becloud the main story body in useful ambiguity, better to enlist spectator interest. It appears in *Terrible Ted* (Biograph, Museum of Modern Art). Motivated by a Wild West dime novel, a boy steals a revolver from a parlor drawer and intimidates police on a brownstone New York street. Inexplicably, the film cuts to a western stage holdup. In turn, Terrible Ted dispatches the bandits, shoots a cardsharp in a bar, saves an Indian girl from a bear, and is captured asleep by Indians. The girl rescues him from the stake, and while counting the scalps of braves he has stabbed, Terrible Ted wakes at home.

A Diabolo Nightmare (Urban, W. R. Booth, director, National Film Archive) has a man entranced by the diabolo, a top-like object that is balanced, spun, thrown up, and caught on a string manipulated with two hand-held sticks. The obsessed figure passes through increasingly nightmarish episodes, evocative first of Edwin S. Porter's *The Dream of a Rarebit Fiend* (Edison, 1906) with a fall from the sky through a ceiling into a home, then of Méliès. The diabolo player journeys underwater, where he tries to teach his game to a Neptune-costumed man. The film concludes in the dreamer's bed.

FARCES

With or without trick interludes, various movies draw from one or another form of stage farce. Two thieves escape capture by hiding in cubbyholes of a bourgeois home including the bathtub: *La Douche d'eau bouillante* (attributed to Méliès but probably not, American Film Institute/Library of Congress). *Mr. Gay and Mrs.* (Biograph, Museum of Modern Art) is very like a nineties stereograph set. The husband flirts; his wife interrupts. In *Under the Old Apple Tree* (Biograph, Museum of Modern Art) tricks are played on suitors who seat themselves beneath the pranksters.

Yale Laundry (Biograph, Museum of Modern Art) describes the chaos that follows when parents leave their daughters in charge of the New Haven Shop. *College Chums* (Edison, Museum of Modern Art) stems directly from a theater farce. A man impersonates his friend's "sister" in order to conciliate an angry fiancée. This film has a multi-image sequence in which lovers speak on the phone, their separate scenes matted against a cityscape, with printed words passing across the sky between. In *Monsieur et Madame veulent une bonne* (Pathé, Georges Hatot, director, Det Danske Filmmuseum), the woman member of a thieves' trio gains employment in a bourgeois home. A confederate is smuggled in by trunk. Males of the household flirt with the woman and hide in the trunk to escape discovery. The film is set in Italy, and its performing style veers radically from typical farce to grotesque *commedia dell'arte* gesture.

Other farces satirize more specific subject matter. *Dr. Skinum* (Biograph, Museum of Modern Art) comments on the vogue for cosmetic surgery. Legs are repaired, a nose bobbed. Weight is lost. Women are stretched and compressed. Here as in other occasional comic bits, a gag triggers memories of later film comedy. The fat woman shrunk to a baby is like the fat man caught in a steam box in W. C. Fields's *The Barbershop* (1933).

CHASES

Chases are many, and they run in two directions: the miscreant pursued, the naïf escaping. *Le Mariage de Victorine (How Bridget's Lover Escaped)* (Méliès, American Film Institute/Library of Congress): a cook's boyfriend eludes pursuers angered at his effect on the dinner service. *Jack the Kisser* (Edison, Museum of Modern Art): outraged victims of an impulsive kisser finally capture him. An old maid and a black woman scuffle over who may kiss Jack tied to a tree.

Wife Wanted (Biograph, Museum of Modern Art): advertising for a mate, a man is pursued by applicants. The winner faints on sight of his many children. *Mind Your Own Business* (Warwick, Jack Smith, director, National Film Archive): boys scrapping after a marble game precipitate combat between the mothers and fathers. The parents pursue the boys.(The film has a very clean match through a door from exterior to interior.) *His Only Pair of Trousers* (Cricks and Martin, A. E. Coleby, director, National Film Archive): a thief steals trousers from a clothesline. Their owner encases himself in a sheet of linoleum and prompts a mayhem of encounters as he rolls from place to place, finally bumping into his quarry.

Stage Struck (Edison, Museum of Modern Art): three country girls are lured into running from home by an itinerant performer. Pursued and finally captured by the parents, the girls' sliding escapes serve to expose skirted legs. *Cheval emballé (The Runaway Horse)* (Pathé, Ferdinand Zecca, director, Museum of Modern Art): when a wheel falls from his cart, a horse bolts, causing a sequence of catastrophes until he returns to the stable. Cuts are consistently developed between the horse eating a bag of storefront oats and his owner, "meanwhile," distracted inside.

[The Police Dogs] (Pathé, possibly not 1907, André Heuze, director, National Film Archive) casts animals in the role of pursuer, tracking down a gang of thieves. *La Course aux potirons (Pumpkins Race)* (Gaumont, Louis Feuillade and Romeo Bozzetti, directors, Museum of Modern Art) is well known and no longer attributed to Emile Cohl.

THE MOTIVATED LINK

For want of a better term, "the motivated link" intends to describe a kind of narrative organization in which separate episodes, characteristically filmed in different or purportedly different locations, have been joined through a single character who is distinguished by some particular motive, eccentricity, or invention.

The Love Microbe (Biograph, Museum of Modern Art): a scientist discovers how to extract love microbes from affectionate couples by inconspicuously drawing specimens from the backs of their necks with a syringe. Reinjecting the microbes into fighting or alienated people in the same fashion (the potion can also be placed in beer!), he accomplishes comic results. "Seen" in a matted point-of-view microscope perspective, the microbes prove to be little, swarming heart-shaped elements.

Liquid Electricity (Vitagraph, National Film Archive): a scientist emulsifies electricity. Sprayed with an atomizer it accelerates (through pixilation) lazy and somnolent subjects. In several instances the scientist himself appears at slowedto-"normal" speed in frame with his high-speed subject. Since this movement was accomplished by decelerating one actor's movements while the other was paced ordinarily (along with tree leaves, shadows, etc.) the effect is particularly unsettling.

"*The Energizer*" (Biograph, Museum of Modern Art): through ingesting a new breakfast cereal, subjects are vitalized into highly energetic conditions. *Une Dame vraiment bien!* (Louis Feuillade, Museum of Modern Art): a pretty woman causes unintentional disasters as she is viewed by Parisian males. *(Short-Sighted Cyclist)* (Eclipse, National Film Archive): dispatched with a note, he runs from one obstacle to another, finally plunging into the Seine. *That Fatal Sneeze* (Hepworth, National Film Archive): a nephew puts quantities of sneezing powder on his uncle's clothing. Sneezing causes objects to fall, an earthquake, blows people away, and results finally in a chase. *Laughing Gas* (Edison, Museum of Modern Art): overdosed at the dentist, a black woman causes hilarity and generally fortuitous results from chance encounters on her journey home. *Deaf-Mutes' Masquerade (Deaf-Mutes' Ball)* (Biograph, Museum of Modern Art): returning drunk from a ball, a deaf-mute disguised in a bear costume causes consternation and is nearly committed to a zoo cage.

In *Hypnotist's Revenge* (Biograph, Museum of Modern Art) a stage mesmerist is stung by a wealthy young man's gibes. The hypnotist follows "Chappie" about, causing him to embrace women, swing from a chandelier at dinner, and try to replace the groom at a wedding. The youth is spared a final commitment to Bellevue when his tormentor relents. *A Suburbanite's Ingenious Alarm* (Edison, Museum of Modern Art): fearful of losing his job, a tardy commuter ties a rope to his leg, extending the loose end out his second story bedroom window so that a friend may wake him in the morning. A drunk secures the other end to a milk wagon. After being dragged through the streets, the employee finally limps to work, unbelievably early. *The Boy, the Bust and the Bath* (Vitagraph, National Film Archive) casts a young woman, her grotesque suitors, and a boy in a boarding house. The boy places a bust bearing her likeness in a bathtub. The men suffer embarassments peeking through the keyhole, but finally trap the boy and soak him. *The Rivals* (Edison, Museum of Modern Art) has two men plotting tricks on one another as they seek the same girl's hand. Both are finally outwitted by a third suitor.

MELODRAMA

Finally there is a series of films that draw on costumes, conventions, and plot contrivances of theatrical melodrama. In *The Fraudulent Solicitor* (Hepworth, Lewin Fitzhamon, director, George Eastman House) a lawyer steals money. Discovered, he kills the client. After a rooftop fight, the murderer is captured. *Røverens Brud* (Nordisk, Viggo Larsen, director, Det Danske Filmmuseum) portrays a police ambush and capture of an outlaw gang, the attempted rescue of the leader by his wife, first foiled, then successful, and finally the couple's death. The bandits' successful escape is eccentrically staged with two identical shots of a passing cart in which the outlaw has been imprisoned. First the wife leaps aboard, then they jump off together.

In *Lost in the Alps* (Edison, Museum of Modern Art) monks' Saint Bernards locate two lost children who appear to be buried in recent Central Park snow. *The Mill Girl* (Vitagraph, National Film Archive) has a working girl suffering sexual harassment from her supervisor. Defended by a mill hand, she later faints during a fire in the factory after enduring further advances. The young man saves her from the building; presumably the villain dies of smoke inhalation in the basement.

The Trainer's Daughter (Edison, Museum of Modern Art) is set at a racetrack. Timing the favored suitor's horse (motivated matte shot to simulate binoculars), the villain bribes a stableboy to dope the animal, but he is overheard by the jockey, who switches horses in their stalls. Villain subdues jockey, who is yet able to warn the fiancée. She herself rides the horse to victory. The approaching race is preceded by a sound-motivated cutaway to the track bugler.

Falsely Accused! (Biograph, Museum of Modern Art) posits a spurned villain who steals plans from the inventor-father's safe. The father is found dead in his (movie) laboratory, his daughter imprisoned. Her boyfriend extracts film from a laboratory camera, learns to process it, and projects images of the actual murder in a courtroom scene. This last sequence is visible in the Museum nitrate print, first with spectators staring at a blank sheet mounted behind the bench, then with the yet-to-be-matted-in murder footage positioned to accommodate the preceding image. Griffith can be identified in the courtroom. His appearance, dating from December, precedes *Rescued from an Eagle's Nest,* which was filmed at Edison the next month. Griffith appears also in *Professional Jealousy* (Biograph, December 1907, Museum of Modern Art). Another point of interest in *Falsely Accused!* is the skillful cut-in of film being developed in a darkroom tray. Vindicating evidence secured through photography dates back to Dion Boucicault, *The Octoroon* (1859).

Jalousie et folie (Pathé, date uncertain, Museum of Modern Art) has the feel of a reenactment, like *The Unwritten Law,* but *mélodrame* itself often derived from lurid news accounts and court records. Finding his wife with her lover, a rural husband loses his sanity. The pair commit him to an asylum; he escapes from the exercise yard. Finding the two together again, the husband strangles his wife and dies in an exchange of rifle fire with the police.

With slight rationalizations, some dozen additional titles might be wedged into one of the above pigeonholes, but these would have little further effect on our inquiry. What shapes do 1907 films take?

The choice of material and its design bear some relation to duration. If an idiom continues early modes (dreams, magic) it tends to be medium length; in the case of trick films, also to unity of time and location. Alternatively, dreams and magic may be accommodated in other generic forms, so that the dream balloon figures as a segment of *The Boaster* (Hepworth, Lewin Fitzhamon, director, George Eastman House) and *The Unwritten Law*. Similarly, *"Teddy" Bears* contains one sequence in which Goldilocks peers through a keyhole and views a primitive, charming moment of puppet animation. A chorus line of little seated teddy bears performs. *La Course des potirons* use reverse motion to animate its pumpkins for the purposes of a chase. *The Water Babies* smoothly shifts from naturalistic exposition to special effects as the chimney sweep descends to an underwater world of Victorian illustration. A bowling ball in *If You Had a Wife Like This* (Biograph, Museum of Modern Art) mysteriously circles each pin, spilling none.

Stage farce, like stage comics, also dates to earliest days. Its character progresses from the simplest of forms (*Vesta Tilley* [Biograph, Museum of Modern Art] merely shows a female impersonator changing costume) to the complications of *College Chums*. Most farces confine themselves to single-set sequences, sometimes with one or another form of split staging or onstage doors for additional paths of entrance and exit. *Cohen's Fire Sale* (Edison, Museum of Modern Art) boasts an especially "authentic" theatrical flat, seeming to continue the perspective of a Hester Street storefront vista. In fact, the mixtures of stylized artifice and the natural curiously characterize 1907 decor, not only shifting modes, as in *When the Devil Drives*, but situating both in a single shot. *The Hooligans of the West* has cavalry fording a real stream that is incongruously laid with large, artificial rocks.

Adaptations, if infrequent, contribute stable, developed narrative skeletons. Interestingly, *The Water Babies* and *Francesca di Rimini* provide some of the most advanced exposition, but their evidence is too minimal for generalizations. Reenactments, in their own way, share qualities with adaption. Each tends to fall into the dramatic strategies of sensational theater in which "key" scenes are linked to create a succession of arresting highlights, like the vignetted illustrations of four-sheet advertising posters. In one respect, adaptations and reenactments share a common advantage, for they draw on audience foreknowledge and thus avoid falling back on popular conventions to depict motives and value-conflict.

By 1907 chases have developed complicated initial business to trigger the pursuits *(Wife Wanted, Stage Struck)* and often integrate the chase with other genres, particularly camera tricks *(His Only Pair of Trousers)*. Such combinations themselves date at least as early as *Maniac Chase* (Edison, 1904). Chases, too, are staged with increasing design. In *Wife Wanted*, the pursued man successively hides in a yard of culvert pipes and a field of haystacks. *[The Police Dogs]* has one skittish canine who predictably fails to surmount a cliff, jump a fence, ford a lake; we may conjecture significance in Pathé's choice to leave this footage at the tail of each shot. Perhaps, too, the conjunction of escape and pursuit provided a formal basis on which rescue films might shortly establish themselves through the introduction of increasingly sophisticated editing.

Like chases, the motivated link provides a form where separate incidents, sometimes almost autonomous, may be joined both to manufacture an entertainment of sufficient length and to heighten effects so that the film overall carries something of a crescendo effect. Indeed, both chase and motivated link comedies easily support propositions made by Henri Bergson in *Laughter,* which first appeared in 1908. Bergson itemized the Jack-in-the-box effect (one stubborn force counteracted by another), the Dancing-jack (a character who is the unknowing pawn of another), and the Snowball (insignificant cause finally culminating in a major consequence). As elsewhere, chases sometimes evoke situations clearly akin to later films. *Wife Wanted* is very like Keaton's *Seven Chances* (1925), just as the devil's escape through an illusory fireplace in *Satan en prison* (Méliès, American Film Institute/National Film Archive) reminds us of Buster's dive through a window in *Sherlock Jr.* (1924).

Melodrama poses the most direct questions with respect to length and plot. In some cases the films are melodrama segments, not condensations like *Uncle Tom's Cabin* (Edison, 1903) which mirrors the truncated 10-20-30 stage entertainment of the nineties, but excerpts of broader schemes. Many suggest one act of a three-act play: crime and apprehension. *(The Fraudulent Solicitor, The Robber's Wife [Røverens Brud])* or peril and rescue (*Lost in the Alps*). Others, such as *The Mill Girl, The Trainer's Daughter,* and *Falsely Accused!* describe more typically conventional evolutions of plot conventions, but we have too little time clearly to explicate the relationships. *The Trainer's Daughter* gives a cloudy picture of actual attitudes shared among father, daughter, boyfriend, jockey, and villain. *The Mill Girl* is somewhat more fully plotted, although its resolutions are hardly tidy. *Falsely Accused!* suggests like relationships between father, daughter, boyfriend, and villain, although we have little understanding why the boyfriend takes film from the movie camera and processes it, and the courtroom denouement is peremptory.[4] A more intensive investigation of narrative form in the evolution of movie melodrama might test the premise that melodrama, in contrast to other idioms, supplied a kind of story closure which encouraged further developments in film exposition: more complicated sets of character interrelationships, and episodes designed to supply other aspects of discourse than plot furtherance, character delineation, for instance.

Watching 1907 over a week's time (how clean the New York streets, how bright the buildings!) may strike the viewer with constant reminders of dime novel graphics (explicit in *Terrible Ted*) or period comics and caricature. One reason for this must be the conditions of cramped framing that often accompany studio setups involving confrontations. The end of *Røverens Brud,* for example, stages a military attack through an outlaw cabin window with such intimacy that each person's firearm is unbelievably point blank: a suicidal shootout. Filmed in exterior, the last scene of *Jalousie et folie* is quite similar.

Another excuse to point up film/comic likenesses is the commonality of

---

[4]Shots are missing from both these Museum of Modern Art titles.

length. A full-page Sunday strip, with its nine-to-twelve panels, tells a story with scope equatable to a half-reel: potentially similar numbers of characters, of incidents and locations.

Finally, comics, stage, and early movies all enjoy a common pool of gesturing and posturing conventions. An example may be drawn from *If You Had a Wife Like This*, a *Bringing Up Father* kind of story. Forced by his shrewish wife to wash the floor, Peck leaves a note (insert): "Gone to the drug store for some headache powder. Will be back soon. Peck." Henceforth he scurries through a series of diversions: poker game, bowling alley, attendance at a music hall Salome dance. Each time, the wife discovers Peck, who narrowly escapes her clutches. In the last scene, she ties him to a chair and forces Peck to watch *her* perform the Dance of the Seven Veils. (Richard Strauss's opera prompted a scandal at the Met early that year.)

Because of the motivated link design, Peck must elude his wife within the confines of a medium long shot at the conclusion of each episode. Such business requires running-in-place frenzy, that is, the actors have to appear to be anxiously pursued and pursuing without escaping the movie camera's purview. Such gesture can be likened to a stage farce where actors must seem to move at greater speed than circumstances allow. Or to a comic strip panel depicting running with a static image.

Well accustomed to chase films, most often executed with diagonal movements and deep perspectives, the viewer easily distinguishes natural states of running from studio contrivances. What fascinates, as with unacknowledged conventions from any period, is the absence of contradiction between the two forms. Stage pursuits are equally acceptable, just as the artificial rocks in *The Hooligans of the West* fail to clash with their location setting.

By this token, films of 1907 trace an entire litany of conventionalized gesture and costume, more often than not deriving from gothic, then domestic, theatrical melodrama with its spilloffs into popular graphics. There is the stage drunk in *The Deaf-Mutes' Masquerade*, bottle upended to tilted head. There is the hand-clasped motion of feminine despair *(The Unwritten Law)* and the mimed confidence between hero and heroine in full view of other parties *(The Trainer's Daughter)*. There is the slapping flirtation of a female impersonator with a prurient male *(College Chums)* that could as well be Jack Lemmon in *Some Like It Hot*. The young boy thrusts his chest in imitation of western bravado in *Terrible Ted*. Battling husbands in *Neighbors* (Biograph, Museum of Modern Art) reconcile and strut, arms around shoulders, inside to drink, looking for all the world like Jiggs, Happy Hooligan, or Flip out of *Little Nemo in Slumberland*. It is an endless list.

One possible use of gesture-coding[5] in such films rests in its correlation to

---

[5] A discussion of visual signals employed in theatrical melodrama will be found in Gilbert B. Cross, *Next Week—East Lynne: Domestic Drama in Performance, 1820–1874* (Lewisburg, Pa.: Bucknell University Press, 1977), pp. 106–41.

plot function, *function* in the broad sense of Vladimir Propp's *Morphology of the Folktale:*[6] a character is what he does or (the equation is reversible) does what he is. For example, one function that figures surprisingly often in early films is the mischievous boy. Because he plays tricks, the mischievous boy regularly serves as an agent to actuate tumbles, practical jokes, and other irritations sufficient to cause chases (like *Max and Moritz, Buster Brown, The Yellow Kid, The Captain and the Kids,* and *Little Jimmy* in period comics). He dates at least as early as Tom Taylor's *The Ticket-of-Leave Man* (1863).

In *The Boy, The Bust and the Bath,* the mischievous boy watches a nearsighted, bandy-legged suitor try to peek through a bathroom door keyhole. The boy clasps his stomach with both hands and bends over in apparent spasms of mirth before jabbing his dupe with a pin. In *The Suitors,* one man views his rival asleep on a park bench, and then places an infant in the sleeper's outstretched hands. He repeats the gesture of the boy in the bathroom hallway; he is serving the function of mischievous boy. In *Yale Laundry,* a group of college boys (identical white sweaters with "Y's" on the chest) play mischievous boy by disclosing a flirtation conducted behind a folding screen. The tramp who steals trousers in *His Only Pair of Trousers* is a mischievous boy, like the sailor in *Under the Old Apple Tree* who drops apples on unwary suitors below, the nephew who puts sneeze powder in his uncle's clothes *(That Fatal Sneeze)*, the drunk who ties the rope to the milk wagon in *The Suburbanite's Ingenious Solution.*

Moving gingerly now between the primitive and something approaching moderate stylistic consciousness, many films of 1907 carry obvious and intentional overtones of fantasy, not limited to special effects or *art nouveau* decor. The strangest of appearances can result from merely converting a French product *(Le Mariage de Victorine)* to foreign soil *(How Bridget's Lover Escaped)*. In *A Seaside Girl* (Hepworth, National Film Archive) a young woman has sought every means to escape the attentions of three smitten men, finally taking a bath cabin into the water and going for a swim, only to find that two of the suitors have seated themselves at the cabin door so that she cannot reenter without harassment. At this point, the third swain, a Scotsman in kilts, wades to her side. They embrace, and he carries her ashore. The sight of a kilted, fully dressed man standing waist-deep in water while embracing a girl in bathing costume all the time watched by two seated males in full dress crouched on a waterbound cabin is bizarre. It hints at the appeal of early movies, some at least, to writers and artists soon to be dadaists and surrealists. Like the hypnotized Chappie swinging from a restaurant dinner party chandelier. Or the inventor of liquid electricity moving in exaggeratedly slow grace while his subjects scurry through their accelerated work schedules and tree leaves flutter wildly. In last analysis, 1907 almost seems to project undated, manic visions of a world we still inhabit.

---

[6]Vladimir Propp, *Morphology of the Folktale,* 2nd ed. (Austin: University of Texas Press, 1968).

BARRY SALT

The Early Development of
Film Form

The years from 1903 to 1917 are the most obscure part of film history, as far as nearly everyone is concerned occupied only by the films of Griffith and Chaplin and a vague intimation of Ince. Although sufficient films from the early years of this century have been available for a number of years to anyone determined to seek them out and view them, it seems that no one has bothered, and the superficial and false commonplaces current for many decades about the early development of film technique have continued to be repeated up to the latest film histories published in English. These mistaken ideas, as far as they go, center on attributing to D. W. Griffith the complete invention of "film language." Griffith may have been the best director working in the years from 1908 to 1915, but that does not prove he invented everything. An outline of the true situation as it developed from 1903 to 1917 follows, based on the examination of hundreds of films of the period, and hopefully to be expanded when more film material comes to light.

INTRODUCTION

There is little to be added to the best accounts of developments up to 1903, for instance that in Jean Mitry's *Histoire du cinéma* (though even this book is not adequate after that date), but there is one minor new point to be made about George Méliès's *L'Affaire Dreyfus* (1899). This concerns an early form of staging in depth in the courtroom scene and in one of the street scenes. In these scenes, apparently unique in Méliès's work and indeed in fictional films of the period, bystanders and observers of the action fill the space between the principal actors, far in the upper background, to the bottom of the frame as seen from a slightly elevated camera position, in a way that copies a common framing occurring in actuality footage of the period. This could be considered to be the first occurrence of a purely "cinematographic" angle in fictional film, but this kind of feature had to wait several years before really being developed in the films of the Vitagraph Co.

At approximately the same time the first "chase" films appeared in England, though the earliest still available seems to be Williamson's *Stop Thief!* of 1901, and as is well known, the possibility of continuous action passing from shot to shot directly cut together without intervening titles was realized. (Strictly speaking there was a small space-time ellipse at each cut already in these first examples.) The other well-known development of this year was in *Grandma's Reading Glass*, made by G. A. Smith, in which long shots of children looking at various objects with a magnifying glass alternate with close shots of these same objects (inside a circular mask). This film and others similar by G. A. Smith were widely imitated in France and elsewhere, e.g. *Scenes from My Balcony* (Zecca, 1901).

1903–1907

1903 saw the application of the *"Grandma's Reading Glass"* device to film narration in *A Search for Evidence* (American Mutoscope and Biograph). In this film, a wife searching for her erring husband peers through a series of hotel bedroom keyholes, and the long shot of this scene is cut directly to a shot of her point of view through the keyhole (vignetted by a keyhole shaped matte). When her husband is finally located the shot of wife and detective breaking through the door is directly cut to a long shot of the inside of the bedroom shot *at 90 degrees* to the angle on the corridor action, and also showing action matching to the shot in the corridor. However, the device of the subjective shot took a number of years to be generalized, as did another development noticeable in the same year, the close-up cut directly into an action scene. In *Gay Shoe Clerk* (Edwin S. Porter, 1903) made for the Edison Co., a true close-up of a ladies' shoe being fitted is cut directly into a long shot of a shoe store scene in which a salesman is fitting the lady with shoes under the eye of her chaperone. The angle of the close-up is the same as that of the master shot, and the matching at the cuts is fairly good, which was not always the case in similar examples in succeeding years.

(Porter may well have been anticipated in the use of this device by G. A. Smith if one believes Georges Sadoul, but many of the dates he gives for other films are too early by a year or two, and the earliest film made by Smith we have using a close shot cut into the course of the action is *The Sick Kitten* of 1903. The instant plagiarism which was such a feature of the early years of the cinema means that absolute priority is rather difficult to establish, but that is no reason for historians not trying to do so.)

The use of a close shot, *not* integrated into the action, either to open or close a film, seems to have been quite common around this time. Apart from the well-known instance of *The Great Train Robbery* (Porter, 1903), similarly *emblematic*

close-ups begin the British films *Raid on a Coiner's Den* and *The Eviction* (both
Alfred Collins, 1904), and also *The Widow and the Only Man* (McCutcheon, 1904,
for American Mutoscope and Biograph). The first shows the hands of three
individuals coming into frame, one with fist clenched, another pointing a pistol in
the opposite direction, and that of a policeman holding a pair of handcuffs; the
second film begins with an eviction notice; and the last begins with shots of the
widow and the only man. *The Widow and the Only Man* also contains a medium
close shot cut into the course of the action, as did a number of subsequent films
from other makers before 1908.

Lighting Effects

It was around 1905 that the major film producing companies, Edison,
Vitagraph, and Biograph, began to use artificial lighting in their studios. In
general this did not make much difference to the appearance of their films
because the banks of mercury vapor tubes (Cooper-Hewitts) were used
sparingly to supplement the main lighting from the diffuse sunlight coming
through the studio roofs, and the light they produced was very nearly equally
diffuse. They were not used to mimic the effect of light coming from a real source
of soft light such as a window, as modern soft lights are sometimes used.
However, there was also from this time some extremely rare use of theatrical type
arc floodlights, and one striking instance is in *The Seven Ages* (Edwin S. Porter,
1905). In one scene in this film the light from a fire falling on two old people
sitting in front of a fireplace is simulated by an arc floodlight in the position of the
fire and out of shot to the side. This is the sole source of light in this scene, and is
possibly the first appearance of such a usage.[1]

It does not seem to have been noticed that the well-known *Rescued by Rover*
(1905) contains a lighting innovation usually credited to Bitzer and Griffith. The
light coming through the window of the set representing the kidnapper's garret
room is produced by a pair of arc floodlights simulating the fall of daylight in an
almost identical arrangement to that in Griffith's *Edgar Allen Poe* of 1909.

However some innovative camera work *was* being done at this time by Billy
Bitzer and F. A. Dobson at Biograph. 1906 saw the appearance of *The Paymaster*,
photographed on location by Bitzer and featuring an available light interior scene
in a watermill in which sunlight coming though windows from the side produces
a strong chiaroscuro effect. In the same year F. A. Dobson produced *The Silver
Wedding* and *The Tunnel Workers*, doubling as director and cameraman, as was
quite usual at this period, and in these films, more by the nature of the sets he had
constructed than by the exact sources of light used, created scenes with

---

[1][Biograph was using artificial light as early as 1903. See ad in *The New York Clipper*,
February 7, 1903, p. 1124—GP.]

illuminated backgrounds and dark foregrounds showing silhouette figures of actors, scenes of a type that were not extensively exploited till a decade later. Dobson mixed studio sets and real locations in the way that was quite standard by this time, but his choice of locations was more enterprising than most. In *The Skyscrapers* scenes of actual skyscrapers under construction are filmed from slightly higher and lower angles as appropriate, *these non-eye-level angles* appearing possibly for the first time in a fiction film.

Cross-Cutting

The earliest recorded appearance of cross-cutting between parallel actions appears to be in *Her First Adventure*, directed by Wallace McCutcheon for American Mutoscope and Biograph in March 1908, which is after D. W. Griffith joined Biograph as an actor, but before he started directing. In this film scenes of the flight of kidnappers are intercut with scenes of a faithful dog searching for a stolen child. It would appear that Griffith took over this established usage as well as others already mentioned and has been granted credit for them ever since. And this is not the end of the story.

1908–1913

In 1908 nearly all films, with very rare exceptions, were at the most one reel in length—that is, 1000 feet running for 15 minutes. Whatever the subsequent form, they commenced with a long explanatory title setting the scene for the action to follow. A fair portion of the production was still made up of "tableau films," in which each scene of the action was shown in one shot invariably preceded by an explanatory title. The scene itself might be staged in long shot in front of a theatre-type set of painted canvas to take one possible extreme, or a realistic constructed set might be used, or at the other extreme an actual place might form the location. It was also possible that the camera might be placed closer to the scene to take either what was called a "French foreground" shot with the bottom of the frame cutting the actors off at the shins, or an "American foreground" in which the actors were only visible from the knees up. Not surprisingly, the use of shots with closer camera tended to be associated with greater naturalism in other elements of the film. Indeed about the beginning of this period the Vitagraph company had arrived at using what was then called "the nine-foot line," that is using actor positions up to nine feet from the camera to play a scene, and so giving what would now be referred to as a medium shot, with the actors only visible from the hips up. In this major group of film types the story told was usually one that in other media would occupy a full-length play or novel, so the series of shot-scenes served the purpose of illustrating the titles which preceded them, and which by themselves almost conveyed the story. The range of possibilities alluded to can be illustrated by *La Dame aux camélias* (Pouctal) with Sarah Bernhardt of 1910 at the theatrical extreme, and two aspects of the Vitagraph Company's production to represent the center and naturalistic extreme of the spectrum: namely J. Stuart Blackton's *Romeo and Juliet* of 1908 and *The Romance of an Umbrella* of 1909.

The category of one-reel films which proved more important for the development of film narration includes Griffith's work at Biograph, but it is really a development of the "chase" type of film widely established before 1908. This type of film had a specially written story involving two or three connected incidents covering a short span of real time and particularly suited to being conveyed without titles before every shot-scene. In other words, the action could appear to move directly from one shot to the next, though usually in fact with a small space-time discontinuity. Virtually all Griffith's Biograph films illustrate this tendency, but it also characterised the Westerns and other action subjects made by the smaller American production companies such as Lubin, Selig, Essanay, etc., around 1909.

In Biograph films scenes were shot exclusively with fixed camera, and the actors were framed in either long shot or medium long shot ("American foreground") with a very limited number of big close-ups of objects important to the action cut into the middle of shots in some films only. These shots would be described in later terminology as "inserts," whereas true close-ups (which at that period were referred to as "busts") are entirely absent from Griffith's films at the beginning of his career. He did, on occasion at this period, use the already well-established device of a medium shot of the actors to conclude the film. His use of a true close-up cut into the body of the action did not occur till around 1911.

As far as camera movements are concerned, Griffith took up the "parallel track" in which the camera moves a fixed distance ahead of actors in a car or on horseback, etc., and which had already been used on occasion in the previous period, but he seems to have had an aesthetic objection to the use of panning shots. This attitude was quite common till well into the twenties, the idea being that panning shots drew attention to the mechanics of filming. That this was the case with Griffith can be seen from those odd occasions when a cameraman supplied him with a pan, such as in *The Massacre* (1912), and it is cut off in the editing just as it starts. An earlier instance of this occurs in *Drive for a Life* (1909), in which a scene involving interplay between actors in two cars, filmed with a car-mounted camera as a parallel track, clearly was shot by the cameraman with a pan at the conclusion of the shot to follow one of the cars diverging from the main road. Again this panning shot was removed in the editing, though even without it the scene has a remarkable intricacy of staging.

Throughout his whole career Griffith never really mastered the use of the angle-reverse angle cut between two actors in a scene, and it remained to others to develop this in interior scenes from 1912 onwards. The lack of this feature, and also the related one of cutting on action, is intimately connected with the way in which he shot scenes for his films. According to Karl Brown's description[2] it was Griffith's practice to create variations in the action of each shot in each take he made of it; so with all takes different in movement, there was no way for the actors or anyone to remember the exact movements they made if it was decided to shoot a closer shot to insert in the master shot. On the other hand, if he decided beforehand to use a close-up at some point, which of course he did on a relatively limited number of occasions, he could not allow as much in the way of acting variations as he customarily preferred to do. Another aspect of Griffith's style that persisted throughout his career and which could already be regarded as conservative by 1910 is that all the actors in his scenes tend to play toward the camera as though to a theater audience, and on the limited occasions when a closer shot is cut into the scene, it is almost always shot from the same frontal direction. In contrast, the Vitagraph company directors were already using an arrangement of actors in the shot in which one or more of them could be in the foreground with their backs more or less turned to the camera in medium shot and the others deeper in the shot, an arrangement that gave the appearance of a natural scene unawares, and which was to become the usual practice in later filmmaking. (See for instance *Love's Awakening* [1910].) Other compositional features found in Vitagraph films alone at this time could be classed together with the foregoing as the discovery of the "cinematographic angle"; for instance the use of skew angles to architectural features, and shooting through doorways from dark interiors, in a way that was not done in still photography. In general the Vitagraph films have an elegance of composition and, where appropriate, of setting and costuming, that is absent from Griffith's work.

Despite what has been said above about Griffith's failure to recognize the importance of cutting on action and "angle-reverse angle cuts" for film construction, there are very rare appearances of these techniques in his films, and they should be mentioned. In *The Squaw's Love* (1911), the squaw jumps from a bluff into the river to escape a pursuer, and a downward angle of her fall from the point of view of her attacker cuts to a long shot of the scene from the other side of the river at the instant the splash of the water forms. This particular instance occurs because the scene was shot with two cameras. And in *The Coming of Angelo* (1913), a climactic confrontation between two leading characters on the seashore is presented with an "angle-reverse angle" pair of medium shots. But there is no question that Griffith did not develop these forms, and on innumerable subsequent occasions in his films when they would have been appropriate he does not use them.

A technique that D. W. Griffith did popularize, though he did not originate, that of cross-cutting between parallel actions, can be studied in his early films

---

[2] Karl Brown, *Adventures with D. W. Griffith* (London: Secker and Warburg, 1974).

such as *Drive for a Life* (1909). It must be pointed out that although we now call this cross-cutting, at that time it was referred to as the "flash-back" or "cut-back" technique, and flashbacks as we understand the term did not exist before 1912. It was the extensive use of cross-cutting that enabled Griffith to do without the use of cutting on action and matching cuts in general as a means of creating filmic movement.

An aspect of film construction that came to be understood in the period we are concerned with was the spatial orientation perceived by the film spectator between the scenes represented in the different shots. To give an example, in all films made around 1908, if an actor exited out of frame right in one shot, and then the next shot showed a different scene, the actor was quite likely to make an entrance from the same (that is right) side of the frame. Although this conforms to the theatrical convention for entrances and exits in succeeding scenes, it is confusing to the unconscious expectations of the film audience, who naturally think of the character as continuing to walk in the same direction for the few seconds before he appears in the next shot from the *left* side. This latter convention established itself by 1913, at least with the more intelligent directors, and its application called for the continuity record procedures described by Karl Brown. Of course more complicated problems of apparent orientation can arise than this, particularly when some reasonable relative orientation of the different scene locations can be deduced by the audience, but these problems can be dealt with by extension of the principle mentioned. A well-known Griffith film that demonstrates lack of awareness of this scene orientation problem at Biograph in 1911 is *The Lonedale Operator*, whereas just about any good film of two years later shows the problem conquered.

The Importance of the Western

The development of Western and other outdoor action subject films in these years is rather difficult to fix precisely at the present time, but it is clear that the physical conditions involved in making Westerns in the countryside predisposed cameramen to make small panning movements of the camera to keep the actors within the frame or even further to keep the picture well composed, despite the difficulty of turning both the camera crank handle and the pan head crank handle simultaneously and in different directions. This can be seen sometimes in G. M. Anderson's films from 1909, and the natural elaboration of these framing movements into definite pans following the actors about the scene has become common in the films Essanay, Kalem, and The American Film Manufacturing Co. made in 1911. Examples can be seen in *The Poisoned Flume* (Allan Dwan, 1911) and *Rory O'Moore* (Sidney Olcott, 1911), and an attempt at the ultimate virtuosic elaboration, a series of combined pans and tilts to follow a group of horsemen on a zigzag path down a hillside, appears in one shot in Dwan's *The Fear* (1912).

But prior to this had occured the capital innovation in this stream of filmmaking, the use of off-eye-line angle-reverse angle combinations of shots, when two people are conversing or otherwise interacting in a film. Obviously it is much easier to get into the use of this device on location than when shooting on sets that lack the side opposite to the principal direction of filming. The earliest example that can be quoted occurs in *The Loafer* (Essanay, 1911) where the shots in question are true close-ups, but the usage must have developed before that date. (It is really necessary to distinguish between the different varieties of angle-reverse angle cuts—the cut from a watcher to his point of view, which was the first to appear as already described; the cut from one long shot of a scene to another more or less oppositely angled long shot which must have happened somewhat later, (the first example that can be quoted is in *Røverens Brud* [Viggo Larsen, 1907]); and the cut between just-off-eye-line angle-reverse angle shots of two people interacting, which is what is under consideration at the moment. The distinction between the first case and the last case can be rather difficult to make in these early years, and indicates the way the last must have developed.)

Titling

During these years a great contribution to narrative speed, economy, and construction was made by the gradual replacement of descriptive or narrative titles by dialogue titles. This development presumably arose in films based on literary classics of one kind or another such as *Romeo and Juliet* (1908) where there was an obvious compulsion to include celebrated lines of dialogue from the original. In keeping with the somewhat conservative attitude to filmmaking at Vitagraph this procedure was very slow to be generalized to their other productions, and in fact it caught on much faster in the Western/action stream of filmmaking elsewhere. For instance in G. M. Anderson's films as early as 1909 there sometimes appear spoken dialogue titles, but like all early occurrences these dialogue titles are not cut into a shot at the moment when they are spoken, but either at the beginning or the end of the relevant shot. By 1911 the use of dialogue titles was fairly common, though not in Griffith's films, but although some are at the point between shots when they would be heard, most are not, and it is doubtful if the principle had yet been realized. (One can see examples in *The Loafer* and *A Tale of Two Cities* by J. S. Blackton.) The dialogue title was generally used by 1913, but in any particular film narrative titles still predominated.

Lighting Techniques

As already remarked, the standard lighting in the better studios was now a mixture of diffuse daylight and diffuse mercury vapor lamp light, but around 1910 supplementary light from arc floodlights on floor stands began to be mixed in, either from the front or sometimes solely from the side. Examples of this latter use can be seen in *Oliver Twist* (1909). Since arc floods are effectively point sources they produce much more definite figure modeling than diffuse light, but for the full benefit of this to be realized the general set lighting has to be reduced in intensity first, and this happened rather more quickly in Denmark than in the United States. Nevertheless, by 1912 entirely arc lit interiors had appeared in American films, for instance in *An Ill Wind* (Weber and Smalley) and *Conscience* (Vitagraph Co.). In the first the key light in a series of office scenes is provided by sets of arc floodlights at one or both sides of the set to give a moderately naturalistic fall of light, and in the second there is heavy chiaroscuro effect lighting from one side source in a waxworks-at-night scene, not to mention general use of arc light for figure modeling. By 1913 arc floodlights were being used on location, as in *Coronets and Hearts*, in which scenes in a real bank and its vault are lit solely with a couple of arcs in what had become the usual disposition: angled at 45 degrees to the scene from either side of the camera. It must be emphasized that this sort of thing was fairly rare in American films at this time, the mass of them still using the earlier diffuse light arrangements. The technique of simulating lamplight by an arc floodlight just out of frame on the side where the oil lamp was standing was finally established by 1913, years after this happened in Danish films.

As far as exterior photography was concerned, the only important development was the introduction of reflector fill light, and this is one of the few cases where the claim for Griffith-Bitzer priority may be correct. Significantly this first occured after 1910 (e.g., *Faithful,* 1910) when the move to filmmaking in California had begun. The harsh middle-of-the-day light in that area produces much less attractive results when used frontally on faces than the more diffuse light usually found in the New York area, so the discovery of back-lighting of figures with direct sunlight plus the reflecting of scattered sunlight onto the front from matte white surfaces was probably inevitable.

Flashbacks

Flashbacks evolved out of the earlier representation of dreams and memories by a subsidiary scene inset within the frame containing the scene showing the dreamer. This technique goes back of course to Zecca's *Histoire d'un crime* (1901), but is slightly troublesome to produce photographically, requiring as it does a double exposure with accurately positioned masks and countermasks in front of the lens. The easier option of total area superimposition of the present and dreamed scene of past events had appeared by 1911 (*After One Hundred Years*) and probably earlier, but the full-blown flashback needed something more than a title to indicate where it started and ended. The fade-out, which had just arrived as a means of concluding a film, was the device pressed into service. For instance in *A Wasted Sacrifice* (Vitagraph, 1912) there is a fade-out on the shot of the rememberer, a cut to the remembered scene, a cut away from it, and a fade-in on the rememberer again. By 1913 the device was well established, but the earlier convention of matting in the remembered scene in one area of the frame was still being used, e.g., in *Atlantis* (August Blom).

In the same year one can see time-lapse within a flashback indicated by the same means as the flashback was entered and left, namely a fade-out and fade-in. This happens in *The Tiger*, made by Frederick Thompson for the Vitagraph Company.

The Missing Link

When we consider, together with the film *The Loafer* already mentioned, such films from 1914 as *Bad Buck of Santa Ynez* (Reginald Barker), which contains scenes cut up into a number of shots taken from many *different* angles, and when we consider that earlier Ince produced films such as *An Apache Father's Vengeance* made in 1912 contain no cutting around at all, then the simplest deduction is that when Ince took over the Reliance company at the end of 1912 he also took over the director who knew how to do this. Reginald Barker was one of the directors for Reliance; he had directed at Essanay in 1910, and when we add in the fact that a fragment of *Wheels of Destiny* (Reliance-Broncho, 1911) shows very advanced cutting around for that year, it rather looks as though Barker is the man who developed the technique of off-eye-line angle-reverse angle cutting, and indeed of cutting around a scene in general. In any case that technique was certainly developed along a path leading through the production companies mentioned.[3]

1914–1917

By 1914 an "Ince style" was a definite option being taken up by a number of directors, though for the reasons already mentioned it is doubtful that the formal aspects of this style were of Thomas Ince's creation, and indeed it may be suspected that the more retarded features of *Civilisation* were due to his personal intervention in the direction. In this style angle-reverse angle combinations of shots are freely applied at appropriate climactic points, though it must be noted that the idea of "not crossing the eye line" had not been established when using this device. (There is an example of this lack in *Bad Buck of Santa Ynez*, in the scene where W. S. Hart meets the widow and the child.) The possibility of following the characters with panning shots is also present, not only in exteriors but also in interiors, e.g., *Typhoon* (Barker, 1914). In 1915 these tendencies were definitely established in such films as *Between Men* (Barker), and another characteristic feature of Ince studio films had also appeared, namely the use of arc spotlights to give backlighting of the figures in interior scenes. However in these films diffuse

---

[3][*An Apache Father's Revenge* does not appear to be an Ince title. There is a 1913 Bronco (Ince) *Wheels of Destiny,* but Reginald Barker was not at Essanay in 1910, nor at Reliance in 1911—GP.]

overhead light still tends to form an important component of the general set lighting. This was not the case in some other places, for example in the work of Alvin Wyckoff (*The Cheat, The Golden Chance*) for Cecil B. De Mille.

De Mille was the leading exponent of a new style of filming that he himself did not develop, but which he adopted with great address. The emergence of this style is apparent in films made in 1914 such as *The Hour and the Man* (Essanay) and *Weights and Measures* (Victor), in which there is a heavy concentration on camera closeness to the action of around medium shot. (This is almost the exact inverse of D. W. Griffith's practice of avoiding medium shots and conducting most of the film in longer shots relieved by a proportion of close shots.) This newly emerging style also tends to involve framing movements, and demands cutting on action with good matching as the actors move from one shot into another as they move about the set. Although it uses close-ups on occasion, this style did not at first include the use of angle-reverse angle close-ups, but these were included by the style's exponents and converts in the next year or two. One instance of this was Ralph Ince, who had recently become a director for the Vitagraph Company.

To some extent allied with these developments was the device of starting a scene with a close shot, rather than showing the whole location in a long shot before cutting in closer, and examples can be seen in *Elsa's Brother* (Van Dyke Brooke for Vitagraph, 1915), and other examples exist in the contemporary works of Maurice Tourneur and Allan Dwan.

Another aspect of shot continuity had reached its definitive formulation by 1914. This was the handling of the movement of actors from one shot to another shot taken in a different location. Previous to this date this transition was dealt with by having the actors walk out of one shot and then walk into another and merely having the directions match. (Though for years after 1914 there were a number of directors active who still could not manage even that much.) But in *Detective Burton's Triumph* (Reliance) the actor is placed in such a position while still within the frame and his direction of movement is so arranged that when the cut is made to the same actor in another different location his movement seems quite continuous to the casual eye, and the space-time ellipse between the shots is concealed. So thoroughgoing is the demonstration of mastery of these weak shot transitions in this film that one is tempted to take it as a consciously virtuoso performance by the unknown director. Strangely, this film, so exceptionally advanced for 1914 in this respect (and also quite forward in most other respects except lighting), entirely lacks dialogue titles, the story being carried by a limited number of narrative titles. Anomalies of sophistication between the handling of the different dimensions of the film medium are not uncommon during this period; for instance crude acting sometimes occurs in a film with good shot dissection, but this is the most singular example noted so far. (Most films make considerable use of dialogue titles by 1914–15, though Griffith was already slipping behind in the proportion he used.)

Generally, compared with the films we have been discussing, D. W.

Griffith's *Birth of a Nation* is technically retarded, though of course other qualities outside our concern at the moment compensate as far as its absolute aesthetic value is in question. In the two hours of this film's duration there is not one use of a subjective shot or more generally of the angle-reverse angle combination, even in scenes crying out for these devices such as Flora Cameron's pursuit by the negro and leap from the cliff. Always the camera moves straight in from the established "audience" side for closer shots. And there are not very many closer shots compared to the usage in the films previously mentioned. Cuts on action are almost completely absent as well, and of course all this still stems from Griffith's technique of using varied improvisation on each take. These features would tend to produce a slow moving film but for the well-known feature of Griffith's style, the cross-cutting between parallel actions. This produces a series of very strong cuts between shots which propel the film forward and compensates for the relatively static nature of the individual shots due to the distance of the actors from the camera and hence the small amount of movement within the frame. Also the cutting in *Birth of a Nation* is slightly faster (average shot length—8 seconds) than the Ince school films, which all have an average shot length of about 10 seconds.

Watching a film such as *His Phantom Sweetheart* (Ralph Ince), one has the subjective impression that it is moving very fast, and this clearly happens because of the relatively large amount of movement within the frame due to the close camera placement which overrides the effect of the somewhat longer shots and "weak" cuts. When one adds in the camera movements used by the Ince school, both a limited number of framing movements and true pans and tilts, one has the direction that the mainstream of cinema was to follow eventually. But not immediately, for a proportion of American films were being made in a style closer to that of Griffith at this time, though usually without his well-planned use of parallel action to give drive to them.

One can indeed point to such films as James Kirkwood's *The Eagle's Mate* of 1914 which show these features, but Kirkwood and anyone else who persisted in this style in America went to the wall even faster than Griffith. (The development of a style depending on quasi-static shots joined by strong fast cuts led away from the mainstream to the avant-garde through Gance and Eisenstein.)

More About Flashbacks

In 1914 a new method of entering and leaving flashbacks through a dissolve began to appear, and for a while coexisted with the earlier fade-out/fade-in convention, sometimes even in the same film, as in *The Man That Might Have Been* (William Humphrey for Vitagraph 1914). This one-reeler has a remarkable complexity of construction, being a series of memories and reveries that contrast the imaginer's real passage through life with what might have been if his son had not died. The use of the dissolve had become practical at this time owing to the addition of frame counters to movie cameras. (Standard on the new Bell & Howell, and then added personally by enterprising cameramen with older Pathés, etc.) The dissolve was not restricted to introducing flashbacks; it also began to be used to cover a suspected mismatch in actor position when making a transition from a longer shot to a closer shot, or indeed even when there was no possibility of mismatch on moving from long shot to close-up. This usage, which continued to be a standard possibility till the latter part of the twenties, can be seen in Ince's *Civilization* (1916) as well as in numerous other films. The dissolve was *not* used to indicate a short time lapse.

Before long other ways of getting into a flashback appeared, for example matting in the past scenes into the center of an insert shot of the letter that inspired their recollection, as in *The On-the-Square Girl* (F. J. Ireland, 1917). But these did not displace the dissolve convention.

Lighting Developments

Even in the small number of dramatic films still available from the time of the First World War one can see important developments taking place in the lighting of both interior and exterior scenes. The earliest detected use of "night-for-night" filming with artificial light occurs in *Their One Love* (Thanhouser, 1915), where an extended night battle sequence is lit with arc floods; sometimes picking out foreground areas with frontal light, in other shots producing silhouette effects with back-lighting alone. (The short "burning of Atlanta" sequence in the earlier *Birth of a Nation* is lit with flares.) However "night for night" shooting did not really become much used until a few years had passed, as was also the case with the use of underexposure on "day-for-night" exteriors. This latter technique can be seen in *The On-the-Square Girl* (1917), but only occasionally thereafter for a number of years.

The main thrust in the development of the lighting of interior scenes in American films was the change to the overall use of *directional* artificial light and the application of this lighting separately to the actors and to the sets. This was a gradual process and has already been alluded to in part. The cameraman who led the way in combining all these elements seems to have been Alvin Wyckoff. By the time he lit *The Cheat* and *The Golden Chance* he was using stronger and weaker arc floodlights from the front to provide key and fill light from the appropriate angles to give good modeling on the faces, and at least some of the time using a back spotlight for more modeling and figure separation from the background. Figure separation is also aided by arranging that the light intensity be lower on the walls of the set than on the figures. Also included in these films are strong chiaroscuro and low-key lighting effects where appropriate, these being produced by lighting limited areas of the scene from the side with a single arc light and not using any fill light at all. This chiaroscuro lighting was applied from above or below eye level as seemed fitting. Of course all these techniques had been applied to lighting isolated scenes in various films before this, but Wyckoff was the first to use them throughout a film with consistency.

In contemporary European lighting practice back-lighting was not used, and it was quite possible to produce good-looking results without it, as the lighting some American films made later than *The Golden Chance* shows, for instance that of *The On-the-Square Girl*. Although not using true back-lighting, this last film does use behind-the-side-lines figure lighting from arc floods in closer shots. The cameraman, Morris E. Hair, also manages to add the features of the lighting of large sets entirely with directional light, and the use of diffusion on floodlights for figure lighting, to those already appearing in Wyckoff's work. Diffusion on floodlights was a notable advance, as it softens the shadow line around the curves of the face, though the original reason for putting glass diffusers in front of arc floodlights may have been an attempt to prevent the "klieg-eye" condition of eye inflammation prevalent among film actors.

Tracking Shots

Inspired by the well-known example of *Cabiria* in 1914, the more adventurous directors in Scandinavia and America took up the occasional use of tracking shots on quasi-static scenes (the "Cabiria movement") in the following years, for example in *David Harum* (A. Dwan), *Civilization* (Ince), *Terje Vigen* (Sjöström), *Himmelskibet* (Hoger-Madsen), etc. At the moment it appears that the last use for a number of years was in *The Blue Bird* (Maurice Tourneur, 1918), but who knows what will turn up as more and more films from the early twenties come to light. During the First World War period the parallel tracking shot also continued to be used on occasion, as it had been earlier.

CONCLUSION

When one looks at a film like *The On-the-Square Girl* made in 1917 one can see all the main features of what was to be the mainstream of cinema in place and working beautifully, and hopefully it has been made clear how this has much less to do with D. W. Griffith and Thomas Ince than is usually supposed.

The other important point that comes out very strongly from a comparative study of films from the 1903 to 1917 period is the lack of fixed meaning in the devices that constitute their form. At one particular date in those years a fade-out could indicate a time-lapse, a flashback, or simply the end of the film, and the same sort of consideration applies to other devices such as dissolves and even camera angles. And yet people then and now appear to have been able to understand the meaning of these films quite easily. The converse situation, in which the same meaning is conveyed by different devices, is illustrated by the telephone conversation problem. Seen from the viewpoint of those early years this was the difficulty of making clear that the two people using the phone are in fact speaking to each other, remembering that before 1910 the two participants in a conversation were always simultaneously visible in the same shot. The first solution offered was simple superimposition of shots of the telephone users, as in *The Story the Biograph Told* (1904), and some time after that the idea of using a split screen showing the speakers in the two halves must have appeared, certainly before 1910 (*Den Hvide Slave-Handel*). Once the idea of cross-cutting between parallel action was established it became possible to cut directly from one phone speaker to another, but the earlier conventions persisted, as can be seen in *Ved Faengslets Port* (1911), in which a phone conversation is first treated by superimposition, and then on a second occasion by simple cutting. Later, in 1913, when cutting between the speakers had become the usual way of treating a phone conversation, it was still possible to use the triptych screen device in the American film *Suspense* (Weber and Smalley). In other words, in 1911 these three conventions for treating the subject matter of a phone conversation existed simultaneously.

This lack of regularity in the significance of style features, which was to become even more marked with the emergence of the avant-garde in the twenties, is one of the main reasons for the failure of attempts to create a science of film considered as a language system. The more film is an art, the less it is a language system. (Consider the treatment of a flashback in *The On-the-Square Girl* described earlier, which is probably a unique case of that handling of the device.) This is not to say that aspects of film cannot be studied by scientific methods, or that there are no regularities in the forms of films at all, just that these regularities are insufficient to be usefully considered as a language system.

MARSHALL DEUTELBAUM

Structural Patterning in the Lumière Films

Despite their hallowed place in film history—or precisely because of it—the earliest films produced by the Lumière company have received virtually no critical attention. Rather, the estimation of their importance appears to have been set ages ago and merely repeated, unquestioningly, in each new history of the motion picture. This traditional opinion, extended as well to all early films, suggests that the aim and pleasure of the first projected films consisted of the simple depiction of motion for its own sake. According to this view, these films—especially the ones produced by the Lumière company—were merely naively photographed views.

Gerald Mast, for example, imputes such a naive quality to these films when he compares them to amateur home movies:

> The first films merely exploited their amazement. The films that Louis Lumière shot for his Cinématographe . . . lasted between thirty and ninety seconds. The camera was stationed in a single spot, turned on to record the action, and then turned off when the action had finished. These films were really "home movies"—unedited scenery, family activity, or posed action—that depended for their effect on the same source as today's "home movies"—the wonder of seeing something reproduced in an unfamiliar and permanent way. Nowhere is the home movieishness of the first films more obvious than in Lumière's *Le Repas de bébé*, which has been duplicated uncounted times in contemporary 8mm. versions.[1]

---

[1]Gerald Mast, *A Short History of the Movies* (New York: Pegasus, 1971), p. 36.

Similarly, Arthur Lennig argues that these Lumière films were only "motion picture snapshots" that present an unmediated view of reality:

> The Lumière brothers had been the first to project films, and were also the first to make them. Entrepreneurs and technicians rather than artists, they took the camera out in the street and photographed such things as a train pulling into a station, waves breaking upon a beach, and workers walking out of a factory. These fifty foot sequences, running just under one minute, were nothing more than motion picture snapshots. Thus was established, although unknowingly, what could be called the documentary aspect of cinema, the recording of unadjusted, unarranged, untampered reality.[2]

These two assertions that the Lumière films reflect an unshaped rendering of reality are extended by Louis D. Giannetti, who declares these films to be "plotless," devoid of any narrative concerns:

> From a strictly historical point of view, the plotless film can be dated almost to the inception of the movies at the turn of the century. The earliest films of the Lumière brothers in France, for example, were not concerned with narrative but with capturing the variety and flux of everyday life. Anything that moved was fascinating for its own sake. Around 1900, movies portraying such events as the arrival of a train or a street parade were enormously popular. These short *actualités*, as they were sometimes called, constituted the first stage of what was later recognized as the documentary movement.[3]

Naturally it is quite comfortable to assess the Lumière films in this manner since any organically conceived history of the motion picture demands that the earliest works be the most "primitive"—in the worst sense of the word. In this view, these unedited films must be naive if the later use of editing demonstrates the transformation of film into an art form. While the opinion that the Lumière films constitute the beginnings of the documentary may provide some saving consolation, this long accepted generality seems to have foreclosed any other assessment.

These descriptions of the Lumière films, however, may be easily tested. Two collections of Lumière films, entitled "Lumière Films—First Programs (1895–1896)" and "Early Lumière Films—1895–1898," are commonly available for viewing from The Museum of Modern Art. The two collections offer twenty-eight

[2]Arthur Lennig, *The Silent Voice: A Text* (Albany, N.Y.: Lane Press, 1969), p. 14.

[3]Louis D. Giannetti, *Godard and Others: Essays on Film Form* (Cranbury, N.J.: Farleigh Dickinson University Press, 1975), p. 137.

Lumière films chosen to represent the various categories of film types listed in the original Lumière catalogues.[4] While some seem, indeed, to be naive, unmediated representations of reality with no pretense of narrative, these terms do not accurately describe most of the films. *Cygnes* ("Feeding the Swans") and *Lions* do seem merely to portray exotic animals in mundane settings. In both films, a keeper throws food to the animals to make them move about; that motion is the dominant subject of the films. Yet few of the other films in this group are quite so minimally a record of simply what happened to be before the camera.

The famous *Sortie d'usine* ("Employees Leaving Lumière Factory"), alluded to by Lennig, offers a startlingly different situation as a close, descriptive analysis of its action reveals. The film begins with the large doors of the factory opening inward. Men and women, on foot and on bicycles, stream through the open doorway and move to the left and right along the sidewalk. Finally, as the last of the workers—a man in a suit and straw hat—emerges from within, the left-hand door is swung shut. Sadoul's brief comment on the film, "on ouvre les portes au début du film, on les ferme à la fin," suggests that far from being a naive record of motion for its own sake, the film reflects a number of carefully chosen decisions about sequential narrative.[5]

Wholly apart from whether the employees were prepared for their appearances and exits, the very shape of the film signals an ordering intelligence at work. To begin with, the film starts and concludes, that is, has a beginning and end, signalled by the movement of the doors through which the workers emerge. In addition, and perhaps more importantly, the action presented by the film is a complete process: the doors open, the workers begin to leave the factory, the last of the workers leaves the factory, the doors close. The film begins with the

---

[4]In addition to the twenty-eight Lumière films on these reels, "Lumière Films—First Programs (1895–1896)" contains an additional short film, *Boiler Loading*, which is not a Lumière film. It does not correspond to any title in the Lumière catalogues and, according to Mrs. Eileen Bowser, curator of film at the Museum of Modern Art, remains unidentified. Several titles for the Lumière films on these reels are spurious. While all titles appearing in my text are the original Lumière titles, in those instances where spurious titles appear on the reels I have added the spurious title, within brackets, after the correct title for the sake of reference. These original titles have been taken from the Lumière catalogue lists reproduced by Georges Sadoul in *Louis Lumière* (Paris: Editions Seghers, 1964), pp. 152–56.

[5]Sadoul, *Lumière*, p. 152. Since I am well aware of the pitfalls in attributing intention to the creation of films, I do not mean my use of the phrase "Lumière films" to suggest that either Louis or Auguste Lumière is necessarily responsible for the conception of these films. On the other hand, since my argument turns on the matter of whether or not these films are naive photographic records, I do mean my description of recurrent structural features over the range of these films to be taken as evidence of a general intention to shape the material to be recorded on film into a coherent whole.

beginning of a sequential process and concludes with that process having run to its own inherent conclusion.

In fact, the film provides two conclusions. The action of the workers leaving the factory ends and offers a conclusion to the process that is the film's subject. In addition, the opening and closing of the doors demarcate the beginning and end of the experiential process of viewing the film. If the movement of the doors offers a framework within which the action occurs, then the opening of the doors is an assertive gesture announcing the beginning of the film and is answered by the closing of the doors which announces its conclusion. In this regard, the movement of the doors serves as structural punctuation.

Less obvious, though even more intriguing, is the way in which the film nearly returns the scene before the camera to the state at which it was when the film began. Both at the beginning and the close, the cinematic image offers only the exterior of the factory seen from the same point of view. So similar in appearance are these opening and closing images to one another, in fact, that if one were to loop the film into a continuous band, the action would appear to be a single periodic event. As will be discussed, several of the Lumière films display this overall structure.

In contrast to these Lumière films, however, the Edison Kinetoscope films of the same period generally reveal little concern with clearly marked beginnings or conclusive endings. Furthermore, few of these films reflect any attempt to match the duration of a depicted action to the length of a film, even though vaudeville performers with polished routines often appeared as their subjects. Though one might expect that these acts could be trimmed as a matter of shaping to fill the length of a Kinetoscope film, the amount of dead time and inconclusiveness in these presentations strongly suggests that nothing akin to the presentation strategies discernable in the Lumière films lay behind the Edison productions.

As this close analysis of *Sortie d'usine* indicates, the brevity of the film and its lack of editing do not prevent it from being a very intricate work. Furthermore, in its self-conscious indication of both the beginning and end of its depicted action, the film reflects a concern with features usually associated with narrative. Put another way, it is remarkable that such a brief film should present a single event in its entirety (the workers leaving the factory) and locate this event within a framework (the movement of doors) that signals the beginning and end of both the film and this action. While *Sortie d'usine* does not tell a story in the usual sense, its organization reflects an order and direction akin to the movement one associates with traditional plot structure.

To understand why this should be the case requires the recognition that most of the Lumière films draw their structure from the inherent processes selected for their subjects. As the following discussion suggests, these processes are either linear and sequential actions in which a series of related events moves toward an inherent conclusion or circular processes in which a series of actions recurs in a regular manner, cyclically, without reaching a conclusion. As the example of *Sortie d'usine* illustrates, both kinds of processes may shape the overall structure of a single film.

Since this description of these films' structures is based on an organizational logic in the arrangement of action to be photographed, rather than on an interpretation of the meaning of the action depicted, the following analysis traces the structure of the films from the most simple linear sort to the most complex combination of linear and circular processes presented in conjunction with one another. Naturally the relationship between these structures and the composition of their images are also noted.

For the time being, the concept of the Lumière films as presentations of various kinds of processes, varying in their completeness, deserves closer attention. If one defines a linear, sequential process as a systematic series of events directed to some end, one might expect certain recurrent details with something akin to a sense of process over the course of these films. As *Sortie d'usine* suggests, for example, the films' structures should reflect the demarcations of a beginning and an end.

To be sure, a number of films present an operational process. *Carmaux: Défournage du coke,* for example, presents the steps of an industrial procedure. As the film begins, a section of steaming coke begins to emerge from a furnace. One man directs a stream of water onto the coke to cool it. Other workmen approach the coke and jab at it with long-handled forks to break up its mass. As the emerging slab finally forms a complete diagonal across the frame, the workmen move in even closer to continue breaking it up.

Significantly, the film begins with the hot coke as it begins to emerge from the oven. The film begins, in other words, with the first step of the process. As the steps of the cooling of the coke and its breakup continue, the mass moves from the upper left of the frame to the lower right. The film concludes, not with the coke entirely cool and broken into pieces, but with the process of removal essentially complete, and the frame essentially balanced in composition.

Much the same operational process is depicted in *Artillerie de montagne: mise en batterie et feu* ("Exercices D'Artillerie") in which the unlimbering of a cannon and its preparation for firing are presented. The film begins with horses drawing a caisson and cannon into view from the right edge of the frame. The cannon is stopped in mid-frame and other cannons can be seen ranged in line into the distance behind it. A soldier unhooks the cannon from the caisson. Three other soldiers join him and they move into action as a battery preparing the cannon for firing. They sight and load the cannon. One soldier stands ready with lanyard in hand to fire the cannon. The cannons in the background have been similarly prepared, and the film ends as one of these is fired.

Here again, the process of preparing a cannon for action begins at the beginning with the arrival of the cannon in much the same way that *Carmaux:*

Défournage du coke begins with the emergence of the coke into view from the oven. The film concludes with all in readiness for the firing of the cannon, signalled by the firing of another cannon nearby, evidence that the process is concluded.

Similarly, *Démolition d'un mur* ("The Falling Wall") carefully presents all the steps required for the completion of the process named in the film's title. The film begins with a group of workmen arranged around a free-standing wall. One man is hunched over an expandable winch with which he applies pressure against the wall. Another man hacks at the foundation of the wall with a pick in order to weaken it further. A third workman stands by with a pick at the ready. The foreman directs the men with the picks away from the wall and orders the man at the winch to apply more pressure. One of the workmen also applies pressure with the head of his pick. The wall topples, cracking at its weakened base. As the dust settles, the three workmen take up picks and begin to break up the debris.

As in the previously cited examples, this film begins with the first steps of the final process of toppling a wall and concludes with the final step completed. While these three films present operational processes as they might be found in reality, the completeness with which they are depicted strongly argues against their being naive "motion picture snapshots" despite their apparently simple content. Two other films depicting operational processes that occur naturally in reality confirm the conscious organizational selection of action for this kind of film.

The apparently simple subject of *Course en sacs* ("Sack Race") receives an unusual visual presentation. The film begins with everything in readiness for the start of a sack race. The contestants are visible at the end of a long street as they await the signal to begin. Crowds of spectators line both curbs of the street, effectively framing the course. As the starter drops his flag, the contestants begin to hop down the street toward the camera. As the last of them reaches the center of the screen, the starter drops his flag again and seven more men begin to hop down the street toward the camera. As the last of this group reaches just the left-center of the frame, the people on the right-hand curb spill into the street to form an ever-closer approaching background behind the last contestants. The very last of these dawdles at mid-frame as the crowd reaches him. He falls down after one of the spectators gives him a playful push. He gets up and hobbles even closer to the camera, followed by the crowd. The film ends with him only half visible at the right edge of the frame and the crowd now quite close to the camera.

Given the process of a sack race—the beginning, the race itself, and the conclusion—two facets of the film are especially noteworthy. The first involves the use of two sets of contestants. Thus not only is the duration of the sack race designed to "fill" the available film, but the second set of contestants assures that the race will always be on the screen. The second set of contestants begins down the course just before the first set disappears from view. Thus the action remains present even though the actors change. In addition, the use of the spectators on the sidewalks as, first, a frame within which the action takes place and, second, as a mass with which to diminish the area within which the action can occur is a masterful stroke. While the race ends with the final contestants reaching the finish line, the film concludes with the disappearance of the field of action as the approaching spectators obscure it from view.

Another remarkable structural use of space occurs in *Scieurs de bois* as an operational process is presented in an unusual way. This process is the cutting of wood. Three woodcutters appear in the center of the frame as they work at the edge of a city street. They are arranged in depth. At the center, furthest from the camera, stands a man sawing a log braced on a saw horse. (The log is parallel to the picture plane.) At the left of center, in front of him, stands a man who splits the lengths of sawed logs into kindling with an axe. At the right of center, closest to the camera, stands a man who gathers up the kindling and stacks it into a holder. As the film begins, the man in the back is sawing a log, the man at the left of center picks up a piece of wood to split, and the man at the right of center picks up some kindling to place in a holder. Interestingly, the holder for kindling is empty when the film begins. At the end of the film, the man in the background is in the midst of cutting a second section of log, the second man has split three pieces of wood into kindling, and the third man has filled the holder more than a third full with kindling.

The orderly arrangement of this process in depth is matched by the decisive choice of having the holder for kindling empty as the film begins. Thus the steps of the process are completed for the first time as the man places an armful of kindling into the holder. The process is allowed to repeat, assuring a certain legibility to the steps involved while also permitting them to appear natural, rather than arranged. To suggest that the action depicted in this film, or the others described, is either naive or an unmediated record of reality as it happened to occur before the camera ignores the conscious arrangement of the beginning and ends of the action to coincide with the physical beginning and end points of the film and fails to recognize the expressive use of space to both clarify the action presented and to focus the viewer's attention on three interdependent actions simultaneously taking place.

A large number of the Lumière films included in these two collections reflect variations of the structural organization described above. Each presents a process, largely described by the film's title, presented in such a way that the beginning of the film coincides with the beginning of the process. None actually begin in the middle of an action. In some instances, the event depicted offers a natural beginning to be captured at the start of the film; at other times, the event seems to have been arranged in such a way that a sense of a beginning is imparted to the material.

The great number of military subjects included in the Lumière catalogue clearly show demarcated beginnings and endings. The orderly execution of military drills, as illustrated by *Artillerie de montagne: mise en batterie et feu*, offered inherent beginning and end points. In some cases, consecutive films were made of the stages of a military maneuver. Thus the Lumière catalogue offered four films (catalogue numbers 182–185) presenting a group of French Cuirassiers in action. The catalogue listing reproduced by Sadoul for these films is incomplete, lacking the title for the third film of the series. For this reason, the English titles for these films, as they appear in the Maguire and Baucus listing, serve better as illustration:

1182. Cuirassiers, Mounting.

1183. Cuirassiers, Wheeling into Line.

1184. Cuirassiers, Charging.

1185. Cuirassiers, Skirmishing.

The above four scenes are the best military subjects ever photographed, the cavalry charge in particular being remarkably exciting. It shows a complete squadron of regular cavalry approaching the camera at full gallop and coming to a sudden halt immediately in the foreground.[6]

The film singled out for comment in the Maguire and Baucus description ("France: Cuirassiers—Melee") typifies the way in which the beginning of an action coincides with the beginning of the film. The film begins with a very long shot across an open plain. Far in the distance, one can see a line of cavalry begin to charge toward the camera with their sabers drawn. When the line of cavalry reaches the camera, however, a curious situation develops. Despite the clear beginning offered by the start of their charge, their arrival at the camera does not provide the conclusion. Their charge over, the soldiers seem uncertain what to do and begin to mill about, individually lowering their sabers after having held them indecisively aloft for an unusually long time.

The difficulty of providing a conclusive ending for this film recurs in a number of films equally remarkable for their clear announcement of a beginning. The *Bains de Diane* ("Swimming Baths at Milan"), for example, begins with a flourish of simultaneous dives into the pool of the swimming club. In addition, the film presents a variety of dives. Two of the first divers begin from handstands. Two later divers perform swan dives. They are followed by a man who performs a twist. Then a man springs from one diving board to another before entering the water. A few more dives fill out the film, but are not performed in any special fashion or order. Thus despite the clearly announced beginning of the film, and the varied dives which serve as the content for the middle section of the film, the

---

[6]*Fall Catalogue, 1897* (New York: Baucus and Maguire, 1897), p. 4. As the American sales agents for Lumière films, Baucus and Maguire retained the Lumière catalogue numbers for the films after a fashion. As these entries indicate, Baucus and Maguire added 1,000 to the original catalogue number.

film ends without a conclusive action. (The action of people diving in to swim also marks the beginning of *Baignade de nègres* ["Baignade de Négrillons"]. Here as well, despite the emphatic action which announces the beginning of the film, the film ends without a clearly conclusive action.)

Both the famous *Arrivée d'un train en gare de Villefranche-sur-Saône* ("*Arrival of Express at Lyons*") and *Repas de bébé* ("Feeding the Baby") reflect a similar structural pattern of clearly announced beginnings without conclusive endings. The *Arrivée d'un train* begins with a view down the station's platform. The platform is filled with waiting people, and the train's engine is just visible in the distance behind them. The train pulls into the station, slowing until the eleventh car stops at the left edge of the frame. The waiting people move toward the coaches and their doors are opened. The passengers begin to alight. Though the film signals its beginnings, literally with the arrival of the train, and offers a process (the meeting of passengers, the passengers alighting from the coaches), the film lacks a defined conclusion.

Repas de bébé similarly lacks a clear conclusion. It begins with all in readiness for the baby's meal, with the infant already seated at the table, flanked by her parents. Though it is more difficult to detect a signal for the film's beginning, the ancillary action of the mother seems to announce it. As the father begins to offer the baby a spoonful of food, the mother begins to prepare a cup of tea for herself. As he feeds the baby, she places one lump of sugar in her cup, pours the tea and stirs it. Just as she begins to stir the tea, the father offers the infant a fresh cookie. The child takes the cookie, is about to bite into it, but suddenly offers it instead to someone off camera as the film ends.

Whether the offering of the cookie to the child was meant to signal the end of the baby's meal, and by extension an end to the film, is difficult to determine. The presentation of the feeding of a baby as a process offers none of the natural beginning and end points inherent in military maneuvers. A comparison of this film, however, with another marked by an inconclusive ending may offer some insight into its design.

Barque sortant du port apparently offers an equally minimal subject—a view of a four-oared boat as it is rowed around a jetty and into open water. Though the progress of the boat does not seem to involve a necessary conclusion, it may well be that such a conclusion was to have been signalled by the film's ancillary action. For while two men row the boat toward open water (as a third man sits in its stern), their progress is watched by two women and two small children from the jetty in the background.

As the boat makes a turn to skirt the jetty, the women point to the boat. When it passes the jetty, one of the women waves at it. Once the boat is past the jetty and in open water, the women turn toward the camera, taking their eyes from the boat. They then appear to ready the children to leave the jetty. In fact, one woman and one child move so far back toward land that they are barely visible at the edge of the frame. It would appear from this much of the film that its conclusion might be signaled by the return of these spectators from the jetty to the shore. This action, at least, would announce that there no longer was anything of import to watch. The film does not offer this as a conclusion, however, since a heavy wave suddenly throws the boat back closer to the jetty and the spectators become motionless.

There is no way to ascertain whether the spectators' departure was preplanned as a conclusive ending for *Barque sortant du port* and rendered impossible by the accidental wave. (As unexpected perhaps as the infant's offer of her cookie to someone off-screen.) However in light of the use made of ancillary figures in *Course en sacs,* and the preparation of the cup of tea which parallels the feeding of the infant in *Repas de bébé,* it remains possible that their departure was such a conscious attempt to organize the whole of the film's action. A closer examination of two obviously fictive Lumière films may offer more insight into the planning many of the films seem to have received.

Often cited as both the first film to tell a story and the first film comedy, *Arroseur et arrosé* depicts all of the structural features previously described. The film begins with the presentation of a gardener watering plants. He occupies the left third of the screen and faces the screen's left edge. As he directs the water toward the left side of the screen, a young boy enters the frame from the right edge. He sneaks quietly toward the gardener and pauses as he reaches a point about one-third of the way in from the right edge. The boy crimps the gardener's hose by stepping on it. The gardener wonders what has happened and, in puzzlement, turns the nozzle of the hose towards his face in order to examine it. Now the boy takes his foot from the hose and the ensuing blast of water hits the gardener full in the face, knocking his hat from his head. The boy tries to run away by moving behind the gardener in the direction of the left side of the screen. The gardener notices him, however, pursues him and catches him just as they pass from view at the left edge of the frame. The frame remains empty for a moment until the gardener drags the boy into view by his ear. He moves with the boy until they both occupy the space at the left of the screen's center. The gardener brings the boy closer to the camera and turns him around so the spanking he gives the boy is clearly visible to the viewer. He lets the boy go after the brief spanking and picks up his hose again. The gardener then assumes the posture and position he occupied at the beginning of the film. The boy quickly exits the frame at the right side, where he originally entered, and the film concludes as it began, with the gardener facing the left edge of the frame, standing about one-third of the way in from that edge, watering the plants.

Several aspects of the film's structure are especially noteworthy. Most notable, of course, is that the event depicted is not discovered but created, not recorded but acted, the whole a unified design. The establishment of the left side of the frame as the domain of the gardener and the right side of the frame as the space for the boy underscores the film's essentially symmetrical presentation. As in *Sortie d'usine,* the film offers a process (the trick played upon the gardener and the boy's punishment for it) within a special demarcative framework. The film begins with an assertion: the gardener is occupied with a task. This is offered as the norm which the boy's prank violates. The return to this norm after the boy's spanking is signaled by the gardener's return to the same task, performed with the same posture, with which he was introduced. The return to this condition· validates the initial assertion and provides the film's conclusive moment. Once again, the first and last images of the film are virtually identical, and a linear action has been presented within a circular framework as a single periodic event.

Another less well known Lumière film of the period, *Partie d'écarté* ("Friendly Party in the Garden of Lumière") similarly presents a linear action within a circular framework. Three men are seated at a table. The two seated across from one another at the left and right sides of the frame are just beginning a game of cards. The third man, seated between them and facing the camera, occupies the center of the frame and watches their play. The man at the left places a coin at the front edge of the table; the man at the right follows suit, placing a coin of his own beside the other's. The man at the right sets down a deck of cards for the other to cut. The man on the right wins the cut and begins to deal. The man in the center, who rapped on the table for a waiter at the same time as the man on the right placed his coin on the table, now sends the waiter off with an order. As the man at the right begins to deal, the man at the left lights a cigar. As the dealer finishes distributing the cards, the waiter returns and leaves three glasses and a bottle of beer with the man in the center.

As the two players begin their card game, the third man begins to pour three glasses of beer. The waiter stands near him to kibbitz. The man finishes filling the beer glasses at the same moment that the man at the left wins the card game and begins to pick up the coins. The three men lift their beer glasses, clinking them together in a toast over the center of the table, and drink. The two players return their glasses to the tray and the man at the left again places a coin at the front edge of the table. As he picks up the cards, the man at the right appears to search through a handful of change for a coin to match the one placed on the table as the new wager.

Once again, the beginning and end points of the film are clearly marked to coincide with a feature of the action depicted. The placing of the first coin at the front edge of the table marks both the beginning of the film and the beginning of the card game. Nevertheless, as an announcement of the beginning of the film, this action remains only an assertion until it recurs at the film's end. At this point, it becomes conclusive, thereby validating the earlier, not because it is a direct sign of the game's conclusion (i.e., an action which inherently marks the end of a card game), but because it signals the beginning of another game. All the while a single card game is the subject of the film, the intricate patterns of simultaneous action and the attendant kibbitzing which amounts to almost a subplot reveal the high degree of organization imparted to the material. The fact that the film is experientially structured around the repeated gesture of the man at the left as he places a coin on the table emphasizes the artistry of the film's achievement. A new game begins as the film ends, but the new game serves to establish the completeness of the earlier one and, by extension, the completeness of what has been offered to view.

As these descriptions of the brief Lumière films illustrate, there is little reason to continue to regard them as naive photographic renderings of natural events which happened to occur before the camera. Even the slightest of the slight events discussed here reveals an attempt to impart a shape to the action depicted. In some cases, the structure was already inherent in the sequential process chosen to be photographed. In others, however, obvious care was taken to mark the beginning of the action depicted in a way that would announce that the first image which appeared on the screen was the initial step, or primary moment, for what was to follow. While the films are largely successful in this aim, as well as in the development of their central sections, some of the Lumière films lack decisive conclusions to announce the completeness of their actions. As I have already suggested in relation to *Barque sortant du port* and *Repas de bébé*, there may have been aleatory reasons for this lack in some cases.

Despite these occasional shortcomings, the sheer structural sophistication of the most complex of these films deserves greater recognition. The use of ancillary actions to signal the beginning and end of a central action and, thereby, create a strong sense of closure for an entire film remains a striking achievement. Similarly, the location of a linear action within a framework that imparts a sense of wholeness to a film by making it seem to be a single example of a periodic event reveals a subtlety of construction one usually associates with later, edited films. Together with these structural traits, the expressive use of space and simultaneity of action to be seen in several of these films strongly argue that it is time to reconsider our evaluation of these films' artistic achievement.

ANDRÉ GAUDREAULT

Temporality and Narrativity in Early Cinema, 1895–1908

But virtually the most important and most significant fact from this point of view is the assumption of an increasingly greater role in the twentieth century by the temporal art for which time is almost the fundamental (and sole) structural principle—the cinema. —Vjaceslav V. Ivanov

Moving pictures tell stories so effectively that they seem always to have told stories, but studying films of the early century permits us, partially at least, to discover how movie narrativity developed. Obviously cinema organizes narrative in various ways; Jancso or Resnais do not operate like Hitchcock or Lelouch, nor do they say the same things. Some filmmakers more or less consciously follow a narrative pattern inherited from long tradition. Others use their talents to subvert the same tradition. Basically, they all draw on similar raw material: shots, sequences, camera movements, characters, dialogue, etc. The differences rest in the assemblage of these ingredients. When one subverts narrative patterns, he necessarily recognizes their existence. Where did the patterns originate?[1]

Despite its promise, film theory is thus far too young to provide ultimate answers to such a consequential question. Partial explanations exist, but much remains to be done. Within this field, besides the very necessary work of rendering early titles, dates, and credits more accurately, a growing number of

---

Translated from the French by John L. Fell.

[1] Lately, we have discussed some of our thesis with David Levy, a colleague from Montreal with whom we are preparing a book on Edwin S. Porter's work. These discussions have been very useful in the development of positions in the following paper.

scholars has undertaken the reconsideration of theses advanced by earlier generations. Many of these previous assertions have served like screens to cloud our consciousness of what actually happened, obscuring how filmmakers really developed the mainstream narrative patterns we know today.[2]

For these reasons, a careful scrutiny of film narrative origins is vital. The following paper seeks a better understanding of how early filmmakers expressed time.

CINEMA AND NARRATIVITY

Despite the usual representation of our earliest films as nonnarrative productions, it is proposed here that narrative has been present since film's inception. The first films (1895–1910) evidenced formal elements of the type found in medieval literature, already constituting a narrative pattern by presenting various expressive materials organized to tell a story.[3] No one would contest the fact that *La Chanson de Roland* is an effective narrative; of course the quality and character of early film narrativity varies. Some films are certainly *not* narrative; however our purpose is not to contrast what is narrative and what is not, but rather to compare two narrative forms which do not deny one another, even though the later one became institutionalized at some point. The earlier pattern developed from what Tom Gunning has called "noncontinuous style," but it is erroneous to consider its qualities as exclusively constituting the ground from which the continuous style evolved.[4]

What characteristics embody mainstream or "institutionalized" narrative form? The question cannot be completely answered for the moment. French scholars speak of transparent cinema (André Bazin), narrative-representative cinema (Christian Metz, Dominique Noguez), continuous narrative style, and linear cinema. Each expression partially accounts for characteristics of narrative form that transform the screen into a transparent frame, providing its audience with a seemingly unmitigated access to reality. A characteristic of the form is its capacity to reproduce subject matter within a pattern of logic consistent with the

---

[2]Noël Burch himself discusses the "Institutional Mode of Representation," which he defines as follows: "Set of (written or unwritten) directives which has been historically interiorized by directors and technicians as the irreducible base of 'film language' within the Institution and which has remained a constant over the past fifty years, independent of the vast stylistic changes which have taken place." Burch, *Correction Please*, leaflet to accompany the film with the same name, directed by Burch in 1978–79, p. 3.

[3]As precisely established by Tom Gunning, "Le Style non-continu du cinéma des premiers temps," *Les Cahiers de la cinémathèque* 29 (Winter 1979):24–34, and Charles Musser, "The Early Cinema of Edwin Porter," *Cinema Journal* 19 (Fall 1979):1–38. This paper returns to the subject at a later stage.

[4]Gunning, "Le Style non-continu," pp. 24–34.

logic of the world it records, excluding whatever elements might serve to break the narrative flow. The exposition frequently proceeds from a linear pattern which arranges the basic elements in a chain of indispensable, intentional links, all operating to further the plot.

Such a narrative form began to develop around 1910, although accurate dating is perilous. A film like David Wark Griffith's *The Musketeers of Pig Alley* (Biograph, 1912) is particularly interesting in this regard.[5] The thoughtful viewer will discern a system atypical either of much contemporary film or of earlier titles. Its fluidity of narrative contrasts with the greater rigidity of the previous period.

To our mind, the degree of narrative fluidity is an essential factor, since this characteristic will prove basic to the narrative form of the ensuing decade. In fact, the valorization of such fluidity serves as a necessary condition for the development of an independent cinematic narrative.

One notices the absence of such flow in the very early films, although in the case of Louis Lumière's work, such an issue is disguised in that each film is a one-shot production.[6] Thus, *L'Arroseur arrosé* (Lumière, 1895) avoids almost every problem of narrative fluidity by staging all its action within a relatively short but continuous camera run. A mischievous boy puts his foot on a gardener's water hose. Puzzled by the stoppage, the gardener imprudently looks into the nozzle. The boy removes his foot and the "waterer" is watered. The gardener pursues the boy, who runs beyond screen frame; the gardener returns him to our view and beats him. All the action unfolds in less than a minute, and problems of narrativity are avoided both because the conceptual model, the narrative anecdote, is so simply contained and because there is only a single shot. (We say "both" because obviously a one-shot film can pose narrative problems. Consider *Gare du Nord* [Jean Rouch, 1964], which, apart from an introductory shot and a concluding one [together less than a minute], is constituted by only one shot[7] lasting at least fifteen minutes.)[8] *L'Arroseur arrosé* is not amenable to potential narrative

---

[5] 1895–1915 film titles are followed by the production company and year of production or copyright in parentheses. For more recent films, the director's name replaces the production company.

[6] Georges Sadoul suggests that the Lumières probably joined four single-shot films on the same subject, a fire exercise. These films would be *Sortie de la pompe, Mise en batterie, Attaque du feu,* and *Sauvetage.* Obviously the Lumière brothers or their employees began at some point to join their films and soon afterward probably produced multi-shot titles. In support of our position, we refer only to the first of the Lumière productions (1895–97), those which initially marked the cinema as an institution.

[7] It is tempting to consider this a one-shot sequence. However, the sequence considered is made up of more than one shot since the introductory shot is necessarily a part of it.

[8] We should note further that this very long shot (probably unique) is undoubtedly made up of two segments. We suspect that Rouch takes advantage of the blackened image in the elevator to join the segments, effacing the edit mark on the sound track. This is done to compensate for limits of the camera's film capacity.

manipulations because of its brevity and because of the isomorphism existing between the film's time-space ordering and the time-space reality it documents. In other words, the simplicity of the film comes from the camera's isolating such a singular, continuous moment fυr its privileged audience. Inventors of the motion picture camera created first the shot, in its time the alpha and omega of film expression, and instituted the era of the one-shot film. Such homogeneity of cinematographic representation was insured by a linear structure operating in terms of an enclosure that permitted no exceptions. As one prepared for shooting, the minimal action-segments were scheduled to appear in a continuous visual field (however their framing might shift) and in a continuous time sequence. The double mobility which characterizes film narrative—mobility of objects depicted and motility of time-space segmentation—had yet to materialize completely. All that was known was the mobility of objects depicted in the frame, a mobility made possible by the new invention which could seize, fix, and reproduce movements of beings and of things. This was the era of what we can term, in the manner of Roman Gubern, "articulation from frame to frame."[9] Scheduled for imminent appearance was the mobility of time-space segmentation: "articulation from shot to shot," the gathering of shots into a sequence.

TEMPORAL OVERLAP

Within such a one-shot system, there is no danger of unmatched cuts or temporal overlap, that is, the repetition of part of an action that concluded the previous shot. A condition for discontinuity is shot multiplicity, since juxtaposing shots from different angles necessarily poses this potential problem by introducing at least two vectors: space and time.

Two successive shots have the capacity to evidence either two separate points of view toward a single space or two distinct spaces.[10] In both cases, the conjunction of shots A and B may describe any one of four time-based narrative alternatives:

1. The time of shot B precedes the time of shot A, that is, a flashback;
2. The final moments concluding shot A are simultaneous with those beginning shot B, that is, a temporal overlap;

---

[9]Roman Gubern, "D. W. Griffith et l'articulation cinématographique," *Les Cahiers de la cinémathèque* 17 (December 1975): 8. Obviously, the word "articulation" carries denotations different from those in linguistics.

[10]To support our demonstration, we will schematize. For a fuller elaboration of spatio-temporal relationships between shots, see Noël Burch, *Theory of Film Practice* (New York: Praeger, 1973), pp. 3–16.

3. The time concluding shot A is rigorously continued into shot B, that is, a matched cut;[11]
4. While immediately successive to the narrative continuity of shot A, the action, in shot B, is temporally discontinuous, that is, an ellipsis.[12] (See the accompanying diagram.)

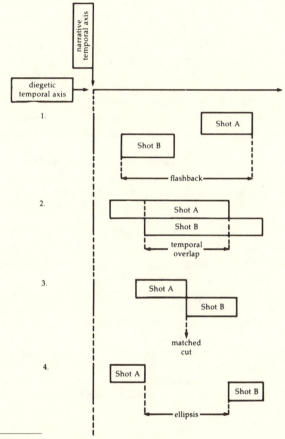

---

[11]In order to provide an impression of rigorous continuity the editor sometimes makes a minimal action overlap (a few images only) or a short ellipsis. Such cuts are made to give the audience an illusion of continuity. For this reason, we include them in our third category.

[12]Francois Baby uses another term, *anamorphosis*, to characterize such a cut, "which (forces) the spectator himself to reconstitute a number of missing elements between two segments." See Baby, "Jacques Godbout rencontre IXE-13 ou du texte au film; quelles transformations?" *Études littéraires* (August 1979), p. 289.

Temporal overlap, when it is used to describe a single, continuous action, may disrupt an audience's sense of that continuity because of the repetition. The repeating action is felt as a kind of jump, obscuring the temporal fluidity. Except for rare occasions, time characteristically presses forward in cinema; even in flashback, time is felt as a *present*. The temporal overlap is perhaps an exception; by repeating some previous action, time seems to be contradicted.[13]

The "technique" of temporal overlap as investigated here disappeared from the screen for many years, returning only with different intentions on the part of Eisenstein, Resnais, and others.[14] Early films under our present consideration use temporal overlaps in an effort to resolve problems of spatial contiguity. As we will see, filmmakers in most cases have repeated action through editing so as to implicate characters displaced between two adjoining spaces, most often spaces separated by a wall. It is as if Griffith's subsequent ubiquitous camera had yet to realize its powers. The camera did not know how to "go through" walls. The narrator, the storyteller, lacked omniscience, perhaps because he had not sufficiently developed a consciousness of his craft, an hypothesis we will examine later.

Although important films containing obvious examples of temporal overlap are often cited in movie histories, this convention has not been the object of close attention. Porter's *Life of an American Fireman* (Edison, 1903) provides a good example, although in this case the phenomenon was obscured by the existence of one version that literally erased the film's principal example of temporal overlap. However, even that version, which appears to us to be inconsistent with the original one, includes at least two other examples that have always been passed over in silence, probably because they are less apparent.[15] It is interesting that of the two possible versions of *Life of an American Fireman*, the one containing editing more compatible with "continuous style," has most often been used. Today that version seems the inauthentic one.

For the sake of clarification, here is a description of the editing of *Life of an American Fireman*. In that film, Porter shows us *from the interior* of a burning house a courageous fireman who unhesitatingly risks his life to perform a rescue.

A woman and her child, overwhelmed by smoke, fall inert onto a bed. A fireman enters the room by breaking the door. He goes to the window and calls for a ladder, throws the woman over his shoulder, and exits by the window. After

---

[13]Here we refer only to short flashbacks. The longer, more important flashback appears more justified and does not suggest impatience, probably, among other reasons, because it serves to explain unfolding action.

[14]Although it is correct to speak of "technique" in some cases, we must remember that many such practices did not have as an explicit goal what we now call temporal overlap.

[15]The reader is referred to Gaudreault, "Detours in Film Narrative: The Development of Cross-Cutting," *Cinema Journal* 19 (Fall 1979):39–59.

a moment the fireman reappears at the window, enters, takes the child, and again climbs out. Finally, two other firemen enter through the window and hose the flames. The shot concludes with a cut (not a fade-out) to black.

Had Porter's film ended here, the spectator would have been deprived of its "climax": on reaching ground, the woman implores the fireman to rescue her child still trapped in the room. Perhaps Porter added the last shot with the intention of showing us the mother's request. This shot runs more or less as long as what has just been described and permits us to witness, once again, *the same action*, this time from the exterior of the building, probably from an onlooker's point of view. Our systemic analysis of the film convinces us that the simple copresence of two different points of view toward one single event justifies their successive presentation, which produces a repetition of the action and finally a temporal overlap that today can only astonish.

In other words, the film's last shot again depicts, this time from another point of view, the action previously seen, yet in an original and incongruous fashion. An overlap of that length is rare among films of the time. Most examples with which we are familiar rather follow the pattern of two other instances in *Life of an American Fireman*. In shot 3 Porter shows us the firemen who, on hearing the alarm, jump from their beds and descend the pole leading to the ground floor; we see each fireman disappear. Shot 4 then reverts slightly; in succession each fireman appears on the ground floor, emerging from the ceiling hole. It is "unlikely" that at the moment when the last fireman is sliding down (end of shot 3) no other fireman has finished his descent (beginning of shot 4), one story lower.

Shots 4 and 5 give us another example of temporal overlap; shot 4 ends when the fire trucks have already exited (toward the camera, which is probably situated near the firehouse doors), and shot 5 begins on an exterior view of the firehouse with the doors still closed. The men then open the door and trucks emerge "one more" time. What we judge significant is that the above-noted overlap and the one constituting the film's final two shots differ in terms of structural intention.

With respect to the earlier two examples, one can conjecture how a more continuous link between the two shots might have been accomplished. The simplest solution would have been to truncate the end of the initial shot (example: at shot 3, one could cut at the moment the fifth fireman disappears through the hole in the floor). Shot 4's beginning might be shortened so that the same fireman is first to descend the pole. At least, such a technique would follow customary practice today. In the case of shots 8 and 9, the solution would have differed. The temporal importance of the overlap works against continuity matching as an ideal answer, since this would deprive the audience of seeing, from interior, the rescue of the mother (beginning of shot 9).

In any case, the preceding action was assumed by the author of the Edison catalogue description, which does not take into account overlapping action.

Alternatively, the ideal solution seems to be the one chosen by the anonymous reeditor of the film from whom we have inherited today's nonauthentic version conserved by the Museum of Modern Art in New York. Here the camera successively passes from interior to exterior (and back again) throughout the unfolding of the drama described by shots 8 and 9. From these two shots, our "anonymous editor" creates a new arrangement composed of thirteen segments.[16] So as to avoid the two elements of action overlapping unreasonably, he has however adopted our initial solution (rejecting parts of shots) when matching several moments (not all, since the editing of the last shots preserves a few examples of slight overlaps, just as between shots 3 and 4). In other words, to the solutions of continuity and fluidity the later editor has added a solution of parallel editing, although it should be emphasized that the parallel editing solution is untypical of the period. Usually parallel editing is unnecessary to the narrative system of Porter and his contemporaries; its utility waits on "continuity filmmakers" to follow, Griffith particularly.

EXAMPLES

Temporal overlap in *Life of an American Fireman* is well known, but there are many other exemplary cases. Although narrative structure in Méliès's films creates very few situations likely to produce action overlaps, his work is not exempt. His films rarely match two shots or present the crossing of contiguous spaces by a character. Méliès is even less likely to match two different points of view on a single action, but *Le Voyage dans la lune* (Star Film, 1902) and *Le Voyage à travers l'impossible* (Star Film, 1904) nevertheless present both phenomena. In the 1902 film, one shot shows the rocket heading through space (the sky) and landing in the eye of the anthropomorphic moon; the next shot locates us on the moon's surface where we again witness the arrival of the rocket. In *Le Voyage à travers l'impossible* the travelers' car crashes into the wall of an inn, breaks it, and enters the building. The next shot shows the interior of the inn before the accident. Customers are at a table; the wall is intact. After a few seconds, the car breaks in and passes through the room, smashing everything.

Two other films produced in 1907 by Star Film involve examples of repeated action editing: *La Douche d'eau bouillante* and *Le Mariage de Victorine*.[17] The action of the latter title takes place both outside and inside a house of which only two rooms are visible, kitchen and dining areas. They seem to be contiguous. The

---

[16]So far no one knows when and why this reediting was done. It seems unlikely to have taken place before 1910.

[17]"Star Film" is more appropriate than "Méliès" since it appears that these two films were directed by a Méliès employee. See John Frazer, *Artificially Arranged Scenes: The Films of Georges Méliès* (Boston: G. K. Hall, 1979), pp. 178–81.

hosts wait impatiently for their meal, which must be served by Victorine, the maid; she is busy with her lover in the kitchen. This situation causes a few crosses of the characters from one room to another, and there is a temporal overlap, but the obvious disorder of the shots in the copy we have viewed (an American Film Institute/Library of Congress print) doesn't allow us to study it more thoroughly. Nevertheless it is interesting that, contrary to general opinion, Star Film seems to have reached a stage competitive with other companies of the time. Indeed, *Le Mariage de Victorine* poses some elements, otherwise absent among previous Star Films, that are consistent parts of the cinematographic "conventions" of the time: exterior locations (the lover rushes outside), close-up as concluding shot (in the AFI version this shot is not final, but the characters' gestures show it is so intended), mobility of the camera between shots, etc.[18] *La Douche d'eau bouillante* also provides examples of repeated action editing. Two robbers hear the host approaching and escape through a door at screen right. The host appears and also exits through the door. A next shot shows the adjacent room. The field is empty, and the two robbers enter and hide, after which the host enters. The same strategem is repeated, but inversely, when all characters return to the first room.

Several other films of the period present similar cases of repeated action editing.

How They Do Things on the Bowery (Edison, 1902)   At a restaurant, a man is turned out by the waiter, who seizes him by the collar and impels him out of the visual field. The waiter takes the suitcase and throws it to him. The last action is taken from inside the restaurant. Then from exterior the waiter throws the man out and ejects the suitcase a "second" time.

A Discordant Note (Edison, 1903)   The first shot shows a character singing out-of-tune at a reception. Guests become enraged, grasp him, and throw him against the background designed as a wall; we see him breaking through the paper flat's surface. The next shot takes us to the building exterior; the wall is momentarily whole, again the victim breaks through it, and now he falls to the street.

The Widow and the Only Man (Biograph, 1904)   Clearly flattered, a woman accepts a suitor's bouquet gift. A close-up shows her inhaling the flowers' scent, but the woman's gestures fail visually to match from shot to shot; rather, they repeat themselves.

The Strenuous Life, or Anti-Race Suicide (Edison, 1904)   A father holds his newborn child, places him on a scale, and mimes his happiness. The next shot, maintaining an identical visual axis, provides a close shot in which the same gestures are repeated.

---

[18]Moreover, it is possible that the original version of that film might have contained a kind of parallel editing.

The Firebug (Biograph, 1905)   In the basement of a family house, a pyromaniac ignites a blaze. Hearing noise, the daughter goes downstairs to investigate. The pyromaniac kidnaps her and flees through a window. A servant sees the firebug fleeing with his captive and pursues the pair through the window. At that moment, the father arrives and undertakes putting out the fire. His wife enters and collapses, as does the maid. The husband carries his wife to the first floor. A following exterior shot shows smoke escaping through the basement window. Then the pyromaniac exits through the window a "second" time, fleeing with his hostage and followed by the servant. As the shot continues, we see the father carrying his wife from inside the house to the veranda and reviving her. The father reenters, secures a gun, and then joins the pursuit.

The Tunnel Workers (Biograph, 1906)   In the anteroom of an excavation site we see a heavy door in the background. As the manager passes through this door, a worker gestures his rage in an aside to the camera. (The manager has recently been discovered philandering with the worker's wife.) The worker then exits through the same door. The next shot is a "reverse angle" from within the excavation, and we see the manager, followed by the worker, pass through the door a "second" time.

TEMPORAL OVERLAP AND REPETITION OF THE ACTION

With the help of these examples and what is presently known of early cinema, it is possible to distinguish three types of situations that facilitate any sort of temporal overlap. Only the first two examples implicate action-repetition, since the third one, we shall see, articulates two disjointed, although simultaneous, actions.

1. **The spatial analysis of a single shot**   When matching a long shot and a closer view of one single action, partial or full repetition of the movements may occur (*The Widow and the Only Man; The Strenuous Life*).

2. **Crossing two contiguous spaces**   When matching two shots with different fields representing two contiguous rooms or spaces, there may be partial or entire repetition of the action. This may happen either through character movement (*A Discordant Note*) or by way of a shift in point of view independent of character movement (*Life of an American Fireman*).

3. **The relationship between two simultaneous actions**   When matching two shots showing two simultaneous actions occurring in noncontiguous spaces, there may be a temporal overlap without repetition of the action. Action A occurs in one space at the same moment that action B takes place elsewhere. For instance, following our analysis of *The Great Train Robbery*, the line of

action presenting the robbery and the robbers' flight takes place apparently simultaneously with the release of the telegrapher and the saloon scene, despite the successive presentation of these two lines of action. On a more limited scale, the film instances another temporal overlap without repetition of action. Shot 3 (the robbery of the mail car) and shot 4 (the struggle on the locomotive) take place simultaneously but are shown successively. (The Edison catalogue specifies this.)

The first two situations alone instance repetition of the action, since only a single action is recorded in these cases. In order to obviate repeated action in these circumstances one would have to operate from a greater consciousness regarding manipulations possible through editing. Later film history provides only rare exceptions to the usual elimination of action overlap, for instance the Odessa Steps sequence (*The Battleship Potemkin*, Eisenstein, 1925) which repeats actions through editing. It is obvious that the descent of two hundred palace steps by the fleeing townspeople would have lasted a far shorter time. However, through editing, the sequence singles out identifiable, individual tragedies (e.g., the woman with the baby carriage) through repeated actions. Other examples include *Persona* (Bergman, 1966), which is somewhat peculiar. Alma's mono- logue is presented twice, consecutively. First the camera shows Elizabeth's reactions alone; the second time we see only Alma. It is somewhat as if Bergman shot the material direct and then in reverse angle, choosing to present each point of view successively instead of alternating one with the other. In its own fashion, this film recalls the ending of *Life of an American Fireman*.[19]

Returning to our earlier examples, it may be remarked that characteristics of *The Firebug* warrant closer attention. Action repetition is caused by factors other than the single temporal overlap; in its unfolding of events, the film presents a particular sort of inconsistency. At the moment we see the action from outside, the time lapse between the servant's exit through the window and the father's exit on the balcony (five seconds) is incongruent with the time of the same action-segment as shown by the preceding shot: the time running from the servant's exit to the moment when the father has climbed the stairway from basement to first floor (fifty-five seconds), quantitatively a time discrepancy of one to eleven. To put it another way, judging by the logic of the exterior shot, there is insufficient time between the servant's window exit and the father's by way of the front door for the father to have undertaken to extinguish the flames, for the maid and wife to have arrived and fainted, and for the father to have climbed the stairway with his wife in his arms as we witnessed in the preceding shot. We might say there has been a kind of ellipsis during the second shot,

---

[19]We will avoid the precedent of Robert Gessner, who saw in the Porter film "a prefigura- tion of *Last Year at Marienbad*" (Resnais, 1961) in "Porter and the Creation of Cinematic Motion," *Journal of the Society of Cinematologists* 2 (1962).

between the exit of the servant and the exit of the father, except that—and this is important to the argument—there has been no shot change to justify such an ellipsis.

In passing we may note that *Life of an American Fireman* presents similar "incongruities." In shot 8, taken from interior, the fireman takes the woman out of the room by the window, disappears down the ladder, and returns in a few moments to save the child. In shot 9, which shows the same action in exterior, we see the fireman descend the ladder with the woman. She regains consciousness and supplicates the fireman to return to the room and save her child. Seen in shot 9, all this action obviously has insufficient time to unfold during the short lapse when the fireman has disappeared from the window in shot 8. The two films' examples demonstrate that early ellipses in cinema were sometimes produced through the manipulation of the unfolding action rather than by the manipulation of the images by editing. By our measure, this is one of the peculiar and unique aspects of early film.

Charles Musser has analyzed the relationship between shots 8 and 9 of *Life of an American Fireman* as follows:

> While, on one level, these two shots create a temporal repetition, on another level each has its own distinct and complementary temporality which taken together forms the whole. When the interior is shown everything that happens takes place in "real" time, while everything that takes place outside is extremely condensed. The reverse is true when the rescue is shown from the exterior. In keeping with theatrical conventions, whenever action takes place off screen, time is severely condensed.[20]

Amplified by analysis of *The Firebug* and other films, Musser's observation leads us to conclude that, in a general way, early filmmakers were more or less consciously considering each shot as an autonomous, self-reliant unit; the shot's objective is to present not a small *temporal* segment of the action but rather the totality of an action unfolding in an homogenous *space*. Between unity of point of view and unity of temporal continuity, the former takes precedent. Before releasing the camera to a subsequent space, everything occurring in the first location is necessarily shown. Spatial anchorage prevails over temporal logic. Stability, persistence, and uniqueness of point of view remain so important that they supersede anachronism.

For such reasons, we strongly support Noël Burch's analysis of the same phenomenon in *Life of an American Fireman*:

---

[20]Musser, "Early Cinema of Porter," pp. 32–33.

However, the fact that once these two shots were filmed, it was decided to connect them in a manner implying an obvious non-linearity rather than disturb the unity of the spatial viewpoint, seems to me to say a good deal about the *alterity* of the relationship these early films entertained with the spectators who watched them. Does it not suggest that the feeling of being seated in a theatre in front of a screen had, for spectators then, a sort of priority over the feeling of being carried away by an imaginary time-flow, modelled on the semblance of linearity which *ordinary time* has for us?[21]

We may note one additional factor that probably worked against interlacing shots or, minimally, smooth matches: the two shots were executed in very different places, probably miles distant: exterior on location, interior in a studio. It is remarkable enough that two such remote spots are joined by editing. We ought not to be astonished by the filmmaker's reticence to do anything more. Further, the shots were not merely remote locations but two different diegetic spaces. To our mind, all these factors worked against intercutting the two units or a simple matching-action continuity that might have been accomplished by trimming either joined end.

In fact, one cannot say such continuities were unknown to the filmmaker of *The Firebug*, which presents a remarkable example between shots 7 and 8 of an extremely precise match, without overlap. At the moment the father struggles with the pyromaniac, an axial cut-in continues our view of the fight by moving from long to medium long shot. We may conjecture that it is from a gathering of various shots incorporating a *single* space (as in this case) that the conception of shot-autonomy begins to lose ground. By cuts and bridges between shots presenting a single and sole action under different angles, the filmmakers begin to regard the action unfolding on screen as equivalent to the continuous flow of the action depicted. Changing of angles provides the viewer with a better vantage on continuous, imperturbably proceeding action. It is the form of live television, where programs are recorded by various cameras that simultaneously cover an (actually continuous) action while a switcher, under a director's discretion, chooses whatever camera will be "on air" at any given moment. In a hockey game broadcast, for example, when we pass from a long shot showing one team advancing the puck to a full shot of one player shooting, there is no danger of disturbing the action.

In cinema such situations differ completely. After recording action in long shot, the director repeats it so as to record the same material in closer view, often with the identical camera—hence problems of matching position, time, speed, and so forth when assembling separate segments as if to simulate live television.

---

[21]Noël Burch, "Porter or Ambivalence," *Screen* 19 (Winter 1978–79): 104.

TEMPORALITY IN THE FOREGROUND

In cases of simultaneous actions occurring in two distinct locations (for instance, two spaces separated by a wall), the conception of an action's inexorable unfolding has, in 1907, yet to dominate the praxis of montage. Indeed, our examples (*La Douche d'eau bouillante, Le Mariage de Victorine*) are far from unique.[22] Produced or registered for copyright in 1907 with one exception the following films all present one or more examples of repeated action editing: *Teddy Bears* (Edison), *Hypnotist's Revenge* (Biograph), *If You Had a Wife Like This* (Biograph), *Lost in the Alps* (Edison), *La Course aux potirons* (Gaumont), and *Rescued from an Eagle's Nest* (Edison, January 1908). So long as insistency of time remains dormant, temporal discrepancy is permitted. We must wait a short while before questions of time are almost obsessively put forward by, among others, D. W. Griffith, who starts to direct in 1908. In most of Griffith's films, temporality assumes dramatic significance for its own sake. The "last minute rescue" becomes a major innovation that implicates the very logic of film narrative since it emphasizes the *time* (last *minute* rescue), and several other "inventions" attributed to Griffith proceed "naturally" from the last minute rescue.

The notion of rescue implies two groups of characters opposed to one another on the level of action: rescuer(s) and threatened person(s).[23] When the threatening agent is not a natural force or object, it becomes a third character function. Moreover, rescuer and victim, remote from one another in order to engender suspense through a last-*minute*, nick-of-*time* arrival, operate in simultaneous time. Under such circumstances, had a filmmaker not shown "genius" to "invent" or to hone parallel editing he might better have remained an actor. We do not wish to denigrate such directors as Griffith, but rather to reposition their work in the context that facilitated it. Parallel editing's infrequency during the chase film era (1903-1908) results largely from dominant story themes. A chase also implicates two action-motivated groups, but (in contrast to the last-minute rescue) its theme works on assumptions of proximity rather than distance: pursuer and pursued may be recorded *within a single shot*. By our reckoning, this is why in almost every chase film prior to 1908, we experience a series of shots in which, without variation, the pursued crosses the visual field and then *within the same shot* the pursuers appear chasing him. Filmmakers favored movement occurring in front of the camera over displacement of the camera between shots. All such films successively show various locations in which the chase occurs, each documenting the action just noted. In general each shot only concludes when

---

[22]See above (n. 18).

[23]It may be noted in passing that these two groups are somewhat like pursuers and pursued of the chase films that just had had their time in the sun (1903–8).

every pursuer (including the eventual laggard one) has exited from the frame.[24]

Viewing these films, we cannot help but wonder at such reticence toward moving the camera before the screen has been emptied of action.[25] Perhaps this disinclination figures in the organization of shots for a film such as *The Firebug*, which really reproduces the same pattern. Everything occurring in the basement of the house has to be shown before the camera moves to the next location. However the effect is not identical in both cases. In a chase film there is no temporal overlap since the camera shifts location with the events. In *The Firebug*, the camera points twice at the "same" space. Had there been no wall, one might see, from exterior, the father rushing down the stairway to the basement. Persistence toward refraining from cutting before everything has taken place within the shot (so as not to frustrate the audience?) has been brought to a point of absurdity. Thus, in *The Police Dogs* (its French title is unknown), produced by Pathé apparently in 1907, a chase begins between a pack of dogs and a group of robbers. The film consists of successive shots showing the robbers fleeing while the pursuing dogs cross the visual field in pursuit. Each shot has its own geographic characteristics: a fence to jump over, a slope to descend. The comic point is that one obstacle is rather hard to overcome and a last dog proves repeatedly unsuccessful in his efforts; in fact, it takes him two or three times to succeed. The dog's attempt is so immoderately time-consuming that one almost forgets the central chase, and the scene induces a comic effect while everything else is not in that mood at all. It is really impossible to be sure whether the filmmaker left this segment intact because of reticence at cutting in the middle of an action to which he chose not to return.

Two other period films present situations eminently favorable to cross-cutting. Their chases take place in automobiles, and at some point a substantial distance separates pursuers and pursued. In both cases situations complicate when the pursued automobile has a breakdown. The films are *The Elopement* (Biograph, 1907) and *Catching a Burglar* (Hepworth, 1908). Different from previous years' titles, these films sometimes show us shots in which only pursuer or pursued appears, for the other agent is too remote to share the camera's field.

---

[24]Films showing such a structure include *The Escaped Lunatic* (Biograph, 1903), *Personal* (Biograph, 1904), *The Lost Child* (Biograph, 1904), *The Maniac Chase* (Edison, 1904), *Stolen by Gypsies* (Edison 1905).

[25]The research referred to in n. 1 has suggested one possible explanation for that apparent reluctance. In a 1904 deposition, Edwin Porter declared that because it was the policy of the Edison studio to attempt to market those longer films in parts as well as in complete versions, he would turn out each of the separate scenes so that it contained what he described as "a fitting and attractive beginning and end." The idea was that each of the separate shots would be reasonably complete and not dependent for its appeal on its position in a sequence. For a more elaborate account of this phenomenon see David Levy, "Edison Sales Policy and the Continuous Action Film, 1904–1906," in part 2 of this book.

Yet there is no cross-cutting, even though a car breakdown would have fitted such a technique well. Difficulty in starting a car enjoins a suspenseful effect that might have been intensified by the simple act of inserting a single shot of the pursuers. Thus, in *The Elopement*, the camera remains fixed until the pursued decide to continue on their way first by walking then by canoe. One can easily see that the device of isolating one of the groups within a certain number of shots (rather than the "classical" chase, which always showed both the groups within each shot) is due more to the mechanization of transportation (because of the greater speeds) than to a different consciousness regarding possibilities of manipulation by editing or, simply, the *mise-en-scène*.

In counterpart, an insistence on temporality is a phenomenon which grows in importance during 1907. By the following year, many themes will emphasize story elements tied to temporality. A film for which Griffith, before directing, provided the script, *Old Isaacs the Pawnbroker*(Biograph, 1908), is particularly interesting. It is the story of a young girl who first visits a charity then a pawnbroker's shop seeking money to buy medicine for her poor, ill mother. The film is constructed in a parallel pattern; during the girl's searches, one inserted shot shows the gravely ill mother, thus emphasizing the emergency. It is easy to locate a kind of prototype for the last-minute rescue which Griffith soon develops in that pattern. Such insistence on "meanwhile" is really striking in its recurrence throughout Griffith's work, evident even before he began to direct.

In interior sets one also notices an increasing number of clocks that sometimes have roles to play. Thus, in *Lost in the Alps* (Edison, 1907), the mother worries about her tardy children, although the clock shows 6:05 (she pointedly looks at it, calling our attention to the time). *Later*, one cannot ignore the clock's indication of the *same time* when we return to the set. The fact that the clock is part of a painted flat insufficiently explains such discrepancy since a year later a film called *Father's Lesson* (Hepworth, 1908) similarly presents a clock that seems painted onto the set but has moveable hands to indicate a different time whenever we return to that set (three times). We must conclude that Porter, who directed *Lost in the Alps*, placed little importance on such details, even when the clock plays a role; the earlier *Great Train Robbery* (Edison, 1903) has an interior set with a clock that from one episode to another also shows the same hour. In contrast, in *The Tired Tailor's Dream* (Biograph, 1907) the clock, which has a very important role, indicates different times from one scene to the next. A man enters and orders his suit to be ready at 5:00 (the clock indicates 4:00). By an axial cut-in the clock, like the tailor who has fallen asleep in his chair, disappears from the field of the camera: the objects animate and the suit is assembled by itself as if by magic. Then we return to the long shot; the clock now shows 5:00. The tailor wakes up, happy at finishing the suit in *time*.

THE SUSPENSE NOTION

For parallel editing (one of the most important narrative devices of cinema) to become systematic, emphasis had to be placed on the physical separation of two conflicting groups converging toward a single place at a single moment. In the construction of the narrative system we are studying, the use of such a device has been useful, if not indispensable. To create a strong identification between the screen and the audience—pretending to the reality of the action, facilitating a strong emotion on the part of the spectator, making the suspense plausible, increasing the efficiency of the close-up—a consistent universe had to be shaped. This was an essential condition. The last-minute rescue, as a basic structure for the construction of a narrative, required it. One cannot hold an audience breathless without withholding the issue of the drama before a particular moment. Porter, who probably had no intention of constructing suspense, provides a contrasting example. In shot 8 of *Life of an American Fireman*, we attend the rescue of the mother and her child, seen from the interior. In shot 9, whatever the wishes of the anonymous author of the film's description, there can be no suspense since no one has any doubt about the outcome of the drama. We only re-see an accomplished action and we know, at the moment when the mother supplicates the fireman to save her child, that the fire will injure no one; the child will be safe. On seeing the film, the anguish referred to by the anonymous writer cannot materialize.

> We now dissolve to the exterior of the burning building. The frantic mother having returned to consciousness, and clad only in her night clothes, is kneeling on the ground imploring the fireman to return for her child. Volunteers are called for and the same fireman who rescued the mother quickly steps out and offers to return for the babe. He is given permission to once more enter the doomed building and without hesitation rushes up the ladder, enters the window and after a breathless wait, in which it appears he must have been overcome with smoke, he appears with the child in his arms and returns safely to the ground.[26]

Griffith seizes on suspense and models it almost always in a last-minute rescue pattern. He will elaborate parallel editing, which necessarily needs a kind of spatio-temporal coherence, despite obvious complexities (many locations, many acting groups), complexity that, as we have said, the "classical" chase film

---

[26]1903 Edison catalogue, quoted by Lewis Jacobs, *The Rise of the American Film* (New York: Teachers College Press, 1968), pp. 40–41.

(1903-1906) avoided by reason of its very character. The recent viewing of films made in 1907 confirms an hypothesis that filmmakers of that period, whatever the exceptions, systematically avoided complicating the structures of their films, perhaps so as not to mislead the audience.[27] The most frequent types of parallel editing (or any similar editing structure) or cross-cutting before Griffith appear to be justified almost exclusively by what is present inside the frame. This is the case with point-of-view shots such as *Grandma's Reading Glass* (Smith, 1900) and *Ce que je vois de mon sixième* (Pathé, 1901) when, in close-up (composed inside a circular matte), we can see various objects viewed by the characters while using a magnifying glass or telescope. It is equally true with films such as *A Search for Evidence* (Biograph, 1903) and *Inquisitive Boots* (Hepworth, 1905): in which we see, inside a keyhole matte, various scenes as if viewed from a hotel corridor. Among the chase films, camera displacement is similarly justified diegetically by the unfolding of events; since the protagonists are moving, the camera has to shift ground from shot to shot. In all such cases, however, the camera does not serve a narrative function *per se*; rather, its presence in each location is justified by the pro-filmic event. It is principally among Griffith's films that justifications for camera displacement assume a narrative dimension. This seems to be the moment when filmmakers start to become conscious of the narrative potential in an instrument previously consigned to recording the single movement of beings and things.[28]

Thus, at the beginning of the century, two different narrative patterns succeed one another. The first articulates shots in a relatively discontinuous fashion, while the second tries to inscribe, in the images' series, a continuous homogenous narrative that provides an illusion of telling itself. Without proposing causal relationships, one may yet remark on the likenesses between the first pattern of film exposition and, as we noted at the beginning of this paper, medieval literature. Early cinema retained a principal characteristic of presenting successions of more-or-less autonomous tableaux. Each element (shot) was not necessarily an instrument of progression, even as late as the chase film. Temporal continuity did not assume dominating importance; rather often, the relation

---

[27] Although our separation between 1900–1906 and 1907 may appear arbitrary, it corresponds to a certain reality. In January 1980 we viewed a substantial part of the existing films of 1907 from all over the world, thanks to Eileen Bowser and Jon Gartenberg of the Museum of Modern Art (New York), who organized and prepared a series of such viewings for scholars. Two years previously, the museum organized a similar screening of 1900–1906 films.

[28] As the reader can see, our analysis concentrates on the American films of the period. More American films are, indeed, available today, but we will surely have to consider those from elsewhere as they are unearthed. The few Pathé titles of 1900–1907 we could see show a relatively good mastery of temporality. *Le Cheval emballé* and *I Fetch the Bread* (French title unknown) show early evidence of parallelism or alternation of simultaneous actions.

between shots was imprecise, even operating in a repetitive mode. All this said, it is worthwhile calling attention to the apparent likeness between such a pattern of narration and that of medieval literature. The following quotation by Erich Auerbach concerning *La Chanson de Roland* applies with equal accuracy to many films produced early in the century.

> Whether one comprehensive representation is replaced by a reiterative enumeration of individual scenes similar in form and progress; whether one intense action is replaced by a repetition of the same action, beginning at the same starting point time and again; or whether finally, instead of a process of complex and periodic development, we have repeated returns to the starting point, each one proceeding to elaborate a different element or motif: in all cases rationally organized condensations are avoided in favor of a halting, spasmodic, juxtapositive, and pro- and retrogressive method in which causal, modal, and even temporal relations are obscured. . . . Time and again there is a new start; every resumption is complete in itself and independent; the next is simply juxtaposed to it, and the relation between the two is often left hanging.[29]

Some authors have gone so far as to identify repeated action editing with the parataxic device often indulged in medieval literature. Considering, among other matters, distances separating the materiality of the linguistic sign from that of the moving picture, we would not venture so far, yet it is fascinating to discover such apparent isomorphism, probably the result of a common attitude shared among Middle Age authors and early filmmakers as both confronted temporality: a parameter no narrative form can elude.

---

[29]Erich Auerbach, *Mimesis* (Garden City, N.Y.: Doubleday, 1957), p. 91.

EILEEN BOWSER

Toward Narrative, 1907:

The Mill Girl

The Mill Girl provides a model for the state of film narrative in 1907. It is not typical of the majority of films made in this year, but it illustrates very well the point reached by film narrative at the time when it was just on the verge of its great post-1907 expansion. It is significant for the elements of narrative technique it uses and also for what it leaves out of techniques available at the time.

The fiction film had already overtaken the actuality film that had dominated production in the first decade of cinema, but the majority of fiction films in 1907 were not very complex narratives. By far the largest number of them were comedies, most of them composed of a series of episodes connected by what John Fell has described as "the motivated link," a device that would be common to all episodes but would not lead very far into narrative modes.[1] An example would be Biograph's *Trial Marriages,* in which a man reads a newspaper article by a society woman recommending trial marriages and is inspired to give a tryout to a series of women, all of whom prove to have different faults considered as potential wives. Such films have a very loose structure and could be shortened or extended without changing the conception very much. Even dramas such as Hepworth's *Pillage by Pillar Box* may begin with narrative intrigue but go on to a chase, the primordial film narrative since 1903. Chase films were composed of repetitious shots and could easily be shortened or lengthened without losing their basic structure.[2] What was wanted, the George Kleine catalogue of 1904 advised its

---

[1] John L. Fell, "Motive, Mischief, and Melodrama: The State of Film Narrative in 1907," *Film Quarterly* 33 (Spring 1980):30–37.

[2] Eileen Bowser, "The Brighton Project: An Introduction," *The Quarterly Review of Film Studies* 4 (Fall 1979):509–38. This contains a description of the form of the early chase film. (French version: "Introduction au projet de Brighton," *Les Cahiers de la cinémathèque* 29 (Winter 1979):7–23.

readers, was "continuous action. There should be no lagging in the story which (the film) tells; every foot must be an essential part, whose loss would deprive the story of some merit; there should be sequences, each part leading to the next with increasing interest, reaching its most interesting point at the climax which should end the film."[3] In 1907, Joseph Medill Patterson reported that "today a consistent plot is demanded. There must be, as in the drama, exposition, development, climax and denouement. The most popular films run from fifteen to twenty minutes and are from 500 to 800 feet long. One studio manager said: 'The people want a story.... we've got to give them a story; they won't take anything else ... a story with plenty of action.... More story, larger story, better story with plenty of action—that is our tendency.' "[4]

In early cinema practice, narrators and/or explanatory titles preceding each shot were frequently employed to carry the burden of the narrative. In 1907–8, an interim aid to narrative was popular, called "talking pictures," with troupes of actors speaking the lines from behind the screen. The Cameraphone and various mechanical methods of recording sound accompaniment were given a try.[5] None of these seemed to be quite satisfactory. Even in 1907, some filmmakers were taking on more of a creative role in the film process, looking for ways to enlist the spectator in the narrative by the way in which it was structured. Only a handful of films surviving from 1907 even try to meet the complexities of an integrated narrative and of these, *The Mill Girl* is an outstanding example. It was made by the Vitagraph Company and copyrighted on September 17, 1907.

The story is a typical melodrama, showing basic emotions, lots of action, and spectacle. It is about a girl working in a textile mill who is subjected to the unwanted advances of her employer. She loves a young man who is a worker in the mill. He comes to her rescue by knocking down the boss. The boss retaliates by hiring two ruffians to beat up the hero. He defeats the thugs on two occasions by his superior strength and wit, but is then dismissed from his job. Free of interference, the dastardly employer again presses his attentions on the girl, but is interrupted by a fire in the factory which brings about his death. The heroine is rescued from the flames by her young man.

This story is told with one intertitle and thirty-one shots, a very high number for its 700' length. There are a couple of Selig films that survive from 1907 that

---

[3]"About Moving Picture Films," in Kleine Optical Company, *Complete Illustrated Catalogue of Moving Picture Films, Stereopticons, Slides, Films* (Chicago, 1904); cited in George Pratt, *Spellbound in Darkness* (Greenwich, Conn.: New York Graphic Society, 1966), pp. 36–37.

[4]Joseph Medill Patterson, "The Nickelodeons: The Poor Man's Elementary Course in Drama," *Saturday Evening Post,* November 23, 1907; cited in Pratt, *Spellbound in Darkness,* pp. 46–52.

[5]Tom Gunning has pointed out that the Cameraphone was used to reproduce vaudeville acts, and he thinks it was never used for narrative. I am indebted to Gunning for a discussion of the ideas in this article.

also contain a lot of shots: *The Girl from Montana* has twenty-six shots in its 900' length and *The Bandit King* has thirty-two shots in 1000'. However, it is difficult to study the Selig films because only a few frames from each shot were used in the paper prints submitted for copyright. We cannot tell how the shots began and ended, and how they were joined. One of the key elements for narrative at this time is how shots were to be linked to articulate the story. Vaclav Tille of Prague, one of the earliest writers on film as an art form, described this question in 1908 when he criticized filmmakers who continue an action from one location to another "without succeeding in linking together all the moments of a moving scene."[6] A survey of the first film reviews published by *The New York Dramatic Mirror* in 1908 reveals a concern for construction and clarity: "A very good theme and a story of real heart interest is spoiled in this film by faulty construction" (June 27th issue); "We have hitherto noted a failing of certain Edison films that they lack clearness in the telling of a picture story . . . this film needs a diagram to interpret it . . ." (July 25); and "It is not often that the Pathé people fail to tell a dramatic story so that the spectators can understand it, but they have done it in this case" (July 25). We haven't yet found a contemporary review of *The Mill Girl*, but we feel confident that its audiences had no difficulty in understanding it.

The Mill Girl contains no close-ups. Close views appeared frequently enough before 1907, first in single-shot "facial expression" films, then as emblematic shots appearing at the beginning or end of the film, representative of the narrative but not part of it. The last shot of *Rube and Mandy at Coney Island* (1903) shows a close view of the protagonists against a black background enjoying the hotdogs they had purchased in the preceding shot at a refreshment stand. The beginning shot of Vitagraph's *The 100 to 1 Shot* (1906) begins with an extreme closeup of a hand holding a fistful of money, another hand entering to crush the bills. These shots stand outside the narrative and do not have an integral function. There are also some surviving examples of close views cut into mid-narrative and mid-scene, in such films as *The Gay Shoe Clerk* (1903), *The Strenuous Life* (1904), or *The Widow and the Only Man* (1904). These close views are not integral to the narrative either, in the sense that they do not advance it. They repeat and underline the action rather than adding to it. They serve rather as a kind of pause. The one exception among surviving early films may be the close view in *The Silver Wedding* (1906). In long shot, the guests at the celebration admire the fine array of silver gifts on a table in the hall and then go into an adjoining room at the rear of the scene. A thief disguised as a delivery man enters the hall, lets in his colleague, and together they close the sliding doors between the two rooms and knock the attendant butler unconscious. They approach the silver-laden table, opening up a

---

[6]Vaclav Tille, "Le Cinéma," *Les Dossiers de la cinémathèque*, 4 (1979). The text has been translated from its original Czech to French and originally appeared in issues of *Novina*, no. 21 (November 6, 1908), no. 22 (November 13, 1908), no. 23 (November 20, 1908), published in Prague.

sack they have brought with them. There is a cut to a much closer view directly on the action and very well matched to the preceding shot This shot shows the thieves stuffing the silver into their bag and leaving the frame. The scene holds for a few seconds, and when we return to the longer view they are no longer in the hall, and the butler is returning to consciousness. At the beginning of the cut-in, there is a continuous time-link, and I think we could consider this close view as integral to the narrative. There could be a question as to whether the time is continuous in the return to longer view, since the thieves are no longer in the shot. However, this use of a close view is very rare for the period. The use of close views was to diminish (although it certainly did not disappear) in the next few years, until revived in a new way, with a new consciousness of its place in the narrative structure. The makers of *The Mill Girl* avoided close views, we think, because they thought of them, as did most filmmakers at that time, as interruptive to the narrative rather than contributing to it. They wanted an action-filled, fully integrated narrative, such as that recommended earlier by the Kleine catalogue.

As the majority of films would do in the next couple of years, *The Mill Girl* maintains something approximating a stage distance, leaving some space visible between the feet of the performers and the bottom of the frame. This space is narrowed in some shots, as the narrative advances to its climactic stages. More important, in a number of the shots the characters enter and leave the frame on the diagonal to the axial plane, coming closer to the camera (to three-quarter shot, heads at the top of frame, knees at bottom of frame) when going in or out of the scene. They move to the center of the frame and the middle distance for the significant action. This has the function of leading the spectator's eye into the scene and centering the important action in such a way that they will not be missed. In many films before this time the significant action may take place at the side of the frame, with so many other actions going on in other parts of the frame as to make it difficult for the modern spectator to "read" the scene. An example would be the scene in the department store in *The Kleptomaniac* (1905), where the lady goes from counter to counter stealing items while customers and employees move about the space, and it is only when she is accused of theft that the significant action occurs in the center of the frame. Whether contemporary spectators were so accustomed to this staging that they could easily "see" the thefts at first viewing, we don't know. It could well be that it was necessary for a narrator to point it out. In any case, the centering of the significant action in *The Mill Girl* illustrates one of the first steps on the part of the filmmaker to direct what the spectator will see.

Further, the diagonal entry and exit from the frame serves as a device to link the shots. This is very clear in the opening two shots of *The Mill Girl*. The first shot shows a gate set in a hedge, surrounded by foliage, representing the home of the heroine. The hero approaches on the path from the right side of the frame, stops in the center to meet the heroine at the gate, and they continue together toward the left, approaching the three-quarter shot as they leave the frame. The following shot at the factory gate shows a group of people entering the frame from the same position at the left, going into the mid-distance, and entering the gate in the center. Among them are the young couple, who stop and pause to talk at the right of the gate until the others have all entered and then follow them into the mill yard. The majority of the shots in *The Mill Girl* follow this kind of direction principle consistently, keeping the action continuous from one shot to the next. There are some shots which begin with characters already in place, and one or two moments when the direction matching seems to fall down. When the employer seeks to escape from the burning factory he exits from left frame parallel to the camera plane, and, with a cut direct on action, he reappears, or his feet do, descending the stairs to the basement, his feet coming down from upper left of frame. In this situation, there is a momentary confusion about the relation of these stairs to the previous space. The cut implies a turn in direction for which no time is allowed between the shots, since he is still visible at the end of one shot and the beginning of the next. A different kind of directional problem occurs when the hero arrives at his home and is followed by the employer and the two thugs he has hired. In the previous shot, the young man has beat up the thugs who were waiting to attack him and left the scene at right while his attackers have fled to the distance, running away from the camera. Following the same direction, the hero enters from the left a scene showing the gate and part of his house, and disappears into the house. Almost immediately the pursuers enter the frame from the left, and one is left with the feeling that they could not be so close behind the man, when they had been running away in the opposite direction in the previous shot. Even though the makers of *The Mill Girl* seem to have had occasional difficulties with it, they clearly saw the possibility of linking the parts of the narrative by directional movement and employed it as frequently as the opportunities presented themselves. It is less used in interior scenes but there is a slight tendency to diagonal even in some of these. The principle was quite rare before 1907, with the exception of the primordial chase film referred to earlier. The chase film consisted almost entirely of diagonal movements from the distance to a close exit at one or the other side of the frame. This movement would be repeated in each following shot, from the distance to the foreground. Once in a while, for the sake of variety, the movement would be reversed, the pursued and the pursuers entering the frame from the foreground and running into the distance. Such shots were quite long, giving time for the participants to run completely through the shot, from the leading actor to the last straggler. As much action as possible was included within the single shot. With the use of horses, cars, and trains in chase films, the action speeded up and the shots became shorter, although the same principle continued to be employed. The construction of the chase film, which might be considered the beginnings of cinematic form, probably suggested the kind of shot linkage exploited by *The Mill Girl*, where the shots are much briefer, and the linkage more controlled.

The Mill Girl does not avail itself of the moving camera, another existing option at this time. Early filmmakers sometimes used a pan to follow action rather than cutting to another shot. They tended to think of the single shot in an isolated manner, as complete in itself. Within the single-shot format, they found many ingenious means to show actions that occurred in more than one location and in consecutive or simultaneous time. In 1907, Edwin S. Porter showed the two participants in a telephone conversation in the same shot (in *College Chums*), each in a circle placed on either side of the frame, the bottom half of the frame consisting of a cityscape to show the space that separated them. This complex shot was to be repeated a number of times for telephone calls, with variations, down through the history of cinema to recent times, but it remained a novel solution and was often used, as here, for comic purposes. For similar reasons, early filmmakers would choose to show the relation between spaces by panning the camera from one to the other, even when the ground to be covered was quite extensive. There are obvious limits to this procedure. The makers of *The Mill Girl* chose instead to show the relation of spaces in alternate shots and to show simultaneity by parallel editing.

The clearest use of parallel editing to be found among surviving films before 1907 appears in *The 100 to 1 Shot* (1906). This was a Vitagraph film, which is enough to make one wonder if the same director (as yet unknown) was responsible for *The Mill Girl*. In the 1906 film the hero wins money at the track that enables him to save the old folks from being evicted. His car is seen approaching the camera on a long straight road; there is a cut to the interior of the home where the eviction is taking place, a return to the car as it makes a turn and stops in front of the house, and in the next shot the hero enters the interior "in the nick of time." It constitutes in embryonic form the "ride to the rescue" that D. W. Griffith was to make his specialty in the coming years. Beginning in 1907, there are several examples of what might be described as parallel editing, none of them, I think, as carefully articulated as in *The Mill Girl*. A Danish film, *For en Kvindes Skyld*, released in August, apparently shows simultaneous action in three locations by cross-cutting between them: the heroine in her room of the castle lets down a rope for her lover, the rival inside a room below hers sees and cuts the rope, and in exterior shots, the lover climbs the rope and falls to his death. The problem with this example is that it exists in two versions, one cut in continuous style and one in noncontinuous style and it has not yet been established which of these may be the original one.[7] *Water Babies*, released in England in November, contains a suggestion of parallel editing in the chase sequence, just one shot that cuts back to the pursuing section of the chase while the one being pursued enters the sea, but this does not seem to be a well-developed example. Edison's *The Trainer's Daughter*, copyrighted in November, contains a cut from the characters in a stable

---

[7]Tom Gunning, "Le Style non-continu du cinéma des premiers temps," *Les Cahiers de la cinémathèque*, 29 (Winter 1979): 24–34.

preparing for a race to the man blowing a horn to signal the start, returning afterward to the interior of the stable. This is one among several instances from this period of such a cut motivated by the characters hearing a sound, and there is an example of it in *The Mill Girl* as well. Biograph's *The Elopement*, made in November and released in December, shows a return to the pursuing car in a chase sequence, but only after the drivers of the leading car have abandoned it and gone through some woods, and out onto a lake in a canoe. As the two cars had previously appeared in the same shots, one not far behind the other, it is evident that the temporal meaning of parallel editing is not understood in the same way as it is in *The Mill Girl*. In France, Zecca made a film called *Cheval Emballé*, released in December, which contains cuts between a horse waiting at the curb and shots of his master making deliveries to various floors inside the building. This alternating sequence continues through a number of shots, while the horse eats stolen grain. In a way, this builds a kind of suspense for the moment when the horse's misdeeds will be discovered, but it has been speculated that it might have been motivated only by a wish to show a lapse of time to account for the diminishing of the grain supply.[8]

The editing of *The Mill Girl*, on the other hand, clearly reveals a spatio-temporal sense of the kind that will form the basis of Griffith's editing not long after he begins to make films. The first sequence that shows this awareness occurs after the hero has had his first confrontation with the employer. The young lovers return to the gate of the film's opening shot and linger there over their farewells. The following shot shows the interior of a low dive where the employer enters and hires two thugs to follow him outside. On a path bordered by bushes, the employer gives instructions and the men crouch in hiding to wait. The next shot returns to the gate, the lovers finally part, and the hero leaves to the right of the frame (observing direction, he is now on his way home). He enters in the next shot the scene where the men lie in hiding to attack him. By returning to the lovers' gate, a degree of suspense about the coming attack has been engendered. However, this example is much more fully developed in the prolonged parallel editing sequence that follows, which is more easily described in a shot list:

Shot 10:   The hero defeats the attackers and exits to right.

Shot 11:   A new location, showing the gate with part of the hero's home behind it. He enters from left, goes in the gate, turns in going up on the porch and disappears into the house at left. Soon after the employer leads his thugs into the scene from the left, they enter the gate and stand talking below the porch.

---

[8]Tom Gunning, in conversation with the author.

Shot 12:   Interior, the hero's bedroom. He enters from right fore-
             ground, goes around the bed, yawns, gets ready for bed,
             closes the window, sits down on a chair to remove his shoes.

Shot 13:   Exterior, another view of the house, the edge of the porch
             visible at left. The employer leads his ruffians in from the left,
             gesticulates upward, and sends the men back out of the
             scene while he stands and waits.

Shot 14:   Interior, a slightly closer view, the hero is in bed. He hears
             something, sits up, puts his hand to his ear (remember the
             example in *The Trainer's Daughter*), goes to the window and
             looks out left.

Shot 15:   The same as #13; the thugs bring a ladder to the wall of the
             house and place it so that the top disappears from sight,
             while the boss gestures silence.

Shot 16:   Interior, the hero is at his window. He turns and makes
             up a dummy in the bed, picks up a stick, and comes to crouch
             behind the foot of the bed, near the camara at right of frame.

Shot 17:   Exterior, the men climb the ladder while the boss holds it at
             the bottom.

Shot 18:   Interior, the hero cups his ear to listen, the thugs raise the
             window and enter, go to the bed, and attack the dummy. The
             hero jumps up, knocks one man to the floor while the other
             flees by way of the window. The hero picks up the fallen man
             and throws him out the window.

Shot 19:   Exterior, the man falls down through the frame and lands on
             the man waiting at the foot, the first thug to flee having
             already left the scene.

Early cinema contains many scenes of characters jumping or being thrown
out windows and doors. More often than not, there is an overlap of time, or
repeated action, as in the most famous example, frequently cited, the rescue of the
woman and child in *The Life of an American Fireman*.[9] The conception of narrative
implied by *The Mill Girl*'s editing represents a fundamental change. It should be
noted, however, that its makers somewhat beg the question of matching cuts on
action by having the exterior of the window remain out of sight, above the frame
line. They follow the same procedure when the hero rescues the heroine from the

---

[9]The original version of this film is discussed in André Gaudreault, "Les Détours du recit
filmique: Sur la naissance du montage parallèle," *Les Cahiers de la cinémathèque* 29
(Winter 1979): 88–101, and by Charles Musser, "Les Débuts d'Edwin S. Porter," in the same
issue, pp. 127–46. Both articles also appeared in *Cinema Journal* 19 (Fall 1979).

flames in the final sequence of the film. He climbs a drain pipe to a window which is not in view, reappears at the window in reverse cut to the interior, lowers her out the window on a rope, and on the return to the exterior, she appears being lowered from somewhere above the frame line, to be followed by the hero as he jumps into the firemen's net. The filmmakers' consistency in keeping the windows out of sight in both cases seems to indicate their consciousness of the difficulties in the direct action cut.

It seems significant to me that the early examples of parallel editing deal with adjacent spaces and not distant ones. This is evidently the first step in the development of the concept. Even the example given from *The 100 to 1 Shot* may be analyzed as adjacent spaces. Early in 1908, however, in a film scripted but not directed by Griffith, *Old Isaacs the Pawnbroker*, there is a clear example of a parallel cut that links quite distant spaces. It serves to express an abstract idea rather than linking continuous action: the child is at the charitable association trying in vain to get help for her sick mother, and a shot is cut in to show the mother at home, trying to rise from her sickbed. It might be thought of as either underlining the pathos of the situation, or as representing the child's thought. In any case, this seems to me to represent a second step in the evolution of parallel editing.

Some of the thirty-one shots of *The Mill Girl* are very short. During the extended interior-exterior editing sequence, there are several that are only 6'. In early cinema style, the spectator needed time to read the contents of a shot. Here, led by screen direction, centering, and by the relation between shots, the audience could grasp the significant action quickly. The filmmaker would no longer give the spectator time to examine all the details of the shot. He controlled the vision of the audience.

The Mill Girl has only one subtitle if the surviving print is complete, and it seems to be.[10] That title indicates a prolonged time lapse: "The next day— Discharged!" The narrative is so well articulated that titles and narrators are not necessary to understand it on first viewing. Even the "Discharged!" of the title would not have been needed, since the pantomime that follows it is clear. The acting is fairly restrained, given the melodramatic nature of the events, but it makes use of the the standard gestures of the melodrama. When the hero finds his girl lying unconscious on her work table amid the smoke of the fire, he pauses a moment to throw his arms high in the air before going about the practical business of finding a rope to lower her out the window. Such broad gestures were needed in order to make emotions visible within the narrative style of 1907. In *The Mill Girl*, one finds this style outlined as a paradigm for the state of film narrative as Griffith found it when he entered the scene.

---

[10]The length of the print examined is 689 feet, and the published length in *Moving Picture World* advertisements is 700 feet. We think the figure is probably rounded off for advertising purposes.

LUCY FISCHER

The Lady Vanishes:

Women, Magic, and the Movies

*Woman is the other, she is all man aspires to be and
does not become . . .Therefore he endows woman with
her nature: the Other—opposition whom he can
touch, conquer, possess, take comfort from, be inspired
by, and yet not have to contend with. She is mystery.*
                    —Simone de Beauvoir

In October and November of 1896, Star Film Company's first year of production, Georges Méliès shot a film entitled *The Vanishing Lady*, which is credited as displaying the director's first use of a cinematic "substitution trick."[1] The "plot" of the film is simple: a lady, in full Victorian garb, is seated in a chair, against the background of an ornate, elaborately-molded wall. A magician (played by Méliès) drapes her body with a fabric cover. When the cloth is removed, the lady has disappeared, and, much to our horror, in her place is a skeleton.

Though the occurrence portrayed is, of course, extraordinary, there is nothing exceptional about the film. It is one of hundreds of such magic films that Méliès produced between the years of 1896 and 1912, films that were imitated by Pathé in France and by Edison in the United States.

It is, in fact, precisely the commonplace quality of the film that is at issue—its status as a cinematic archetype, or even cliché. By 1896 the trick film paradigm had been established: such works would involve a *male* magician performing acts of wonder upon a *female* subject. To make a lady vanish was, after all, Méliès first idea for a substitution trick. In subsequent films he would elaborate upon this basic situation. Thus, in *Apparitions fugitives* (1904) Méliès would levitate a female subject and in *Extraordinary Illusions* (1903) reconstitute her out of a mannequin's parts. In *L'Enchanteur Alcofrisbas* (1903) Méliès would conjure women out of

---

[1] Paul Hammond, *Marvelous Méliès* (London: Gordon Fraser, 1974), p. 30.

flames and in *Extraordinary Illusions* turn them into men. From film to film the superficial persona of the male magician figure would tend to vary—from the traditional nineteenth-century stage magician in *Ten Ladies in an Umbrella* (1903) to the Roman god in *Jupiter's Thunderbolts* (1903)—but his function would remain the same: to perform feats of wonder upon a female subject.

Though we are all accustomed to crediting Méliès with the birth of film magic, the implications of that genre for the *image of women* have not been examined. In addition to being the "father" of film fantasy, Méliès may also have to stand as the inadvertent patriarch of a particular cinematic vision of women.

In all fairness to Méliès, however, his personal role in authoring such a vision is highly qualified. For, as we know, many of the screen creations associated with Méliès are, in truth, derived from the antecedent tradition of theatrical magic. Méliès, himself, was a stage magician; prior to making films he had purchased the Théâter Robert-Houdin in 1888. Thus it is to the legacy of theatrical magic that we must turn to find the roots of this cinematic image of woman—a vision which Méliès and others eventually "grafted" onto the screen.

When one begins to examine the history of stage magic, one finds that the situation of male magician and female subject—so common to the trick film genre—is simply a convention borrowed from theatrical magic. In the course of an entire book on the history of stage magic (*The Magic Catalogue* by William Doerflinger) only two examples of female magicians were ever cited.[2] One involved a woman named Adelaid Herrman, who originally served as magician's assistant to her husband Alexander, and then assumed his role when he died. The other reference was to Dorothy Dietrich and Celeste Evans, a team of magicians specializing in "dove illusions." Clearly, this text does not constitute a definitive study of stage magic, and one would assume that other female magicians have, indeed, existed and performed. But the paucity of references to women magicians at least makes clear the exceptional nature of that status, and the tenacity with which the model of male magician and female subject is maintained.

It is precisely the dominance and immutability of that paradigm that makes one begin to suspect that sexual role-playing is *itself* at issue in the rhetoric of magic, and that perhaps in performing his tricks upon the female subject, the male magician is not simply accomplishing acts of prestidigitation, but is also articulating a discourse on attitudes toward women.

In approaching the phenomenon of theatrical and cinematic magic in this fashion I am making certain assumptions. Like Roland Barthes in his studies of wrestling and striptease in *Mythologies*, I will assume that the conventions of magic are not simply arbitrary, incomprehensible actions, but rather elements in a coherent social "sign system" that can be read for its cultural meaning.[3] The

---

[2]William Doerflinger, *The Magic Catalogue* (New York: E. P. Dutton, 1977), pp. 21, 41.
[3]Roland Barthes, *Mythologies*, trans. Annette Lavers (New York: Hill and Wang, 1972), pp. 15–25, 84–87.

notion, however, that the significance of magic involves a submerged discourse on sexual politics, is a speculation—a working hypothesis that must be tested through an examination of magical practice.

To begin that investigation, let us return to the basic archetype of male magician working wonders upon the female subject, and commence to read it for its implications. Perhaps the act most typical of trick films is that of simply *conjuring* a woman. In Edison's *Mystic Swing* (1900) a series of women are made to appear on a moving trapeze; in Biograph's *Pierrot's Problem* (1902) a clown-magician produces two girls from behind his voluminous pantaloons. In *Ten Ladies in an Umbrella*, Méliès makes women appear and disappear with the help of an unlikely prop; in *The Ballet Master's Dream* (1903) a sleeper conjures women as part of an oneiric fantasy.

Accustomed as we are to this particular magical trope, it is easy to accept it as a mere "given" of the rhetoric of magic, and therefore to neglect to pursue its implications. But if we regard it as meaningful and begin to consider its significance, various issues come into focus.

On the most obvious level, the act of the male magician conjuring women is simply a demonstration of his *power over the female sex.* Woman has no existence independent of the male magician; he can make her appear when he wants her and disappear when (to paraphrase de Beauvoir), he wishes no longer "to contend" with her. Woman is thus a function of male will.

In the rhetoric of magic the conjured woman is also a *decorative* object—to be placed here and there like a throw pillow or a piece of sculpture. Thus, in countless trick films (like *Jupiter's Thunderbolts*) women appear in tableaux "arrangements"—like dried flowers or fruit.

On another level, the act of conjuring and "vanishing" ladies tends to *dematerialize* and *decorporealize* the female sex—to relegate woman to the level of "spirit." Thus, to paraphrase de Beauvoir again, magical practice literalizes the notion of woman as "Other," as unfathomable "mystery."

Often, however, in these trick films, woman's immaterial status takes on a particular inflection. Rather than function simply as a spirit, she is cast specifically as a *figment of the male imagination*. This notion is most apparent in the trick films involving the magician as dreamer. In Méliès's *The Clockmaker's Dream* (1904), for example, the main character falls asleep and has an oneiric fantasy of a bevy of women who emerge from a grandfather clock. Similarly, in *The Ballet Master's Dream* (Méliès, 1903) a man dreams about a series of dancing women. In these films the narrative openly situates the women within the male imagination, and casts them as sexual fantasies.In other films their status as sexual fantasy is less literal and explicit, yet why else would Méliès bother to conjure so many ladies from an umbrella?

Thus far, however, our inquiry has only scratched the surface and has viewed the act of conjuring women as a flexing of the male sense of power over the passive, ethereal female sex. But from another viewpoint, the male's need to exert his power can be seen as belying the *opposite* impluse: rather than evince his sense of strength in relation to women, might it not bespeak his perception of relative weakness? In other words, the gentleman doth protest too much. If our male magician is so sure of his own power over woman, why must he so relentlessly subject us to repeated demonstrations of his capability?

It is in response to that question that I must advance another speculation. Might it be that in addition to demonstrating the male sense of power over the female, the practice of magic also evinces certain deep-seated male anxieties concerning the *female's power over him*? According to this reading the male magician is not so much attempting to demonstrate his potency over the female, as he is to *defuse or exorcise her potency over him*. What aspects of magical practice might corroborate such a reading? And, furthermore, what psychological and cultural evidence is there to support such a notion of male "anxieties" regarding women?

As a starting point for the investigation of these questions, it is useful to examine the reverse situation of the magic "paradigm"—that is, the model of a female magician performing tricks upon the male. As mentioned earlier, in the history of theatrical magic such female magicians are rare, and their occurrence is no more common in the archives of cinematic magic. Several films of this kind do exist, however, and their portrayal of the female magician is most telling.[4]

There is, for example, a marvelous film of 1905 made by Edison entitled *A Pipe Dream*, which opens with a medium close-up of a woman smoking a cigarette, seated against a black background. She begins rather playfully to blow smoke into her outstretched hand, and, out of nowhere, a tiny man appears, on bended knees, upon her palm. The little homunculus seems to be pleading with the woman, as though asking for her hand in marriage. She laughs at him cruelly, and begins to close her palm; her homunculus disappears. Perplexed, she tries again to conjure her little man, but cannot repeat the trick.

What is interesting about this film is its characterization of the female "magician"—one fraught with anxiety and ambivalence toward women. Unlike the camera set-up for most magic films, that of *A Pipe Dream* renders the scale of

---

[4]Thus far I have based my research largely on the Library of Congress Paper Print Collection as well as on those trick films available through commercial distribution. Further research would have to be done into archival holdings and trick film descriptions to ascertain precisely how uncommon female magicians were in this genre. Eileen Bowser and Bob Summers of the Museum of Modern Art have informed me that, based on the screenings at the International Federation of Film Archives (FIAF) Brighton Conference, female magician figures were most common in Pathé films. This has been born out by my examination of *The Red Spectre* and *Transformation*, discussed later in this article. [Fischer's ensuing point concerning *A Pipe Dream* is underlined by the fact that the film indicates a man to be the dreamer—GP.]

the woman huge, particularly in comparison to her diminutive little man. She is a literalization of the overpowering female, the Amazon, or the awesome, domineering Mother, as seen by a child-man. Thus, she is a figure of considerable terror. Psychologists might have something to say about her as well, particularly about how her depiction evinces certain classic male fears concerning women. In her article, "The Dread of Woman" (1932), for example, Karen Horney speaks of the psychic importance of the male child's anxieties regarding his mother, and Horney's language seems custom-made for the film. She discusses the young boy's perception that his genital is "much too small for his mother's" and how he "reacts with the dread of his own inadequacy, of being rejected and derided." Such, of course, is the fate of our homunculus.

The film has other implications as well. The fact that the woman smokes a cigarette marks her, according to Victorian mores, as dangerously loose and "masculine," and thus invests her magician-status with a degree of perversity. Furthermore, it is significant that when she tries to repeat her trick, she fails, as though her magical powers were accidental, or beyond her control.

Another film of the period, *The Red Spectre* (Pathé, 1907) is interesting to examine in this regard as well. The narrative of this film involves a competition between a male magician (dressed as a devil, in skeleton costume) and a female conjurer (dressed in courtly attire). Ultimately, the woman magician reduces the male to a folded costume, and appropriates his black cape. Again, a certain anxiety regarding the figure of the female magician is apparent, particularly her perceived ability to get the better of the male.

In point of fact, throughout the history of myth and religious practice, when women have been "granted" magical powers by men, those powers have most often been regarded as evil or dangerous. We rarely find an image of a harmless female magician, playfully conjuring people and objects. Rather, she is cast as a figure of great perversity. According to Greek legend, for example, the magical Circe turned the companions of Ulysses into pigs and wild beasts; and in Venezuelan mythology, the love-goddess, Maria Leonza turned men into stone.[5] Similarly, the legendary Sirens were bird-women who played magical music on their lyres and lured sailors to a watery grave. Even in contemporary mythos, the tainted figure of the prostitute is said to turn "tricks" upon her "johns." Thus, in all of these cases, women who practice magic seem to do so at the expense of men.

In terms of the history of the Christian religion, the most compelling female "magician" is, significantly, the witch—clearly a figure of great terror. Though male witches, or *incubi*, were thought to exist, the notion of witchcraft was strongly identified with the female of the species, or *succubi*. That perverse magical powers were associated with womanhood in particular is apparent in the *Malleus Maleficarum*, a handbook, on witchcraft written by two Dominican monks in 1484. According to that influential text: "Perfidy is more found in women than

---

[5]Wolfgang Lederer, *The Fear of Women* (New York: Harcourt, Brace, Jovanovich, 1968), p. 57.

in men . . . since they are feebler in body and in mind, it is not surprising they should come under the spell of witchcraft."[6] Furthermore, woman "is more carnal than man as is clear from her many carnal abominations." Thus all witchcraft is seen to stem from "the carnal lust which in women is insatiable."[7]

What these few examples demonstrate is the flip side of the male magician/female subject paradigm. In the cases where women magicians exist, they are figures of awe and dread. This makes clear the fact that woman is not always perceived as *powerless*—a passive prop. Rather woman's power is often acknowledged, but it is viewed as perilous and perverse. Perhaps, the male magician is not only performing tricks upon the female; he is preventing *her* from performing more dangerous tricks upon *him*.

Thus the rhetoric of magic may bespeak a *fear* of the female, rather than the exuberant display of male superiority that marks its surface. The male magician's obsessive need to "dematerialize" women by making them vanish, may in fact, betray his fear of female "carnality," as much as it displays his own sense of power.

But what precisely are the nature of these male fears, and what cultural/psychological evidence is there to support their existence? First of all, several texts have been written on the subject: *The Fear of Women* by psychoanalyst Wolfgang Lederer, and *The Dangerous Sex* by H. R. Hays.[8] Furthermore, various psychologists have produced essays on the topic, like Gregory Zilboorg's "Masculine and Feminine . . .," Karen Horney's "The Dread of Woman," and Frieda Fromm-Reichmann and Virginia Gunst's "On The Denial of Women's Sexual Pleasure."[9] Freud himself spoke of male anxieties toward women in *Totem and Taboo*.[10]

In most interpretations, this fear of woman centers on the female genital. According to Freud, in his essay "Medusa's Head," the female genital posits the threat of male castration and is thus viewed with terror.[11] In other remarks in *Totem and Taboo* Freud questions whether the male fear of woman might not stem

---

[6]H. R. Hays, *The Dangerous Sex* (New York: G. P. Putnam's Sons, 1964), p. 141.

[7]Hays, *The Dangerous Sex*, p. 141.

[8]Cited in nn. 6 and 7.

[9]Gregory Zilboorg, "Masculine and Feminine: Some Biological and Cultural Aspects," in *Psychoanalysis and Women*, ed. Jean Baker (New York: Penguin, 1977), pp. 96–131; Karen Horney, "The Dread of Women," in her *Feminine Psychology*, ed. Harold Kelman (New York: Norton, 1967), pp. 133–46; Frieda Fromm-Reichmann and Virginia Gunst, "On the Denial of Women's Sexual Pleasure," in Baker, ed. *Psychoanalysis and Women*, pp. 86–93.

[10]Sigmund Freud, *Totem and Taboo* (1913), in *The Basic Writings of Sigmund Freud*, A. A. Brill, trans. and ed. (New York: Random House, 1938), pp. 807–930; as discussed in Lederer, *Fear of Women*, pp. 2–7.

[11]Sigmund Freud, "Medusa's Head," in his *Sexuality and Love*, ed. Philip Reiff (New York: Collier Books, 1963), pp. 212–3.

from a fear of being "weakened" by her, as he is in the sexual act.[12] In much of the writing on the subject mythology has served as cultural evidence. Myths, for example, provide the suggestion that men may also fear women's procreative powers because they perceive them as entailing the reverse power of *death*. Frieda Fromm-Reichmann and Virginia Gunst cite the following Persian myth of creation as proof of such an anxiety:

> In that myth a woman creates the world, and she creates it by the act of natural creativity which is hers and which cannot be duplicated by men. She gives birth to a great number of sons. The sons, greatly puzzled by this act which they cannot duplicate become frightened. They think: "Who can tell us, that *if she can give life, she cannot also take life.*"And so, because of their fear of this *mysterious ability of woman*, and of its *reversible* possibility, they kill her [italics mine].[13]

Thus, once more woman's sexuality is linked to mutilation or death: if woman can conceive life, can she not also take it away? If the womb is a bearer of life, might it not also be a tomb?

This irrational fear of female "magic" is apparent in many of the trick films. In *The Red Spectre* it seems significant that the woman magician manages to kill the *male* devil, reducing him to a disembodied skeleton. In several other films, women are associated with death and skeletal symbolism. Méliès's *The Vanishing Lady*, for example, when the woman disappears she is replaced by a skeleton, an occurrence which also happens in Edison's *The Mystic Swing*. Perhaps this fear of women explains why so many magic films involve tricks in which women are turned into men, thereby annihilating their disturbing sexual status. In *A Delusion* (Biograph, 1902) a female model turns into a man each time the photographer looks into the camera lens. In *The Artist's Dilemma* (Edison, 1901) a woman turns into a clown.

Given this basic fear of imagined female powers, it is not surprising to find the iconography of theatrical and cinematic magic plagued by a rampant *hostility* toward the female subject. In fact, it is this very aggression that makes the theory of male fear more plausible. If the male magician only wished to "play" with the female subject, why has he devised for her such a chamber of horrors?

For instance, in many trick films women are symbolically dismembered. In Biograph's *A Mystic Reincarnation* (1902) a male magician conjures female body parts, then turns them into a woman. In *Extraordinary Illusions* (1903) Méliès takes out mannequin limbs from a "magical box" and through stop-motion photography transforms them into a flesh and blood woman.

---

[12]Discussed in Lederer, *Fear of Women*, p. 3.

[13]Fromm-Reichmann and Gunst, "On the Denial of Women's Sexual Pleasure," p. 88.

In other films (like *Apparitions fugitives* [1904], *L'Enchanteur Alcofrisbas*, and *The Red Spectre*) women are levitated, an action which likens them to corpses in advanced states of *rigor mortis*. In such a posture they also impersonate the model Victorian wife—whose sexuality was entirely dormant. According to H. R. Hays, women of the era engaged in intercourse "in a sort of coma, apparently pretending that nothing was happening [since] the slightest sign of life on [their] part would have been a humiliating admission of depravity."[14]

In the canon of theatrical magic tricks, of grandiose "stage illusions," we find a catalogue of magical misogyny. Thus we have such tricks as "Rod Through Body" in which a sword is placed through a woman's torso, "Dagger Chest" in which a series of knives are placed into a box around a woman's head, "Shooting a Woman Out of a Cannon," "Sawing a Woman in Half," "Shooting Through a Woman," and finally "The Electric Chair."[15] Such tricks cannot simply be viewed as jovial and naive demonstrations of imagined male powers, as a harmless flexing of the masculine ego. Rather they must be regarded as symbolic acts of considerable violence.

But certainly not *all* of magical practice involves a thinly disguised hostility toward women. What about such trifles as pulling rabbits from hats, or flowers from cones? Though it is true that such tricks do not suggest male aggression toward women, they can, nonetheless, be seen as constituting a submerged discourse on male-female relations. For when one begins to examine those sleights-of-hand so characteristic of magic tradition, one is struck by how so many of them center on the theme of *creation*: men pulling rabbits out of hats, making flowers grow from canes, bringing mechanical automata "to life." All of these acts seem like symbolic representations of *birth*, and their occurrence at the hand of the male magician seems to bespeak an envy of what is, essentially, the *female procreative function*. Significantly, most of these magical births take place with the aid of a highly phallic object—a "mystic" cone, or a cane, or perhaps an "enchanted candle."

Since my proposed reading of these tricks presumes a notion of male envy of the female procreative function, it would be well to examine that subject before proceeding any further. In the canons of psychoanalytic literature, we are, of course, more familiar with a theory of the *reverse* situation, of the female's alleged envy of the male. According to Freud in his formulation of "penis envy," during a young girl's "phallic phase" (3–7 years), she sees a naked man and realizes that she "lacks" a penis. As Freud would have it the psychological consequences of the young girl's perception are devastating and far-reaching: "She develops, like a scar, a sense of inferiority ... she begins to share the contempt felt by men for a sex

---

[14]Hays, *The Dangerous Sex*, p. 215.

[15]These tricks are listed in Doerflinger, *Magic Catalogue*, as well as in *Dunninger's Complete Encyclopedia of Magic* (New York: Spring Books, n.d.).

which is the lesser in so important a respect. . . . Even after penis-envy has abandoned its true object, it continues to exist . . . in the character trait of jealousy."[16] Thus in traditional psychoanalytic theory it is the female who is seen as biologically deficient and envious of the male.

Early on in the history of psychology, voices were raised in protest against Freud's construal of sexual relations. And many of those who countered his claims did so by advancing an opposing notion of the male envy of the female for her procreative life-giving powers. Thus, writing in 1926, Karen Horney states:

> from the biological point of view woman has in motherhood, or in the capacity for motherhood, a quite physiological superiority. This is most clearly reflected in the unconscious of the male psyche in the boy's intense envy of motherhood. . . . When one begins . . . to analyze men . . . one receives a most surprising impression of the intensity of this envy of pregnancy, childbirth and motherhood, as well as of the breasts, and of the act of suckling.[17]

Similarly psychoanalysts Fromm-Reichman and Gunst state:

> Men are not only unconsciously afraid of women as child-bearers but many men are also envious of this ability of women. . . . We know it from our clinical practice. . . . We hear so much about penis envy but it is not fashionable in a patriarchal culture to talk about birth envy, although many of us know it exists.[18]

In discussing the issue of male envy, many psychoanalysts have felt the need to venture into the field of anthropology. Thus in 1944 psychoanalyst Gregory Zilboorg wrote an essay, "Masculine and Feminine," in which he posited male envy as a determining force in the creation of primitive culture:

> The male who first overcame the woman by means of rape was hostile and murderous toward the female. . . . But despite all his economic and sadistic and phallic superiority, man could not fail to discover that woman . . . still possessed a unique power over mankind. She could produce children. . . . Thus man, who hated the woman-mother, must have envied her too. . . .[19]

---

[16]Sigmund Freud, "Some Psychological Consequences of the Anatomical Distinction Between the Sexes," in Freud, *Sexuality and Love*, p. 188.

[17]Karen Horney, "The Flight from Womanhood," in Horney, *Feminine Psychology*, pp. 60–61.

[18]Fromm-Reichmann and Gunst, "On the Denial of Women's Sexual Pleasure," p. 91.

[19]Zilboorg, "Masculine and Feminine," p. 124.

Zilboorg's assertions are clearly hypothetical, but many practicing anthropologists have documented concrete evidence of the male envy of the female. Margaret Mead, for example, in a chapter on "Womb-Envying Patterns" in *Male and Female*, demonstrates how male initiation rituals of South Sea island societies evince anxieties that are suppressed in Western society:

> In our Occidental view of life, woman, fashioned from man's rib, can at most strive unsuccessfully to imitate man's superior powers and higher vocations. The basic theme of the initiatory cult, however, is that women, by virtue of their ability to make children, hold the secrets of life. Men's role is uncertain, undefined and perhaps unnecessary. By a great effort man has hit upon a method of compensating himself for his basic inferiority. Equipped with various mysterious noise-making instruments . . . they can get the male children away from the women, brand them as incomplete and themselves turn boys into men. Women, it is true, make human beings, but only men can make men.[20]

Thus, Mead casts male initiatory rites as elaborate, compensatory "magic tricks."

Another researcher in the field of male envy is Bruno Bettelheim, who, in his book *Symbolic Wounds*, describes the primitive ritual of *couvade*, by which the husband of a parturient woman enacts a rite in which he mimics, and even appropriates the child-bearing act:

> The [pregnant] woman works as usual up until a few hours before birth; she goes to the forest with some women, and there the birth takes place. In a few hours she is up and at work . . . as soon as the child is born the father takes to his hammock and abstains from work, from all food but weak gruel . . . and is nursed and cared for by all the women of the place. This goes on for days, sometimes weeks.[21]

What these various quotes from psychologists and anthropologists demonstrate is that there exists a body of literature in which male envy of the female's procreative function is established and considered a crucial aspect of sexual dynamics. Given that most cultures are patriarchal, however, it is clear that such feelings are not openly acknowledged, and indeed are concealed and suppressed. How is man to maintain and justify political power over woman if the truth of his awe and envy of the female sex comes out? In the "primitive" societies described by Mead and Bettelheim, this envy is released in the form of established cultural

---

[20]Margaret Mead, *Male and Female* (New York: William Morrow, 1949), pp.102–3.

[21]Bruno Bettelheim, *Symbolic Wounds: Puberty Rites and the Envious Male* (New York: Collier oks, 1971), pp. 109–10.

rituals. In modern Western society, however, such sanctioned avenues of expression do not exist, and envy wears more oblique disguises.

It is my contention that the rhetoric of magic is one of those disguises, one of those cultural artifacts in which the male envy of the female procreative powers is manifest. Yet what is there about magical practice that supports such a reading?

I have already mentioned the general emphasis in conjuring tricks on the notion of creation or birth, be it rabbits from a hat, women from umbrellas, or automata that move. But there are many standard magic tricks which evince a more overt symbolism. Within the canon of theatrical magic there are, for example, a whole series of tricks which involve the central prop of an egg. *Dunninger's Complete Encyclopedia of Magic* lists such tricks as "Eggs Extraordinary," in which a designated card is found within an egg. "Miraculous Eggs" in which a ring is produced from an egg, and "The Coin in Egg."[22] *The Magic Catalogue* notes tricks with even more tendentious implications. A trick entitled "Human Hen," for example, is described as follows:

> Egg after egg . . . are produced from magician's (or friend's) mouth. They are placed into a clear bowl, or tray in plain view of everyone. You can make as many eggs as you wish appear. Mouth is seen as empty after each egg is removed. Eggs are real and can be cracked open to prove so.[23]

Shades of Professor Unrath and The Blue Angel.

Other tricks, not specifically involving eggs, have similar birth implications. One entitled, "Baby Trousseau Production" entails a male magician and a male subject:

> Performer shakes hands with person who helped him, notices a ravel on their [sic] collar. When he pulls it, it is really a tape, and as he continues to pull, audience sees that it is a long string of fluttering dolls clothes in all colors. This causes a big laugh which gets bigger when a baby nursing bottle seemingly full of milk and complete with nipples, shows up on the end of the tape line.[24]

In a similar vein, one reads in the history of stage magic of a turn-of-the-century Mongolian conjurer, Chin Ling Foo, who "was noted for his production of large bowls of water or small children from an apparently empty cloth."[25]

---

[22]*Dunninger's Encyclopedia,* pp. 139, 262, 278.

[23]Doerflinger, *Magic Catalogue,* p. 123.

[24]Doerflinger, *Magic Catalogue,* p. 113.

[25]Doerflinger, *Magic Catalogue,* p. 26.

While these tricks tend to mimic the procreative act, the canon of "escape tricks" evince a male anxiety about the birth process itself. In *Houdini on Magic*, for example, the trick of "The Spanish Maiden" is described in terms that foreground those fears:

> [The Spanish Maiden] is shaped like a human body and the front is painted to resemble a maiden. The device hinges open at the side and both sections of the interior are lined with iron spikes. When you enter the device, you take a position between the spikes. The front is then closed, so that the spikes completely trap you within. Padlocks are attached to staples on the outside of the Maiden to prevent you from opening the device. Nevertheless, soon after the cabinet is placed over the Spanish Maiden, you make your escape.[26]

The history of trick films evinces similar associations of magic and birth. The Star Film catalogue lists such Méliès films as *Prolific Magical Egg* and *Marvelous Egg Producing with Surprising Developments*, both of 1902. And in *The Brahmin and the Butterfly* (1900) the character of a male magician conjures a caterpillar from an "egg shaped cocoon," which then turns into a beautiful princess.

Many other films, though devoid of overt egg symbolism, nonetheless display a submerged iconography of birth. In *Pierrot's Problem*, for example, the magician-clown seems to give birth to two young women from out of his baggy pantaloons (though he eventually "combines" them into one huge "Great Mother" of a woman). Similarly, it is telling that so many magic films (like *The Red Spectre* and *L'Enchanteur Alcofrisbas*) employ as their settings caves and grottoes. For according to historians of myth, like Mircea Eliade, these locales have commonly been associated with the world's womb in primitive Earth-Mother cults.[27] Finally it is interesting to note that many magician's props seem to embody womb symbolism. One thinks of the classic "magic box," so nicely labeled as such in Méliès's *Extraordinary Illusions*. One notices as well the countless films (like *The Red Spectre* and *L'Enchanteur Alcofrisbas*) in which women are conjured from urns, as though to literalize the notion of womb as "magic vessel."

Thus in many magic films, the prestidigitation performed by the male magician seems to have relevance to the issue of birth. It is as though through magical practice the male can symbolically imitate, or even appropriate, an aspect of female procreative powers.

It is interesting to note in this respect the existence of a magic film that runs

---

[26]Walter B. Gibson and Morris N. Young, eds., *Houdini on Magic* (New York: Dover, 1953), 118.

[27]Mircea Eliade, *Myths, Dreams and Mysteries*, trans. Philip Mairet (New York: Harper, 1960), 17.

counter to this example, a film in which the role of female as procreator is not suppressed. In an extraordinary Pathé trick film of ca. 1906, entitled *Transforma-tion,* a *female* magician conjures live male and female babies out of a series of flowers and vegetables, and ends the film with the children bouncing blissfully on her knee.[28] Thus the subtext of female procreation which seems masked in most examples of magical practice, is, in this film, somehow liberated, or brought to the surface.

In summary, then, the rhetoric of magic—in its theatrical and cinematic varieties—constitutes a complex *drama of male-female relations.* In the guise of the magician figure, the male enacts a series of symbolic rituals in which he expresses numerous often-contradictory attitudes toward woman: his desire to exert power over her, to employ her as decorative object, to cast her as a sexual fantasy, to exorcize her imagined powers of death, and to appropriate her real powers of procreation.

At various points in this essay I have mentioned how the genre of the trick film owes its heritage to the legacy of theatrical magic. Yet the question arises as to *why* the conventions of stage magic were so easily translated onto the screen. Is there something *specific* to the cinematic medium that makes it appropriate for the conventions of magic, and if so, what implications might this have on the issue of women and film?

Clearly, the very nature of the cinematic medium links it with magic, for the photographic process has always held for people a magical aura. Though grounded in physical realities, photography still strikes us as producing an image "conjured" (albeit "developed" in a wash of Kodak chemicals).

Historically, *motion* picture photography had even stronger ties to magic. One of the early predecessors of the film projector was, of course, the magic lantern, a device which projected painted, often animated slides. Clearly cinema, with its use of photography and its perfection of the illusion of movement, created even a more "magical" image of life. As Parker Tyler has written:

> Camera trickery is really camera magic, for illusion can be freely created by the movie camera with more mathematical accuracy and shock value than by sleight-of-hand or stage illusion. The very homogeneity of cinema illusion—the images of the actors themselves are illusive, their corporeal bodies absent—creates a throwback in the mood of the spectator to the vestiges . . . of ancient beliefs . . .[29]

---

[28]Again, as mentioned in n. 5, it is significant that this film is attributed (by Reel Images, its distributor) to Pathé.

[29]Parker Tyler, "From *Magic and Myth of the Movies* Preface," in *Film Theory and Criticism,* ed. Gerald Mast and Marshall Cohen (New York: Oxford University Press, 1974), p. 586.

It is interesting that among the trick films of the era are some whose iconography provides a commentary on the perceived magical qualities of the film medium. In *A Spiritualist Photographer* (Méliès, 1903), for example, a male magician appears on stage with a huge empty picture frame. He fits blank paper into the frame and stands a woman before it. As a torch burns beneath her, she magically dissolves onto the photographic paper. The magician rolls up the print and the flesh and blood woman reappears.

This same play with conjuring the image of women appears in *The Red Spectre*. As part of the devil-magician's competition with his female counterpart, he produces not live women but the *image* of women on a movie-type screen. Having done this, he lies beneath the ersatz screen and peers lasciviously at his nubile creations.

Several things can be concluded from the activities portrayed in these two films. First, they establish that the photographic act is seen as a kind of conjuring: producing a cinematic image is viewed as a "magic trick" equivalent to those one might perform on stage. Secondly, they demonstrate how readily the magic of the film image was associated with the image of the *female*. As theatrical magicians had obsessively made live women appear on stage, so the film magicians might conjure their images on screen.

Still another film of this era seems to literalize the notion of the cinematic apparatus as a magical device for producing women. In Méliès *The Magic Lantern* (1903) we find the characters of Pierrot and Harlequin in a children's play room. Early on in the film they assemble a huge magic lantern and project its light on the wall. After a while, however, they become curious about what is inside the lantern's cavity. They open it up and, as though from a mechanical birth chamber, a stream of women swarm out.

Thus the legacy of magic in film is twofold. On the superficial level, there is cinema's historical inheritance of the conventions of stage magic, as manifest quite literally in the trick films of Edison, Pathé, Méliès, and others.[30] On a deeper level, however, is the primitive association of the film image itself with a conjured magical illusion.

Given the "sexual politics" of magic, what might the implications be, for the portrayal of women in film, of the association of cinema and magic? Clearly, this is a complex question that cannot be summarily answered; but several preliminary speculations present themselves. There would seem to be, within the history of cinema, a group of male filmmakers who strongly identify the directorial role with that of a magician. Often, they are directors who display a great ambivalence toward women in their films (an exception is Jacques Rivette who, in *Celine and Julie Go Boating*, openly invests the two female main characters with magical

---

[30]For the most complete discussion of the influence of magicians on movies, see Erik Barnouw, *The Magician and the Cinema* (New York: Oxford University Press, 1981).

powers). Orson Welles, for example, in *F for Fake* (1973), flamboyantly adopts the stance of a master conjurer; but in his earlier film, *Lady from Shanghai* (1949), he casts Rita Hayworth as a perversely magical ensnarer of men. Jean Cocteau, in *The Testament of Orpheus* (1959), flaunts his own and cinema's trickery, but in his earlier *Orpheus* (1949) reveals woman (in the figure of Eurydice) to be the true source of magic in life and in art. Busby Berkeley, of course, is an obvious pledge for this fraternity, conjuring women from safely off-screen with all the male bravado that Méliès displayed so guilelessly on stage.

There is also the case of a director like Ingmar Bergman who, though admitting the lure of the cinema's magic, seems more qualified in his enthusiasm for the conjurer's posture. In his film *The Magician* (1958) he creates the character of Albert Vogler, a rather morose and somber magician who stands in contrast to the wry and mischievous figures cut by Méliès or Welles.[31] Significantly, within the narrative of *The Magician* the issue of the relation of women to magic is foregrounded. An old woman in Vogler's magic troupe seems to have more powers than he does and, in fact, brews all the potent medicines that he sells. Yet, typically, she is regarded as a witch, and never performs on stage. Various male members of the magic troupe utilize their association with magic to control women. Tubul sells the cook, Sofia, a "love potion," and Simson woos the naive Sara by telling her how "magic attracts women." Most interesting of all, is the fact that for half the film Vogler's wife and magician's assistant, Manda, is disguised (at his request) as the male, Aman—a name that is an anagram for "Manda," but also for the English words "a man." Finally, another character in the film, Mrs. Egerman, believes that Vogler has the power to bring back her deceased child. Throughout the film the magician's powers are cast in terms that suggest the cinema. Thus Vogler's act involves magic lanterns and shadows projected on screens; and he has the power to summon huge disembodied faces, which seem like nothing so much as film close-ups.

Bergman, himself, admits that his own fascination with cinema began with the childhood gift of a magic lantern, complete with a set of colored glass fairy-tale slides. But it was the acquisition a few years later of a film projector that had a profound effect upon the young director; and Bergman's recollection of that childhood experience makes clear his almost unconscious association of the powers of women, magic, and the cinema. Thus he speaks of his own first encounter with a "vanishing lady":

> When I was ten years old I received my first, rattling film projector, with its chimney and lamp. I found it both mystifying and fascinating. The

---

[31]My comments on *The Magician* are, unfortunately, based on the published screenplay, since I was unable to view the film at the time of writing this piece. See Ingmar Bergman, *Four Screenplays of Ingmar Bergman,* trans. Lars Malmstrom and David Kushner (New York: Simon and Schuster, 1960).

first film I had was nine feet long and brown in color. It showed a girl lying asleep in a meadow, who woke up and stretched out her arms, then disappeared to the right. That was all there was to it. The film was a great success and was projected every night until it broke and could not be mended any more.

This little rickety machine was my first conjuring set. And even today, I remind myself with childish excitement that I am really a conjurer...[32]

---

[32]Ingmar Bergman, introduction to *Four Screenplays*, pp. xiv–xv. Most of the films that I have discussed in this article will soon be available on a single reel through Film Circulation, the Museum of Modern Art.

TOM GUNNING

An Unseen Energy Swallows Space:
The Space in Early Film and Its Relation to American Avant-Garde Film

In the natural sciences there is the concept of the pseudomorph, a
phenomenon that closely resembles another phenomenon—rock or plant—
without truly being related. The relation of a pseudomorphic to an authentic
paradigm is that of a counterfeit to an original: a surface deceit that conceals a
number of internal differences, an attractive appearance of affinity that cloaks
a basic discontinuity in genus and species. As a historian of cinema with interests
in both early film and in the achievements of the American avant-garde film, I
must confess that the relations I will describe between the two movements are, to
some extent, pseudomorphic.[1] The immense gulf separating the technical,
economic, and ideological aims of the pioneers of cinema from those of the avant-
garde films made in the U.S. since the 1940s can be bridged only by the most
dubious leap of faith. My conscience as a film historian finds it necessary to stress
that we are dealing here not with a continuous tradition but with a relation traced
over an abyss.

Perhaps it is the true function of history not to leap over but to confront such
abysses. Comparing early film to recent films of the American avant-garde frees
the early works from the ghetto of primitive babbling to which the progress-
oriented model of film history has assigned them. If we cease to see early films
simply as failed or awkward approximations of a later style, we begin to see them
as possessing a style and logic of their own. In many respects this style (and, as I
hope to show, particularly its approach to space) is different from that of later

---

[1]This article originally was presented in slightly different form as a lecture at the Whitney
Museum of American Art on November 15, 1979, as part of a series of lectures and films
entitled "Researches and Investigations into Film: Its Origins and the Avant-Garde,"
organized by John G. Hanhardt, curator of video and film at the Whitney.

commercial film. Although this "difference" is not the same "difference" by which the American avant-garde separates itself from commercial cinema, a comparison is illuminating. I must add that the impetus for the comparison comes partly from avant-garde filmmakers themselves, from artists such as Ken Jacobs, Ernie Gehr, Hollis Frampton, and others who have directly included elements from early films in their own work. Likewise, it was undoubtedly my encounter with films by these and other avant-garde filmmakers that allowed me to see early films with a fresh eye.

Historically it has been one of the strategies of modern art to define itself by uprooting itself from immediate traditions in Western art, relating itself instead to an alien tradition. One might say that to compare *Les Demoiselles d'Avignon* to African sculpture is to misunderstand the purposes and contexts of Picasso, on the one hand, and primitive art, on the other. But to ignore such a comparison is to miss one of the strongest statements this modernist painting is making about its relation to tradition. And a particularly rich comparison can be made if one avoids lifting certain formal elements from the traditions in which they appear, in order to compare them in some spaceless, timeless realm, but rather, observes closely the context and project of modernism that makes this fissure in tradition an integral part of what modernism defines itself to be.

For Walter Benjamin, the invention of cinema was the most advanced example of the shattering of tradition caused by the appearance of mechanical reproduction.[2] I find that films from cinema's first decade most clearly reveal the new perceptual and aesthetic experience that this form of mechanical reproduction introduced. In the way these films restructure both traditional representations of space and the relation of spectacle to audience we may find a link to avant-garde practice that is more than pseudomorphic.

I have chosen three films from film's first decade, all of which show a unique representation of space on the screen and a particular relation between audience and spectacle. Although all three of these films differ in the way they define these relations, they have in common the fact that their approaches were gradually abandoned during the period 1908–13 and nearly forbidden in commercial cinema in the decades following. This transition period from 1908 to 1913 is an important one. During this time we see the first broad economic organization of the film industry, the first moves on the part of production companies to attract a middle-class audience, and the dominance of narrative cinema over actualities, along with the development of the basic syntax of narrative film. All of these traits can be seen reflected in the films D. W. Griffith made during this period for the Biograph Company.

---

[2]Walter Benjamin, "Art in the Age of Mechanical Reproduction," in *Illuminations* (New York: Harcourt, Brace, Jovanovich, 1968). This article is strongly indebted to Benjamin's ideas.

My first example is George Méliès's *Le Mélomane* from 1903. Here an eccentric music master (played by Méliès himself) leads his female companions into a strange landscape dominated by a large utility pole bearing power lines, standing against a dark sky. He tosses a large musical clef up onto the power lines, redefining the space as that of a musical staff. Using his own detachable and self-multiplying head for notes, he then proceeds to compose a tune.

The comparison of Méliès to the films of the avant-garde is such a cliché of film history that it has almost been forgotten. In the late 20s and early 30s the Surrealists embraced the retired filmmaker, discovered selling toys and candies in Montparnasse Station, acknowledging their common delight in transformations and the marvelous. Partly mediated through the Surrealists, the heritage of Méliès can be seen in the films of the first generation of American avant-garde filmmakers: Maya Deren, Harry Smith, Kenneth Anger, Stan Brakhage, and others. But what I would like to focus on is less the films by Méliès that involve the metamorphosis of people, objects, and settings through stop-motion than those films, nearly as numerous, which explore the magical effects of multiple exposure.

In stop-motion, Méliès found a convenient and effective cinematic equivalent of the trap doors, fake panels, and quick light changes that allowed transformations in his Théâtre Robert-Houdin. Multiple exposure also had its stage antecedents in the reflections on glass (known as "the Pepper's Ghost Illusion") or the use of black backgrounds which could render dark shrouded figures invisible. In a number of Méliès's films a black area in the set left an area of virginal film on the camera negative onto which a new image could be fixed when the film was rewound in the camera. This allowed an illusion not possible on the stage, the multiple reproduction of a single figure. In the essay on filmmaking he wrote in 1907, Méliès recounts the nightmare it could be to make such a film.[3] With all the effects created in the camera, it was always possible that a scene requiring six superimpositions, with rigorous control of placement and movement, would suddenly tear on the fifth shooting and have to be begun all over again. Nonetheless the genre fascinated him and, apparently, his audience.

Most often, it was Méliès himself who was reproduced in this manner, his head more often than his full figure. In *Le Mélomane* a number of Méliès's faces grin and grimace at us from their positions on the musical staff. The black sky has become the ground on which numerous images of the same face can be printed. In *L'Homme d'orchestre*, Méliès reproduced himself seven times as the various members of an orchestra, each one playing a different instrument. Reproductions of his detached head appear in *The Man with the Rubber Head*—in which Méliès inflates a duplicate of his own head to enormous proportions until it explodes—and *A Fine Joke on My Head*, in which he torments his free-floating head with cigar smoke.

---

[3]This essay is reprinted in Georges Sadoul, *Georges Méliès* (Paris: Edition Seghers, 1961).

All these films can summon up a comparison to the avant-garde and surrealist traditions in film through their destruction of the principle of identity and their possible psychoanalytic associations. They can be seen as ancestors of the triple Maya Deren seated around the dining-room table in *Meshes of the Afternoon* (1943). However, Deren's sense of psychodrama is missing in Méliès, and with it the illusionistic three-dimensional space of the surrealist depiction of the dream. A more accurate description of Méliès's films notes their playfulness, their delight in the phenomenon of photographic reproduction.

The space of Méliès's films, with its predominantly stage-like tableaux and theatrical blocking, has most often been related to the space of the turn-of-the-century theater—specifically Méliès's own Théâtre Robert-Houdin. For those primarily familiar with his longer narrative films—*A Trip to the Moon, Fairyland,* or *The Kingdom of the Fairies, The Palace of The Arabian Nights, An Impossible Voyage,* etc.—this may seem accurate. However, a film like *Le Mélomane* (as well as sequences in his longer films) presents a different space. The space is defined as a surface bearing the imprint of several images that create an ambiguous area of often contradictory orientations. This is evident in *Le Mélomane* as the painted backdrop of power lines against a night sky becomes transformed into the flat space of musical notation. The head-notes embody this double nature, appearing both as notes on a page and as grimacing faces. The multiplying of the same face further emphasizes the surface of the film as the repository for multiple reprintings.

This type of ambiguous space reappears in a number of Méliès's films involving superimposition or primitive matting. In *The Magic Lantern,* a circular insert reveals a close-up of the two dolls seen prancing below. The insert is explained as a projection from the magic lantern shown in the shot. No explanation is given for the circular insert in *Au Clair de la Lune, ou Pierrot malheureux,* which at one moment is the moon and at the next becomes a wildly rolling eye and arching eyebrow. In these films a conflict in scale further creates the impression of a collage-like space within which contradictory spatial images have been united.

A fertile comparison within the American avant-garde to this aspect of Méliès would be the sequence that begins part 4 of Stan Brakhage's *Dog Star Man,* in which four layers of superimposition of the film's protagonist start to rise from the ground. The comparison should be made not only on the basis of the multiple images of the same figure, but also in the way this multiple superimposition transforms the space of the screen into a matrix of contradictory spaces, as it often does throughout *Dog Star Man.* Brakhage has acknowledged his admiration for Méliès (referring however to his set designs rather than to his use of multiple exposure), and has described Méliès's films as an attack on Western painterly perspective.[4]

---

[4]Stan Brakhage, *The Brakhage Lectures* (Chicago: Good Lion Press, 1972), p. 22.

But a gap in intentions appears. Brakhage's image functions as a metaphor for the division of identity that forms the basis of his mythic film. Méliès's space is also metaphorical, with its reading of power lines as a musical staff. But it is a self-contained metaphor of the process of the trick itself, the conflict between film as a representation of three-dimensional figures and as a flat repository for printed images. Likewise the ambiguous flowing together of Brakhage's superimpositions creates a sort of abstract-expressionist space quite alien to Méliès.

Méliès's approach to cinematic space was soon to be eclipsed. Even before the economic collapse of his production company, Star Film, this earlier mode of filmmaking was nearly abandoned. By 1911 practically the only films released by his firm were the westerns produced by his brother Gaston in Texas. Already by 1908 (if not earlier) the trick film—once the major fictional genre of early cinema—had lost its popularity. One American reviewer claimed the audience lost interest once they learned how the trick was done. The ascendency of the narrative film with its verisimilitude of space sounded the death knell of Méliès's style. It must be stressed that the attitude toward the camera that nearly disappeared with Méliès was not, as has often been claimed, simply that of a recording device for a theatrical spectacle. It is more correct to say that Méliès saw the camera as a sort of printing press that could imprint film with an ambiguous figure midway between letters and objects, like the grinning half notes in *Le Mélomane.*

My next example of the unique space of early film is that of a film of a man framed at the waist. The man grimly contemplates a pistol and places it next to his temple. Then stopping abruptly, he looks directly out from the screen, points his finger toward the audience/camera, and laughs. The title of this single shot Edison film from 1902 is *The Burlesque Suicide.* This film raises another issue of the relation between the camera and the space before it. The direct look and its accompanying gesture shatters the fictional suicide, revealing it as a joke on the camera (or more accurately, on the audience, who now occupies the area beyond the frame previously occupied by the camera). The acknowledgment and engagement of the audience by the actor creates a different sort of ambiguous spatial relation because it indicates that the space on the screen is not a self-contained fictional world, but can be directly linked to the space of the spectator.

This is not at all infrequent in films before 1908. It appears most often in comic films with the actor letting the audience in on a joke. In comic films, this aside to the audience probably never entirely disappears, even with the coming of sound, although it is modified. Perhaps its most interesting appearance in early movies is in erotic film (again a tradition that continues in some pornographic films, but outside the dominant forms of filmmaking). Frequently, as in Biograph's *From Show Girl to Burlesque Queen* (1903), a woman undressing before the camera will stare directly at the camera as though meeting the gaze of the spectator. This seeming acknowledgment of the presence of the spectator-voyeur gives these films much of their erotic power.

A Pathé film from 1902, *Le Coucher de la Mariée,* shows the problematic relation such an erotic glance has to the space of the narrative. In this film a woman undresses in a set of a bedroom. A man watches her from behind a screen on the right. Although the woman appears unaware of the voyeur included within the frame, her gaze, gestures, and expressions indicate she is aware of, and acknowledges, the observing camera/audience. We as spectators have a privileged erotic relation to the woman not shared by the man within the space of the fiction.

One may see this playing to the camera as the translation of a stage device to the screen. Nineteenth-century melodrama, vaudeville, and burlesque all had traditions of asides (not to mention the soliloquies of Elizabethan drama), of turning to the audience and directly addressing it. However, the effect in film is different. The actor does not turn and acknowledge the gaze of an actually present audience, but that of the camera. The audience does not greet the eyes of a flesh and blood actor, but that of his image on the screen. This dialectic of presence and absence (which is the most radical departure of film from theater) is underscored by the ghost-like meeting of glances. It is interesting that films revolving around such confrontations of the audience were often shot in medium close-up. The larger scale of the image allowed the actor's straightforward stare to be the center of attention. Further, films of this sort were often only a single shot in length. We find the large scale of image not only in *Burlesque Suicide* but also in the famous closing shot of Porter's *The Great Train Robbery* with its outlaw firing into the audience/camera. The Edison catalogue for this film informed exhibitors that they could place this shot either at the beginning or end of the film.[5] This advice reveals an era in which the exhibitor still made major decisions in the construction of a spectacle, but also shows the problematic role of this offscreen glance in a multi-shot fictional film. The outlaw who fires at the audience is difficult to integrate into the world of the fiction. As Noël Burch has phrased it, this shot "seems to hover on the fringe of a diegesis which cannot assimilate it."[6]

A direct look at the camera was later seen as sabotaging the developing space of narrative cinema, and it became taboo. As an offscreen glance became one of the ways shots were linked together and a synthetic space was created, a glance like this directed at the audience/camera would undermine these connections. We find this change in the actor's relation to the camera discussed and argued for a few years later by the most influential and sophisticated film reviewer of the time, Frank Woods, who wrote for the *New York Dramatic Mirror* under the name "The Spectator."

In 1910, particularly, Woods attacked playing to the camera as contrary to the

---

[5]The catalogue description can be found reprinted in George Pratt, ed., *Spellbound in Darkness* (Greenwich, Conn.: New York Graphic Society, 1972), pp. 34–36.

[6]Noël Burch, "Film's Institutional Mode of Representation and the Soviet Response," *October* 11 (Winter 1979): 79.

principles of film. For Woods, the unique "illusion of reality" in film depended not on the dropping of stage conventions, but on ignoring the presence of the camera. "Picture acting," he declared, "is far more convincing and effective when the players appear to be ignorant that there is a camera taking their picture. Facial remarks directed at the camera destroy the illusion of reality."[7] This pretended absence of the camera implied a new relation between spectator and screen: "We the spectators are not part of the picture, nor is there supposed to be a camera there making a moving photograph of the scene."[8] This taboo on looking at the film's place of origin (which reminds me a bit of orthodox Judaism's stricture against looking at the sexual organs) and its resulting forbidding of direct engagement of the audience became one of the bases of the enclosed fictional space of the classical narrative film.[9]

The relation of the avant-garde film to the enclosed fictive space of classical cinema has always been one of divergence. A history of the form of American avant-garde film could be written around the strategies used to create new relations between spectator and film. Such filmmakers as Brakhage (*Blue Moses*), George Landow (*Remedial Reading Comprehension; Wide Angle Saxon*), and Robert Nelson (*Bleu Shut*) have used direct address to the audience. However the important issue here is not the similarity these later films bear to the audience engagement images of early film (the avant-garde filmmakers' sources for this technique were undoubtedly not early film). Rather the difference both forms share with classical narrative film's relation to the spectator reveals the point of comparison. Of course there is a world of difference between early cinema before the imposition of the taboo of looking at the camera and the conscious violation of that taboo by later radical filmmakers.

My final example of the space in early film is called *Panorama of the Flatiron Building*, a Biograph film from 1903. This "actuality" begins by observing the base of the then tallest building in New York City with the traffic and pedestrians moving around it. The camera tilts up somewhat jerkily until it views the top of the building. The film then ends. This film carries an obvious similarity to a number of films of the avant-garde in which camera movement within a space determines the whole structure of the film. However this film, in which the camera imitates the gesture of the rube in the big city craning his neck to see the top of the first skyscraper, may seem quite conventional and its relation to the

---

[7] "The Spectator," in the *New York Dramatic Mirror*, April 10, 1910.

[8] Ibid., June 25, 1910.

[9] Readers of recent film theory will find here rich historical evidence to relate to the theory of the "suture" as propounded by Jean-Pierre Oudart, Stephen Heath, and others. A history of the use and avoidance of the direct glance at the camera would be fascinating, not only in such experimental directors as Eisenstein and Godard, but also in such classical directors as Griffith, Ford, and Hitchcock.

avant-garde the most pseudomorphic. The camera here accepts, portrays, and explores the illusionary deep space of travelogues and picture postcards. Its resemblance to the relation between form and camera movement in films typified by Michael Snow's *Wavelength*, ◄————►(*Back and Forth*), and *La Région centrale* seems at first quite accidental. This film does not use the aspect of duration (it lasts a little over a minute, compared to *La Région centrale*'s three hours) nor does it accomplish the transformation of space by camera movement that Snow's films exhibit.

However, this "panorama" represents a genre of considerable importance in films made between 1900 and about 1907, one which reveals another peculiar relation between spectator and the space represented on the screen. Writing the history of camera movement from the perspective of later narrative cinema, one might suppose that it began as a subsidiary to narrative action. The camera moves when something in the shot moves. One thinks of the tracking shots following the galloping Klan in *The Birth of a Nation*, or the pan which keeps the outlaws in frame as they move toward their horses in *The Great Train Robbery*. But as this film (and others related to it) shows, camera movement began as a display of the camera's ability to mobilize and explore space. The "content" or purpose of this film is as much a demonstration of the camera's ability to tilt as it is the Flatiron Building.

We find a plethora of such films in early cinema, based on camera movement from a variety of vehicles as well as from the camera's moveable tripod. In the Library of Congress Paper Print Collection we find circular pans of a number of man-made and natural wonders. Niagara Falls is shown the most often, but other sights filmed in this way include the Jones and Laughlin Steel Works Yard, the Market in Cairo, Egypt, Le Champs de Mars, the Electric Tower at the Pan American Exposition, and so on. Cameras were catapulted into space by means of subway cars, freight trains, aerial balloons, street cars, gondolas, and the moving boardwalk at the Paris Exposition in 1900.

The International Expositions that crowd the first years of the twentieth century seem especially to spawn such films. The Paris Exposition in 1900, the Pan American Exposition in 1901, and the St. Louis Exposition in 1904 were all recorded by a variety of moving cameras. The 1900 Exposition also saw the most ambitious attempt to exploit such films—the Cineorama of Grimoin-Sanson. This attraction showed scenes photographed from a balloon on a circular screen serviced by ten projectors. Unfortunately the heat of the projection room caused the projectionist to faint, and the Cineorama was closed as a fire hazard.[10] A more modest and far-reaching means of exhibition was introduced at the St. Louis Exposition. Known as Hale's Tours, this attraction projected films on a front wall of a projection room designed to resemble a train car complete with a conductor

---

[10]See the account of the Cinéorama in Georges Sadoul's *Histoire générale du cinéma*, vol. 2 (Paris: Editions Denoël, 1948), pp. 93–99.

who called out the location shown in each film, sound effects simulating airbrakes and the clickety-clack of the track, and a mechanically produced swaying and rocking of the car. After the exposition, Hale's Tours opened in nearly every major American city, reaching a peak of 500 shows in 1905. In most cities Hale's Tours were the first theaters to show a program consisting entirely of films.[11]

The experience to be reconstituted in these films is the thrill of motion and its transformation of space. Although a large part of their appeal was clearly as a cheap form of vicarious tourism for the masses, the experience was also uniquely cinematic. The sense of penetration of space by the unseen camera gave the spectator an almost uncanny feeling. An early reviewer for the *New York Mail and Express* described Biograph's moving camera film of the Haverstraw Tunnel in this way:

> The way in which the unseen energy swallows up space and flings itself into the distances is as mysterious and impressive almost as an allegory. A sensation is produced akin to that which Poe in his "Fall of the House of Usher" relates was communicated to him by his doomed companion when he sketched the shaft in the heart of the earth, with an unearthly radiance thrilling through it. One holds his breathe instinctively as he is swept along in the rush of the phantom cars. His attention is held almost with the vise of fate.[12]

Exhibition situations like Hale's Tours both gave a reassuring context for this experience (the audience is on a train) and played with it (everyone knew they weren't really on a train). Film historian Charles Musser has found a lecture from 1901 which accompanied a showing of a film of a tilt up the Electric Tower at the Pan American Exposition (a film much like our *Panorama of the Flatiron Building*) which explains the camera movement as the rising and descending of a balloon. The desire to provide a place for the spectator related to the movement within the spectacle reveals the enjoyable anxiety the audience felt before the illusion of motion.

Interestingly the idea of providing an onlooker as a sort of stand-in for the audience appears in some early films and then seems to be dropped. One of the earliest surviving panorama films, Edison's *Mt. Tamalpais RR No. 2* from 1898, angles the camera so that a woman tourist is seen in the foreground watching the landscape unwind around her. But the vast majority of these panoramas present the landscape unmediated. Our only connection with it is the unseen, but experienced, camera.

---

[11]See Raymond Fielding, "Hale's Tours: Ultrarealism in the Pre-1910 Motion Pictures," in part 2 of this volume.

[12]Quoted in Robert C. Allen, "Vaudeville and the Film, 1895–1915: A Study in Media Interaction" (Ph.D. dissertation, University of Iowa, 1977), p. 131.

The name given to many of these films—panorama—announces their ancestory in popular entertainments before cinema. Huge circular paintings, static or moving, of historical events or wonders of nature were a standard feature of fairs or the theater districts of great cities in the nineteenth century. Daguerre's Diorama, with effects of light and transparency, was only the beginning of complicated ways of presenting landscapes, some of which were in motion. But the photographic illusion of motion awaited, of course, the arrival of motion pictures. Even today amusement parks have attractions employing motion pictures to give an illusion of movement in ways that descend from the Cineorama and Hale's Tours.

However, before we relinquish this particular relation of spectator to screen to the amusements of popular culture, the implications of this experience of motion and landscape needs to be probed, particularly in the context of its period. In 1914, ten years after the opening of Hale's Tours, the cubist painter Fernand Léger was to write:

> When one crosses a landscape by automobile or express train it becomes fragmented; it loses in descriptive value but gains in synthetic value. The view through the door of the railroad car or the automobile windshield in combination with the speed has altered the habitual look of things.[13]

It was to this and similar transformations in perception caused by modern life that Léger attributed the new look of modernist painting. The similar effect of the views from speeding vehicles on Futurist painting and manifestos is well known.[14]

In fact, several panorama films seem to be deliberately undercranked in order to cause the spectator a sort of vertigo. A film taken from a boat by Biograph in 1903, *Down the Hudson,* uses extreme undercranking at points to produce dizzying effects of speed. The rate of cranking varies throughout the film, so that a spectator would become aware of its mechanical creation. Such effects could also be created by the projectionist in the days of hand-cranked projectors. Showman Lyman Howe often ended his program of films with an attraction called *The Runaway Train* in which a wildly overcranked projector caused a film taken from a train in the Alps to plunge down inclines and across bridges, creating a sensation in the audience.[15]

These borrowed landscapes, this mechanical reproduction of the route of the

---

[13]Fernand Léger, "Contemporary Achievements in Painting," in *Functions of Painting* (New York: Viking, 1973), p. 11.

[14]See "The Founding and Manifesto of Futurism" in *Futurist Manifestos,* ed. Umbro Appolonio (New York: Viking, 1973).

[15]*Motography,* July 1911, p. 5.

tourist, ultimately referred back to the camera, the "unseen energy" that invaded space and transformed it. Perhaps this primal experience of the camera devouring space was not that distant from the experience of Snow's gyrating camera in *La Région centrale*. In any case the movies deserve to be seen as ancestors of a film experience that has recently reappeared. It is interesting to see that camera movement films of this sort also did not survive in later cinema, or were radically altered. After an initial success Hale's Tours found audiences dwindling. Perhaps this explains Selig Polyscope's (which supplied some of the films used) change in its product. The catalogue description of their *Trip over Cripple Creek Short Line* reads as follows:

> A special train over the famous Cripple Creek short line is in picture constantly and on the rear platform is a group of pretty girls in summer dress. Their smiling faces and gestures add much to the picture and give a touch of novelty never before attempted.[16]

Travelogues began to appear (or, as early exhibitors called them, "scenics"), which tended to have actors portraying tourists as mediators for the audience's enjoyment of distant places. The landscape itself, the "view," was now more important than the experience of motion.

We can see an interesting absorbing of this kind of camera movement into the space of narrative film in D. W. Griffith's *The Country Doctor* from 1909. The film opens with a slow pan across a springtime valley. The pan leads us to the house from which the doctor and his family emerge. Instead of simply exploring space, here the camera movement serves as an establishing shot, bringing the spectator into the world of the narrative. The film ends with a reversal of this pan, moving away from the doctor's house back into the larger world. The two pans serve to bracket the world of the film and define the space of narrative.

These three examples from early cinema show approaches to space and attitudes toward the spectator that were either eliminated or greatly transformed by the development of narrative cinema in the decade after 1908. Their relation to avant-garde films which later proposed alternatives to this system of narrative space is not simple. Certainly early filmmakers envisioned no aesthetic project like that of the avant-garde filmmaker. It is dubious that any of these films were thought about aesthetically at all. However, they display quite nakedly new relations to the representation of space that the camera made possible. Some of these possibilities were rediscovered by the avant-garde. But every rediscovery is a recreation. In this case tasks and roles that were unimaginable to the filmmakers of cinema's first decade are implied.

Regina Cornwell, in a discussion of the ambiguous relation between early

---

[16]Fielding, "Hale's Tours."

film and the avant-garde, noted the paradox contained in the title of Ernie Gehr's film, *History*. The simplicity of this film caused Michael Snow to declare, "At last, the first film."[17] Yet as Cornwell points out this film could not have been made until the early 70s.[18] History is what divides the approaches of early film from those of the avant-garde. If one of the projects of the avant-garde is to return to the origins of cinema, that return can only be historically aware. Early cinema offers a number of roads not taken, ambiguities not absorbed into commercial narrative cinema. But for the avant-garde these need not be seen as history's dead-end streets. They can be inspirations for new understandings of tradition and for new films.

---

[17]Quoted in Ernie Gehr, "Program Notes by Ernie Gehr for a Film Showing at the Museum of Modern Art, New York City, February 2, 1971, at 5: 30 PM," *Film Culture* 53–55 (1972):37.

[18]Regina Cornwell, "Progress Discontinuous," *Artforum* 18 (April 1980):60–67. Ms. Cornwell's article was originally presented as part of the series of talks (see n. 1) at the Whitney Museum.

EILEEN BOWSER

Griffith's Film Career Before
The Adventures of Dollie

The time is 1907. An inventor of a motion picture camera is brutally murdered in his workshop, stabbed with his own paper cutter. His daughter is found beside the body, clutching the murder weapon, and is accused of the crime. Her lover, convinced of her innocence, searches the scene of the murder for clues. He finds the inventor's camera with a roll of film still inside. The inventor, it turns out, had been testing his invention at the time of the murder. The young man takes the film into the darkroom. Cut to close-up to show the process of developing in the chemical bath. In the courtroom, he proposes to show the film as evidence of the heroine's innocence and the identity of the real murderer. The fellow holding up the left-hand corner of the sheet serving as a screen is strangely familiar. It is David Wark Griffith, making a prophetic entrance in motion pictures holding up the blank screen that will be so wonderfully filled by him in the years to come. At least, we'd like to think of it as his film debut. We know that it was before he played in *Rescued from an Eagle's Nest,* which is usually cited.

Linda Arvidson's account of her husband's first or second film at Biograph describes him as riding horses in the wilds of Ft. Lee.[1] We can't identify any film to match that description. *Falsely Accused!,* the film described above, was made in the Biograph studio on 14th Street on December 26, 27, and 28, 1907, photographed by Griffith's future colleague, Billy Bitzer. As Griffith's bit part is confined to the courtroom scene, he probably worked on only one of those three days. The screen he holds up in the film is blank because the scene to be projected on it was to be matted in. It was filmed separately and appears in the original negative at the end of the film in the correct size to fill the blank screen. A system of double

---

[1]Linda Arvidson, *When the Movies Were Young* (New York: Dutton, 1925), p. 31.

printing for each projection print must have been used, since optical printers were not yet in use and the Biograph camera did not permit doing matte shots in the camera. The film could not be run back through the camera again because it was unperforated stock which had the holes cut in during the filming by a device in the camera. The same double printing method must have been used to make the matte shots for *Bobby's Kodak*, filmed at about the same time, and for *Those Awful Hats*, directed by Griffith in January 1909. This was a day when prints were all assembled by hand, and the number to be made was not that large. There is a good view of Biograph's 68 mm. camera in *Falsely Accused!*, though not in close-up.

Rescued from an Eagles's Nest was filmed in the Palisades across the river in New Jersey the following week (January 2 and 7, 1908). Although this was not Griffith's first film appearance, it was probably his first leading role. As the woodsman saving his baby from the clutches of an eagle, he is virile and heroic and overacts to the point of being "hammy," but no more so than most film actors at the time. He was far from realizing the restraint demanded by the intimacy of the motion picture camera. Most people view this film in the context of the later Griffith films and see it as crude and primitive. But when it is seen in the context of the other films of its period,[2] it is a fairly average melodrama, using the conventions of what must have been a stage presentation as well as the conventions of the chase film as established in the pre-Griffith period,[3] and combining painted backdrops with reality as many films of the time did. One can believe that contemporary audiences found it exciting.

Griffith's next screen experience probably occured a week later (January 15–20) at the Biograph studio, as an extra in *Classmates*, photographed by Bitzer. This was an elaborate production, utilizing two earlier Biograph actuality films as part of the fictional plot. Griffith plays only a bit, but gets quite a lot of footage as an energetic and none-too-graceful dancer at the Harvard college ball. On February 7, Griffith was back at Edison, with another bit part as one of the dancers at a ball (already typecast?) in *Cupid's Pranks*. This is an imaginative trick film, with horizontal and vertical split screens showing Cupid in conjunction with actuality films of New York skyscrapers. Split screens were one of early cinema's devices for relating separate spaces in one frame. Next, according to Kemp Niver, Griffith played a principle role in *The Princess in the Vase*, made at Biograph on February 10 and 14.[4] We have not been able to confirm this in repeated screenings of the film.

---

[2]This paper is based on films seen during a Film Research Seminar organized at the Museum of Modern Art, January 1980, dedicated to the year 1907 and the first part of 1908, to investigate the state of film narrative at the time Griffith entered films.

[3]The conventions of the early comic chase films are outlined in my article "The Brighton Project: An Introduction," *Quarterly Review of Film Studies* 3 (Fall 1979): 524–25.

[4]Kemp R. Niver, *Motion Pictures from the Library of Congress Paper Print Collection, 1894–1912* (Berkeley: University of California Press, 1967), pp. 79–80.

We don't mean to say that Niver is wrong but only that we find it difficult to recognize Griffith in his makeup in the role of the lover of an Egyptian princess of ancient times and reincarnated in modern times. Another problem complicates the identification. Our print varies from that described in the *Biograph Bulletin* and the description of the paper print by Niver. To enter into this problem would take me too far from my present topic. However, this is probably Griffith's fifth film appearance.

His next film work is as scriptwriter for *Old Isaacs the Pawnbroker* (photographed by Marvin on March 17, 18, and 19). This film is of much more interest in the light of his future career. According to Linda Arvidson, this was "the first little cinema drama of which he was the author and which was immediately put into the works. . . ."[5] Although she wrote this many years later, we are inclined to believe her memory to be correct in this case. It would have meant an extra $15 or so at a time when they were glad to get $5 a day for an acting assignment. That is good reason for remembering.

The film is about the efforts of a little girl to get help for her invalid mother, about to be evicted from her poverty-stricken home. The child visits the offices of the Amalgamated Association of Charities, a big bureaucracy where she is sent from one office to the next without being given any immediate help. In desperation, she takes her mother's old shoes to the pawnbroker, and when they are refused, she returns with her doll. The pawnbroker, moved by this pathetic sight, questions her and finds out about the dire straights of the little family. He comes to the rescue in time to stave off their eviction, bringing food and clothing. The drama is enlivened with additional characters who visit the pawnbroker's shop—a drunken Irish washerwoman, a burglar, I don't remember who else. The poor people belong to various ethnic immigrant groups and are shown at last to have more sensitivity then organized charity. The Jewish pawnbroker, stereotyped in appearance, is not stereotypical in his behavior. He is courageous, as shown by his fight with the burglar. He is sensitive, generous, and kind, as shown by his treatment of the little girl. We know that Biograph deliberately attacked ethnic prejudice in this film by the words of the *Biograph Bulletin* issued with it, which states that it "dissipates the malignant calumnies launched at the Hebraic race."[6] The bitterness against organized charities and reform movements was to show up a number of times in Griffith's films, in such Biograph films as *Simple Chairty* (1910), *The Reformers, or the Lost Art of Minding One's Own Business* (1913), and, the most well-known example, the modern story of *Intolerance*. The theme of the pathetic child who brings about change in the lives

[5]Arvidson, *When the Movies Were Young,* p. 40.
[6]*Biograph Bulletins, 1896–1908,* compiled by Kemp R. Niver (Los Angeles: Locare Research Group, 1971), p. 344.

of the adults around her is very common in Griffith's Biograph films and also in the work of other filmmakers of the period.

The most interesting aspect of *Old Isaacs the Pawnbroker*, looking forward to what Griffith was to do as a director, is the appearance of parallel editing to link distant events occurring in the same time frame. At least, it seems to be in the same time frame, although one must never be overconfident in interpreting the intentions of a filmmaker at this time. Examples of parallel editing were already in existence even if not clearly articulated. The first decade of cinema adapted what Tom Gunning has called the noncontinuous style, with each filmed action (single shot) autonomous in itself.[7] Action was frequently repeated when a new viewpoint was needed (a new location). The style, derived from the magic lantern shows, cartoons, and similar preexisting sources of pictorial narrative, had begun to reach its limits in the push toward longer and more complex narratives in the nickelodeon era, when the narrator-showman no longer ran every film show. Its conventions were to be gradually abandoned by most filmmakers as they began to consider alternate ways to link the actions of the narrative in space and time. By 1907, one can find films where cuts are made on action and movement continues from one shot to the next instead of being repeated. The earliest editing steps appear to have been taken as an attempt to relate actions in adjacent spaces (usually interior/exterior spaces), and quite a few of them might be interpreted as the need to show visual equivalents of sounds, sounds to which the characters react. (Were these sounds meant to be heard by the audience, through the use of effects during a performance?) In Vitagraph's *The Mill Girl*, copyrighted September 17, 1907, the hero in his bedroom reacts to some sound he hears from outside, and prepares for an impending attack by thugs climbing a ladder outside his window. There are several cuts back and forth to exterior and interior scenes before the men enter the window. In *The Trainer's Daughter* (Edison, copyrighted November 15, 1907), the characters in the horse stable preparing for a race react to an intercut shot of a man blowing a horn to start a race. In *Chiens Policiers* (made in France by Eclipse, believed to be in 1907), a group of policemen are walking along and seem to hear something, looking out of frame. In the next shot there is a robbery in process. We return to the police, who then run out of frame and enter the scene of the robbery in the next shot. In *Francesca di Rimini* (Vitagraph, copyrighted September 4, 1907), the Hunchback looks up and out of frame as though he heard a sound, there is a cut to an approaching messenger, and then we return to the Hunchback as the messenger enters the scene. Not every example of the beginnings of parallel editing can be related to a sound, however. In *Cheval emballé* ("The Runaway Horse"), made in France by Zecca and released December 21, 1907, the horse waiting for his master making milk deliveries inside the house eats the sack of grain on the sidewalk, with several cuts between

---

[7]Tom Gunning, "Le Style non-continu du cinéma des premiers temps," *Les Cahiers de la cinémathèque* 29 (Winter 1979): 24–31.

the simultaneous actions. A few hints of parallel editing begin to enter the conventions of the chase film as well, in such films as Vitagraph's *One Hundred to One Shot* (1906) and Biograph's *The Elopement,* made in November 1907.

In no other film we have seen up to this time is there any example of parallel editing of the kind found in *Old Isaacs the Pawnbroker.* It is, to be sure, only one shot. In the midst of the sequence where the little girl is going around the offices of the Amalgamated Association of Charities, there is cut in one shot of her invalid mother at home, trying to rise from her sickbed and falling back on her pillows. The action then continues at the charity offices. The only reason we can imagine for the interpolation of this shot is a deliberate intent to underline the pathos or the irony of the situation. This is precisely the kind of thing Griffith was going to do very early on in his career as a director. The cut is unusual as well because it links events that are presumably quite distant, not in the adjacent spaces. Griffith was to turn the newly-minted formal devices of cinema to expressive use as no one else had done. One can hardly believe that the novice screenplay writer could have written the specific shot into his little scenario, or that he might have been hanging around the studio to suggest it. It is a tempting thought, though. There was something about Griffith that convinced the Biograph management to offer him a chance at directing. If it wasn't his idea to insert that shot, whoever did do it may have started an idea in Griffith's mind. It seems a remarkable coincidence, if I do not exaggerate the importance of this shot, that it should have turned up in a film made from a Griffith script.

Linda Arvidson reports that Griffith played the leading role in *The Music Master,* made April 7 and 9 at the Biograph studio. I have not seen this film and don't know of any existing copy. Judging by the description in the *Biograph Bulletin,* it appears to have used as a model Edison's *Fireside Reminiscences,* made in January of the same year. In both films a man sitting by his fireside remembers episodes from his past, which are matted into the scene. In *Fireside Reminiscences,* the scenes are placed in the fireplace, while the description of *The Music Master* only says "on the wall" there appears "a phantasmagorical portrayal of his thoughts. . . ." The illustration shows the side-lighting effect from the fireplace that was later to be hailed as an innovation in Griffith's *A Drunkard's Reformation.* In fact, Bitzer had utilized dramatic side-lighting long before, very effectively in *The Paymaster,* made in June 1906. The tendency to express all temporal and spatial relationships in one shot in early cinema style led to interesting solutions such as the matting in flashback cuts.

On April 18 and 20, Biograph made an animation trick film called *The Sculptor's Nightmare,* in which Griffith, Mack Sennett (some time before his official "debut" in films), and Eddie Dillon made appearances. The members of a political club cannot agree on which candidate to support at the forthcoming convention. They storm the studio of a sculptor to commission busts of the rival candidates. The sculptor has a nightmare in which lumps of clay form themselves into busts of Taft, Fairbanks, Bryon, a "Teddy" bear, and then Roosevelt himself.

Griffith's bit is very small, but the film itself is interesting for an unusually well-matched (for the time) cut to reverse angle, when the crowd of politicians come to the studio. The sculptor stands at his open door, arm raised in alarm; the next shot reverses to inside the studio, showing his back, arm still upraised, in much the same position on the screen. There are also a couple of cuts to a closer view in midscene, but this is not at all unusual in films before 1908.

Linda Arvidson identifies *When Knights Were Bold* (April 22) as the only joint appearance of herself with her husband. The wigs, makeup, and costumes of the sixteenth-century English court and the great distance of the actors from the camera make it difficult to recognize them, at least in our print, which is quite incomplete due to deterioration of the original nitrate. Arvidson contradicts herself on the point of "only joint appearance" when she mentions a mutoscope called *A Studio Party* in which she and Griffith both played.[8] There is no such title listed for the time period, although the Biograph production records include numerous suggestively titled mutoscopes, but she may well have been mistaken about the title.[9] We haven't been able to identify it.

Another script by Griffith, *'Ostler Joe,* was made on May 7, 8, and 9, Bitzer at the camera and Griffith in a principle role as the seducer of a married woman. Based on a poem by George R. Sims which had been the basis of a popular stage presentation by Mrs. James Brown Potter, the script is typical of Griffith's material in the Biograph years. A happy family, composed of an honest working man (Tony O'Sullivan), his innocent wife, and their baby, is broken up when Griffith lures the lady away to a gay lifestyle. The baby dies and the fallen woman ends deserted, poor, and dying, while her faithful, now white-haired husband waits at her bedside. On May 22 and 24, Griffith played another extra role, as a customer in a restaurant in *Man in the Box,* a thriller remade from Biograph's 1905 *The Great Jewel Mystery.* On May 28 and 29, Griffith got a close-up in *At the French Ball,* in clown makeup, as a man who attends a costume party where his wife is also present, each unknown to the other. They begin a flirtation, which leads to disaster. This is a film I haven't seen, and must depend on Niver's account.[10]

Another Griffith script, *At the Crossroads of Life,* was filmed June 2 and 4, photographed by both Bitzer and Marvin. Once again, Griffith plays an evil seducer of young women. The daughters of a minister shock their father by playing at amateur theatricals. They go to a professional audition, and one of them is hired by the New York Opera Company. She is tempted to go astray by Griffith, but she really would prefer to go back home. Not quite able to admit this to her father, she sends him a telegram asking him to come see her performance. Father

[8]Arvidson, *When the Movies Were Young,* p. 45.

[9]Production records of the Biograph Company, Special Collections of the Library, Museum of Modern Art, New York.

[10]Niver, *Motion Pictures from the Library of Congress Paper Print Collection,* p. 10.

arrives backstage just in time to break up the planned seduction. Marion Leonard plays the heroine and Robert Harron has a bit part as the backstage call boy. The scenes of girls changing clothes in the dressing room recall the many Biograph erotic films of the time. The film's style is that of the earlier period. All the scenes are shot at a "stage distance," and there is the use of a split screen effect (really the wall of a flat) to separate the backstage areas and bring two simultaneous actions in adjacent spaces into one shot.

Griffith seems to have specialized in villain roles, playing an abductor in *The Black Viper* (made June 6 and 22) who meets his deserved fate in hand-to-hand combat with the hero, and a western holdup man (a good bad-man type) in *The Stage Rustler*, a tragic western for which he wrote the script, made June 10 and 13. I haven't seen either of these, which exist in the Library of Congress Paper Print Collection, and so this little study of Griffith's early film career is not complete. Whether every film he might have appeared in is mentioned here we do not know. Linda Arvidson said that Griffith made the rounds of Lubin, Kalem, and other studios, but was not hired. Still, perhaps there was a forgotten day of work here or there that will turn up one day. Griffith continued to make small appearances now and then in the Biograph films he directed. He was ready to step in when another extra was needed. One of the slyest such moments occurs in *The Adventures of Billy* (1911), a scene reminiscent of Hitchcock's deliberate appearances in his films. Little Billy is a bootblack, a poverty-stricken child. He (really she, played by Edna Foster) approaches a tall man sitting leisurely on a bench at the edge of the frame, not far from the camera, and the man turns his head ever so slightly into profile until he is recognizable as the director of the film.

It may be concluded that my real interest in this study of Griffith's career in films before he began to direct is not so much his performance as an actor, which has nothing much to recommend it, as it is to examine the state of filmmaking as it existed in 1907–8 and especially his experience of it, with a view to better understanding what he did when he took over responsibility for Biograph's productions. It is more than ever necessary to underline that Griffith was not an inventor of the cinematic devices for which he used to be credited in the older film histories. It is more complicated than that. His role was to consolidate what had been done sporadically by earlier filmmakers. His early films were a culmination of ideas rather than some newly-born film language. It was his ability to see the expressive possibilities in them that led him to become the first creative artist of American cinema.

Bibliography

Allen, Robert C. "Vaudeville and Film, 1895–1915: A Study in Media Interaction." Ph.D. dissertation, University of Iowa, 1977.

Allister, Ray. *Friese-Greene: Close-up of an Inventor*. London: Marsland, 1948.

Amengual, Barthelemy. "*The Life of an American Fireman* et la naissance du montage," *Les Cahiers de la cinémathèque* no. 17 (Christmas 1975).

Baker, Larry. "A History of Special Effect Cinematography in the United States, 1895–1914." M. A. thesis, West Virginia University, 1969.

Balio, Tino, ed. *The American Film Industry*. Madison: University of Wisconsin Press, 1976.

Barnes, John. *The Beginnings of the Cinema in England*. New York: Barnes and Noble, 1976.

Barr, J. Miller. "Animated Pictures." *Popular Science Monthly* 52 (December 1897): 177–88.

Benfield, Robert. *Bijou Kinema: A History of Early Cinema in Yorkshire*. Sheffield, U.K.: Sheffield City Polytechnic, 1976.

Bessy, Maurice. *Louis Lumière, inventeur*. Paris: Prisma, 1948.

_____ . *Méliès*. Paris: Anthologie du cinéma, 1966.

_____ , and Lo Duca, Giuseppe. *Georges Méliès*. Paris: J.J. Pauvert, 1961.

Black, Alexander. "Photography in Fiction." *Scribner's* 18 (September 1895): 348–60.

_____ . "The Camera and the Comedy." *Scribner's* 20 (November 1896): 605-10.

Bowser, Eileen. "The Brighton Project: An Introduction." *Quarterly Review of Film Studies* 4 (Fall 1979): 509-38.

Bromhead, A. C. *Reminiscences of the British Film Trade.* Proceedings of the British Kinematograph Society, offprint no. 21. British Kinematograph Society, 1933.

Brownlow, Kevin. *The Parade's Gone By. . . .* New York: Knopf, 1969.

Burch, Noël. "Porter or Ambivalence." *Screen* 19 (Winter 1978–79): 91–105.

Card, James. "Problems of Film History." *Hollywood Quarterly* 4 (Spring 1950): 279–88.

Ceram, C. W. [Kurt Wilhelm Marek]. *Archaeology of the Cinema.* New York: Harcourt, Brace, 1965.

Chanan, Michael. *The Dream That Kicks.* London: Routledge and Kegan Paul, 1980.

Cinema and Bioscope Magazine, nos. 1–4, 1906–7.

Cook, Olive. *Movement in Two Dimensions.* London: Hitchinson, 1963.

Currie, Barton W. "The Nickel Madness." *Harper's Weekly* 51 (August 24, 1907): 1246–47.

Deslandes, Jacques. *Le Boulevard du cinéma.* Paris: Editions du cerf, 1963.

———. *Histoire compareé du cinéma.* Vol. 1, *De la cinématique au cinématographe, 1826–1896.* Tournai, Belg.: Tornai Casterman, 1968.

———, and Richard, Jacques. *Histoire comparée du cinéma.* Vol. 2, *Du cinématographe au cinéma.* Tournai, Belg.: Tornai Casterman, 1966.

Deutelbaum, Marshall A. "Process and Circularity in Primitive Film Narrative." Ph.D. dissertation, University of Rochester, 1978.

———. ed. *"Image": On the Art and Evolution of the Film.* New York: Dover, 1979.

Dickson, Antonia and Dickson, W. K. L. "Edison's Invention of the Kineto-Phonograph." *Century* 48 (June 1894): 206–14.

Dickson, W. K. L. *Biograph in Battle.* London: Fisher Unwin, 1901.

Dickson, W. K. L. and Dickson, Antonia. *History of the Kinetograph and Kinetophonograph.* 1895. Reprint. New York: Arno, 1970.

East, John M. "Looking Back—When Croydon Was the Film Capital of Great Britain." In *Film Review, 1977–78,* edited by F. Maurice Speed. London: W. H. Allen, 1977.

Fay, Arthur. *Bioscope Shows and Their Engines.* Tarrant Hinton, U.K.: The Oakwood Press, 1966.

Fell, John L. *Film and the Narrative Tradition.* Norman, Okla.: University of Oklahoma Press, 1974.

———. "L'Articulation des rapports spatiaux." *Les Cahiers de la cinémathèque* 29 (Winter 1979): 81–87.

Fielding, Ray. *A Technological History of Motion Pictures and Television.* Berkeley: University of California Press, 1967.

Forty Years of Film History, 1895–1935: Notes on the Films. London: British Film Institute, n.d.

Frazer, John. *Artificially Arranged Scenes: The Films of Georges Méliès.* Boston: G. K. Hall, 1979.

Gartenberg, Jon. "Camera Movement in Edison and Biograph Films, 1900–1906." *Cinema Journal* 19 (Spring 1980): 1–16.

Gaudreault, André. "Detours in Film Narrative: The Development of Cross-Cutting." *Cinema Journal* 19 (Fall 1979): 39–59.

Gessner, Robert. "The Moving Image." *American Heritage* 11 (April 1960): 30–35.

Gifford, Denis. *The British Film Catalogue, 1895–1970.* Newton Abbot, U.K.: David and Charles, 1973.

Grau, Robert. *The Business Man in the Amusement World.* New York: Broadway, 1910.

_____ . *Theater of Science.* New York: Broadway, 1914.

Gunning, Tom. "Le Style non-continu du cinéma des premiers temps." *Les Cahiers de la cinémathèque* 29 (Winter 1979): 24–34.

Haas, Robert Bartlett. *Muybridge: Man in Motion.* Berkeley: University of California Press, 1976.

Hagan, John. "L'Erotisme des premiers temps." *Les Cahiers de la cinémathèque* 29 (Winter 1979): 72–79.

_____ . "Les Actions simultanées." *Les Cahiers de la cinémathèque* 29 (Winter 1979): 34–40.

Hamilton, Harlan. "Les Allures du cheval: Representées par la photographie instantanée." *La Nature,* December 14, 1897.

Hammond, Paul. *Marvelous Méliès.* New York: St. Martin's, 1975.

Hampton, Benjamin B. *A History of the Movies.* 1931. Reprint. New York: Dover, 1970.

Hendricks, Gordon. *The Edison Motion Picture Myth.* Berkeley: University of California Press, 1961. Reprint. New York: Arno, 1972.

_____ . "A New Look at an Old Sneeze." *Film Culture* no. 22–23 (1961): 90–95.

_____ . *Beginnings of the Biograph.* 1964. Reprint. New York. Arno, 1972.

_____ . *The Kinetoscope: America's First Commercially Successful Motion Picture Exhibitor.* New York: The Beginnings of the American Film, 1966.

_____ . *Eadweard Muybridge: The Father of the Motion Picture.* London: Secker and Warberg, 1975.

Hepworth, Cecil M. "Those Were the Days." In *The Penguin Film Review* 6 (1948): 33–39.

———. *Came the Dawn: Memories of a Film Pioneer.* London: Phoenix House, 1951.

———. *Animated Photography: The ABC of the Cinematograph.* 1900. Reprint. New York: Arno, 1970.

Hepworth, Thomas Cradock. *The Book of the Lantern.* 1899. Reprint. New York: Arno, 1978.

Holman, Roger, comp. *Cinema 1900/1906: An Analytical Study by the National Film Archive (London) and the International Federation of Film Archives.* 2 vols. Brussels, Belgium: Fédération Internationale des Archives du Film, 1982. Vol. 1: *Brighton Symposium, 1978.*Vol. 2: *Analytical Filmography (Fiction Films), 1900–1906.*

Hopkins, Albert A. *Stage Illusions and Scientific Diversions.* 1897. Reprint. New York: Benjamin Blom, 1967.

Hopwood, Henry V. *Living Pictures.* 1899. Reprint. New York: Arno, 1970.

Huettig, Mae D. *Economic Control of the Motion Picture Industry.* Philadelphia: University of Pennsylvania Press, 1944.

Hulfish, David. *The Motion Picture: Its Making and Its Theater.* Chicago: Electricity Magazine Corporation, 1909.

———. *Cyclopedia of Motion-Picture Work.* Chicago: American School, 1911.

———. *Motion Picture Work.* Chicago: American School, 1913.

"An Interview with J. Stuart Blackton." *The Moving Picture World,* December 19, 1908.

Jenkins, C. Francis. *Picture Ribbons.* Washington, D.C.: H. L. McQueen, 1897.

Jenkins, Charles Francis and Depue, Oscar B. *Handbook for Motion Picture and Stereopticon Operators.* Washington, D.C.: Knega, 1908.

Jenkins, Reese V. *Images and Enterprise: Technology and the American Photographic Industry, 1839–1925.* Baltimore: Johns Hopkins, 1975.

Jobes, Gertrude. *Motion Picture Empire.* Hamden, Conn.: Archon, 1966.

Jowett, Garth. *Film: The Democratic Art.* Boston: Little, Brown, 1975.

Lahue, Kalton C., ed. *Motion Picture Pioneer: The Selig Polyscope Company.* South Brunswick, N.J.: A. S. Barnes, 1973.

Levy, David. "The 'Fake Train Robbery': Les Reportages simulés, les reconstitutions et le film narratif américain." *Les Cahiers de la cinémathèque* 29 (Winter 1979): 42–56.

Leyda, Jay. *Kino.* London: Allen and Unwin, 1960.

Low, Rachel. *The History of the British Film. Vol. 2, 1906–1914.* London: Allen and Unwin, 1949.

———, and Manvell, Roger. *The History of the British Film, 1806–1906.* London: Allen and Unwin, 1948.

MacDonell, Kevin. *Eadweard Muybridge: The Man Who Invented the Motion Picture.* Boston: Little, Brown, 1972.

"Making the First Picture Play." *Harper's Weekly* 38 (October 13, 1894).

Malthête-Méliès, Madeleine. *Méliès l'enchanteur.* Paris: Hachette, 1973.

Marey, Etienne Jules. *Movement.* 1895. Reprint. New York: Arno, 1970.

———. "The History of Chronophotography." *Smithsonian Institution Annual Report for 1901.* Washington, D.C.: Smithsonian Institute, 1902.

Matthews, Brander. "The Kinetoscope of Time." *Scribner's* 18 (December 1895): 733–44.

May, Lary Linden. "Reforming Leisure: The Birth of Mass Culture and the Motion Picture Industry, 1896–1920." Ph.D. dissertation, University of California, Los Angeles, 1977.

———. *Screening the Past: The Birth of Mass Culture and the Motion Picture Industry.* New York: Oxford University Press, 1980.

Mitry, Jean. *Histoire du cinéma. Vol. I.* Paris: Editions universitaires, 1967.

Moving Picture World, 1907–27.

Musser, Charles. "The Early Cinema of Edwin Porter." *Cinema Journal* 19 (Fall 1979): 1–38.

Muybridge, Eadweard. *Muybridge's Complete Human and Animal Locomotion: All 781 Plates from the 1887 Animal Locomotion.* New York: Dover, 1979.

Niver, Kemp R. *In the Beginning: Program Notes to Accompany One Hundred Early Motion Pictures.* New York: Brandon Books, n.d.

———. *Motion Pictures from the Library of Congress Paper Print Collection: 1894–1912.* Berkeley: University of California Press, 1967.

———. *The First Twenty Years: A Segment of Film History.* Los Angeles: Locare Research Group, 1968.

———. ed. *Biograph Bulletins, 1896–1908.* Los Angeles: Locare Research Group, 1971.

Optical Lantern and Cinematograph Journal 1–4 (1904–7). Sometimes published as *Kinematograph Journal: Incorporating Lantern Weekly.*

Optical Magic Lantern Journal 1–12 (1889–1903).

"Our Visits." *The Moving Picture World,* February 1, 1908.

Patterson, Joseph Medill. "The Nickelodeons." *Saturday Evening Post*, November 23, 1907. Anthologized in *The Saturday Evening Post Treasury*, edited by Roger Butterfield. New York: Simon and Schuster, 1954.

Paul, Robert W., Hepworth, Cecil M., and Barker, W. G. *Before 1910: Kinematograph Experiences*. Proceedings of the British Kinematograph Society, offprint no. 38. British Kinematograph Society, 1936.

Perry, George. *The Great British Picture Show*. New York: Hill and Wang, 1974.

Pierce, Lucy France. "The Nickelodeon." *The World To-Day* 15 (October 1908): 1052-57.

Pratt, George C. *Spellbound in Darkness: A History of the Silent Film*. Greenwich, Conn.: New York Graphic Society, 1966.

Projection Lantern and Cinematograph, nos. 1–12 (May 1906–September 1907).

Quigley, Jr., Martin. *Magic Shadows*. Washington, D.C.: Georgetown University Press, 1948.

Ramsaye, Terry. *A Million and One Nights. 1926*. Reprint. New York: Simon and Schuster, 1964.

Richardson, F. H. *Motion Picture Handbook 1910*. New York: The Moving Picture World, 1910.

Robinson, David. *Origins of the Cinema: Catalogue of an Exhibition Presented by Cumberland Row Antiques Limited, July–August 1944*. London: Cumberland Row Antiques Limited, 1964.

Sadoul, Georges. "English Influence on the Work of Edwin S. Porter." *Hollywood Quarterly* 3 (Fall 1947): 41–50.

_____ . *Histoire générale du cinéma*. Vol. 2, *Les Pionniers du cinéma: De Méliès à Pathé, 1897–1909*. Paris: Les Editions Denoël, 1947.

_____ . *British Creators of Film Technique*. London: British Film Institute, 1948.

_____ . *Histoire générale du cinéma*. Vol. 1, *L'Invention du cinéma, 1832–1897*. Paris: Les Editions Denoël, 1948.

_____ . *Louis Lumière*. Paris: Editions Seghers, 1964.

_____ . *Histoire du cinéma mondial: Des origines à nos jours*. Paris: Flammarion, 1968.

_____ . *Georges Méliès*. Paris: Éditions Seghers, 1970.

_____ . *French Film. 1953*. Reprint. New York: Arno, 1972.

Salt, Barry. "Film Form, 1900–1906." *Sight and Sound* 47 (Summer 1978): 148–53.

Sklar, Robert. *Movie-Made America*. New York: Random House, 1975.

Slide, Anthony. *Early American Cinema*. New York: A. S. Barnes, 1970.

Sopocy, Martin. "A Narrated Cinema: The Pioneer Story Films of James A. Williamson." *Cinema Journal* 18 (Fall 1978): 1–28.

Spehr, Paul C. "Some Still Fragments of a Moving Past." *The Quarterly Journal of the Library of Congress* 32 (January 1975): 33–50.

———. *The Movies Begin: Making Movies in New Jersey, 1887–1920*. New York: Newark Museum and Morgan and Morgan, 1977.

———. "Filmmaking at the American Mutoscope and Biograph Company, 1900–1906." *The Quarterly Journal of the Library of Congress* 37 (Summer–Fall 1980): 413–21.

Spottiswoode, Raymond. "The Friese-Greene Controversy: The Evidence Reconsidered." *Quarterly of Radio, Film and Television* (Spring 1955).

Talbot, Frederick Arthur. *Moving Pictures: How They Are Made and Worked*. Philadelphia: J. B. Lippincott, 1912.

Thomas, David B. *The Origin of the Motion Picture: An Introductory Booklet on the Pre-History of the Cinema*. London: Her Majesty's Stationery Office, 1964.

Trutat, Eugène. *La Photographie animée*. Paris: Gauthier-Villars, 1899.

Vardac, A. Nicholas. *Stage to Screen: Theatrical Methods from Garrick to Griffith*. Cambridge, Mass.: Harvard University Press, 1949.

Walls, Howard Lamarr. *Motion Pictures, 1894–1912*. Washington, D.C.: Library of Congress, 1953.

Walsh, George Ethelbert. "Moving Picture Drama for the Multitude." *The Independent* 64 (February 6, 1908): 306–10.

Waters, Theodore. "Out with a Moving Picture Machine." *Cosmopolitan* 40 (January 1906).

Wenden, D. J. *The Birth of the Movies*. New York: Dutton, 1975.

Index of Film Titles

General Index

Designer: Rick Chafian
Compositor: Al's Typesetting
Text: 9/11 Palatino
Display: Palatino and Palatino Bold
Printer: Vail Ballou Press
Binder: Vail Ballou Press